Claus Schünemann/Günter Treu
BAKING, THE ART AND SCIENCE
A Practical Handbook for the Baking Industry

Claus Schünemann/Günter Treu

BAKING

THE ART
AND
SCIENCE

A
Practical Handbook
For The
Baking Industry

Published by Baker Tech Inc., Calgary, Alberta, Canada

ISBN 3-7734-0113-2. First Edition 1986
German copyright 1984 Neue Gildefachverlag
GmbH & Co. KG, Alfeld

ISBN 0-9693745-0-X First English Edition 1988
© Baker Tech Inc.
Box 208, Sub P.O. 158
Calgary, Alberta, Canada T1Y 6M0

Baker Tech Inc., Publications Division
Project Manager: Volker Baumann
Technical Advisor: Brian Hinton

English Edition Project Team
Editorial and Design Consultants:
WordsWork Comprehensive Communications Inc.
Editor-in-chief: Ron Shewchuk
Copy editor/project coordinator: Sandra Dawson
Art Director: Ray Heinrich
Translator: Christina Ackerman
Editorial Consultant: John Carstairs
Technical Assistance: Nick Oleynick
Cover: design by Garry Kan; photo arrangement by
Eileen Harwood; products supplied by City Bakery
(Calgary) Ltd.
Cartoons: Ulf Marckwort
Printing: Cal Oka Printing Ltd.

Printed in Canada

Preface

Volker Baumann

In 1986 I ordered a copy of *Technologie der Backwarenherstellung* through a German baking journal. At that time I was working as a technical consultant for a milling company, and I hoped the new textbook would be a useful addition to my modest collection of books about baking.

When the book arrived in the mail I was impressed and excited. In my 25 years as a working baker, I had never seen a more comprehensive and practical resource. Here was a single reference book packed with straightforward information on baking techniques, current techology and specialty products.

Not only was *Technologie der Backwarenherstellung* filled with practical information; it was also a pleasure to look at, with hundreds of color photographs and illustrations. It seemed that no matter where I opened it, I would find something interesting and useful. It perfectly filled the gap in my library between complex scientific manuals and commercial recipe books.

In the following weeks I showed *Technologie* to my colleagues in the baking industry. They too were impressed, and encouraged me to make the book accessible to English-speaking bakers. Inspired by their enthusiasm and support, I obtained the rights to the English version and put together a team of experts to prepare the book for publication. Two-and-a-half years later, I am pleased to be writing this preface to the first English edition, which we have entitled *Baking, The Art and Science*.

Of course, without the excellent scholarship of the original authors, Claus Schünemann and Günter Treu, we would not have a book at all. The German edition was designed to meet the technical requirements of the West German educational program for apprentice bakers. It was written as a textbook, and is divided into convenient sections, allowing the book to be used as a quick reference tool as well as for in-depth study.

Baking, The Art and Science covers nearly every facet of baking, including raw materials, ingredients, working methods and processes, standards and quality evaluations. The book takes into account technological, mathematical, financial and legal aspects of the baking industry, as well as hygiene, accident prevention, environmental protection and economical use of energy.

The German authors and publisher have endeavored to make this textbook as appealing and easy-to-use as possible, and the English edition is presented in the same spirit. Where appropriate, the techniques and terminology have been adapted to North American standards.

I hope *Baking, The Art and Science* succeeds in bringing its readers the wisdom and expertise of the German baking industry. My heartfelt thanks are extended to all who helped bring this book to the English-speaking world.

Sincerely,

Volker Baumann
President, Baker Tech Inc.
November 1988, Calgary

How to use *Baking, The Art and Science*

The following items are provided for ease of orientation:

— table of contents
— index

The book has a modular structure for ease of understanding. The text of the various chapters provides essential study information. In addition, the following items are provided for further clarification:

— figures, illustrations and cartoons,
— clearly structured tables,
— basic recipes and sample recipes,
— schematic representations of working and production processes.

This book contains study aids. They are identified using colors:

— memoranda, tables (light red)
— important information, summaries, basic recipes (red)
— references, suggestions (blue)
— additional information (light yellow)
— statements, observations based on the tests (yellow)

PLEASE NOTE: All sample recipes in this book are based on flour with a protein content of 10%. Because protein content may vary from region to region, the liquid component of the recipes may need to be adjusted.

Table of Contents

Wheat Flour and its Applications

The Use and Application of Rye Flour

Production of Whole-grain and Specialty Breads

Production of Sweet Yeast-raised Goods

Products Made with Special Doughs and with Batters

Appendix

Wheat Flour and its Applications

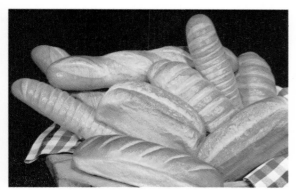

Fig. 1 **French breads**

Fig. 2 **Small French crusty roll varieties**

Bread Varieties

Wholesale and retail bakers produce many varieties of French bread and French crusty rolls. As shown in *Figs. 1-3*, the number of varieties is endless. By making one or two simple adjustments to the make-up procedure and to the formula, bakers can give their customers a welcome change.

The growing popularity of variety breads can be explained by a change in consumer tastes. European breads and buns have a higher value in the eyes of consumers than the standard North American products.

The consumer wants bakery products that:
— taste good;
— can be easily digested; and
— are fresh from the oven.

By using the right combinations of ingredients and the right tools, today's baker can make all this possible.

What determines the composition of French breads?

French breads *are basically made with little or no sugar and fat content, and are generally made with white flour.*

The addition of a small percentage of rye flour (up to 10%) is a common practice.

Fig. 3 **An assortment of country-style rolls**

Food Regulatory Guidelines

1

*More about bread weights and sizes can be found in the chapter entitled **Recommended Weights for Bread**.*

Crusty breads should weigh at least 500 g. Smaller products like submarine and hoagie rolls can weigh less than 250 g. There are no government regulations as to the weight of these products.

Composition of Crusty/French Varieties

Crusty French breads contain the following ingredients:

— white flour
— water and/or milk
— yeast
— salt
— baking additives

The following ingredients can also be used:

— shortening
— sugar
— rye flour (up to 10% of total flour)
— sesame seeds, poppy seeds, caraway seeds, and cracked wheat (used for decoration and flavoring)

Fig. 4   **Vienna roll (folded)**

Fig. 5   **Vienna rolls (cut)**

Fig. 8   **Rose rolls**

Fig. 6   **Club rolls**

Fig. 9   **Crusty rolls**

Fig. 7   **Kaiser rolls**

Fig. 10   **Pressed Rolls**

Categories of French and Crusty Roll Products

The first distinction made by consumers is between small and large bakery products.
Large products include:
— white bread, baked in a pan
— white bread in oblong, compact form, baked without a pan
— French white bread in oblong, longer form
— long baguettes (long, fat-free type of French bread)
— sandwich breads baked in square, enclosed pans

Fig. 11 **Pressed milk rolls**

Small crusty rolls are categorized according to these features:	Examples:
— type of liquid added	➤ milk rolls water rolls
— shape	➤ round rolls long rolls line rolls double rolls crescents pretzels
— method of shaping	➤ folded rolls pattern cut rolls cut rolls pressed rolls plain rolls
— appearance	➤ French rolls club rolls rose rolls star rolls hamburger rolls round rolls double/submarine rolls
— addition of other grain products	➤ rye rolls coarse or fine rolls whole-wheat rolls graham rolls
— special additives	➤ cheese rolls onion rolls bacon rolls poppy, sesame and caraway seed rolls
— special processes	➤ soft pretzels bagels

Fig. 12 **French bread varieties**

Joe thinks: *"All white breads and rolls are made from one and the same dough. So why all these varieties? You're tricking the customers!"*
Is this true?

Fig. 13 **Siamese (Twin roll)**

Comparing French Crusty Bread to Light Rye Breads

French crusty bread differs from light rye breads in a number of ways. French bread:

- ➤ has more volume;
- ➤ has a lighter, golden yellow crust;
- ➤ has a softer, spongier texture;
- ➤ has a lighter crumb color;
- ➤ has a more delicate aroma;
- ➤ stales more quickly;
- ➤ because of lighter texture, is less filling; and
- ➤ is easier to digest.

Fig. 14 **Baguette rolls**

Fig. 15 **French crusty and rye bread scaled at 500 g each for comparison**

Flour and its Baking Qualities

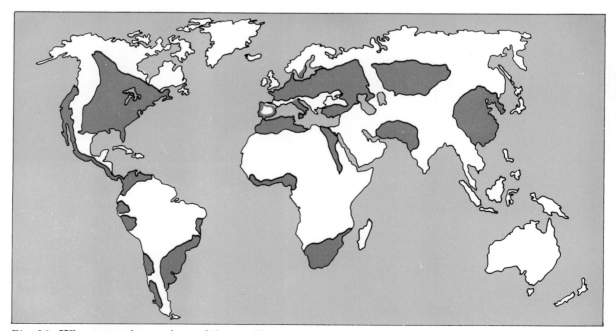

Fig. 16 **Wheat-growing regions of the world**

Wheat Flour — Origin and Production

Wheat can be grown in many parts of the world. It is cultivated as far south as Argentina and as far north as Finland, and from sea level to 3,000 metres above sea level in China. Certain environmental factors can influence the growth of wheat, including temperature, precipitation, frost-free period and soil type.

Wheat belongs to the grass family. In itself, it is not a single species, but a group of species within the genus **triticum**. The wheat species may be placed in three groups according to the number of pairs of chromosomes.

The groups are called: **diploid**, includes triticum monococcum L (einkorn); **tetraploid**, includes triticum durum (durum wheat); and **hexaploid**, includes triticum vulgare host or common bread wheat.

* *The baking ability of flour depends on its characteristics.*

The following factors are considered when evaluating the baking ability of flour products:

➤ how much water flour can absorb to form dough, or "water absorption"
➤ dough consistency obtained
➤ fermentation process and fermentation stability
➤ baking ability

Bread-making flour can have varying baking qualities which depend on the following:

➤ type of wheat used (growing conditions such as climate, weather, soil, fertilizers used)
➤ milling process

Additional Information

As the biggest wheat producer in the world, North America also has the highest surplus of wheat. Wheat from the U.S.A. and Canada has a very high protein content and exceedingly high baking qualities. In Europe, North American wheat varieties are mixed with locally grown wheats (miller's grist) to produce strong flours suitable for bread-making.

Look at the map of the world (opposite page) with the wheat producing regions highlighted. Try to interpret which conditions are favorable and which ones are unfavorable for the growing of wheat.

Fig. 17 **Wheat field**

Fig. 18
Grains: wheat, rye, barley, oats

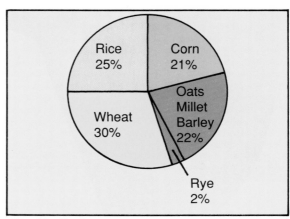

Fig. 19 **Grain types as percentages of total world grain production**

5

Food for Thought: *Look at Fig. 19 showing percentages of grain varieties. It is interesting to note that, although rye flour holds a relatively small proportion of the world consumption, it has a dominant position along with wheat flour in European markets.*

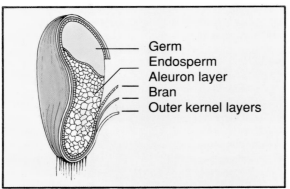

Fig. 20
Longitudinal cut through a wheat kernel

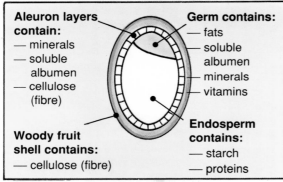

Fig. 21 **Nutritional value of the grain components**

Fig. 22 **White breads made with light wheat flour (left) and dark wheat flour (right)**

Evaluate the possible reasons for the difference in volume and color of these two loaves.

	Water	Albumen	Minerals	Fat	Starch	Celluose, Pentosan, Soluble Sugars
Bran	15	10	7	0	0	68
Germ	15	33	5	12	0	35
Aleuron layer	15	25	10	8	0	42
Endosperm	15	10	0.5	1.5	70	3

Table 1 **Composition of Grains**

Components of Wheat Grain

Make a longitudinal cut through a wheat kernel and observe the following components:
— endosperm (the flour body) 83.5%
— germ (the seedling) 2.5%
— bran (the shell) 14%
The endosperm consists primarily of:
starch   (70-73%)
protein   (10-14%)
water   (14%)

During the milling process, the **endosperm** yields the flour.

The **aleuron layer** surrounds the endosperm. This thick, honeycomb-shaped layer is particularly rich in minerals and soluble albumen. It also contains more fat and enzymes than the endosperm. Dark flour contains a large percentage of aleuron layer.

The **germ** is located at one end of the grain and has the ability to produce a new plant. The germ is rich in soluble albumen, fat, minerals and vitamins. The small shield separating the germ from the endosperm contains a large amount of vitamin B.

Flour containing germ cannot be stored for long periods of time because of its high enzyme content. The germ reduces the baking ability of the flour and causes the flour components to decompose.

The **bran** acts as the shell, holding the germ and the endosperm. The outer fruity layer, consisting of several cell layers, is woody and cannot be digested. The shell underneath gives the grain its characteristic color.

Flour in the center of the endosperm is of a different quality than the flour found in its outer layers.

Flour made from the center of the wheat kernel endosperm:	Flour made from the outer layer of the endosperm:
➤ is lighter;	➤ is darker;
➤ contains more starch;	➤ contains less starch;
➤ contains less albumen (protein);	➤ contains more albumen (protein);
➤ contains more gluten;	➤ contains less gluten;
➤ contains fewer soluble sugar substances;	➤ contains more soluble sugar substances;
➤ contains fewer vitamins;	➤ contains more vitamins;
➤ contains fewer enzymes;	➤ contains more enzymes;
➤ contains the less branny part of the wheat kernel.	➤ contains larger quantities of shell parts of the grain.

Remember:
Flour made from the center part of the flour body (wheat kernel/endosperm) has a better baking ability. Flour made from the outer layers of the endosperm has more nutritional value.

Flour Milling

Fig. 23

Flour is the starting point of all baking products and, therefore, must have the highest standards of quality and consistency.

Preferred qualities of flour:
— *light-colored, high-gluten flour for the finest bakery products*
— *light-colored, balanced-gluten flour for white flour products*
— *medium-light colored, lower-gluten flour for mixed flour products*
— *dark, lower-gluten flour for dark, mixed flour products*
— *cracked grain for cracked wheat/rye products*

The milling of grain is aimed at producing flour with high baking qualities. Although it is technically possible to grind the grains in one single phase, the end result would be a fine, dark granular flour that would ***not*** have the qualities needed for baking. But it would not be possible to obtain the desired baking quality from this product by means of sifting or other steps.

The miller must use a milling process that produces:

— lighter-colored and darker-colored flour; and
— flour with baking qualities that can be predetermined.

The miller solves this problem through the use of various phases in the grinding of the wheat. This grinding process is called ***multi-phase milling***. Various phases of careful grinding, sifting and separating of bran in four to five grinding phases, and in a number of streams, yield a large number of milled products of different colors and compositions.

The large number of millstreams allows the miller, through blending, to obtain flour with different baking qualities. In order to ensure that grain ground in the first phase does not result in fine, dark, granular flour, the miller uses the following methods:

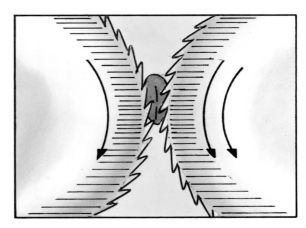

Fig. 24 **Shearing action of the break rolls in a flour mill**

7

The Modern Milling Process

— First the grain is cleaned.
— During the **preliminary cleaning process**, foreign material such as chaff, weed seeds, small stones and dust is eliminated.
— During the **final cleaning process**, undesirable grain components such as the outermost kernel layers, any sprouted protrusion from the germ portion, and the small beard tuft are removed.

The grain is conditioned (tempered) with moisture and heat prior to grinding in order to achieve a higher flour yield and to obtain very light-colored flour. The wheat stands for 9 to 18 hours of tempering, which uses a steam-heat process to obtain the proper condition for grinding. The grinding process is as follows:
— the grain is crushed between corrugated steel rollers (**first break**);
— the particles are sorted in a sifter, according to size, into:
    — fine flour (first break flour or first break release)
    — coarse flour
    — farina (coarser material)
    — coarse, larger pieces containing endosperm, bran and germ

Prior to further grinding of the coarse fractions (coarse flour and farina), further removal of bran is made. Bran with adhering endosperm is separated during sifting and sent to the **second break** roller system.

During the second sifting, the coarsest material goes to the **third break** and so on up to **four breaks**. (Some mills have as many as **five break** systems.) Finally, after the coarse fraction leaves the bran finisher, there is no endosperm left, and the remainder is packed off as bran. The germ becomes flattened by the rollers and is removed at the third break.

Only a small amount of germ can be recovered. The majority is lost in the "shorts" — a mixture of bran, germ and endosperm — and some is reduced to flour particle size and remains in the flour.

The sifters separate the fragments called "middlings" from the finer bran particles. A whole floor in the flour

Thomas says: *I can understand how, at the cleaning process, larger and lighter foreign material can be separated from the wheat. But how are weed seeds, small stones and metal shards separated?*

Before milling, the grain is tempered (moistened).
➤ *This strengthens the bran, making it easier to separate from the endosperm without excessive powdering.*
➤ *The endosperm loses some of its firmness, allowing it to break into smaller parts.*

The two grooved steel rollers are adjusted very wide during the first break.
➤ *The grain is partially crushed during the first stage, opening up the endosperm for further reduction. With each reduction, more flour is extracted from the wheat kernel.*

One of the steel rollers runs faster than the other (advance movement or speed differential).
➤ *This allows for more efficient breakage of the wheat kernel.*

mill is devoted to the sifters. From the sifter, the middlings travel to the purifiers, which classify particles as to size by screening, and which use air currents to separate the heavier particles (endosperm) from the lighter ones (bran).

The endosperm fragments are now ready for reduction rollers, which will grind them into flour. These fragments will once again be subjected to finer sifters and rollers to produce fine flour. The reduction is repeated until all that is left are the shorts, which are used for animal feed. Each break produces flour and, in turn, each reduction produces flour.

These become the **streams** from which the miller will produce the final flour, by first combining streams into **divides** and then combining portions (or all) of the divides in specific ways to form **grades** of flour.

Flour Treatment

In the past, the aging and bleaching process of flour was accomplished by prolonged storage. This is now achieved by the use of bleaching and maturing agents. Maturing agents, such as potassium bromate, ascorbic acid, azodicarbonamide and benzoperoxide (bleaching agent) are used in concentrations of 5 - 50 parts per million (ppm). These agents are added to the flour in powdered form, with starch acting as the diluent.
The level of treatment varies with:

— different flours and their degree of extraction;
— different wheat varieties, their origins and conditions of growth;
— length of storage prior to milling; and
— intended use of the flour.

Flour Types

Hard Wheat Flours

Top Patent ➤ 0.35 - 0.40% ash content/11.0 - 12.0% protein
Uses: Danishes, sweet doughs, yeast doughnuts and smaller volume breads and buns.

First Baker's ➤ 0.50 - 0.55% ash content/13.0 - 13.8% protein
Uses: All purpose strong baker's flour, breads, buns, soft rolls and puff pastry

First Clears ➤ 0.70 - 0.80% ash content/15.5 - 17% protein
Uses: A dark, very high protein flour used as a base for rye bread production; poor color not a factor in the finished product.

Second Clears ➤ Low grade flour, not used in food production. Constitutes less than 5% of flour produced by a mill.

Soft Wheat Flours

Cake Flour ➤ 0.36 - 0.40% ash content/7.8 - 8.5% protein, chlorinated to 4.5 - 5.0 ph.
Uses: High-ratio cakes (cakes with a high amount of sugar and liquid in proportion to flour), angel food cakes and jelly rolls.

Pastry Flour ➤ 0.40 - 0.45% ash content/8.0 - 8.8% protein, chlorinated to 5.0 - 5.5 ph. (also available unchlorinated)
Uses: Cakes, pastries and pies.

Cookie Flour ➤ 0.45 - 0.50% ash content/9.0 - 10.5% protein
Uses: Cookies and blended flours. For large-scale manufacturers, flour can be chlorinated to the user's specifications.

Whole-wheat Flour ➤ Various bran coat granulations produce coarse to fine whole-wheat flours.

Rye Flours

Light Rye ➤ (75% extraction) 0.55 - 0.65% ash content
Uses: Can be blended up to 40% with white flour without a major loss of loaf volume.

Medium Rye ➤ (87% extraction) 0.65 - 1.00% ash content
Uses: Up to 30% blend with white flour.

Dark Rye ➤ (100% extraction) Limited to 20% flour blend before significant volume reduction occurs in the product.

Rye Meals ➤ Fine/medium/coarse/pumpernickel and flaked. Consist of a variety of broken or cracked rye grains after being classified in a series of sieves.

Other Flours

Stone-ground Flour ➤ (100% extraction) Usually untreated and, because of germ content, is subject to limited shelf life.

Cracked Wheat/Rye ➤ Available in coarse, medium or fine granulations.

Semolina ➤ A fine meal consisting of particles of coarsely-ground durum.

Extraction Rate: *indicator of the percentage of flour obtained from a given amount of grain.*

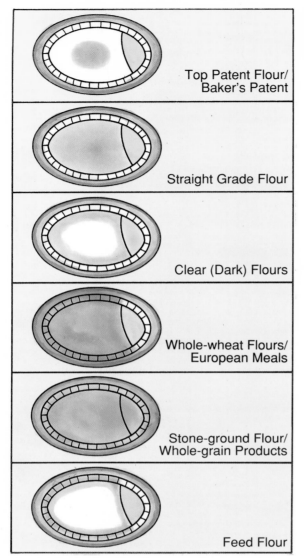

Fig. 26 **Grain classification according to the degree of grinding (blue color)**

Top Patent Flour/
Baker's Patent

Straight Grade Flour

Clear (Dark) Flours

Whole-wheat Flours/
European Meals

Stone-ground Flour/
Whole-grain Products

Feed Flour

Explain the composition of the flour types shown in Fig. 26.

Meal has a medium to coarse composition. It contains all the components of the grain, except the woody shell. In Europe, the germ is removed from the meal in a special milling process. **Whole-grain products and stone-ground** *flour contain all of the components of the grain, including the germ. Only the outer, woody shell is eliminated from the grain prior to coarse grinding. Stone-ground flour can be stored for up to 4 weeks, under normal storage conditions, without losing a significant amount of vitamins and quality. If stored longer, the flour can lose baking ability and aroma due to the enzyme activity of the germ.*

The most important data about flour production:

➤ *A wheat kernel consists essentially of:*
  • *the endosperm*
  • *the aleuron layer*
  • *the bran*
  • *the germ*
➤ *The endosperm consists of:*
  • *starch (up to 70%)*
  • *albumen (protein) (up to 17%)*
  • *water (up to 15%)*
  • *other substances: fat, sugar, enzymes, minerals*

Flour from the center part of the endosperm is of a higher baking quality than flour from the outer layers. To obtain flour with different degrees of lightness in color and different baking qualities, the flour mill uses careful milling procedures known as the multi-stage grinding process and divide blending. Flour can also undergo a variety of other treatments such as oxidization, bleaching, and the addition of enzymes.

The Components of Wheat Flour

Look at a sample of wheat flour. The flour looks white throughout. But it is actually composed of a large number of substances that can have different effects in terms of baking technology.

Each flour is also different. A modern flour mill offers flours with uniform baking abilities, but because the wheat to be milled differs in terms of composition and quality, this uniformity is not always easy to achieve.

Composition and baking qualities of wheat flour depend on:
➤ *the type of wheat;*
➤ *the growing conditions, such as climate, soil and fertilizers used; and*
➤ *various other factors, such as storage conditions, grinding process used and degree of grinding.*

Table 3 (bottom of page 11) reveals the following characteristics of wheat flour:

Wheat flour is primarily composed of starch. The water content is amazingly high, although the flour seems to be powdery and dry. The protein content is as high or higher than in an egg.

The next few pages will examine the suitability of wheat flour for the production of bakery products, taking into account the composition of the flour.

The Protein Content of Flour

Test 1

Prepare a dough from:
50 g patent flour
+ 30 ml water
+ 1 g salt

Let stand for 30 minutes, then wash the dough, while kneading it carefully under a thin water jet *(Fig. 27)*.

Catch the falling dough pieces in a cheesecloth and the water in a bowl underneath. The washing process is finished when the washing water is clear.

Observation:
Of 80 g of dough, about 15 g remains. The remaining dough is cohesive and gummy and, after a short resting period, becomes sticky. It can be stretched without breaking and contracts when released.

Conclusion:
The remaining dough consists of moist, sticky albumen (protein) which is insoluble in water. This substance is called gluten. A large number of dough properties are united in the moist gluten.

Test 2

Weigh the moist gluten and dry it in a dryer or in an oven at low temperature. Then weigh the dried gluten *(Fig. 29)*.

Observation:
The dry gluten weighs about a third of the moist gluten.

Conclusion:
When incorporated into a dough, the gluten absorbs about twice its own weight in water. Therefore, gluten can swell.

Remember:
Weight of the dry gluten from a dough made with 100 g of flour equals the percentage of the gluten-producing albumen in that flour.
The difference in weight between moist gluten and dry gluten equals the absorption capacity of the gluten-producing albumen.

Wheat flour albumen is not a homogeneous material. It is composed of many albumen materials with varying properties:

Fig. 27
Washing gluten from the dough

Reference: *Keep the washing water from Test 1 for the tests on **Carbohydrates of Wheat Flour**.*

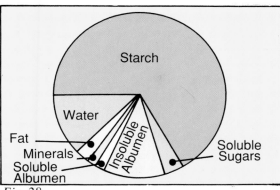
Fig. 28
Composition of Wheat Flour

The average composition of top patent flour
73.5% carbohydrates, which are composed of: — 71% starch — 2.4% soluble sugar — 0.1% cellulose 13% albumen (protein), which is composed of: — 12% gluten-forming albumen — 1% water-soluble albumen 14% water, which contains: — 1% fats — 0.1% minerals

Table 3

11

Fig. 29

Moist gluten and baked, dried-wheat gluten

Food for thought:

100 g of wheat flour can absorb 60 g of water.
100 g of wheat flour contains 10 g of gluten producing-albumen.
10 g of gluten can absorb (bind) 20 g of water. How high is the water-absorbing capacity of the non-gluten remainder of the flour substance?

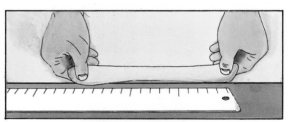

Fig. 30 **Gluten extension test with a ruler**

Reference: *Keep the washing water from Test 3 for Tests 4 and 5.*

Remember:

Light-colored wheat flours contain less albumen than dark-colored wheat flours, but they are of a higher baking quality.

Fig. 31

* *The major part of the albumen has a gluten-forming effect when incorporated into a dough.*
* *The remainder of the albumen becomes liquid when incorporated into a dough.*

Technically, only the gluten-forming protein (albumen) is of significance:

Properties of Gluten-forming Albumen:	Effects on Baking Process:
● It is insoluble in water.	➤ When incorporated into a dough, it absorbs twice its own weight in water.
● It can swell.	
● When swollen, it binds together.	➤ It gives the dough its cohesion.
● When swollen, it is elastic.	➤ It makes the dough elastic and workable, giving it firmness.
● When swollen, it can contain gases.	➤ It keeps the fermentation gases in the dough and makes the dough light.
● It coagulates when heated.	➤ It solidifies when baked and provides for preliminary texture.

Test 3

Wash out gluten samples from top baker's patent flour, baker's patent and straight grade flour. Let the samples stand for a few minutes, then extend each sample slowly along a ruler *(Fig. 30)*.

Observation:
The gluten sample made from the top baker's patent flour can be stretched, but only with difficulty. When released, it contracts almost completely.
The gluten sample made from the baker's patent flour can be stretched easily and, when released, it contracts only slightly.
The gluten sample made from the straight grade flour can be stretched very easily and very far, but it has a tendency to tear.

Conclusion:
Doughs made of flour from the centre of the grain kernel (top baker's patent) are very elastic and difficult to form. Flours with these properties are called **high-gluten flours**. Doughs made from flour from the outer layers of the kernel are less

(cont'd.)

elastic and break easily when formed. Such dough properties are called **short**. Flours yielding short doughs are called **low-gluten flours**.

Differences in the baking properties of bread flours are primarily caused through fluctuations in the character and in the percentage of protein present.

The following principle applies:

<blockquote>

* *The baking ability of bread flour is determined by the gluten/protein.*
</blockquote>

Fluctuations in the composition and quality of the other flour components have only a slight influence on baking quality.
The **miller** will choose grain primarily based on the quality of the gluten. The **baker** is not directly interested in the quality of the flour albumen; he judges the flour solely on its baking performance.
Through additives, the baker can change the baking properties of wheat flour. To improve the characteristics of the dough (workability, proofing stability, proofing tolerance), the properties of the gluten must be changed.

Proofing is allowing dough to "rest" in a warm, moist, controlled environment.

<hr>

How to affect the properties of gluten

➤ *By adding salt:*
The quantities of salt usually added for bread and bun doughs make the gluten more solid and the dough becomes more elastic. Too high a quantity of salt significantly reduces the swelling ability of the gluten and the dough is "short."

➤ *By adding fat:*
A small increase to the amount of fat makes the gluten more elastic; the dough is smoother and has a greater fermentation stability. Higher additions of fat make the dough "short."

➤ *By adding baking additives:*
Baking additives which firm up the gluten are suitable for low-gluten flours. The miller already adds ascorbic acid (vitamin C) to the flour. L-Cysteine (amino acid) has the same effect.

➤ *Additives reducing the effect of the gluten, such as protease (enzymes decomposing gluten) or cystine (amino acid) are suitable for high-gluten flours.*

➤ *Baking additives containing emulsifiers generally improve the properties of gluten.*

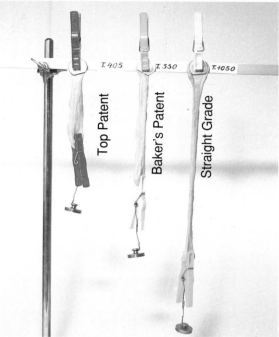

Fig. 32 **Stretch test**
In this test, 20 g weights are attached to samples of dough. The samples are judged after 30 minutes and again after 60 minutes.

<hr>

Additional Information

*Flour albumen consists mainly of **gliadin**, **glutenin**, albumin and globulin.*
Gliadin and glutenin make up about 85% of the flour albumen. They form gluten when water is incorporated into the dough.
Albumin and globulin dissolve in water when incorporated into the dough.
*Mill laboratories measure **gluten quality** through the determination of its **sedimentation value**.*
*These methods are discussed in more detail in the chapter entitled **Evaluation of Wheat Flour**.*

<hr>

Carbohydrates in Flour

Starch

Have you ever thought about what causes flour to have a white color?
The answer to this question can be derived from the following test.

<hr>

Test 4

Use the bowl of washing water from the washing process of the gluten. After a while, the washing water forms a white layer at the bottom (*Fig. 33*). Mix the washing water with iodine (iodine-potassium iodide solution).

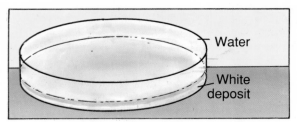

Fig. 33 **Settled washing water from the washing process of the gluten**

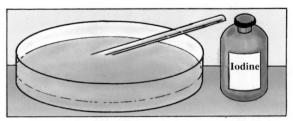

Fig. 34 **Agitated washing water mixed with iodine**

Iodine is a chemical used to determine the presence of starch.

Fig. 35 **Mix starch and water**

Fig. 36 **Filter the starch slurry**

Fig. 37 **Measure filtered water**

Figs. 35 -37 **Water-absorbing capacity of raw starch**

Observation:
The white deposit turns violet-blue when iodine is added *(Fig. 34)*.

Conclusion:
Wheat flour contains starch, which is insoluble in cold water.

Test 5

Use the washing water of a light-colored flour (from *Test 3*).
Carefully pour off the clear washing water above the deposit.
Dry the starch deposit in a dryer at 50°C (or at low temperature on a heating element).
Weigh the deposit.

Observation:
When rubbed between the fingers, the dry deposit turns into powder. The dry deposit weighs about 35 g.

Conclusion:
The properties of starch do not change in cold water. Wheat flour contains about 70% starch (35 g/50 g = 70%).

Test 6

Mix 20 g of wheat starch with 20 ml water. Filter the slurry (a coffee filter can be used).When no more water runs through, measure the water in a measuring cylinder *(Figs. 35 -37)*.

Observation:
A moist starch deposit remains in the filter. The water filtered through measures about 10 ml.

Conclusion:
When incorporated into a dough, the starch of the wheat flour absorbs about half of its own weight in water.

Test 7

Stir 10 g of wheat starch into 100 ml of water and heat the slurry while stirring continuously. Measure the temperature at all times *(Fig. 38)*.

Observation:
At about 60°C, the slurry starts to thicken. When it starts to boil, the slurry turns into a glossy, pasty mass.

Conclusion:
Wheat starch turns pasty between 60°C and 88°C and, in the process, absorbs water.

Carbohydrates (cont'd.)

Wheat contains many forms of carbohydrates.
The main component is starch.
The remainder is composed of soluble sugars, cellulose and pentosan.

Wheat Starch	
Properties:	**Effect:**
* Wheat starch is insoluble in cold water.	➤ Starch is the solid substance of the dough, even after incorporation into the dough.
* Wheat starch cannot swell in cold water, but brings a limited amount of water into the dough.	➤ Starch causes water to accumulate at the surface of the dough.
* Wheat starch becomes pasty between 60°C and 88°C, and this process also causes the starch to absorb water.	➤ Starch binds the dough-water during the baking process, creating a firm texture in the bread.
* Wheat starch can be decomposed by enzymes.	➤ Products of decomposition of the starch are sugars such as dextrine, malt sugar and dextrose. They improve fermentation of the dough and deepen the brown color of the crust.
* Wheat starch can be decomposed in a dry state through the application of heat.	➤ During baking, dextrines form on the crust. Heat makes them turn yellowish, and later brown. Through condensing vapors or application of moisture, the dextrines form a shiny layer.

During the baking process (wheat flour), the starch can absorb, through thickening, considerably more water than the dough provides. Therefore, instead of a paste, a firm texture is achieved. This texture is caused exclusively through paste formation of the starch during baking.

This indicates that starch is the most important flour component for the texture of the product.

For dough formation and dough characteristics, starch is of little importance.

Remember:
Starch forms the texture during baking.

. Additional Information

Light-colored flours from the center of the wheat grain contain more starch than flour from the outer layers, and absorb less water than dark-colored flours when incorporated into the dough. Therefore, the texture of bakery products made of light-colored wheat flours is drier.

Fig. 38 Determination of the paste-formation temperature of the wheat starch

Soluble Sugars

Test 8
Mix dark wheat flour or fine cracked wheat with water until a liquid slurry is obtained. Let the slurry stand for 20 minutes, then filter. Mix the filtrate with a **Fehling solution** and heat it.

Observation:
The filtrate turns red (*Fig. 39*).

Conclusion:
Flour contains soluble sugars.

Fig. 39 Demonstration of sugar in flour

15

Soluble malt sugar, dextrose and dextrine vary in complexity, with dextrine being the most complex and dextrose the simplest.

Soluble Sugars	
Properties:	*Effect:*
— *Dextrine, malt sugar and dextrose are water-soluble.*	➤ *Through the liquid added, they are distributed evenly in the dough.*
— *Malt sugar and dextrose (but not dextrine) can be fermented.*	➤ *They improve yeast fermentation and thus make the dough lighter in texture.*
— *Dextrine, malt sugar and dextrose turn brown when heated.*	➤ *They make the crust turn brown.*
— *Malt sugar and dextrose taste sweet.*	➤ *They enhance the flavor of the product.*

Wheat flour contains between 1.5% and 3% soluble sugars.

The soluble sugar content is:	
low:	*high:*
— *in light-colored wheat flour;*	— *in dark-colored wheat flour;*
— *in fresh flour;*	— *in flour which has been stored too long;*
— *in flour with a low water content;*	— *in flour with a high water content;*
— *in flour derived from dry-ripened and dry-harvested grain.*	— *in flour derived from moist-ripened and moist-harvested grain; flours derived from germinating grain have a particularly high soluble sugar content (refer also to* **Growth**, *in the chapter entitled* **Evaluation of Rye Flour**).

The addition of appropriate additives will improve the sugar balance of a dough made from wheat flour (refer to the chapter entitled **Baking Additives for Wheat-flour Products**).

These additives are:
— soluble, fermentable sugars;
— starch digesting enzymes; and
— baking malt.

Cellulose and Pentosan

The shell of the grain primarily contains indigestible components: *cellulose* and *pentosan*.

Cellulose and pentosan contain the following properties which are important to the baking process:

Properties:	Effect:
— *Cellulose and pentosan are insoluble in water.*	
— *Cellulose and pentosan can swell significantly.*	➤ *They absorb a large amount of the liquid added during dough preparation; this is why dark flour rich in shell material has a high dough yield.*
— *When swelling, pentosan forms a gel.*	➤ *The slimy texture has a negative effect on the dough properties; doughs made of flour rich in shell material are somewhat sticky-moist and short. The corresponding effects are a reduced fermentation stability and tolerance. The end product is therefore small in volume and has somewhat dense cells.*
— *Cellulose and pentosan do not change during the baking process.*	➤ *They remain swollen during the baking process. Bakery products made of flour rich in shell material therefore have a more "humid" texture and keep fresh longer.*

Dark-colored, finely-ground flour has a high bran content.

Light-colored, coarser-ground flour has a low bran content.

Cellulose and pentosan are bulking materials and are nutritionally important.

> **Remember:**
> *Flour rich in bran material has a low baking ability:*
> — *because the cohesiveness is low; and*
> — *because cellulose and pentosan have a negative effect on the properties of dough.*

Water in Wheat Flour

It is hard to imagine that wheat flour, which is so powdery-dry, contains water, but a simple test can prove this.

Test 9

Place some wheat flour into a test tube.
Heat the flour sample over the flame of a Bunsen burner while shaking the tube.
Hold the test tube at an angle and heat only the lower part.

Observation:
Water precipitation occurs in the upper part of the test tube (*Fig. 40*).

Conclusion:
Wheat flour contains water.

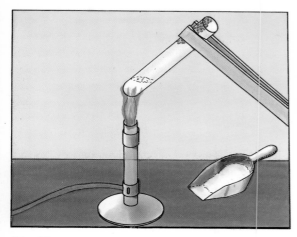

Fig. 40
Demonstration showing water in flour

The water content of ripened wheat flour fluctuates more than any other flour component. The water content depends on ripening and harvesting conditions and should not exceed 15%.
In the case of moist wheat, the water content must be reduced through drying prior to storage of the wheat. Wheat flour with too high a water content changes during storage, which in turn has a negative effect on the baking properties.

Remember:

Wheat flour with too high a water content:
— does not store well; and
— loses some of its baking abilities.

Wheat flours with a high water content	
Changes during storage:	*Effects on quality:*
— Have a tendency to form lumps.	➤ Sifting causes a loss of time and flour.
— Get moldy after a short storage time.	➤ The flour, and therefore the baked product, smells or tastes moldy.
— Attract insects.	➤ Flour consumption and contamination by insects results in losses to the baker.
— Are very rapidly decomposed by their own enzymes.	➤ Starch digestion causes the soluble sugar content to rise, favoring dough fermentation and crust browning. But this process, proteolysis, causes a reduction of dough properties; doughs have a lower fermentation stability. Therefore, the volume of the end product is small with large cells.

In addition to the negative changes during storage, flour with a high water content has economical disadvantages for the baker:
— During dough preparation, flour absorbs less of the added water and the baker obtains less dough.
— The baker has to pay the same amount for flour containing a lot of water as for flour with a normal water content. However, most water level corrections are made in the milling process.

Fats of Wheat Flour

Test 10
Stir a small amount of ether into 5 g of dark-colored wheat flour (whole-wheat/first clear flour) (*Fig. 41*).

Be careful when handling ether; do not inhale the vapors; no open fire; no sparking electrical equipment!

Let the solution stand for a few minutes and then filter the slurry (*Fig. 42*). Let the filtrate solvent evaporate in an open dish (*Fig. 43*).
Be sure the work area is well-ventilated to prevent the accumulation of ether vapor.

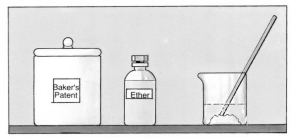

Combine flour with ether.

Filter the slurry.

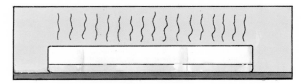

Let the solvents of the filtrate evaporate.

Figs. 41 – 43 **Demonstration of fat in flour**

Reference: *The effects of fat addition to a wheat dough are discussed in detail in the chapter entitled Baking Additives for Wheat-flour Products.*

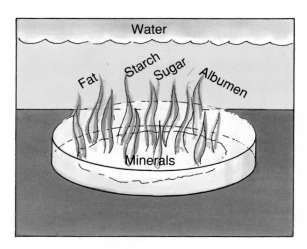

Fig. 44 **Principle of flour incineration**

Observation:
An oily liquid remains in the glass dish. When mixed with water, it forms greasy patches on the water surface. On blotting paper, it leaves a greasy spot.

Conclusion:
Wheat flour contains fat.

Wheat flour contains between 1% and 2% fat.

Dark-colored flour contains more fat than light-colored flour.
Fats have a positive effect on the elasticity of the gluten. Therefore, flour fat has an influence on baking properties.
Slight fluctuations in the fat content of the flour have, however, no influence on its baking properties.
The positive effect of flour fat can be increased by adding specific amounts of baking additives.

Minerals in Wheat Flour

Test 11:
It is recommended that this test be done in laboratories only.
Weigh on a precision scale 5 g of top patent flour and 5 g of second clear flour. Place each of the samples into a heat-resistant dish. Incinerate the samples at a temperature of about 900°C. When the residue looks colorless, the incineration is finished.
Weigh the residue.
(When performing tests to determine the type of flour, the water must be removed through drying prior to incineration.)

Observation:
A glassy, translucent layer has formed at the bottom of the dish. Of the top patent flour sample, about 20 mg remains; of the second clear flour sample, a residue of 80 mg remains.

Conclusion:
Wheat flour contains components called minerals that cannot be burned, and the amount of these minerals varies with the type of flour.

Dark-colored flour is rich in minerals, whereas light-colored flour has a low mineral content.

* *Components of wheat flour that cannot be burned (ashes) are minerals.*

Minerals have a positive effect on the gluten properties during the baking process. Normal fluctuations in the composition and quantity of minerals in wheat flour have, however, no influence on the baking properties. In spite of its higher mineral content, dark-colored wheat flour has a lower baking ability than light-colored flour.

The aleuron layer of the wheat kernel, representing the outer layers of the endosperm, has the highest mineral content. Therefore, the mineral content of wheat flour is used as a gauge of the amount of outer shell in the flour.

Wheat Flour Enzymes

Test 12

Cook a starch solution composed of 1 g of wheat starch and 1 litre of water. Let the solution cool to 40°C. Add an iodine-potassium iodide solution to a small portion of the sample.
Mix the remainder of the solution with an amylase (an enzyme that helps change starch into sugar) solution. Now repeat the iodine test every few minutes.

Observation:

The starch solution without the amylase turns violet-blue when iodine is added (presence of starch). The samples containing amylase turn more and more reddish with iodine, until finally the red color also disappears.

Conclusion:

Amylase decomposes starch into dextrines (red color).
Amylase further decomposes starch into complex and simple sugars (no red color).

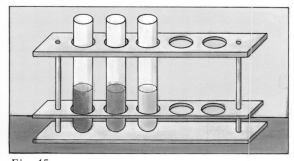

Fig. 45
Iodine sample in starch paste containing amylase

Sample 1 still contains starch.
Sample 2 contains dextrine and no starch.
Sample 3 contains single and double sugars; it contains no starch or dextrine.

Temperature scale for paste formation of wheat starch:	
Average value for the start:	60°C
Average value for the finish:	88°C
Total completion:	98°C

Flour Enzymes	
Properties:	**Effect on the baking process:**
— *Amylase decomposes flour starch into dextrines, malt sugar and dextrose. Maltase decomposes malt sugar into dextrose.*	➤ *Amylase and maltase have a small effect during flour storage and are particularly active in a moist-warm dough. The yeast ferments the sugar in the dough and, in the process, produces gas which gives the dough a light texture. Amylase continues to break down the starch into sugars, even in the last fermentation phase of the dough. The non-fermented sugar reinforces the brown color of the crust.*
— *Protease decomposes the albumen of the flour.*	➤ *Albumen decomposition starts during storage of the flour and accelerates in a moist-warm dough. Thus, the gluten is weakened. Normally, flour used for white-flour products has enough gluten to tolerate a decrease. Doughs made of low-gluten flour lose elasticity and fermentation stability. Products made of such doughs have a small volume and large cells.*
— *Lipase decomposes the flour fats.*	➤ *Fat decomposition is noticeable only in flour that has been stored too long. The flour turns rancid and is considered spoiled. Such flour has also lost gluten through simultaneous albumen decomposition and can no longer be used for baking.*

Total decomposition of wheat starch is possible only when alpha and beta amylase act together. Ripe wheat contains only beta amylase. Alpha amylase is produced only during germination and, therefore, sprouted flour contains a high amount of alpha amylase.

Beta amylase attacks only the ends of the starch molecule and, in the process, separates the malt sugar. Alpha amylase, however, separates dextrine inside the starch molecule. The decomposition of starch through amylase proceeds especially fast:

— at temperatures between 50°C and 65°C; and
— when starch is present in the form of a paste.

Unlike rye starch, wheat starch is decomposed only slightly by amylase during baking. Baking additives containing alpha amylase will, therefore, not have a significant effect on wheat flour doughs.

Flour amylase starts to lose its effect at 70°C. At this temperature, only a small amount of the wheat starch has turned into a paste and, therefore, the main part of the wheat starch can no longer be decomposed.

Food for Thought:
What rules for flour storage can you derive from the knowledge of the effect of enzymes?

Enzymes regulate the metabolism in animal and plant organisms.

Enzymes effect the synthesis and decomposition of organic matter. Enzymes become active only within a certain temperature scale, and only when sufficient moisture is present.

These enzymes play a major role in the **decomposition** of the wheat kernel.

Of all parts of the wheat grain, the germ has the highest enzyme content. Because flour products containing parts of the germ are rapidly decomposed by the enzymes of the seed, the germ is separated from the grain during milling. After only a few weeks, the baking ability of such products is reduced and they spoil very rapidly.

Dark-colored wheat flours are characterized by a higher enzyme activity than lighter-colored ones because of the higher content of parts from the outer layers of the grain.

The period of time for which ground products can be stored is, therefore, largely determined by the amount of enzymes in the wheat.

The enzyme activity is particularly high in:
— whole-grain products;
— flour containing grain from partially sprouted wheat;
— flour with a high water content; and
— dark-colored flours with a high bran content.

In the case of flour with a low maltose content (low content of malt sugar), a stronger enzymatic decomposition is needed to achieve higher baking qualities. Flour with a low amylase activity (too low a starch decomposition through enzymes) is therefore enriched with amylase in the mill and also by the baker with baking additives.

Summary of the Most Important Facts on the Significance of Flour Components

* *Top patent flour is essentially composed of the following:*
  about 71.0% starch
  about 2.0% soluble sugar
  about 11.5% protein/gluten
  about 14.0% water
  about 2.5% minerals and other components

* *The baking ability of wheat flour is determined by the quality of its gluten materials:*
  — gluten absorbs twice its own weight in water during dough preparation
  — gluten transfers its properties to the dough
  — gluten holds fermentation gases in the dough

* *Soluble sugars in wheat flour improve the fermentation process of the yeast in the dough and enhance the browning of the crust.*
  Starch digesting enzymes (amylases) separate fermentable sugars from the starch in the dough, thereby improving the sugar balance.

* *The texture of a bakery product is created through the formation of starch paste.*

* *Wheat flours with too high a water content (more than 15%) can only be stored for a short period of time before spoiling.*

Evaluation of Wheat Flour

Fig. 46

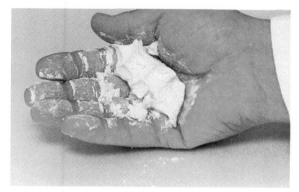

Fig. 47   **Compression test: Flour is too moist**

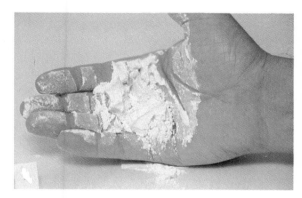

Fig. 48   **Compression test: Flour is normal**

The baking quality of flour is not usually indicated on the package, and the most a baker will know about the flour purchased is the approximate protein content.

What practical methods can be used by a baker to evaluate the freshness, storage and baking qualities of wheat flour?

In general, a baker can evaluate the quality of a flour only after a product has been baked. There are simple tests that can be performed which allow a baker, to a limited extent, to detect large deviations from the desired condition of the flour. However, fluctuations in flour quality are so minor that most defects could be discovered only in laboratory tests.

If a baker encounters a situation where an analysis of a flour sample is necessary, most flour mills can provide a complete testing service.

> *Wheat flour must meet the following requirements:*
> — *It must yield products with the desired characteristics.*
> — *It must produce doughs with the qualities required for the baking process.*
> — *It must store well.*

Simple Tests for Flour Evaluation

Determination of the Water Content (Compression Test)
Compress the flour in your hand, then open your hand again.

> *Evaluation:*
> — *Very dry flour falls apart like powder.* ➤ *No indication of deficiencies.*
> — *Normal flour falls apart in big clumps (batches).* ➤ *No indication of deficiencies.*
> — *Moist flour remains compressed.* ➤ *This flour cannot be stored and its baking ability has been reduced.*

Joe says:
"What's the use of evaluating flour in the bakery? Once the flour has been delivered, it's too late!"
What do you think?

21

Determination of the "Touch" Test

Rub a little bit of flour between your thumb and index finger.

> *Evaluation:*
>
> — *The flour has a* ➤ *No indication of defi-*
> *rough touch.* *ciency.*
>
> — *The flour has a* ➤ *The baking ability could*
> *smooth touch.* *be reduced. Such flours*
> *may be derived from soft*
> *wheat varieties, which*
> *have a lower baking*
> *ability compared with*
> *flour made from hard*
> *wheat.*

Determination of Flour Color

Check samples of top patent flour and straight grade flour. It may be difficult to detect any differences in color. Under artificial light, it is even possible to confuse a light rye and a wheat flour, which are similarly light in color. Depending on the grain variety and the milling process used, flour has a characteristic color. The whiteness of the flour is caused by the flour starch.

The yellowish color of wheat flour and the gray-blue color of rye flour is caused by the outer shell of the grain.

The **Pekar test** makes it easier to distinguish between flour varieties.

> **Test 13**
>
> On a flat, dark board press the flour samples with a spatula.
> Make sure the samples are close together, but do not mix.
>
> **Observation:**
> Differences in color are clearly recognizable.
>
> **Conclusion:**
> Misleading shadows on the surface of the flour samples are eliminated when the samples are pressed flat against the board.
>
> **Continuation of test:**
> Now, dip the flour samples at a slight angle into a water bath until no air bubbles rise to the surface. After taking the samples out of the water, carefully let the water run off.
>
> **Observation:**
> Differences in color are even more apparent.
>
> **Conclusion:**
> The bran particles on the flour surface swell and the color of the flour becomes more distinct.

Fig. 49 **Pekar test:**
Dip the flour sample at an angle into a water bath

Fig. 50 **Pekar test: Evaluate the flour samples**

> *Fresh, high-quality flour has a matte gloss.*
> *Flour that is old and decomposed has a chalky, dull appearance.*

The absence of flour gloss is primarily caused by the decomposition of fats and similar materials such as carotene.

Determination of Flour Odor

Scatter a little bit of flour and smell it.

Flour must have a pleasant, fresh odor. If a slightly foreign odor is detected, the cause should be determined.

If the cause is harmless, it is possible to evaluate the usability of the flour by baking a test product.

When the flour smells moldy or rancid, the baking ability is also reduced.

> *A foreign odor can have many causes:*
> — *Grain diseases,*
> — *Sprays (pesticides),*
> — *Disinfecting agents (acquired in storage or transportation),*
> — *Fungi,*
> — *Mites and insects,*
> — *Enzymatic decomposition (rancid flour).*

Evaluation of Flour Through Baking Tests

Even fresh flour can result in an unsatisfactory end product. Deficiencies can have various causes. The flour may not have good baking properties, or the production method used may not sufficiently take into account the properties of the flour.

In order to obtain a satisfactory baking result, take the following steps:

— mix the flour with flour of another batch. This reduces and often neutralizes the deficiencies.
— make changes in the production method such as dough temperature or resting time.
— make changes in the formulation such as yeast level or type of baking additive used.

An experienced baker can usually trace baking problems to deficiencies in the product and take corresponding steps to correct them.

Sending flour samples to be tested by an expert is often impractical; a trial batch is the simplest way to determine deficiencies.
Here are a few tests that can be conducted by the baker to determine deficiencies in the formulation or production method.

When conducting a test, apply the following principles:	
— *Make a list.*	➤ *quantity of ingredients* ➤ *temperature* ➤ *time* ➤ *evaluation data*
— *Use practical test quantities.*	➤ *test results are relevant only for operations when a certain quantity is used (minimum size for test runs with rolls is 1 kg of flour).*
— *Be precise; otherwise results lose relevance.*	➤ *Take precise temperatures of* — *the ingredients,* — *the proofer,* — *the oven,* — *the room.* ➤ *Weigh exactly:* — *ingredients,* — *dough pieces.* ➤ *Time exactly:* — *mixing times,* — *resting time,* — *intermediate proofing time,* — *final proof,* — *baking time/ temperature.*

— *When conducting multiple tests, make sure the test conditions are uniform.*	➤ *Only one component can be changed in any one test (for example, only the quantity of salt or type of baking additive used).*
— *When conducting single tests, make sure they are conducted more than once for comparison purposes.*	➤ *Different results from test to test indicate improper procedures.*
— *When evaluating the results, record **all** results, regardless of their status.*	➤ *dough quantity,* ➤ *dough condition,* ➤ *fermentation process,* ➤ *yields,* ➤ *product volume,* ➤ *crust and texture,* ➤ *appearance and taste*

Joe says: *"We have no time for trial runs! Besides, they are worthless. A good baker uses his experience to get better results."*

What do you think?

Food for Thought: *Why do results from very small test quantities yield less useful information?*

Test bakeries in flour mills conduct tests to examine the baking behavior of the flour produced. This ensures that commercial batches with the required baking properties can be produced.

Flour mills generally use standardized baking tests. Because the corresponding equipment is not available, standard baking tests are difficult to run in a bakery.

Standard baking tests include:

— *Pan-baked Products Test *)*
— *Round Products Test *)*
— *Rapid Mix Test *) (for rolls)*

---

*) For more information on these tests, refer to the publication entitled **Approved Methods**, Eighth Edition, by the American Association of Cereal Chemists.

Flour Evaluation Through Laboratory Tests

In addition to conducting simple tests and trial baking runs, flour mills, companies producing ingredients, and research institutes use chemical and physical methods for flour and dough examination.

Such methods determine the precise baking behavior of flours.

The results lead to ways of improving the baking ability of flour.

A bakery does not have the prerequisites for flour tests of this kind. Therefore, these methods will not be discussed in detail. The following is an overview of the customary methods of examination used in the baking industry.

Additional Information
Determination of Water Content

Principle: Wheat flour is dried in an electric drying chamber. The weight-loss is measured. Or: The water content is measured based on the electrical conductivity of the flour.

Purpose: To determine the storability of the flour.

Evaluation of the storability of flour:
Water content:
over 16% = cannot be stored
about 15% = limits storage
under 15% = good storage

Table 4

Determination of Acid Value*)

Principle: The acid value of the flour is determined by means of a standardized method (refer to the chapter entitled Evaluation of Bread).

Purpose: The acid value is an indication of the degree of flour decomposition and, therefore, of the baking properties to be expected.

Acid value index of wheat flour (baker's patent):
1.7 = normal; no indication of deficiencies.
2.5 = somewhat high; deficiencies possible.
3   = quite high; the flour is too old, the baking ability reduced.
4   = too high; the baking ability is greatly limited; the flour is spoiled.

Table 5

Determination of Moist-Gluten Content*)
Principle: A specific method is used to eliminate, through washing, and to weigh the moist gluten from a wheat flour dough.

Purpose: The quantity of the moist gluten affects the baking ability of the flour.

Evaluation of the moist-gluten quantity:
over 27%   = high
20 - 27%   = average
under 20% = low

Table 6

Determination of the Sedimentation Value*)
(Sediment=Deposit)
Principle: Using a standardized method, wheat flour is treated with color and milk acid. In the process, a measurable deposit of flour albumen forms in the test tube.

Purpose: The sedimentation value, in connection with the value of the moist-gluten determination, provides useful information about the baking properties of the flour.

Evaluation of dough properties using the sedimentation value of the flour:
over 40   = very good
30 - 40   = good
20 - 29   = satisfactory
under 20 = unsatisfactory

Table 7

Determination of the Fall Number*)
Principle: A water-flour slurry is heated in a boiling water bath and yields a flour paste. Depending on amylase activity, the flour paste is more or less solid.
The time, in seconds, it takes a standardized object to sink to the bottom is the fall number.
Purpose: Conclusions can be drawn from the fall number regarding the activity of the alpha amylase and the fermentation process taking place in the wheat-flour dough.

Evaluation of dough gassing power using fall number:	
under 200 =	high amylase activity: too high a content of fermentable sugars.
200 - 300 =	average amylase activity: desirable sugar balance in the dough.
over 300 =	too low an amylase activity: the dough has low gassing power.

Table 8

Determination of the Maltose Number

Principle: The flour enzymes are left for one hour at 27°C in a water-flour slurry.

---

*) For more information on these tests, refer to the publication entitled **Approved Methods**, Eighth Edition, by the American Association of Cereal Chemists.

The quantity of the sugar is then measured.

Purpose: *To determine the enzyme activity in the flour. The maltose number relates directly to the gassing power of the flour.*

Methods of Determination of Dough Properties
So far, only one component and its influence on the baking properties of wheat flour has been examined at one time. Results of single-component tests may indicate the potential baking behavior of the flour, but the baking result does not always confirm these conclusions.
More reliable conclusions can often be drawn from the properties of the dough as a unit.

Determination of the Mixing Resistance of Doughs Made From Wheat Flour (Farinogram)

Principle: *The resistance of the dough against the kneading arm during the mixing process is recorded by means of a standardized measuring method.*
*The mixer equipped with such a measuring device is called a **farinograph**. The diagram showing the resistance of dough is called a **farinogram**.*

Purpose:

— *To determine the amount of water the dough can absorb. This indicates the dough firmness and the dough yield.*
— *To determine the degree of softening of the dough when mixed for too long. This will reveal information as to the dough's stability.*

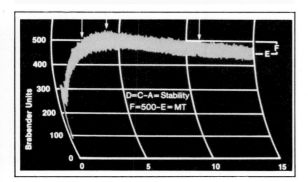

Fig. 51
Farinogram: Normal curve of a strong flour

The farinogram shows the following values:

— *water-absorbing capacity of the flour,*
— *dough development time = time elapsing until the highest point in the curve is reached,*
— *dough stability = time elapsing between crossing the 500 line and falling below the 500 line,*
— *softening of the dough = magnitude of curve decrease after 10 and then after 15 minutes.*

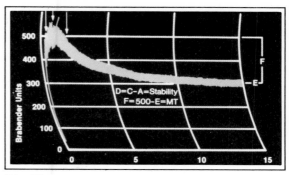

Fig. 52
Farinogram: Normal curve of weak flour

Determination of Dough Elasticity (Extensogram)

Principle: *Using a standardized procedure, dough strings are formed after varying dough resting periods, then extended until they break.*
The extension resistance and the length of extension are measured and recorded.
*The extension device is called an **extensograph**. The extension diagram is called an **extensogram**.*

Purpose: *To establish the elasticity of the dough. The extension diagram provides conclusions regarding the dough properties, in particular:*
— *handling properties,*
— *fermentation stability,*
— *fermentation tolerance.*

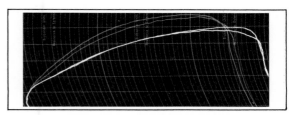

Fig. 53   **Extensogram of a strong flour**

The extensogram shows the following values (among others):
— *extension resistance of the dough = the higher the curve, the bigger the resistance to extension*
— *extensibility of the dough = the longer the curve, the more extendible the dough*

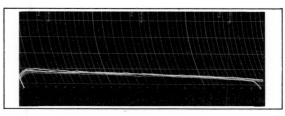

Fig. 54   **Extensogram of a weak flour**

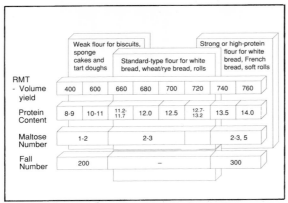

	Weak flour for biscuits, sponge cakes and tart doughs		Standard-type flour for white bread, wheat/rye bread, rolls				Strong or high-protein flour for white bread, French bread, soft rolls	
RMT - Volume yield	400	600	660	680	700	720	740	760
Protein Content	8-9	10-11	11.2-11.7	12.0	12.5	12.7-13.2	13.5	14.0
Maltose Number	1-2		2-3				2-3, 5	
Fall Number	200			–			300	

Fig. 55 **Quality profile of top baker's flour**

* RMT = Rapid Mix Test
Standard Baking test for Bread

Flour Storage
Changes Occurring in Flour During Storage

Changes occur in flour during storage not only because of its enzyme content, but also because of other micro-organisms.

Changes:	Effects on the baking process:
— Starch is decomposed into soluble sugars. As the percentage of fermentable sugars in the flour increases, the starch content decreases.	➤ **Effect:** *Improvement of the sugar balance in the dough. Yeast fermentation and crust browning are improved. When flour is stored for too long (more than two months), the high soluble sugar content has a negative effect. The crust of white flour products turns too brown. The brittleness of the crust decreases noticeably after the finished product has been stored for two to three hours.*
— Albumen and fats are decomposed and the acidity in the flour increases.	➤ **Effect:** *Flours with normal baking ability yield doughs with better properties. However, when the flour is stored too long, dough stability, fermentation stability and fermentation tolerance are reduced (refer to the chapter **Fermentation Stability/ Fermentation Tolerance**). The finished product has a small volume and somewhat large cells. The use of very old flour has a negative effect on the taste of the finished product.*

The baking ability of wheat flour made from freshly-harvested grain is improved during the first one to two months of storage due to the enzymatic changes occurring during that time. This is called the "maturing" of the flour.

Flour mills eliminate the need to mature fresh flour through the addition of ascorbic acid and malt flour.

The following general rule applies to the quantity of flour to be stored:

* The flour supply must last at least one week. A smaller supply can cause loss in production (in case of delivery delays).

* The flour supply should not exceed the requirements for six weeks. Longer storage entails the risk of reduced quality of the flour.

Suggestion: *Find out how many bags of flour are stored in a local bakery. Calculate the number of days for which the flour supply will last. Compare the storage time with recommendations made above.*

Flour Storage in Silos

Many bakeries store flour in silos, while others still use conventional paper bags.

There are a number of good reasons for storing flour in silos:
➤ *purchase of flour at economical prices*
➤ *ease of handling*
➤ *time savings*
➤ *minimal dust development*
➤ *reduced risk of storing flour for too long (old flour is not necessarily used first)*
➤ *better conditions for hygienic storing*
➤ *no empty bags need to be disposed of*

If the reasons are so convincing, why don't all bakeries store their flour in silos?
Reasons for not using silo storage could include the following:
— lack of suitable location,
— lack of profitability (in very small bakeries),
— lack of capital,
— subject to region and location of the mill.

Flour silos can be put up just about anywhere — in buildings and outside — providing temperatures remain stable. Flour storage in silos is almost free from problems.

Modern flour silos comprise the following equipment:

Storage silo	=	Silo cell made of synthetics, special steel, sheet steel or reinforced concrete
Conveying equipment	=	Suction or pneumatic equipment transporting the flour in pipes to the bakery; metering screws for horizontal transportation
Screening machines	=	For hygienic reasons: to eliminate impurities. For technological reasons: to loosen up and ventilate the flour in order to improve dough formation and maturing
Mixing equipment	=	Mixing of flours of different quality or for mixed bread from two or more cells
Weighing equipment	=	Precision and time savings
Flour dust evacuation equipment	=	To avoid losses; for environmental protection
Control equipment	=	To control the work flow: conversion of basic recipes, metering of flour quantities, ingredients and water added, compilation of storage data

Possible disadvantages of silo storage are:

* *Separation of flour* ➤ *Small flour particles are blown to the silo walls during filling; larger particles concentrate in the center.*

* *Formation of condensation water* ➤ *Cooling-off of the inner silo wall causes condensation to form. This results in crust formation and moldiness on the inner walls.*

* *Evacuation problems* ➤ *Flour condenses and gets stuck above the evacuation funnel.*
Or: Due to the weight of the flour, it piles up at the joints, seams and curbs of the silo's inner wall.

* *Flour dust deposits* ➤ *The dust formed during filling and emptying settles above the flour surface at the silo wall.*

Caution!
Explosion hazard! During the operation of silos, explosive dust mixes with air inside the silo. Therefore, avoid ignitable sources of every kind in rooms where silos have been erected.

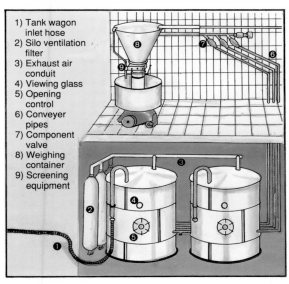

1) Tank wagon inlet hose
2) Silo ventilation filter
3) Exhaust air conduit
4) Viewing glass
5) Opening control
6) Conveyer pipes
7) Component valve
8) Weighing container
9) Screening equipment

Fig. 56 **Schematic representation of a silo plant**

Fig. 57 **Electronically controlled equipment for weighing, temperature adjustment and sifting**

Fig. 58 **Flour storage in outside silos**

Fig. 59 **Flour storage in inside silos**

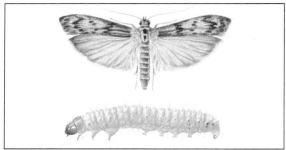
Fig. 60 **Moth (12 mm) and larva (18 mm)**

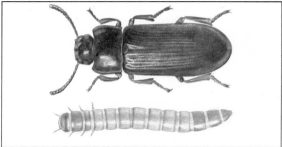
Fig. 61 **Confused flour beetle (16 mm) and mealworm (24 mm)**

Flour Spoiling Through Insect Contamination

Despite high hygienic standards in modern bakeries, insects can still be found. Even constant cleaning cannot prevent flour from collecting and forming crusts in cracks or grooves in walls, floors and equipment. Insects, most of which spin webs or cocoons, find their way into bakeries and multiply in these crevices.

An insect prevention program should include:
— inspection of incoming ingredients
— storage facilities off the floor
— good stock rotation
— regular check of inaccessible places
— store all refuse a good distance from the bakery
— purchase insect control devices such as electrical grids, ultra-violet lights or automatic pyrethrum aerosol dispensers

> *The most frequent flour insects are:*
> ** Confused flour beetles → eggs → mealworm*
> ** Flour moth → eggs → larvae*
> ** Flour mites → eggs*

Flour mites cannot be detected by the eye.

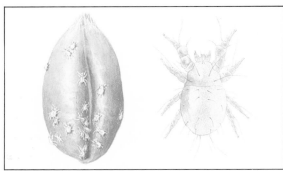
Fig. 62 **Flour mites on a wheat grain**

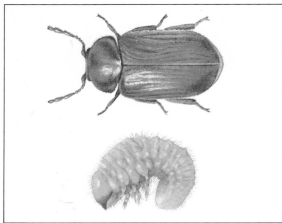
Fig. 63 **Bread beetle (3.75 mm) and larvae (4.8 mm)**

28

Summary of the Most Important Requirements for the Storage of Flour	
Store in a cool place!	➤ *Warmth (over 20°C) accelerates flour decomposition through enzymatic action. The baking properties of flour are reduced after a short storage period. Cold storage (below 10°C) leads to difficulties in the temperature regulation of the dough. Therefore, if necessary, insulate storage or silo chambers to avoid extreme hot or cold temperatures.*
Store in a dry place!	➤ *Flour attracts moisture. Moisture promotes the activity of flour enzymes and micro-organisms and rapidly reduces the baking properties of flour.*
Store in a well-ventilated place!	➤ *Flour is compressed when stored vertically in bags and silos and therefore becomes warmer. Flour gives off water when stored and therefore increases the moisture content in the air. For these reasons, it is important to ventilate storage areas and silo chambers. Store flour bags on pallets no less than six inches (15 cm) off the floor. Do not let full flour silos "rest" for a long period of time without removing the flour.*
Store in a clean place!	➤ *Dusty storage rooms encourage the breeding of insects. Flour silo cells must be emptied several times per year, freed from residual flour clinging to the inside walls, and treated with a pesticide to reduce the risk of insects.*
Protect against foreign odors!	➤ *Foreign odors can occur through:* *— coats of fresh paint;* *— cleaning agents;* *— disinfectants or pesticides;* *— mold; and* *— attacks by insects.*

Baking Additives for Wheat-Flour Products

Fig. 64

A baker tests a new baking additive. In spite of uniform baking conditions and uniform flour, problems arise:
— the dough has a different quality
— the dough is not easy to work with
— the rolls show deficiencies in quality
How is this possible?

Joe comments: "The baking additive is no good!" But, the answer may not be as simple as this.

In the past, bakers may have used baking additives containing mainly malt. Today new additives are based on an emulsifier.

The traditional method for bread production may have to be adapted to the specific effects of the new baking additives.

Baking additives are different from the usual ingredients found in flour:

* *Wheat-flour baking additives are generally used, depending on their composition, for specific improvement of the production and quality of wheat-flour products.*

Joe says: *"Baking additives are baking additives! They all contain the same things!"*
What do you think?

Fig. 65 **Rolls made without baking additives (also made without the addition of sugar and fat)**

Fig. 66 **Cross-section of a roll made without baking additives (also made without the addition of sugar and fat)**

Note the rough texture.

no malt   2% malt

Fig. 67 **Dough for pan-baked white bread without baking additive (left), and with baking malt (right), at identical proofing times**

Give a reason for the difference in dough volume.

Units of quantity for pure malt flour (Diastatic)	
per kg of flour	per litre of water
15 - 20 g	25 - 33 g

Ingredients in Baking Additives (for wheat flour)

Depending on their composition, baking additives have different effects.

The components of baking additives can be divided into two groups, based on their effects:

Components:	Effects:
I. — malt sugar	➤ better dough fermentation
— other sugar produced by starch	➤ better browning of the crust
— alpha and beta amylase	➤ better brittleness
	➤ bigger volume
II. — fats	➤ better dough quality, in particular better preparation properties, higher fermentation stability, higher fermentation tolerance
— emulsifying agents	
— milk materials	
— ascorbic acid	
— cystine and L-cysteine	➤ bigger product volume
	➤ better bloom
	➤ better and longer lasting crustiness
	➤ texture with finer cells
	➤ longer fresh-keeping qualities

Baking Additives Containing Diastatic Malt

Malt is the oldest baking additive. It is produced from germinated grains (barley).

Many years ago, it was added to the dough unmixed, in the form of malt flour or malt extract (liquid malt). Today, malt is found in many mixed baking additives.

The active components of malt are:
— malt sugar (maltose); and
— starch-digesting enzymes, especially alpha-amylase, besides other enzymes.

Effects of Malt:
— *Maltose (malt sugar) ➤ is yeast food and therefore promotes fermentation.*   *This reduces the fermentation time. The lighter texture of the final product is demonstrated by a larger product volume and a better crust.*

— *Maltose improves the browning of the crust.*

— *Starch-digesting en- ➤ zymes (amylase) separate fermentable sugars from the flour starch during the fermentation process, but also during the baking process.*   *This ensures sugar supply for the yeast up to the final baking phase. The sugar required for browning is still produced during the final proof.*

— *Malt has a positive effect on the taste of the product.*

The manufacturer's recommendations for the amount of baking additives in flour must be strictly followed, especially in the case of additives containing enzymes.

Too large a quantity reduces the crustiness and the elasticity of the texture.

Baking Additives with Amylase Compound

Amylases are starch-digesting enzymes produced from barley (grains) or from cultures of micro-organisms. As a rule, fungal and bacterial amylases are used for the production of additives.

Like malt, additives containing amylase compounds enhance the fermentation of the yeast and the browning of the crust.
Their effect, however, is different from that of malt because amylase compounds:

— have hardly any effect on the gluten. Contrary to malt, they do not contain any albumen-digesting enzymes.
— improve the fresh-keeping properties of the flour.

Baking Additives With Sugars Produced From Starch

Sugars produced from starch include corn syrup, glucose and dextrose (fructose). They are produced by conversion of starch with the aid of acids or enzymes (starch hydrolysis). Sugars produced by starch are components of many baking additives, improving the activity of the yeast and browning of the crust.

Baking Additives with Fat Components

Some additives contain fat in conjunction with emulsifying agents.
Shortenings improve the gluten properties, creating a smoother and more elastic dough. This leads to improvements of the:

> — *workability of the dough; and*
> — *fermentation stability and tolerance.*
>
> *Therefore the bakery products:*
> — *have a larger volume;*
> — *have a texture with finer cells;*
> — *can be cut more easily; and*
> — *keep fresh longer.*

Baking Additives with Emulsifying Agents

For additives of this type, shortening-like emulsifiers are added. Since they can attach to fats and also to water, emulsifying agents contribute to a finer distribution of fats (fat of the flour) in the aqueous dough phase.

Food for Thought: *Why can excessive addition of baking additives containing enzymes lead to a reduced elasticity of the texture?*

Fig. 68
Left: Roll with 1% addition of fat, but without malt Right: Roll with 1% addition of fat and 1.5% addition of malt

Suggestion: *Find out which baking additives are used in a local bakery.*

Try to find out which active materials these baking additives contain. Often, brand names suggest the composition of the product.

Caution: *Baking additives containing diacetyl tartaric acid esters of monoglycerides and diglycerides (emulsifying agents) cannot be used for milk products!*

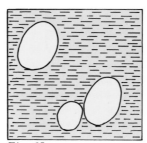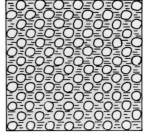

Fig. 69
Fat distribution in water without emulsifying agents (left), and with emulsifiers (right)

Emulsifying agents also have an influence on the characteristics of the gluten. The gluten becomes smoother, more extensible, and also more elastic. The effect of an emulsifying agent is reinforced through intensive mixing, which leads to a better cohesiveness of the gluten.

Effects of emulsifying agents:	
— dough is easier to work with	higher product volume
— higher fermentation stability (good capacity to hold gas)	improved crustiness, texture with finer cells
— higher fermentation tolerance (insensitivity to overfermentation)	products keep fresh longer

The following emulsifiers are used for baking additives:
— lecithin, a natural product from soya beans; and
— monoglycerides and diglycerides.

Emulsifiers are available in pure form for large manufacturers, but normally are purchased by the baker in a diluted form for several reasons:
— lower inventory costs
— less chance in scaling errors

The amount of emulsifiers to be added for the production of rolls is about 2 to 3% of the flour quantity.

Thomas says:
"I don't think it's right to use additives containing chemicals for the production of bakery products!"

Is this statement correct?

Additional Information

In order to obtain malt products, barley or wheat grains are made to germinate at high air humidity. This causes the activated enzymes to convert the flour substance. From the point of view of baking technique, the high production of alpha-amylase, dextrine, maltose and protease (albumen-digesting enzymes) is significant.

Alpha-amylase, in conjunction with beta-amylase of the flour, converts flour starch into fermentable sugars in the dough.
Amylase is made inactive only at baking temperatures exceeding 70°C.
Through malt, the dough is also enriched with active protease which weakens the gluten.

Reducing the gluten content of a high-gluten flour has a positive effect on the dough properties. Low-gluten flour, however, suffers a reduction in baking properties.

Amylase compounds from bacterial cultures and mold fungus contain no albumen-digesting enzymes. Therefore, they can also be used in conjunction with low-gluten flour.
Bacterial amylase differs from fungal amylase with respect to its insensitivity to temperatures. It loses its effectiveness at 75°C and is destroyed at 95°C.

The use of bacterial amylase for white-bread production is contested, because it is possible that a part of the amylase is not destroyed during baking. This causes the starch to decompose in stored bread; the resulting released moisture keeps the bread fresh longer. But there is also a danger that the texture will become too moist and inelastic.

Emulsifiers used for baking additives include natural lecithin, monoglycerides and diglycerides of fatty acids, as well as monoglycerides and diglycerides in conjunction with acetic acid and diacetyl tartaric acid (diacetyl tartaric acid ester = DATEM). Monoglycerides and diglycerides have a composition similar to that of fats.
(Fig. 70)

*Emulsifiers make suitable baking additives because of their capacity to relieve the tension at the surface of fat and water. In the dough, the **hydrophilous** parts of the emulsifiers attach to the aqueous dough substances, and the **lipophilous** parts attach to the fatty dough substances. Therefore, a homogeneous fat-water system is created in the dough.*

In some emulsifiers such as DATEM, an interaction occurs with the flour albumen which considerably improves the dough properties. Baking additives with DATEM are particularly used in cases where a large product volume is desired.

Certain emulsifiers cause a delay in starch decay. Consequently, the product stays fresher longer.

Ascorbic acid (vitamin C), cysteine and cystine (amino acids) are among the gluten-changing materials in baking additives. Additives containing ascorbic acid improve the dough properties and, therefore, the quality of the products.

Some flour is enriched with ascorbic acid at the flour mill and, in case of a low enzyme activity in the flour, also with malt flour or fungal amylase.

Cysteine reduces the extension resistance in gluten, significantly increasing the dough properties.

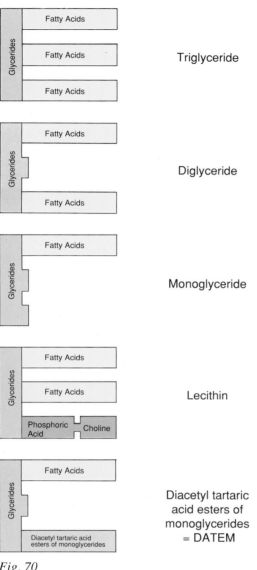

Fig. 70
Composition of glycerides

The Role of Shortening and Sugar as Dough-Improvers

Many consumers have the perception that products made without baking additives are of considerably higher quality.

As proof, they refer to the crusty, tasty roll of the "good old days," without any additives.

A clear answer:

Today it is nearly impossible to meet consumer demands for quality without the use of baking additives.

When mass-produced baked products were first introduced, quality was compromised in some cases, and this reduced quality was associated with additives. However, minimum quality products can be produced without baking additives.
This can be accomplished with the addition of:
— fat; and
— sugar.

A small addition of fat to the dough (about 1%) improves, even without the use of emulsifiers;
— the dough property;
— the fermentation stability; and
— the fermentation tolerance.
This gives bakery products:
— a larger volume;
— a finer-celled texture; and
— a tender-brittle crust.

Increasingly higher additions of fat produce a soft texture and crust, similar to cake, and change the taste of the products.

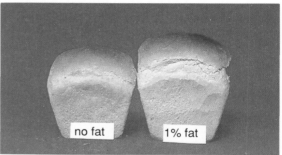

Fig. 71
Pan-baked bread without baking additives with no fat (left), and with 1% fat addition (right)

Compare the volume and the color of the crust of both breads.

Fig. 72
Pan-baked bread with no fat, and with 1% fat addition (cross-section)

Compare the texture of both breads.

A small amount of sugar added (1 to 2%):
— improves dough fermentation (especially in the initial phase);
— increases browning of the crust;
— increases the volume (but only slightly); and
— improves the crustiness.

33

Increasingly high additions of sugar can slow dough fermentation, reduce the dough properties and the quality of the baked product. The crust browns deeply and the crustiness disappears too quickly.

The addition of fat and sugar has disadvantages compared to the use of a mixed baking additive based on emulsifiers:
— *The fermentation stability and the fermentation tolerance are reduced.*
— *The product volume is smaller.*
— *The quality of the final product is lower.*
Small deficiencies in the regulation of the dough temperature and the fermentation time clearly affect the quality.

Fig. 73

Pan-baked white-flour bread without baking additives (left), and 1% addition of sugar (right)

Compare the color of the crust.

Fig. 74 **Pan-baked bread, with and without the addition of sugar (cross-section)**

Compare the texture of the bread.

Use of Wheat-Flour Baking Additives

Rules for the application of additives:

— *Baking additives are incorporated into the dough with all other ingredients.*
Exception: In the case of doughs prepared with a sponge dough, such as for baguettes, additives are incorporated at the dough stage.
— *Additives cannot be mixed together without a trial bake test, even if they come from the same manufacturer.*
— *Respect the manufacturer's instructions regarding quantities to be used.*

Summary of the most important information on baking additives for wheat-flour products

— *baking additives for wheat-flour products improve*	➤ *dough development*
	➤ *properties of the dough*
	➤ *fermentation stability and tolerance*
	➤ *product quality*
— *baking additives for wheat-flour products contain*	➤ *sugars*
	➤ *enzymes*
	➤ *fats*
	➤ *emulsifiers*
— *baking additives prevent*	➤ *bread diseases such as mold and rope*

Reference: *Information on mold and on measures to prevent mold is contained in the chapter* **Mold as a Bread Disease**. *Rope is discussed in the chapter entitled* **Rope as a Bread Disease**.

The Importance of Salt in Baking

The Effects of Salt on Dough, on Fermentation and on the Baked Product

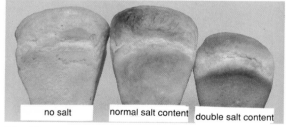

Fig. 75

Products shown with varying salt content: without salt (left), with a normal amount of salt (center), and with a double amount of salt (right)

Compare the color of the crust and the volume of the product.

In general, bread baked from dough with inadequate salt content tastes bland and unappetizing.

Ask the consumer why salt is added to bread and the answer will automatically be: "To improve the taste!"

In fact, salt is the most important flavor enhancer in the production of baked goods.

Have you ever forgotten to add salt to a dough? When did you first notice it?

An experienced baker can detect the omission of salt in a dough by one of the following characteristics:

→ the dough "flows" — it has a low degree of firmness

→ the dough is not very elastic

→ the dough shows signs of "wild fermentation"

→ the dough is sticky and wet

→ proofing tolerance is greatly reduced

→ the volume of the finished product is small and pale in color

→ the crust of the finished product is hard and brittle and it splinters

→ the baked product has uneven cell structure

→ the finished product tastes bland

The addition of salt, up to the optimum quantity of 1.8% (baker's percent), improves the baking properties of the flour. Larger or smaller quantities of salt lead to deficiencies during the baking process.

Effects of Salt Additions	
Effect:	**Effect on the baking process:**
* Salt reduces the solubility of the gluten.	This increases the resistance and the elasticity of the gluten and maintains these properties for a long period of time.
* Salt reduces the swelling capacity of the gluten.	This gives the dough: • a better firmness, • better properties during make-up, • a better fermentation stability, and • a higher fermentation tolerance. The effects are: • a larger volume of the final product, • a finer texture, • finer cells, • the product is easier to cut, • prolonged shelf life.
* Salt slows the enzymatic breakdown of the gluten.	
* Salt counteracts the fermentation activity of the yeast.	This allows for better control over the fermentation process, and the products brown better.
* Salt improves the taste.	

Bakery products without salt have a reduced quality. This also holds true for products with too much salt. Typical deficiencies of doughs or products containing **too much salt:**

→ The dough is "wet," "short" and "flows;" it is difficult to work with.

→ The dough fermentation is delayed/slowed down.

→ The end product is small in volume.

→ The crust browns very fast.

→ The texture shows dense cells.

→ The product tastes too salty.

Fig. 76 Doughs with varying salt contents: without salt (left), with normal salt content (center), and with a double amount of salt (right)

Compare the "firmness" of the doughs.

Fig. 77 Fermentation (proofing) behavior of doughs without salt (left), with normal salt content (center), and with a double amount of salt (right)

Compare the proofing rate.

Use of salt in wheat-flour products:	
30 g per litre of liquid	= 3.0%
18 g per kg of flour	= 1.8%

Table 9

Food for Thought: *Bakery products containing salt brown well, whereas products without salt brown only slightly.*
Question: Does salt brown when heated?
Answer: No.
Then why do products containing salt brown better?

Many experts claim that yeast and salt should not come into concentrated contact. Do concentrated salt solutions reduce the rising power of the yeast?

Test 14

Crumble 15 g of compressed yeast into small pieces and mix with 5 g of salt.
Let this mixture stand for 15 minutes.

Observation: The dry salt-yeast mixture becomes liquid.

Conclusion: Salt withdraws cell water from the yeast.

Continuation of the test: From this salt-yeast solution prepare a dough made from 250 g bread flour, 140 ml of water and the corresponding quantity of other ingredients.

Observation:
The dough ferments as usual and yields a product free from faults.

Conclusion:
The fermentation enzymes of the yeast retain their fermentation capacity in a concentrated salt solution. Fermentation activity stops in concentrated salt solutions, but, when adequately diluted, becomes active again.

Fig. 78 **Salt-yeast mixture: After a resting period of 15 minutes (left), freshly prepared (right)**

When the salt and yeast amounts required for dough preparation remain in a mixed state for more than an hour, fermentation is slightly delayed.

Concentrated salt solutions destroy the yeast cells; the yeast can no longer multiply. The fermentation enzymes, however, retain their fermentation capacity.

Food for Thought: *Experts base their salt calculation on the total weight of the formula.*
Bakers calculate the amount of salt in two ways: based on total liquids, based on flour weight.

What reasons support each method of calculation? Or is it completely irrelevant how the amount of salt is calculated?

Properties of Salt

Salt is a mineral found in the earth and in the ocean. Salt is a compound of sodium and chlorine (sodium chloride = NaCl).
Common salt is:

— soluble in water;

— attracts water (hygroscopic); and

— has a sharp taste (salty).

Commercial Types of Salt and Their Suitability for the Baking Process

Stone salt is mined.
Compared with other commercially available salts, stone salt has a lower degree of purity. Compared to boiled salt, it dissolves somewhat slower in water.
Coarse stone salt should therefore be dissolved in water before it is incorporated into the dough, as undissolved salt crystals make the dough too moist and reduce its workability.

Boiled salt comes from a concentrated solution of stone salt or ocean water. When the liquid has evaporated, the residue is a fine-grained boiled salt.
Because of its purity and its ability to quickly dissolve in water, boiled salt is better suited for the baking process than stone salt.

Saline salt is boiled salt produced from spring water containing salt. It is comparable to normal boiled salt.

Summary of the most important characteristics of salt

* *When salt is added in normal quantities, it improves:*
   — *the properties of yeast-raised doughs; and*
   — *the fermentation stability and tolerance, therefore achieving a larger volume and a finer texture of the end product.*
* *Because salt slows down the activity of the yeast, it is possible to control the fermentation process, and more sugar remains for browning of the crust.*
* *Usual amounts of salt to use for doughs are:*
   — *18 g per kg of flour; and*
   — *30 g per litre of liquid.*

The Leavening of Wheat-flour Doughs

During the production process, bakery products are leavened. Why?
Because products that are not leavened:
— are heavy (in proportion to their volume);
— have a very small volume;
— have a slimy, inelastic texture;
— are sticky when cut;
— are chewy;
— have little aroma;
— take a long time to digest; and
— are not wholesome.

Only very flat bakery products (such as pita bread) can bake thoroughly without leavening. In ancient times, people made unleavened bread, first from fresh and later from fermenting dough pastes. The fermentation gases leavened the bread. Later, bakery products were leavened by means of sour dough or yeast foam, a product from fermentation.
To produce "sweet" leavened bakery goods, egg foam and steam were used and are still used today.
Leavening has a distinctive influence on the quality of baked goods.

The influence of leavening is apparent in the:
— *volume of the product;*
— *crust;*
— *texture;*
— *taste;*
— *wholesomeness; and*
— *fresh-keeping properties (shelf life).*

Bakery products are leavened with:

- *Yeast and sourdough* = *biological leavening*
- *Steam and air* = *physical leavening*
- *Baking powder, soda and ammonia* = *chemical leavening*

Bakers primarily use yeast as their leavening agent.

The production of baked goods with biological leaveners requires extensive knowledge and experience.

This is why homemakers, for example, often use chemical leaveners instead of yeast in their home-made goods.

Fig. 79
Unleavened and leavened bread (made from the same dough quantity)

Fig. 80
Well-leavened (left) and poorly-leavened (right) textures

Remember:
In most cases, unleavened baked goods are not suitable for consumption (poor digestive qualities).

Yeast as the Leavening Agent

Fig. 81 **Compressed yeast (baker's yeast)**

37

Yeast as a Living Organism

Yeast is alive! Where does yeast come from? Where does it live?

Yeasts are everywhere: in bodies of water, in the air — in all living matter.

Yeasts make their presence known through their decaying activities: food and juice residues start to ferment and finally spoil. Yeast cannot be detected by the human eye without a microscope.

> * *Yeast consists of micro-organisms and is ranked among the lower fungi.*

There are 349 different yeast species that can ferment sugar into carbon-dioxide gas and alcohol. Man has made use of this capacity of yeast since ancient times to make alcoholic beverages. Today, common baker's yeast is a specially-grown strain of **Saccharomyces Cerevisiae**.

Fruit juices containing sugar were fermented solely through their natural yeast content. Later, **wild yeast** was used to cultivate fungus species with specific properties. Such **cultured yeast** species are beer, wine and baker's yeasts.

Function of the Cell Components

Look at yeast cells under a microscope.

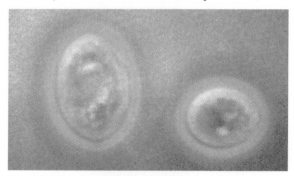

Fig. 82 **Micro-photograph of yeast cells**

Observation: Round to oval cells swim in the solution. They appear translucent and colorless. In the cell, blurry rings and dots in irregular sizes are visible (*Fig. 82*).

In *Fig. 83*, the cell components of the yeast are represented in simplified form.

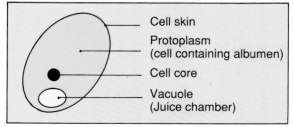

Fig. 83 **Drawing of a yeast cell**

Cell skin
Protoplasm (cell containing albumen)
Cell core
Vacuole (Juice chamber)

The **cell membrane** of the yeast is semi-permeable. Only water, gas and dissolved material can permeate the membrane. This cell membrane allows the yeast to absorb oxygen and nutrients and to give off enzymes and other substances into its environment. This process is also known as osmosis.

The **cell content** consists primarily of water and fine-grained albumen material (protoplasm). This is where all life develops, and where the enzymes for the decomposition of the absorbed nutrients and for the development of cell substances are produced.

The yeast gives off certain enzymes into its aqueous environment in order to decompose large-molecule nutrients (albumen composed of many amino acids). The yeast cell can absorb only small-molecule nutrients such as simple sugars through its cell membrane. The enzymes break down the large-molecule nutrients to create food the yeast can absorb.

Yeast enzymes can decompose the following nutrients:

➤ sugars, such as dextrose, fructose, beet and cane sugar, maltose
➤ albumen
➤ fat

Certain substances, such as starch, dextrine and lactose, cannot be directly fermented by the yeast without the addition of enzymes contained in flour.

The **cell core** is the center of all cell activities and carries all the genes.

The **vacuole** is a chamber in the yeast cell which is filled with cell juice. When there is not enough nutrition, the juice chambers enlarge and the cell chamber containing protoplasm shrinks.

Activities and Living Conditions

> *Yeast needs sugars, but also albumen or nitrogenous minerals, to stay alive.*

In a dough (wheat flour), yeast feeds on dissolved matters of flour, such as malt sugar, some dextrose and albumen. The food supply for yeast in the dough can be specifically improved by adding sugar or baking additives. In general, the dough is an ideal nutrient provider for the yeast.

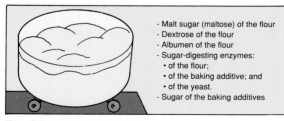

- Malt sugar (maltose) of the flour
- Dextrose of the flour
- Albumen of the flour
- Sugar-digesting enzymes:
  • of the flour;
  • of the baking additive; and
  • of the yeast.
- Sugar of the baking additives

Fig. 84
Yeast food in a dough

It needs water to absorb nutrients and can absorb them only in a dissolved state.

A dough made from wheat flour contains enough water for the yeast to become active. Softer, more moist doughs favor yeast activity.

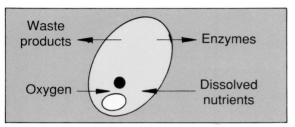

Fig. 85 **Water is a prerequisite for the osmotic action**

Yeast needs warmth to live.

Yeast in dough is active between 0°C and 55°C. At temperatures less than 20°C and over 40°C, the rate of growth is significantly reduced.
Yeast cells die at temperatures of more than 60°C. Yeast can survive for a few weeks at temperatures as low as -20°C, but it gradually loses its fermentation capacity.

The most favorable temperature for yeast to multiply is between 20°C and 27°C; optimum multiplication of yeast is achieved at around 26°C.
The optimum temperature for fermentation lies between 27°C and 38°C; yeast ferments best at 35°C.

Therefore, a dough must be stored at a specific temperature for the activities of the yeast to occur rapidly.

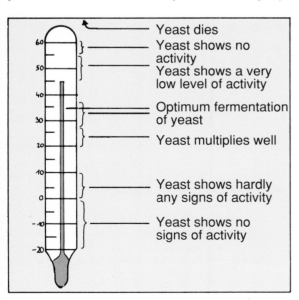

Fig. 86 **Activity of the yeast in relation to temperature**

Yeast needs oxygen to stay alive.

Yeast needs oxygen to "burn" nutrients and to multiply.
Doughs made from wheat flour contain a limited amount of oxygen.
Oxygen enters the dough through the sifting of flour, the water added and the mixing of the dough.
However, the oxygen content in the dough is of no importance in the formation of fermentation gas and for the multiplication of the yeast because:
— formation of fermentation gas is secured through a chemical process which does not involve oxygen; and
— the time period elapsing between dough preparation and baking is too short for the yeast to multiply.

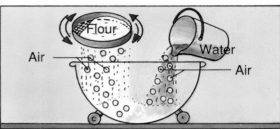

Fig. 87
Incorporation of air into the dough through sifting the flour and through adding water

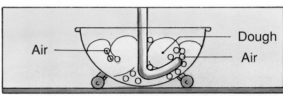

Fig. 88 **Incorporation of air into dough through intensive mixing**

Yeast needs energy to live.

It has two ways of gaining energy:
➤ respiration
➤ fermentation

Respiration

As yeast absorbs nutrients from the dough, it uses oxygen to separate the sugar into carbon dioxide and water and, in the process, energy is released.
Yeast can "breathe" nutrients in this way, provided that:
— sufficient oxygen is available; and
— the temperature is not much higher than 26°C.

Respiration is represented in the form of an equation:
$C_6H_{12}O_6 + 6\,O_2 \rightarrow 6\,CO_2 + 6\,H_2O$ Sugar + Oxygen → Carbon dioxide + Water

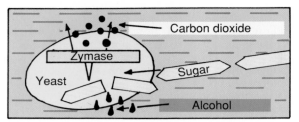

Fig. 89 Schematic representation of alcoholic fermentation

Process of alcoholic fermentation in the form of an equation:
$C_6H_{12}O_6 \rightarrow 2\,CO_2 + 2\,C_2H_5OH$ Sugar → Carbon dioxide gas + Alcohol

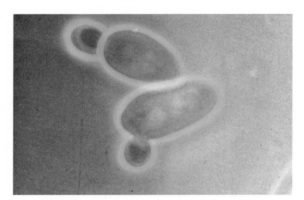

Fig. 90 **Micro-photo: "budding"**

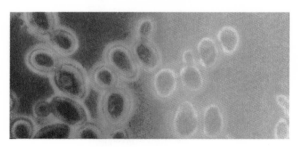

Fig. 91 **Micro-photo: formation of a growth colony of yeast cells**

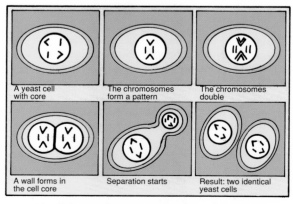

Fig. 92 **Schematic representation of yeast multiplication**

40

Fermentation

During the fermentation process, the yeast uses the fermentation enzyme, *zymase*, to separate dextrose into carbon dioxide gas and alcohol.

Yeast ferments sugars provided that:
— there is a lack of oxygen; and
— the temperature of the nutrient solution (dough) is between 27°C and 38°C.

> **Remember:**
> *The following are unfermentable:*
> ➤ *cellulose*
> ➤ *starch*
> ➤ *dextrine*
> ➤ *lactose (milk sugar)*

In a bakery that is not automated, doughs are usually prepared at temperatures between 24°C and 27°C. The small oxygen content in the dough is quickly "breathed in" by the yeast. Therefore, the sugar dissolved in the dough is fermented due to a lack of oxygen. The products of the fermentation process remain in the dough. A small amount of the carbon dioxide gas dissolves in "free dough water" into a liquid carbonic acid. A small amount of the fermentation gas evaporates. The majority of the carbon dioxide is trapped in the gluten strands and is therefore prevented from leaving the dough. As a result, fermentation gas cells form in the dough and alcohol formed partly evaporates during baking. The remaining alcohol has a favorable effect on the taste of the baked product.

> **Remember:** *Fermentation gases produced by the yeast aerate the dough.*

Multiplication

Compared with other plant organisms, yeast has a much better chance of survival in spite of harsh environmental conditions. It is independent from climate and soil conditions. It is not dependent on any location and can survive for hundreds of years as a spore.

Under favorable living conditions, yeast multiplies through the separation of cells.

Under unfavorable living conditions, when water and nutrients are lacking, the yeast forms spores.

The *cell separation* develops as follows:

The cell core migrates to the cell wall of the yeast cell. It splits up and forms a daughter cell. The daughter cell multiplies in the same way while it is still growing and tied to the mother cell.

A colony develops. Later, the daughter cell separates from the mother cell. The multiplication process continues for as long as the conditions for multiplication are present *(Figs. 90 - 92)*.

The *spores* form as follows:

Once the nutrients of a solution are used up, the yeast becomes dormant and feeds on its reserve material. When the nutrient solution and the yeast cells dry out, the cell core separates and forms spores. The spores are insensitive to heat and cold. The slightest breeze carries them anywhere. Under dry conditions, the spores can live forever. When spores fall into a nutrient solution, they germinate into yeast cells.

Yeast Evaluation

How is yeast properly stored?
In order to find the correct answer, the following must be established:
— what are a baker's yeast requirements?
— what changes does the yeast undergo when stored?

Requirements of Yeast

→ *Baker's or compressed yeast must have good gassing power.*
→ *Yeast must have good storage properties.*
→ *Yeast must produce enzymes that help mature the dough.*
→ *Yeast contributes to the formation of the aroma of breads.*

Test 15 (Fermentation test):

For this test, yeast samples of various commercial brands, yeast samples with various storing properties and yeast samples requiring different storage methods can be used.
In the test, the following kinds of yeast are available:
Sample A = fresh yeast
Sample B = yeast that has been stored for three weeks at room temperature
Sample C = yeast that has been stored for three weeks in a refrigerator
Prepare three doughs each from 100 g of flour, 65 ml of water and 5 g of yeast samples A, B and C. The dough temperature shall be 30°C.
Separate the doughs and press one-half of each into a fermentation cylinder. Let the samples rise at a temperature of about 32°C. Evaluate the samples after 30 minutes.

Observation:
The doughs of samples A and C have risen nearly to the same extent; the dough of sample B has not risen as much as the dough prepared with the other samples (*Fig. 93*).

Parallel Test 16 (gassing test):
Form the other half of each of the three samples into a ball. Place the balls into beaker glasses filled with warm water (32°C).

Observation:
First, the dough balls fall to the bottom. After a short while — approximately three to seven minutes — the dough samples rise to the surface of the water. Probably, samples A and C will rise simultaneously, sample B a little bit later (*Fig. 94*).

Conclusion:
The yeast of dough sample B has a lower rising power. The cause for this is inappropriate storing.

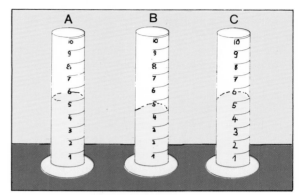

Fig. 93　**Fermentation test**

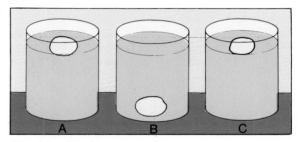

Fig. 94　**Gassing test**

Remember: *Gassing power is the quantity of carbon dioxide formed by a certain amount of yeast under controlled conditions.*

Food for Thought:
A baker uses three-week-old yeast to make rolls. He establishes that the yeast still has good gassing power. Why is the same yeast possibly unsuitable for the production of fancy yeast bakery products?

Taking into account the requirements with regard to gassing power and taste, properly stored yeast can be used for about:

— four weeks to produce regular baked goods; and
— two weeks to make fancy yeast goods (*Fig. 95*).

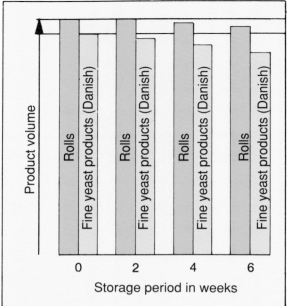

Fig. 95
Volume yield of rolls and other yeast products made from two, four and six-week-old yeast

Fig. 96 **Fresh yeast and yeast that has been stored too dry**

Fig. 97
Older yeast that has been stored dry – leaves dry yeast residue on the paper

Food for Thought:
The type of wrapping material used has an influence on aging or spoiling of yeast. Why do some yeast manufacturers use waterproof wrapping materials for compressed yeast, even though the yeast may spoil faster?

Yeast Storage

Yeast contains up to 75% water. The remainder of the yeast is primarily composed of albumen. Therefore, the yeast offers ideal living conditions for saprogenous (decomposing) organisms.

Changes occurring during storage:	Effects on the baking process:
— Yeast dries out.	➤ No effects on the gassing power and taste.
— Yeast uses a part of its own substance as a nutrient.	➤ Reduced gassing power.
— Yeast decomposes and putrifies.	➤ Loss of gassing power and bad taste.

When the yeast is drying out, it does not immediately lose a part of its gassing power, but the degree of dryness is an indicator of the period of time it has been stored.

Yeast showing symptoms of dryness is usually weakened through *autolysis* (self-fermentation), and can have a reduced gassing power.

Once a yeast package has been opened— even if it is stored in a refrigerator — it is suitable for use for only a few days. The outer yeast layer dries rapidly and forms a hard crust, which does not combine well with water added during the mixing process.

Evaluation of Freshness

When comparing baker's (compressed) yeast in batches that have been stored for varying periods of time, check the package it comes in:

* *Waterproof packages:*
➤ *slow down the drying-out process and the browning of the yeast; and*
➤ *favor decomposition of the yeast.*

* *Water-permeable packages:*
➤ *accelerate the drying-out process and the browning of the yeast; and*
➤ *slow down the decomposition of the yeast.*

* *Yeast is considered spoiled for baking when it no longer possesses sufficient gassing power.*
* *Yeast is spoiled for sanitary purposes:*
➤ *when it has an unpleasant taste or smell;*
➤ *when it is moldy; and*
➤ *when it has a rotten appearance.*

With this information, one can determine whether or not yeast is spoiled.

Methods of Evaluation	Characteristics of Fresh Yeast	Characteristics of four-to-eight-week-old yeast	
		Air access in storage	Airtight storage
Unwrapping	Paper detaches easily	Paper comes off with difficulty; small pieces of yeast stick to the paper	Paper sticks to the yeast; a smeary film remains on the paper
Smell and taste test	Pleasant fermentation smell, no foreign smell	Bitter, unpleasant; brown spots — gray	Somewhat putrid
Surface color	Creamy-gray	Brown specks — gray	Gray
Scratching the surface with a fingernail	Smooth but sticky; produces ripples on surface	Small pieces of yeast come off	Smeary, smooth grooves
Breaking of the yeast	Uneven break with a contoured surface	Yeast falls apart in small pieces	Stringy, rubbery extension until it breaks
Dissolving in water (slurry)	With ease and without residue	With difficulty, residues remain	With ease and without residue
Surface condition	Smooth-dull	Cracked, dry surface	Smeary surface

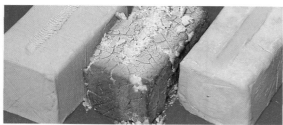

Fig. 98 **Yeast evaluation:**
Scratching the surface with a fingernail. Fresh yeast (left), older yeast stored in a dry environment (center), older yeast stored in an airtight environment (right)

Recommended Storage for Compressed Yeast

Store in room (if no refrigeration is available):	
— very cool, best between 4°C and 7°C	➤ to prevent the yeast from drying out quickly
	➤ to reduce the speed of "autolysis" through the enzymes of the yeast
— in a dry, well-ventilated environment	➤ to prevent the yeast from molding and putrifying rapidly
— protected from foreign odors	➤ to prevent odors from being transmitted into the bakery products
Store in refrigerator:	
— airtight	➤ to prevent the yeast from drying out

Fig. 99 **Yeast evaluation: Breaking test. Fresh yeast (left), older yeast stored in a dry environment (center), older yeast stored in an airtight environment (right)**

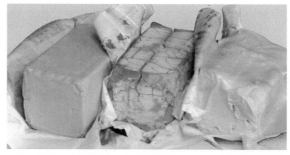

Fig. 100 **Fresh yeast (left), yeast stored in a dry environment (center), and frozen, then defrosted yeast (right)**

Food for Thought:
How often should yeast be delivered to a bakery?
Should freezing be implemented in certain cases?

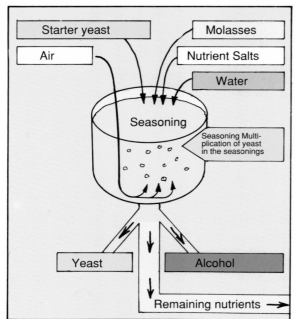

Fig. 101
Simplified graph of yeast production

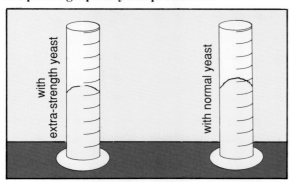

Fig. 102 **Fermentation test with normal yeast and with extra-strength yeast: gassing power**

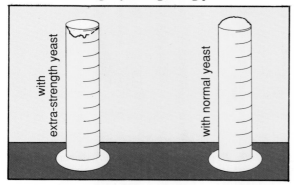

Fig. 103 **Fermentation test with normal yeast and with extra-strength yeast: sensitive to over-development**

Evaluate the gassing power of compressed yeast and extra-strength yeast, and its influence on fermentation tolerance of doughs, based on the two fermentation tests (Figs. 102 & 103).

Disadvantages of freezing yeast:
— The procedure is uneconomical because:
- freezing uses up energy;
- freezing takes up freezer space;
— The quality is reduced because:
- frozen yeast loses its gassing power over a period of time; and
- defrosted yeast must be used up immediately to avoid spoilage (it turns soft, smeary).

Yeast cultivation

Because yeast is a living organism and it cannot be manufactured, it is cultivated in special plants.

* Yeast is cultivated in bacilli cultures.

Appropriate strains of yeast cultures are multiplied in phases to yield the starter yeast.
For mass production, the yeast is made to multiply in huge fermentation tanks. The nutrient solution is provided with oxygen via ventilation systems.
After total consumption of the nutrient solution, the yeast is separated from the remaining nutrient matter by separators (centrifuges) and filter presses.

Additional Information

For yeast cultivation, the necessary nutrients are added to the nutrient matter:

— sugar in the form of molasses ➤ *molasses contains up to 50% beet sugar and 10% minerals*

— nutrient salt containing nitrogen and phosphorous ➤ *with these compounds, the yeast produces cell albumen*

With the aid of a ventilation system, the nutrient solution:
— is provided with oxygen; and
— is temperature-controlled.
The usual temperature for the multiplication process lies between 20°C and 26°C. Lower temperatures increase the yeast yield; higher temperatures increase alcohol production.

Extra-Strength Yeast

As the name indicates, this kind of yeast has stronger gassing power than normal yeast.
But why is it produced, and why isn't all yeast extra strength?
It is necessary to clarify what kind of advantages and, possibly, what disadvantages this type of yeast has compared to normal compressed yeast.

Additional Information

For production of compressed yeast, a nutrient solution made of molasses (residue from sugar production) is used.

Several yeast generations are fed primarily on beet sugar. Such cells orient their enzyme balance directly towards the decomposition of beet sugar.

Baker's (compressed) yeast ferments the beet sugar in doughs better and faster than any other sugar. Yeasts adjust their enzyme production only gradually to the other sugar types present in dough.

Extra-strength yeast is cultivated from yeast cultures which simultaneously ferment both beet sugar and malt sugar.

Such yeast types can readily ferment the malt sugar present in dough. Due to the continuous supply of malt sugar through starch decomposition in the dough, extra-strength yeast guarantees a good gassing power, even in the last fermentation phases of the dough.

Extra-strength yeast is actually less sensitive to concentrated sugar solutions than normal baker's yeast and, therefore, is especially well - suited for doughs containing high amounts of sugar.

Dry Yeast

Dry yeast plays a major role in the commercial and industrial production of baked goods because of its long shelf life and convenient storage.

Instant active dry yeast is powdery and needs no dissolving, but is added dry to the flour immediately before the dough is formed. This type of yeast is gaining in popularity, but there are disadvantages involved in its use. For example, instant active dry yeast has an unfavorable reaction with spices such as cinnamon.

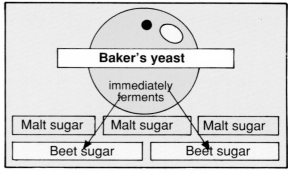

Fig. 104 **Effect of normal (baker's) yeast**

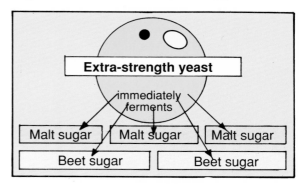

Fig. 105 **Effect of extra-strength yeast**

Dry yeast is of increasing importance:

— for areas without fresh yeast supply; and
— as a back-up supply for emergency and in households.

The water content is only 7% (fresh yeast contains about 75% water).

Granular yeast is one type of dry yeast (active dry yeast) and must be dissolved in water (29°C to 32°C). Because it is very concentrated, up to 60% less active dry yeast is required to achieve the same effect as fresh yeast. A small amount of sugar added at the dissolving stage promotes its activation. This type of yeast can be stored for up to one year without any loss of gassing power.

Summary of the most important facts on yeast as a leavening agent

* *To live, yeast needs food, warmth and moisture, as well as oxygen, to enable it to multiply.*
* *Baker's yeast directly ferments simple sugars like fructose and dextrose and, indirectly, beet/cane and malt sugars. It does **not** ferment starch, dextrine and lactose (milk sugar).*
* *During the fermentation process, yeast converts sugars into carbon dioxide gas and alcohol = alcoholic fermentation.*
* *Yeast must be stored in a cool, dry environment and must be protected against drying out and against foreign odors.*

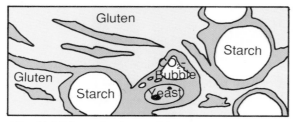

Fig. 106 **Water balance of the yeast in the dough**

Explain the following schematic representation.

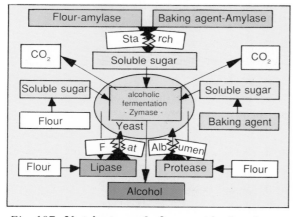

Fig. 107 **Nutrient supply for yeast in dough**

Explain the nutrient supply for yeast with the aid of this diagram.

The Formation of Gas and Cells

Gas Formation

Yeast will find ideal living conditions in a dough: water, nutrients, warmth and some oxygen.

The **water** in the dough is partly fixed and partly free. The major part of the water is fixed by the gluten-forming proteins; a smaller part by the bran particles of the grain. Free water is found on the surface of the starch grains and of the swelled gluten strands, as well as in the free spaces of the flour substance.

The yeast has access to the free water. The water-soluble flour and ingredients dissolve in this water.

The enzymes found in the flour, the yeast and the baking additives are active in this water film.

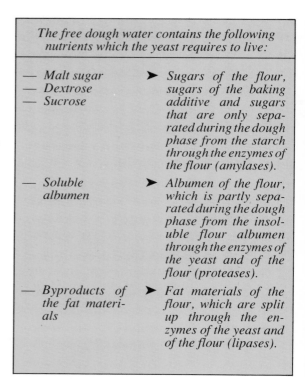

The free dough water contains the following nutrients which the yeast requires to live:

— Malt sugar — Dextrose — Sucrose	► Sugars of the flour, sugars of the baking additive and sugars that are only separated during the dough phase from the starch through the enzymes of the flour (amylases).
— Soluble albumen	► Albumen of the flour, which is partly separated during the dough phase from the insoluble flour albumen through the enzymes of the yeast and of the flour (proteases).
— Byproducts of the fat materials	► Fat materials of the flour, which are split up through the enzymes of the yeast and of the flour (lipases).

How long does it take for yeast to ferment in dough?

The yeast starts to ferment in dough as soon as adequate living conditions are present (when the ingredients are mixed together).

As soon as nutrients are present in a dissolved state, the yeast starts to ferment the sugar for the purpose of producing energy.

The products separated — carbon dioxide and water or alcohol — are given off by the yeast into its environment. (The swelled gluten traps the gas in the dough.)

46

Each yeast cell is surrounded by a gas bubble, which gets bigger and bigger. The dough "rises," is "leavened," and increases in volume.

Cell Formation

When evaluating the "crumb" of a baked product, descriptions such as "large cells," "dense cells" or "fine cells" are often used. To enhance the understanding of these terms, the following diagram shows three typical cells.

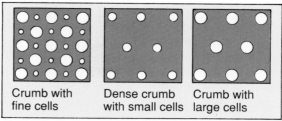

Crumb with   Dense crumb   Crumb with
fine cells   with small cells   large cells

Fig. 108
Schematic representation of cell structures (cells)

Crumb Type:	Description:	Effect:
* Crumb with fine cells	= a large number of small-to-medium-sized cells with tender, thin walls	➤ large volume; tender crumb; keeps fresh for a long time
* Dense crumb with small cells	= a small number of small-to-medium-sized cells with thick, dense walls	➤ small volume; firm, rigid crumb; firm, tough crust; keeps fresh for a short time only
* Crumb with large cells	= a large number of medium-sized to large cells, with partly dense, thick walls	➤ small volume; coarse, firm crumb, keeps fresh for a short time only

Cell formation in yeast-raised products occurs only prior to baking. During baking these cells enlarge, but no new cells are formed.

The assumption that yeast-raised products are leavened only through the activity of the yeast is wrong.

When flour is added to water, fine cells start to form in the dough. In and between the flour particles, air is trapped and partially remains in the dough.

The air content is increased even more through sifting of the flour.

Baking tests have shown that baked products made with sifted flour have a larger volume than those made with unsifted flour.

During mixing, punching and rounding, air is incorporated into the dough. A large number of very fine air bubbles, hardly visible to the eye, are produced in the dough.

> **Test 17 (Cell Formation):**
> Form a piece of dough (50 g is sufficient) immediately after mixing and bake this piece without delay.
> **Observation:**
> The baking time is longer than usual and the dough piece seems to be heavy. The crumb is very dense, but it has small cells.
> **Conclusion:**
> Cells start to form in dough during the mixing stages.

The carbon dioxide quantity produced by the yeast during the mixing stage is very small due to the short mixing time. But even this small amount of carbon dioxide (CO_2) contributes to the formation of the first fine cells in the dough.

> **Cell formation starts during dough preparation by:**
> — incorporating air through addition of ingredients;
> — incorporating air during mixing; and
> — through the fermentation gas of the yeast.

Joe thinks:
"Who cares whether the yeast ferments during the mixing stages or later! Cells can form only after the mixing of the dough!"

Is this true?

No matter how much carbon dioxide has developed through the yeast, alone it cannot produce the desired amount of fine cells in the dough. Cells occur only in those places in the dough where yeast cells ferment. A dough with these kinds of cells yields a crumb that has large, dense cells with thick walls.

To create a large number of tiny cells, the gas must be distributed in the dough. This is accomplished through punching and/or rounding of the partially-developed dough and through intensive working of the dough during finalization and shaping.

The small-and medium-sized cells turn into a multitude of very fine cells. When the dough is worked through, some fermentation gases escape. But the very small cells are not destroyed in the process. Unlike larger cells, very small cells are able to endure strong mechanical stress.

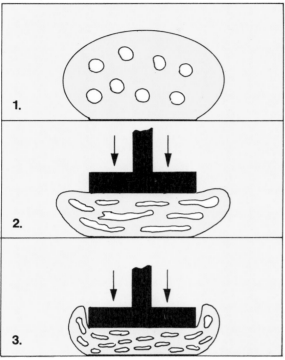

Fig. 109 **Formation of very fine cells in the dough through compression of the partially-developed dough**

For obtaining high-quality baked products, the formation of very fine cells is an important prerequisite. Only a large number of small-and-medium-sized cells with thin, tender walls ensures a high quality of the final product.

Remember:
The very fine cells in the dough are created through:
➤ *the formation of a sufficient quantity of gas;*
➤ *the distribution of the gas in the dough; and*
➤ *manipulation enhancing the capacity of the dough to retain the gas (punching).*

There are many ways to enhance fermentation of the yeast so that a large quantity of carbon dioxide is produced in a very short time.
Most of these measures have, however, a negative effect on the dough properties and on the quality of the product.
All regulating measures must therefore never be evaluated from one point of view (such as an improvement of the fermentation process). All deciding factors having an effect on the quality must be taken into consideration.

The competence of the baker to regulate processes such as mixing, resting periods and proofing, with the objective of creating a high quality product, is referred to as ***dough handling***.
The importance of this process is explained further in the following chapter.

Joe says: *"The cells in the dough are formed through multiplication of the yeast!"*

Thomas says: *"This cannot be true! It takes yeast two to four hours to produce the first daughter cells!" Who is right?*

Summary of the most important facts on gas and cell formation in the dough

* *Yeast ferments sugar in the dough. The carbon dioxide separated in the process forms cells which increase in size.*
* *Many fine cells are created through:*
— *sifting of the flour prior to its incorporation into the dough;*
— *intensive mixing; and*
— *punching and rounding of the partially-developed dough.*

The Dough-Handling Process

Yeast dough changes its properties gradually from the initial preparation phase to the final baking stage:

➤ *Immediately after mixing, the dough is still somewhat moist and overextended.*
➤ *Later the dough relaxes and becomes drier. The extension resistance increases, the extensibility decreases. The dough becomes "shorter" and tears easily when manipulated.*
➤ *The older the dough, the more its capacity to hold gas is reduced; it loses in fermentation stability.*

During their development, yeast doughs briefly attain the dough properties desired for make-up. This degree of maturity is a prerequisite for the production of high-quality bakery products.

A competent baker ***processes*** dough in such a way that it reaches its ***maturity*** at the desired point in time.

Hygiene, Safety and Environmental Protection

The preparation of dough requires a high degree of technical knowledge. Before performing this task, ensure that the following principles are respected with regard to:

- ➤ *hygiene;*
- ➤ *safety; and*
- ➤ *environmental protection.*

* *Wear working clothes that are hygienic and appropriate.*

Dirty clothes (or street clothes) could be carriers of micro-organisms. Only clothes that can be washed at boiling temperatures will meet hygienic requirements. Light-colored clothes are required to reveal dirt.
Clothes must cover the whole body to avoid the contact of body sweat, which contains bacteria, to any product.

* *Hair must be covered with a hat and/or hairnet.*

Long, unprotected hair can be caught up in moving operating equipment, such as a mixer, and cause serious accidents!
And, of course, hair found in bakery products is unacceptable.

* *Wear safe footwear!*

For safety at work, shoes with good foot support and non-slip soles are absolutely necessary.

* *Make sure your hands are always clean — especially during the mixing and make-up stages!*

If a baker's hands show open wounds or cuts, he should not be involved in the preparation, manipulation or make-up stages. Festering wounds are prohibited when working with food (staph contamination). This could lead to food poisoning, especially when contact is made with low acid foods.

* *Smoking in storage and production areas is prohibited!*

Anyone smoking during dough preparation or make-up is guilty of negligence.

* *Ensure that, at the beginning, during and at the end of a working day, bakery equipment and tools are totally clean!*

Cleanliness in a bakery attracts prospective clients. No one wants to buy bakery products that have been contaminated with dust or bacteria.

Joe says:
"*During baking all micro-organisms are killed! So why the need for hygienic regulations?*"
What do you think?

Reference:
The most frequent causes for accidents and the most important measures for accident prevention in the preparation of dough are dealt with in the chapter entitled **Mixing and Make-up of Dough**.

Fig. 110 **The hat must cover the hair!**

Food Regulatory Guidelines:

It is illegal to produce bakery products if their consumption constitutes a health hazard.

The use of adulterated ingredients and products made from spoiled ingredients is prohibited.

Reference:
Special instructions on how to clean electrical equipment are given in the chapter entitled **Types of Mixers**.

During production, regular cleaning activities are necessary. Dirt, dust and spillage must be eliminated.

The same care must be used when selecting ingredients.

➤ Only potable water (drinking quality) may be used for any preparation of food and a good supply of hot water should be available for cleaning purposes.

➤ In some instances, flour should be sifted prior to use. Do not use any flour swept up from surfaces, no matter how clean! Very fine dirt particles and germs cannot be eliminated through sifting.

➤ Do not use any ingredients which have an unpleasant odor! Such ingredients should be considered spoiled.

Food for Thought:
A country bakery uses water from a well and has done so for a generation. The theory is that this water is purer than tap water from a reservoir. What are your thoughts on this?

* *Avoid unnecessary flour dust development!*

During the last few years, the professional disease "baker's asthma" has increased in frequency. This is caused by fine-grained dust particles of the flour which impair the function of the respiratory organs. In a bakery there are three important causes of flour dust creation:

— emptying flour bags into a mixer or bin
— the initial mixing period (the first minute of mixing)
— dusting of flour on working tables, cloths, and baskets during the make-up phase

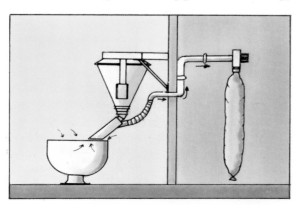

Fig. 111 **Flour dust removal through suction during dough mixing**

Explain the schematic representation of flour dust removal through suction.

New mixers are available with a dust-reducing cover (*Fig. 138*).

Steps in the prevention of dust development:

➤ *High-speed mixers without dust-containing covers should always be operated in first gear during the initial mixing phase.*
➤ *When dusting work tables, avoid stirring up large dust clouds.*
➤ *Take advantage of flour dust-reducing suction equipment (Fig. 111).*

Various Kinds of Fermentation Processes

In principle, there are two fermentation processes:
— direct fermentation
— indirect fermentation

* *Direct Fermentation = the dough is prepared in only one working phase.*

* *Indirect Fermentation = the dough is prepared in two or more working phases; first a sponge dough is made, then the actual dough.*

Direct fermentation is primarily used in today's production processes.
The use of indirect fermentation has advantages as well as disadvantages.

Indirect fermentation	
Advantages:	*Disadvantages:*
— *yeast savings (not applicable to sponge doughs with a short maturing time);*	— *higher fermentation losses (not applicable to sponge doughs with a short maturing time)*
— *formation of a higher proportion of aromatic materials;*	— *requires more time*
— *when using high-gluten flour:*	— *when using low-gluten flour, deficiencies occur in the quality of the final product*
• *a higher product volume,*	
• *better crust and crumb;*	
— *better aeration of the product;*	
— *longer shelf life*	

Food for Thought:
Are sponge doughs made in your bakery? If so, find out why these sponge doughs are prepared.

Treatment of Sponge Doughs:

* Sponge doughs are made only from flour, water or milk, and yeast. A small amount of sugar — up to 2% of the flour content used — can also be added.

* Sponge doughs must "mature." Depending on the method used, the maturing time is from 30 minutes to eight hours.

* Sponge doughs with a short maturing time must be kept warm; those with a longer maturing time have to be kept cool.

* Sponge doughs must be kept soft.

For white-flour products, some of the advantages of indirect fermentation can be achieved through the use of baking additives.

However, this does not apply to the development of the aroma of a product. Therefore, the use of sponge doughs for many breads has increased in recent years.

In many bakeries, indirect fermentation with a long maturing time is used mainly for specialty breads or to obtain more flavor.

Additional Information

Sponge doughs with a long maturing time undergo a profound transformation process. The enzymes present in flour and yeast transform considerable quantities of the flour substance into a soluble state. The metabolism of the yeast does not only yield alcohols and carbon dioxide, but also a multitude of other products of separation. After a resting period of about three hours, the yeast cells start to become active and the yeast multiplies.

In addition to yeast, the dough contains a number of other bacteria which enter the dough through the flour. Due to the long maturing time of the dough, these bacteria can also germinate and multiply. The products of metabolism of the bacteria and the products of separation from the yeast metabolizing the flour substances have an influence on the aroma of the baked product.

During the long fermentation time of the sponge dough, the flour loses much of its baking ability. This loss is primarily due to the separation of the gluten. Therefore, only part of the flour (20 to 30%) is incorporated into the sponge dough when indirect fermentation is used.

Preparation of Ingredients

Let's assume a baker has to prepare the ingredients for a dough for crusty rolls.
The first step, of course, is to **read** the recipe!

The basic recipe indicates the following:
— quantity of ingredients needed (often given only in "baker's per cent," based on flour being 100%)
— desired dough temperature
— yield
— process details such as mixing time, resting times, baking temperature and baking time

Recipe No.	Basic recipe for: crusty rolls		
Ingredients:	per 100 kg Flour	per litre Water	per Press
Bread flour	100.0 kg	1.670 kg	1.000 kg
Water	60.0 kg	1.000 l	0.600 kg
Yeast	6.0 kg	0.100 kg	0.060 kg
Salt	1.8 kg	0.030 kg	0.018 kg
Baking additives	1.8 kg	0.030 kg	0.018 kg
Total dough-weight:	169.6 kg	2.830 kg	1.696 kg

Weight per Press (of dough) .... 1700 g
Dough temperature .... 25 °C
Mixing time .... 7 min.
Resting time .... 8 min.
Baking temperature .... 230 °C
Baking time .... 20 min.

Table 10

The recipe is the quantity of ingredients required for the desired quantity of dough.
The recipe for crusty rolls can be calculated easily: the quantity of ingredients indicated on the basic recipe for a batch of rolls is multiplied by the desired number of batches (see example).

Example: Recipe for 25 batches (presses) of crusty rolls	
25 x 1.000 kg Flour	= 25.000 kg
25 x 0.600 kg Water	= 15.000 kg
25 x 0.060 kg Yeast	= 1.500 kg
25 x 0.018 kg Salt	= 0.450 kg
25 x 0.018 kg Additives	= 0.450 kg

Table 11

Supplies of Wheat Flour

Maintaining an adequate supply of wheat flour requires long-term planning. The supply of flour should be sufficient for at least one week, but should not exceed more than six weeks.

* *Too small a flour supply makes frequent purchases necessary and has the following disadvantages:*
— *Loss of price advantage, which could be achieved through large-scale purchases.*
— *Frequent changes in the production method due to variations in the flour quality.*
— *Differences in the dough temperatures due to flour which has not yet adjusted to the storage temperature.*

The quantity of flour required for dough preparation is scaled and where applicable, sifted. In the case of silo storage, sifting of flour takes place automatically during scaling.

The purposes of flour sifting are:
— to eliminate impurities;
— to dissolve flour lumps; and
— to enrich flour with air.

The air in the flour improves the formation of very small cells during mixing.

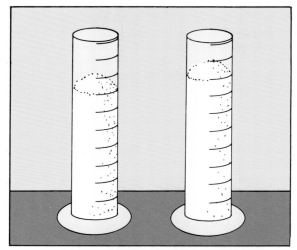

Fig. 112 **Volume of unsifted flour (left), and of sifted flour (right)**

Preparation of Liquid Added to Dough

The liquid added is the only dough ingredient in which the temperature can be easily changed.

* *The desired dough temperature is regulated by the temperature of the liquid added.*

The temperature of the liquid added is essentially dependent on:
— the desired dough temperature;
— the flour temperature; and
— the friction obtained during mixing.
In addition, the room temperature, the temperature of the other ingredients and, where applicable, the temperature of the sponge dough, have an influence on the desired dough temperature.
The following simplified statement applies:

* *The average temperature of the flour and of the water, plus the increase in temperature during mixing (friction) determine the dough temperature (refer to the example in Table 12).*

Example 1: Calculation of dough temperature	
Flour	16°C
+ Water	24°C
=	40°C
40:2 = Average temperature	20° C
+ Friction	6°C
= Dough Temperature	26°C

Table 12

The following formula is used for the calculation of the temperature of the liquid:

> *Desired dough temperature*
> *- Friction*
>
> *= Average temperature*
>   *of flour and water*
>
> *Average temperature x 2*
> *- Flour temperature*
>
> *= Liquid temperature*

Example (without sponge dough): Calculation of Liquid Temperature	
• Desired Dough Temperature	25° C
• Friction	4° C
• Flour Temperature	16° C
Desired Dough Temperature	25° C
- Friction*	4° C
= Temperature Before Mixing	21° C
Temperature Before Mixing x 2 =	42° C
- Flour Temperature	16° C
= Water Temperature	26° C

Table 13

* Friction varies according to the type of mixer used, mixing time and firmness of dough.

To determine the friction factor, the following example can be used:

> *Desired dough temperature*
> *- Friction*
>
> *= Average temperature*
>   *of flour, water and sponge dough*
>
> *Average temperature x 3*
> *- Flour temperature*
> *- Sponge dough temperature*
>
> *= Liquid temperature*

• Desired dough temperature		22°C
• Friction factor		3°C
• Flour temperature		17°C
• Temperature of sponge dough		20°C
	Desired dough temperature	22°C
-	Friction	3°C
=	Average temperature	19°C
	Average temperature x 3 =	57°C
-	Flour temperature	17°C
-	Sponge dough temperature	20°C
=	Water temperature	20°C

Table 14

Remember:

➤ *Cool sponge doughs or extremely cold flours can be compensated for, to a limited extent, only by the temperature of the liquid added:*

— *a 50°C liquid will reduce the fermentation ability of the yeast.*

— *a 55°C liquid will destroy the fermentation ability of the yeast.*

➤ *The further the temperatures are from the flour, sponge dough and the liquids, the higher the deviations will be from the desired dough temperatures.*

Temperature regulation and measuring of liquids is done:

— by the use of a thermometer;
— in semi-automatic temperature-regulating devices; and
— in fully-automatic digitally-controlled water-tempering devices.

What temperature is best suited for the production of white-flour products?

* *The dough temperature is optimal when the dough yields the highest quality of products - - assuming that the rest of the production process is error-free.*

The optimum dough temperature depends largely on the intensity and duration of the mixing process. Doughs prepared in slow-speed mixers are susceptible to faster maturation and should be kept cool for best results.

Doughs prepared in high-speed mixers age more slowly. The cause is better swelling of the dough through intensive mechanical treatment of the flour components. The higher friction will, however, compensate for the temperature adjustment.

The dough temperature has an influence on
* *the dough properties:*
➤ *Doughs prepared under excessively cool conditions mature very slowly. They remain "young" or "green" for a long time.*

— *they are moist*
— *they are sticky and runny*
— *they are not firm and they "flow"*

➤ *Doughs that are made under excessively warm conditions (especially doughs that have been mixed for a long time) mature very fast and get "old" very fast.*
— *they are dry and tend to form a skin*
— *they firm up very quickly*
— *they turn "short" very rapidly*
— *they lose fermentation stability*

* *the behavior during fermentation:*
➤ *Doughs that are prepared under cool conditions ferment very slowly.*
➤ *Doughs prepared under excessively warm conditions reach the peak of their gassing power during mixing or even during make-up.*

* *the quality of the final product:*
➤ *Products from excessively warm doughs:*
— *have small volume;*
— *have a pale crust;*
— *have large cells with thick walls; and*
— *have a reduced shelf life.*

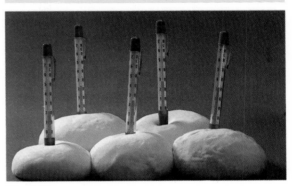

Fig. 113
Checking dough temperatures

Fig. 114 **White bread made at a normal dough temperature (left), and under an excessively high dough temperature (right)**

Data (to *Fig. 114*)
Mixer: High Speed

Dough temperature:	28°C	33°C
Resting time:	15 min.	10 min.
Intermediate proof:	45 min.	35 min.
Baking time:	30 min.	30 min.

Compare and evaluate:
— *the volume;*
— *the crust color; and*
— *the cells/crumb texture.*

53

Approximate Values for the Dough Temperature of Wheat-flour Doughs		
Type of mixer:	Mixing time:	Dough temperature:
Low Speed Mixer	20-30 min.	approx. 23°C
Rapid Mixer	12-15 min.	approx. 25°C
Intensive Mixer	8-10 min.	approx. 26°C
High-Speed Mixer	4- 6 min.	approx. 28°C
Blender-type Mixer	1- 2 min.	approx. 29°C

Table 15

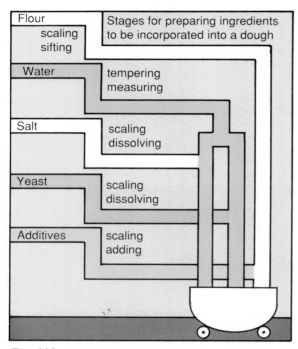

Fig. 115

Preparation of Salt, Yeast and Baking Additives

There is no set sequence in which salt, yeast and baking additives are to be added to the dough.
In general, all these ingredients are added at the same time. Dissolving or slurrying of the yeast and salt in the liquid to be added is recommended to obtain good distribution in the dough.
If instant active dry yeast is used, it should be mixed — like milk powder — with the flour.
The addition of fat at a later stage aids in the lubrication of the dough.

Ready-Mix Flour (pre-mixes) and Ingredients

Flour mills offer mixes for all types of bakery products, from bread mixes to cake and cookie mixes.

> * Mixes are a combination of ingredients for specific bakery products. They contain all durable ingredients in adequate proportions.

In most cases only water and yeast must be added (eggs and water for cakes and cookies). Some changes in mixing and handling procedures are necessary.

Mixes offer the following advantages:

— Less work ➤ This reduces the production costs.

— Quality control and consistency ➤ The possibility of wrong quantities of salt or other ingredients is eliminated. Deficiencies in quality due to an inappropriate ingredient are also eliminated. Using a mix also saves time by eliminating the need to scale many different ingredients.

Food for Thought: In spite of the advantages of using ready-mix flours, a large majority of products are still made from "scratch." What are the reasons for this?

Joe thinks: "The reason is quite obvious! The consumer does not like products made with extra chemicals!" Evaluate Joe's statement.

Salt-Yeast Method

The salt-yeast test in the chapter entitled **The Effect of Salt on the Baking Process** has shown that salt in concentrated form is not or is only minimally detrimental to the yeast when exposed for a short time.
The so-called salt-yeast method can even be advantageous.

The Method:

The salt and yeast required for dough preparation is dissolved, or slurried, in 10 times the quantity of water (in relation to the salt quantity).
The water temperature should not be higher than 23°C. The solution must sit at least four hours but no longer than 48 hours.

Process:

Salt withdraws a considerable amount of liquid from the yeast cells until the salt concentration in the cell and the solution is equally high. This process is called **plasmolysis**.
The salt solution is enriched with the cell albumen and enzymes of the yeast. Most of the yeast cells become inactive in the process. The fermentation enzymes, however, essentially maintain their fermentation capacity. A small loss is compensated for by a somewhat larger addition of yeast (about 1% of the flour).

> **Effect:** The processing properties of the dough are significantly improved, as well as the fermentation stability and fermentation tolerance.

Most doughs usually become dry and "short" after the optimum dough maturity threshold is exceeded. Their capacity to hold gas is then rapidly decreased.

The released cell liquid of the yeast provides the desired degree of moisture to doughs made with this salt-yeast solution. Such doughs retain their moisture for a longer period and can mature without deteriorating. Dough pieces can surpass full maturity without resulting deficiencies.

Example of the Salt-Yeast Method
• Quantity of Dough ....43.0 kg
Total ingredients: Flour ....25.0 kg Water ....15.0 kg Salt ....5.0 kg Yeast ....2.0 kg Baking Additive ....5.0 kg
Ingredients for the salt-yeast solution: Salt ....5.0 kg 10-fold Amount of Water.......................5.0 kg Yeast ....2.0 kg
Dough ingredients: Salt-yeast Solution ....7.5 kg Water ....10.0 kg Flour ....25.0 kg Baking Additive ....5.0 kg

Table 16

Food for Thought: *Which ingredient of a dough should determine the calculation of the other ingredients: the water or the flour?*

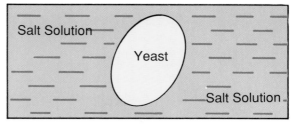

Fig. 116 **Salt-yeast solution: beginning**

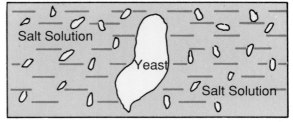

Fig. 117 **Salt-yeast solution: later**

Additional Information

Many bakers calculate the ingredients based on the quantity of liquid added, rather than the quantity of flour. However, the proportion of flour to water will fluctuate when the water absorption rate of the flour is higher (determined by the protein content). An example of how to correctly calculate the proportion of ingredients is shown below.

Example:	
Flour quantity as determining factor:	*Water quantity as determining factor:*
Per kg of flour, 18 g of salt must be used (1.8%). Calculation of salt quantity to be used for dough, rolls or buns, when 60 litres of water are used per 100 kg of flour: *100 x 0.018 kg = 1.8 kg of salt* *Calculation of salt quantity to be used for white bread dough, when 54 litres of water are used per 100 kg of flour:* *100 x 0.018 kg = 1.8 kg of salt*	*30 grams of salt must be used per litre of water. Calculation of salt quantity to be used for dough (rolls/buns), when 60 litres of water are used per 100 kg of flour:* *60 x 0.030 kg = 1.8 kg of salt* *Calculation of salt quantity used for white bread dough, when 54 litres of water are used per 100 kg of flour:* *54 x 0.030 kg = 1.62 of salt*

Because flour makes up the largest portion of dough, changes in the ratio of flour to water cause only slight deviations when calculated in relation to total flour content.
Nutrient concentration in the dough water is the most important factor for the activity of the yeast in the dough. Deviations in the sugar-salt concentration of the dough water are smallest when the liquid added is the determining factor for the other ingredients.

Firmness of the Dough — Dough Yield

It is customary in many bakeries to measure only the quantity of liquid added, but not the quantity of flour. During the initial mixing stages, more flour is added to the dough until the firmness is satisfactory to the baker by means of a simple hand test.

As a normal procedure, **this method is not recommended:**
The hand test is an imprecise measuring method because the firmness of dough varies. The baker risks differing dough properties and fluctuations in the quality of the product.

Fig. 118 **Dough pieces made with a firm dough (left), and a soft dough (right)**

Fig. 119 **French bread made with a firm dough (left), and with a normal dough (right)**

Fig. 120 **Kaiser rolls made with a firm dough (left), and with a normal dough (right)**

Fig. 121 **Vienna rolls made with a normal dough (left), and with a soft dough (right)**

Joe prepares two doughs of equal firmness, but the flour is from two different shipments. 1 litre of water is used for each dough. Flour I yields 2.660 kg of dough Flour II yields 2.810 kg of dough. Joe maintains: "Flour II is better! It yields more dough!" What do you think?

The scaling of all ingredients is of utmost importance. Scaling flour eliminates guess work, produces consistent doughs and eliminates overheating of doughs (due to overmixing, while adding flour or water constantly).

Some of the consequences of soft and firm doughs:

Characteristics and effects of doughs	
Excessively firm:	*Excessively soft:*
— *are difficult to mix*	— *are less firm and therefore "flow"*
— *are too stiff (difficult to weigh)*	— *are sticky to work with*
— *fermentation process is slower*	— *dough pieces easily lose their shape*
— *are difficult to shape*	— *finished product remains fairly flat; it has a tendency to form "footing"*
— *products show poor symmetry*	
— *volume is smaller*	— *volume is smaller*
— *product will show a pale crust*	— *crumb shows uneven, large cells*
— *crumb shows dense cells and often has a streaky texture*	— *product has a deep brown crust*

The water absorption rate of the flour may change from time to time. This is not a significant variable for the small bakery, but needs to be closely monitored in large industrial operations.

The quantity of water that flour can absorb depends on the following factors:	
— *the degree of fineness of the flour* ▶	*dark-colored flour absorbs more water than light-colored flour, because the proportion of swollen grain components increases with the degree of fineness of milled flour*
— *the composition of the flour* ▶	*high-gluten flour generally absorbs more water than low-gluten flour*
— *the water content of the flour* ▶	*the higher the water content, the lower the water absorption capacity*
— *the dough temperature* ▶	*doughs that are kept warm during mixing absorb more water than doughs that are kept cool*

Only an experienced baker can determine the optimum dough firmness.

Evaluate the firmness of the dough.

In order to compare the water absorption capacity of flour, it is expressed in terms of **dough yield.**

* The dough yield is the quantity of dough obtained from 100 weight units of flour.

Example: 100 units of flour and 60 units of water = a dough yield of 160.

The dough yield number is of two-fold importance for practical use:
● It helps to determine the flour-water ratio, which allows for doughs of equal firmness.
● It makes it possible to express the evaluated optimum dough firmness with an index number.

The flours from the last harvest have yielded the following quantities of dough*:
— for manual make-up doughs (for rolls and buns): dough yield = 156 to 162
— for automated systems, (bun lines, overhead systems): dough yield = 152 to 156
— for white bread production: dough yield = 150 to 156
* These are European examples; North American dough yields are generally higher.

Additional Information

The dough yield can be used as an index for the water absorption capacity of flour, but cannot directly be used for the calculation of dough quantities. In practice, other ingredients are also used:
— ingredients increase, through their quantity proportion, the dough yield
— ingredients change, through their properties, the dough yield

In practice, fermentation and scaling losses, as well as losses through dust development of the flour (in the initial blending stage), must be considered.
For calculation of quantities of dough, the following terms are of importance:

Net dough yield	= *Quantity of dough obtained with 100 kg of flour and quantity of water.*
Gross dough yield	= *Quantity of dough obtained with 100 kg of flour, the quantity of water and other ingredients.*
Real dough yield	= *Quantity of dough obtained with 100 kg of flour, the quantity of water and the other ingredients, minus losses due to fermentation and small scaling inaccuracies.*

Dough Mixing and Development

Test 18:
1. Blend 3 parts of flour and 2 parts of water.
2. Blend 3 parts of wheat starch and 2 parts of water.

Observation:
Flour and water yield a dough. Starch and water yield an aqueous slurry.

Conclusion:
Wheat flour has dough-forming properties.

Fig. 122 **Dough made from flour and water (left); slurry made with starch and water (right)**

When preparing a yeast dough for rolls or buns in a mixer, the following observations can be made:
In the first stage a mixture of flour, ingredients and water is obtained in the form of loose strands. Gradually this mixture turns into a sticky, moist dough. Finally the dough loses its thick, sticky consistency; it becomes smoother and dryer.

If the mixing process is not interrupted in time, the moisture content and the stickiness of the dough increase again.

The dough development proceeds in phases, without distinct transition:

1. Phase ➤ *Blending*
2. Phase ➤ *Dough formation*
3. Phase ➤ *Dough development*
4. Phase ➤ *Over-mixing*

Blending Phase

In the initial dough preparation phase, the condition for the formation of dough is created through the **blending** of all ingredients.

The distribution of all ingredients, the individual flour components, and especially the water, continues up to the end of the mixing process.

Dough Formation Phase

Dough formation commences as soon as flour comes into contact with water.

Dough formation proceeds as follows:
— *the swollen flour components absorb water*
— *the swollen flour components stick together and form a network of gluten strands*
— *the water-soluble substances, such as sugar and salt, start to dissolve*

Additional Information

The gluten-forming proteins in wheat flour do not appear in single molecules, but in the form of **colloids**. *These are conglomerates of many protein molecules of microscopic size. They have the capacity to trap water between the individual molecules.*

The gluten-forming proteins absorb twice their own weight in water.

Flour starch in pure form is not (or only minimally) able to swell. It is, however, able to deposit about a third of its own weight in water on its surface.

The shell components of the flour contain a large percentage of expandable materials: pentosan, cellulose, hemi-cellulose. Therefore, dark-colored flour/whole-wheat (which is rich in shell components) absorbs more water than light-colored flour.

Through swelling, the gluten-forming substances increase their surface. During mixing of the dough, the swollen albumen substances are pressed together, moved against each other and stretched, sticking together to form a network. This is how gluten is formed, which in turn forms the dough texture. The gluten network contains other dough components.

Dough Development Phase

Immediately after its formation, a wheat-flour dough is not yet sufficiently developed to be processed into bakery products. For proper development, the dough must be mixed intensively.

Fig. 123 **Effect of mixing on the fermentation stability: intensively mixed dough (left), and under-mixed dough (right) under identical conditions**

Reasons for insufficient suitability of under-mixed doughs:	
— *The swelling of the dough is insufficient.*	➤ *The dough is difficult to work with; it is sticky. This can be partially compensated for by increasing the resting period of the dough.*
— *The water-soluble substances, such as salt, sugar and albumen, are not yet sufficiently dissolved.*	➤ *The dough remains very moist; the nutrient content in the dough water is not yet optimal for the yeast to become active.*
— *The proportion of incorporated air and of fermentation gases in the dough is still very small.*	➤ *The dough lacks the required small cells; they are no longer achievable to the extent desired, even with the fermentation gases forming after mixing phase.*
— *The fat substances of the flour, or the fat through addition, have not yet sufficiently emulsified.*	➤ *Therefore, the dough does not yet have the desired condition.*

Deficiencies due to under-mixed doughs are:
— small volume;
— insufficient development;
— insufficient "bloom*" of the crust; and
— coarse crumb.
***Bloom** is the surface appearance of bread, cakes, flour, etc. The bloom of bread or of the crust of bread refers to the gradations and tints of color produced by carmelisation.

Fig. 124 **Effect of the mixing on the quality of the product: Vienna rolls made with an under-mixed dough (left), and with a properly mixed dough (right)**

Compare the volume and shape.

Through intensive mixing, the flour components are well-distributed in the dough, thus enhancing the swelling of the flour. The reduction in the amount of free dough water causes the dough to firm up.

Friction during mixing increases; the dough warms up. Therefore the gluten properties and the fermentation stability are improved.

A longer mixing time and a warmer dough temperature favor the fermentation process of the yeast. Fermentation gases are incorporated into the dough texture at the same time as air.

The volume of the dough increases. After the mixing stage is finished, the dough has very small cells which persist during subsequent phases.

The mixing is completed when the dough has reached its highest development stage.

In most bakeries this moment is determined based on experience.

* *The moment the dough reaches optimum development is the ideal mixing time.*

How to determine the optimum mixing time:
— the dough reaches its highest degree of firmness
— the dough is less moist; it has a soft, smooth texture
— the dough detaches from the mixing bowl and arm during mixing
— the dough has a smooth, lighter-colored surface
— by the window test; a piece of dough is stretched lightly with the fingers:
— if it breaks too easily, the dough is under-mixed;
— if it becomes nearly clear - like a window - the optimum mixing time has been reached.

* *The time from the start of mixing to optimum dough development is referred to as the **dough development time**.*

Fig. 125
Effect of mixing on the volume of dough: Dough volume of under-mixed dough (left), and of intensively mixed dough (right)

Joe says:
"What has the mixing time got to do with the quality of the product?! I know from my colleagues, that in some bakeries the dough is mixed for only 90 seconds and in others for more than 10 minutes. And all of them bake good rolls!"

Fig. 126 **An intensively-mixed dough**

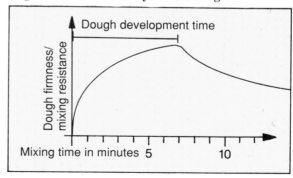

Fig. 127 **Dough development as a function of mixing resistance and time**

Explain this diagram.

What factors determine the mixing time?	
— The mixing speed:	➤ As the mixing speed increases, the dough development time decreases.
— The mixer:	➤ The larger the proportion of dough constantly worked by the mixer, and the higher the compression of the dough, the shorter the dough development time.
— The dough temperature:	➤ As the temperature increases, the development time decreases; warmth enhances swelling of the dough.
— The firmness of the dough:	➤ In the case of firm doughs, the desired degree of swelling of the dough is achieved earlier due to a higher flour content and the higher degree of warming (caused through the higher friction in firmer doughs).
— The flour quality:	➤ Doughs made with high-gluten flour take longer to develop than doughs made from low-gluten flour.

Reference: *For approximate values for the optimum mixing time, refer to the chapter* **Mixers**.

The mixing time is primarily determined by the type of mixer used and the mixing speed.

Other factors, such as dough firmness, temperature or flour quality have only a limited effect on the optimum mixing time.

Fig. 128 **Vienna rolls made with an intensively-mixed dough (left), and with an over-mixed dough (right)**

Phase of Over-Mixing

What are some of the symptoms of an over-mixed dough?
— decreasing firmness during mixing
— increasingly shiny-moist dough surface
— increasing extensibility of the dough
— "flowing" of the dough

Over-mixing causes these product deficiencies:
- *small product volume*
- *poor coloration of the crust*
- *bland-tasting product*
- *reduced shelf life (fresh-keeping qualities)*

A dough has been over-mixed when the dough properties and the quality of the product are lower than those of comparable doughs for which a shorter mixing time was used.

Additional Information
Over-mixing of the dough causes excessive stress on the gluten strands and the gluten structure is destroyed. In the process, incorporated dough water is released again.

A small degree of over-mixing can be compensated by a longer resting period. The dough recovers in most instances.

The baker has no means at his disposal to compensate for excessive over-mixing.

The degree of over-mixing a dough can endure, without becoming deficient, is called **mixing tolerance**.

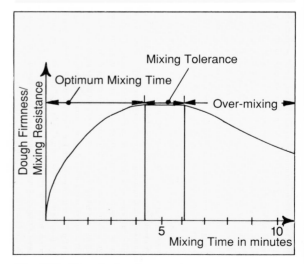

Fig. 129 **Dough development**

Explain this diagram, in particular:
— optimum mixing time
— mixing tolerance
— over-mixing

Summary of the Most Important Information on Dough Mixing and Development

* The period of time from the start of mixing to optimum dough development is referred to as the **dough development time**.
  It includes:
  — the blending phase;
  — the dough formation phase; and
  — the dough development phase.
* **Intensive Mixing**
  — reduces the fermentation time
  — improves the dough properties
  — improves the quality of the product
* **The optimum mixing time** depends on the mixers used and mixing speed.
* **Over-mixed doughs** lead to deficiencies in the product.

Mixers

There are several types of mixers available for the baking industry.
Evaluate the mixing systems and requirements in your bakery.

Requirements From Mixers

Bakers require:	Industry offers:
* Optimum dough development in a short period of time	➤ Mixing systems with high intensity (high degree of effectiveness and high mixing speed)
* Suitability for all dough types	➤ Mixers with variable speeds and proper attachments
* Suitability for various dough sizes	➤ Mixers with uniform effects on large, but also on extremely small doughs
* Yeast activation (successful stimulation of the fermentation process) during mixing	➤ Mixers that accomplish the blending and the slight warming of the dough during mixing
* Formation of very small cells during mixing	➤ Mixers that ensure strong aeration of the dough during mixing
* Easy dough transportation	➤ Mobile mixers; tilting, lifting-tilting equipment

* Simple and easy handling	➤ Elements for easy handling within a small radius from the work place
* Easy servicing	➤ Long servicing intervals; easy access for lubricating parts and changing oil
* Easy cleaning/ sanitizing	➤ Rounded angles and corners on all outside equipment parts; impact-resistant, smooth paint; bowls and accessories made of stainless steel
* Little environmental impact	➤ Low-noise and low vibration machine operation; moving rollers with a synthetic finish; dust-proof bowl cover
* High safety standards	➤ Automatic switch-off devices when the protective grid or the bowl-cover is removed or opened; safe electrical connections

Types of Dough-mixers

Mixers are categorized according to:
— the mixing intensity; and
— the mixing system used.

Percussion Mixer

One-arm lifting mixer

Double-cone mixer

Spiral mixer

Twisting mixer

Circular impact mixer

Fig. 130 **Schematic representation of mixers**

Categorization According to Mixing Intensity	Rotations per minute (RPM)	Approximate Mixing Time	Mixing System
Dough blender	2000 — 3000 1000 — 1500	approx. 60 seconds approx. 120 seconds	Circular impact mixer
High performance mixer	200 — 300	4 — 6 minutes	Twisting mixer (planetary system mixer)
Intensive mixer	120 — 180	8 — 10 minutes	Percussion mixer with two gears Spiral mixer with two gears Double-cone mixer with two gears Intensive-plus mixer with two gears
Rapid mixer	60 — 90	12 — 15 minutes	Lifting mixer with two gears Twisting-lifting mixer with two gears
Slow-speed mixer	25 — 40	20 — 30 minutes	Twisting-lifting mixer

Mixing Systems

The **circular impact mixer** operates based on the principle of a blender. At the bottom of the bowl a mixing tool/blade rotates at high speed.

In the last phase of dough development, the dough warms up very quickly. This is caused by the conversion of friction into warmth, which increases as the dough becomes firmer.

The dough begins to overheat as soon as the optimum mixing time is slightly exceeded, and this can lead to deficiencies in the product. An attempt to correct the dough firmness, through the addition of flour liquid after dough formation, also leads to over-mixing.

Fig. 132 **Horizontal mixer (small version)**

The **spiral mixer** belongs to the category of intensive mixers. The spiral mixing arm protrudes from the bowl wall to the center. The rotating bowl continuously feeds the dough to the mixing spiral. The temperature increase of the dough is approximately 5° C. Spiral mixers are very efficient, even for dough sizes that use only a small per cent of their maximum capacity.

Fig. 131 **Circular impact mixer/blender**

Fig. 133 **Spiral mixer**

Depending on its mixing speed, the *lifting mixer* belongs in the category of fast mixers or intensive mixers. The mixing arm lifts while the bowl rotates, therefore increasing the mixing effect. The increase of temperature during the operation of the lifting mixer is very low and is higher during the operation of the intensive mixer.

Fig. 134 **Schematic representation of the operation of a lifting mixer**

The *twisting mixer* belongs to the group of high-performance mixers. Its two twisting arms are installed off-center in the mixing bowl and move in opposite directions. The rotating bowl increases the mixing effect through continuous re-feeding of the dough. The friction on this mixer is higher than 5°C.

Fig. 135 **Twisting mixer**

Twisting/lifting mixers fall into the group of slow mixers. They are suited for rye and coarse meal doughs, but are also sufficient for wheat-flour doughs.

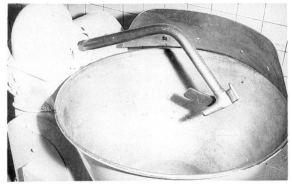

Fig. 136 **Twisting/lifting mixer**

Additional Information
High-speed mixers are best suited for high-performance bakeries, and are easily incorporated into an efficient production line.

They are the only mixers that ensure reduced fermentation time (refer to page 65), a prerequisite for continuous dough make-up without (or only little) resting time. In large-scale bakeries, high-performance mixers are used with other equipment to increase the capacity of production.

In fully-automated plants, the metering of ingredients, temperature regulation, feeding, mixing and dough development are performed under ideal conditions and high-performance mixers are essential.

Continuous mixers have a high hourly performance. Here the dough is not prepared by conventional means, but rather in a continuous process. The ingredients are added in an infinite stream to the blending and mixing chamber of a metering plant. The dough leaves the mixer as a continuous strand and is fed into the make-up plant.

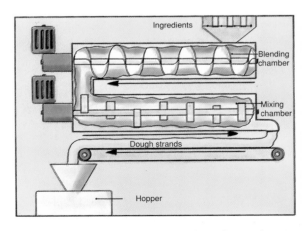

Fig. 137 **Schematic representation of a continuous mixer (dough preparation in a continuous strand)**

Joe is smart! *He has taken the protective covering off the mixing bowl. This way he can scrape the sides of the bowl and remove the sticky dough while the machine is still running.*

How smart is Joe?

Fig. 138
Spiral mixer with a bowl cover (in accordance with safety regulations) to protect anyone from injuries caused by the mixing arm or from breathing flour dust

Caution!
Repair work on electrical installations and equipment must be done only by a certified electrician.
This applies also to the repair and exchange of electrical outlets.
Machines must be equipped with protective devices to prevent electrical shocks. Defective repair work on electrical devices can be deadly.

Mixing equipment should be operated and cleaned only by responsible people. Young baker apprentices should operate equipment only under the supervision of experts.

Dangers Associated with Working on Mixers

The installation of electrical equipment and its subsequent operation should follow local safety regulations for the protection of operators.

The most dangerous areas of mixers are:
— *areas where the mixing arm moves along the bowl-wall; where hands and arms can be caught and bruised or severed; and*
— *rotating attachments in the form of hooks, paddles or whips on planetary mixers, or spirals and blades on other mixers.*

Protective devices on mixers must be designed so that access to the dangerous areas is **prevented,** and that access from the front is at least **made difficult.**

All mixers must be constructed so that the mixer stops as soon as the protective cover is lifted or removed. The cover above the mixing bowl must also prevent or reduce flour dust development and inhalation. (Fig. 138)

What could cause a mixer to stop suddenly while preparing a dough?
Possible causes are:
➤ a broken fuse:
 ● through short-circuiting,
 ● through excessive charge (overloading);
➤ interruption of a current conductor in the plug, in the electrical outlet, in the motor connection; or
➤ sliding of a drive belt.

If the safety device switches off again immediately after having been switched on, a short circuit is the probable cause.
If a fuse blows (breaker switches off) again, but only after the mixer has been running for a while, the electrical circuit is overloaded. The cause for this could be that the dough currently mixing is too large or too firm for the capacity of the mixer.

If the fuse is intact, an interruption in the electrical current conductor could be the cause.
If the motor of the mixer continues to run after the attachments have stopped operating, it is possible that the drive belt is not transmitting power from the drive to the attachment. After correcting the tension of the drive belt, the machine is ready for operation (follow the instruction manual).

Maintenance of Mixers

Modern mixing equipment requires little maintenance. A good system of preventive maintenance will:
— keep the machines operational;

— increase the life expectancy of equipment; and
— prevent hygienic problems.

The following maintenance work should be performed on a weekly basis:

* *Check the oil level in the gear casing: the time intervals at which oil changes are required are indicated in the operating manual. Modern mixers normally have a fully-automatic pulsating oil supply. An oil change is required only after several years of operation.*

  ➤ *Gear wheel drive and chain drive are destroyed after a short period of operation if the oil film between metal parts is interrupted.*

* *Lubricate bearings; grease cups/nipples are provided for that purpose. With modern equipment, greasing occurs automatically.*

  ➤ *Bearing lock will occur after a while if the lube film is not adequate.*

* *Lubricating of guide rollers, spindles, stops, driving and steering rolls.*

* *Control of drive belt tension.*

In a bakery, a high amount of dust develops within a short time. An initially sticky and later solid dirt layer develops rapidly through steam condensing on equipment and tools.

This dirt layer, rich in nutrients, is an ideal breeding ground for micro-organisms, mites and insects.

The equipment should therefore be cleaned daily. Hot water is used to wash off the dust, but adding detergent to the hot water increases the cleaning effect.

Bowls and mixing arms must be rinsed with clear water. Once a week the machines should be cleaned with a disinfectant solution. After this procedure, *rinsing* with hot water is essential.

The use of disinfectants reduces the risk of transmitting germs to products and reduces bacteria to safe levels.

A good sanitation program should be applied in all bakeries.

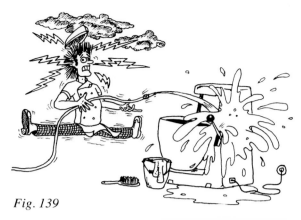

Fig. 139

Caution!
Do not clean equipment with a hose or other similar devices; a dangerous short circuit could result!

Remember:
Do not remove dried-on, heavy duty dirt with a metal scraper or scouring agent. This would cause rusty spots on the equipment or roughening of the synthetic finish. When wiping the equipment, ensure dirt does not get into the small grooves.

Dough Fermentation

Dough cannot be shaped immediately after mixing, even if physical strength is applied. The outer dough layer will break. However, shaping of the dough is possible after a short resting period.

A young dough can be shaped after a short resting period, but is initially very sticky. This applies especially to under-mixed dough prepared under cool conditions.

Products made from such doughs (without a resting time) are of low quality, even if all other steps of the fermentation process are implemented. The crumb of such a product is poorly aerated and shows signs of thick cell walls. A resting period prior to make-up is essential.

* *Dough maturity is the most favorable condition prior to make-up.*

Doughs, which have not matured enough are called *young doughs*. Doughs which have exceeded the optimum degree of dough maturity are called *old doughs*.

Fig. 140 **Rolls made from a young dough (left), and with a dough of optimum maturity (right)**

Fig. 141 **Roll made with an old dough**

Remember:
Prior to make-up, dough has to rest.
Dough-swelling has to be adequate before make-up.
A minimum amount of fermentation gases must form before the dough can be made up and shaped.

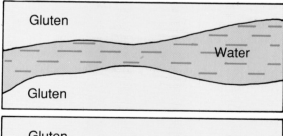

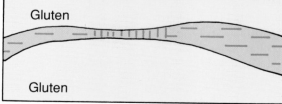

Fig. 142
Young dough: The gluten has not sufficiently swelled; it can be moved; it " flows " (above)
Old doughs: Adequately swelled gluten strands stick together. The dough has "firmness" (below)

Dough and product faults due to young doughs:	old doughs:
— the dough is sticky and "flows"	— the dough surface is very dry
— the dough is poorly aerated	— the dough is poorly aerated
— the product volume is small	— the product volume is small
— poor bloom	— the product is rough — the crust color is pale
— the crust is dark and shows brown spots	— the crumb is dry and crumbly
— the cells of the crumb have thick walls	— the product has a bland taste

Dough fermentation starts at the mixing stage and continues to the point when the yeast is killed in the baking process.

Doughs that are made fairly warm reach their optimum maturity at the end of the mixing process.

Swelling Maturity

After the mixing stage, the flour components are not yet completely swelled.

In wheat-flour doughs, approximately 80% of the liquid added is permanently absorbed immediately after mixing. The remaining 20% is free. The liquid is trapped between the gluten strands on the surface of the dough substances and on the inner and outer walls of the gas cells. The water film is still very strong on these interfaces shortly after mixing.

The high degree of moisture on these surfaces immediately after mixing causes:
— stickiness of the dough;
— high extensibility of the dough; and
—"flowing" of the dough.

Through progressive swelling, the dough loses its stickiness. The dough becomes increasingly "shorter" and "firmer."

Additional Information

*The **swelling maturity** is the time when the moisture is balanced on the inner and outer interfaces of the dough.*
The degree of dough moisture has a strong influence on the dough characteristics, in particular:
— the workability of the dough; and
— the dough properties favoring the formation of very small cells.

Too high a degree of moisture on the inner walls of the fermentation gas cells prevents, during the punching stage, the cohesion of the inner cell walls.

The strong water film on the cell walls isolates and presses the walls together. Instead of many very small cells, a few flat cells form.

When swelling maturity begins, the cell wall moisture is so low that cells pressed together on the inner walls stick together, and the gases remaining in the dough form very small cells.

Dough Fermentation — Dough Maturing

In order to achieve dough maturity, the dough must swell and the yeast must undergo fermentation. Fermentation gases form cells in the dough.

The gas cells are a prerequisite:

— for formation of very small cells during working of the dough; and

— for rapid development of the dough-swelling process.

When cells form, the dough increases its inner surfaces, and the free dough water is distributed over larger interfaces. This enhances swelling.

Maturing of the dough is favored:
— *through dough preparation in a warm environment*
— *in firm doughs;*
— *through a high proportion of yeast;*
— *through baking additives containing fat and emulsifiers; and*
— *through intensive mixing.*

Additional Information

In continuous preparation of wheat-flour doughs (the customary process for industrial roll production) the possibilities of an accelerated dough maturing process are fully realized.

Doughs are made firm (dough yield 152 - 155) and prepared under warm conditions (28°C to 30°C). They are mixed in high speed (horizontal) mixers. Dough maturity is achieved at the time the mixing is completed. A short resting time, usually the time it takes to transport the dough to the overhead system, is sufficient to relax the dough.

When the dough is prepared at temperatures of more than 30°C, optimum dough maturity is achieved during the mixing process. Such doughs are "old" and show corresponding deficiencies as a result.

Fermentation Tolerance

* *Fermentation tolerance is the period of time dough can endure from the time of maturity to the moment of make-up, without negative effects on the quality of the eventual product.*

The fermentation tolerance is increased:
— through the use of strong (high-gluten) flour;
— through dough preparation in a cool environment;
— through a small proportion of yeast used, and through baking additives containing emulsifiers.

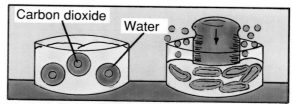

Fig. 143 **Young dough: cell walls are very moist; when pressed together, they yield few, flat cells**

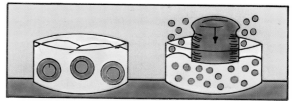

Fig. 144 **Mature dough: cell walls are only somewhat moist; when pressed together, they yield many small cells**

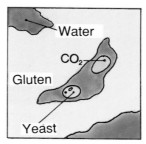

Fig. 145 **Dough swelling as a function of dough fermentation; the larger the cells grow through fermentation gas formation, the more the cell wall moisture is reduced**

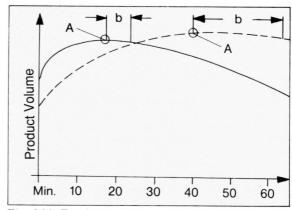

Fig. 146 **Product volume as a function of dough resting time**
———— : Curve for dough # 1
---------- : Curve for dough # 2
Point "A" signifies the time of optimum dough maturity. The distance "B" signifies the extent of fermentation tolerance

Evaluate dough # 1 and # 2 based on the schematic graph.

67

Summary of information on dough maturing
* *Dough maturity is the optimum moment for the make-up process.*
* *Dough maturing encompasses swelling maturity and a minimum fermentation activity of the yeast in the dough.*
* *Maturing of the dough is accelerated through:*
— *dough preparation in a warm environment;*
— *preparation of a firm dough;*
— *the use of high proportions of yeast;*
— *intensive mixing; and*
— *the use of baking additives containing fat and emulsifiers.*

Fig. 147

During the baking process, products lose weight = baking loss

	Baking weight	Baking loss
Rolls	50 g	17 - 20%
	45 g	18 - 20%
White bread	500 g	14 - 16%
	1000 g	11 - 13%

Table 17

Fig. 148 **Bakery products during cooling lose weight = cooling loss**

The Make-up Process

The make-up procedures for rolls, buns and breads vary from manual to semi-and fully-automated equipment.

Manual make-up is limited to only a few bakeries or bakeries too small to warrant modern equipment.

Commercial bakeries use semi-and-fully-automated equipment for efficiency and consistency.

Scaling of Dough

As soon as dough has reached its optimum maturity, it is divided into smaller portions for bread and roll production.

This weighing of dough pieces, commonly referred to as **scaling**, is carried out by manual or automated equipment, such as "scale-o-matic" devices and overhead hoppers.

The baking and cooling loss must be taken into account at the time of scaling the dough so that the desired weight (net weight of the product) is achieved. The weight loss during baking, cooling and storage is caused by evaporation of moisture. Cooling loss and storage loss are commonly included in the term **baking loss**.

> * *The actual baking loss is the weight loss occurring during baking and cooling.*

For calculations pertaining to baking loss, the values shown in *Table 17* are very helpful.

Fig. 149

During storage, bakery products lose weight (storage loss)

Reference: *The application of weights and measures varies from country to country. Some guidelines are given in the chapter* **Weight Loss for Wheat-flour Products.**

Fig. 150
The percentage of baking loss is low in large volume products

Fig. 151
Baking loss percentage is high in smaller baked items

Fig. 152
Compact products, such as those shown, have a lower baking loss

Fig. 153
The baking loss is higher in long, thin products

The following example will show how a calculation is made to compensate for a baking loss. Calculation for a press of rolls (36 pieces); finished roll to weigh 45 g.
The weight loss estimated during baking and cooling is approximately 18%.

Solution: 45 g x 36 pieces = 1620 g dough
dough = 100%
- baking loss = 18%

Product = 82%

$$82/100 = 1620/x$$
$$82x = 100 (1620)$$
$$x = \frac{100 (1620)}{82}$$

$$100\% = 1975.60 \ g$$

1,975 g of dough is needed for one press of rolls producing 36 rolls.

Fig. 154 Products with high-density crumb structure have less of a baking loss

Fig. 155 Higher baking loss is common in products with a large cell structure

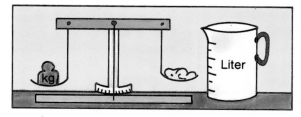

Fig. 156
Some methods of scaling and measuring:
Scaling by a balance scale (left), and measuring volume in a marked container (right)

Most bakeries still use the manual method for scaling dough. However, the application of dough dividers has become more popular in recent years.

Dough dividers measure the volume rather than the weight of the dough. By adjusting the measuring piston, a relatively high degree of accuracy can be achieved.

Dough scales and dividers do not have to comply with government regulating agencies for their accuracy, as the net weight is the deciding factor.

Remember:
1. *Baking loss is the weight loss during baking.*
2. *Baking loss is principally related to the weight of the dough.*
   Weight of dough = 100%

69

Rounding

After the scaling process, the dough pieces are given a round shape either by hand or by an automatic dough-rounder.

The purpose of this process is to:
➤ *eliminate air pockets;*
➤ *achieve a uniform tension in the dough;*
➤ *achieve a smooth dough surface;*
➤ *provide basic shape for molding into a uniform dough piece; and*
➤ *distribute yeast cells and dough temperature evenly throughout.*

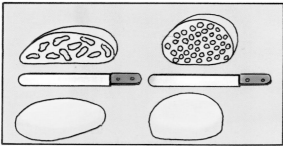

Fig. 157 **Unshaped, partially proofed dough piece (left), and rounded dough piece (right), shown in cross-sections**

Intermediate Proof

The rounded dough pieces are subject to a further resting period, which is generally referred to as **benching**, **bench time** or **intermediate proof**.

* *Intermediate proofing is the period between rounding and molding.*

The intermediate proof has a dual purpose:
— relaxation of the dough
— fermentation development

Without intermediate proofing further shaping is not recommended, as the strong dough tension from the rounding process causes:
— the outer dough skin to break easily (*Fig. 158*);
— the dough pieces to shrink back; and
— unnecessary strength requirements for molding.
Dough pieces should have a soft, smooth surface before shaping.

Fig. 158
Torn dough skin, due to overexertion during make-up

70

Moist and sticky dough surfaces caused by excessive air humidity or by covering dough with plastic bags make the shaping more difficult, regardless of hand make-up or make-up by a bread-molder/sheeter. This can lead to deficiencies as shown in *Fig. 159*.

In contrast, dough pieces that are rough-dry do not close after rolling and this also leads to deficiencies.

Fig. 159
Poor breakage due to high moisture/humidity (left), lack of moisture (right), compared to a normal, deficiency-free roll (center)

Shaping

There are many different shapes, varieties and forms for white-flour products. The following shapes are part of the more customary selection:
➤ long shaping, for white bread and sandwich loaves,
➤ folding of rolls
➤ pressing and stamping of rolls (Kaiser rolls)
➤ rolling of crescent rolls
➤ special shaping for soft pretzels
➤ twisting methods for braids

The shape of buns and rolls is accomplished by using a specialized form of equipment called a **bun-rounder**. This machine is common in any modern bakery.

The following roll varieties are given a round shape and do not need further manipulation:	
— *hamburger buns*	➤ *round shape, flattened before proofing*
— *dinner buns and rolls*	➤ *round pieces set together in rows, usually three to five dozen per baking sheet; for dinner rolls, the round pieces are set apart usually one to two dozen per baking sheet*
— *poppy and sesame seed rolls*	➤ *round pieces, moistened with egg wash and dipped into seeds*

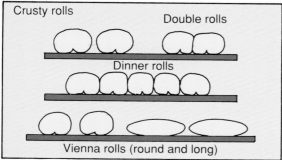

Fig. 160

These roll varieties are made up without intermediate proof

> *The following roll varieties are given their final shape after intermediate proofing:*
>
> — *folded rolls* ➤ *The round pieces are depressed*
> *(when ma-* *by the palm of the hand, then*
> *c h i n e -* *given a long, oval shape by roll-*
> *folded, the* *ing on a table top. If a mechanical*
> *intermedi-* *sheeter is used, the pieces are*
> *ate proofing* *flattened first, then caught by a*
> *is omitted)* *wire-attachment and rolled into*
> *an oval shape.*
>
> — *p r e s s e d* ➤ *Pressed rolls are given a depres-*
> *rolls* *sion in the center with a round,*
> *wooden piece (doughnut stick,*
> *the end of an wooden spoon or by*
> *mechanical means).*
>
> — *Kaiser rolls* ➤ *These dough pieces are hand-*
> *stamped or subjected to one of*
> *many forms of semi-and-fully-*
> *automated stamping devices.*

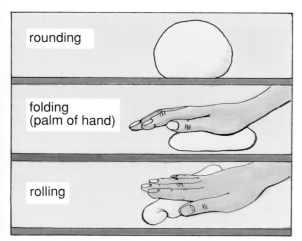

rounding

folding
(palm of hand)

rolling

Fig. 161 **Folding procedure of Vienna rolls**

For white bread or sandwich bread-types, the dough pieces are given a long shape after the intermediate proofing period.

When a machine is used for this purpose, the length of the loaf is achieved by first being flattened, then rolled under a metal plate.

The approximate length of the various dough pieces for white bread is as follows:

Bread Type	Baking Weight	Length
— French bread, baked on baking pans or sheets	500 g / 750 g / 1000 g	approx. 30 cm / approx. 30 cm / approx. 50 cm
— pan-baked white bread & sandwich bread	500 g	approx. 25 cm
— baguettes	250 g / 500 g	approx. 40 cm / approx. 75 cm

Sandwich Bread

The traditional methods for forming sandwich breads can have the following disadvantages:
— concave sidewalls during baking and
— crumb with irregular cells (*Fig. 162*).
The four-piece, twist and cluster methods of dough forming alleviate the above problems.

Fig. 162 **Concave sidewall formation due to poor molding technique**

Fig. 163 **Note the effect of too much flour during sheeting and molding**

Four-Piece Method

The semi-proofed (round piece) is pressed flat, rolled to form a dough strand, separated into four pieces, then placed into the pan as shown in *Fig. 164*. This method is primarily used for special effect.

71

Fig. 164 **Four-Piece Method**

Twist Method

The semi-proofed round piece is cut and rolled into two separate strands. The strands are then twisted together as shown in *Fig. 165*.

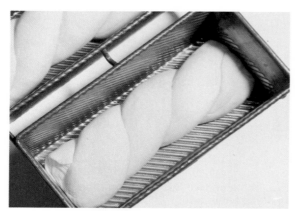

Fig. 165 **Twist Method**

Cluster Method

Round pieces, normally used for rolls, are placed in rows of two by five and then pressed down.

Fig. 166 **Cluster Method**

Types of Make-up Equipment

Bakers can use a variety of machines and equipment for the make-up procedure of doughs.
The use of such equipment allows bakers to achieve:
— ease of operation;
— more economical production; and
— higher productivity.

The following factors should be considered when choosing bakery equipment, depending on type, volume and capacity:

* *Profitability*	➤ *The cost of acquisition and operation of the machine or plant must be justifiable through lower cost production.*
* *Space requirements, taking into consideration the work process*	➤ *The location of the machine or plant must allow a trouble-free, continuous work process with short transportation channels.*
* *Planning of operations*	➤ *Before purchasing an individual machine, make sure it is compatible with an existing or planned operation.*

Manufacturers of bakery equipment offer sizes fitting any and every bakery, small and large operations, from semi-to-fully-automated plants with minimal space requirements.

Complete make-up plants consist of a combination of mixers, automated scaling devices, rounders, overhead-proofers and sheeters.

The semi-automated plants differ from the fully-automated plants through the requirement of human labor.

Equipment for Roll and Bun Production

Even the smallest bakeries usually use a bun-rounder of some sort for the make-up of rolls and buns. These machines are available in both semi-automated and fully-automated forms (*Fig. 167*).

Fig. 167 **Bun divider/rounder machine; fully-automated design**

Thirty-six times the dough weight of a roll is scaled and shaped into a round form (head or press). After a short period of intermediate proofing, the heads are pressed flat, then placed on the machine plate.

These bun-rounder plates (metal or plastic) are inserted into the opening of the machine. For semi-automated operation, the cutting-head of the bun-rounder is lowered on the plates containing the large dough piece and pressed flat. The cutting device is then activated and through oscillating action, the cut pieces are then rounded.

For fully-automated machines, only two buttons are depressed to obtain the same results.

Fully-Automated Divider/Rounding Systems

These systems are designed for larger bun/roll operations and are the first stage of a **bun line**, a fully-automated system from start to finish.

The system shown in *Fig. 171* has the following functions:

— dividing and scaling by volume measuring
— rounding of individual dough pieces
— placement of rounded dough pieces on a strip conveyor belt

Additional Information

For continuous bun-production operation, a semi-to-fully-automated system is needed.

Fig. 168 **Completely manual make-up of dough**

Fig. 169 **Semi-automated make-up operation**

Fig. 170 **Fully-automated production line**

Fig. 171 **Fully-automated divider/rounder system (scaling by volume)**

73

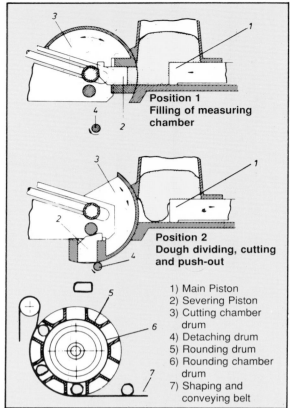

Position 1
Filling of measuring chamber

Position 2
Dough dividing, cutting and push-out

1) Main Piston
2) Severing Piston
3) Cutting chamber drum
4) Detaching drum
5) Rounding drum
6) Rounding chamber drum
7) Shaping and conveying belt

Fig. 172
Work principle of an automated bun divider/rounder, based on the piston principle

Doughs should not have any (or only little) fermentation time for processing in semi or fully-automated dividing systems. Dough temperature, firmness and mixing intensity must be adjusted accordingly to gain the optimum maturity at the time of make-up.

*The dough is fed into a **hopper** in large piece form or as a dough strand via a feeder conveyor. Various systems can be used for the dividing process. An older dividing system consists of dividing dough into strips, then cutting each piece for scaling on a balance scale.*

With modern equipment, dividing is usually achieved by the use of a metering piston device (hopper). This device can be adjusted if corrections of the dough weight are necessary.

Dough sheeters/molders are used for the shaping of bread and rolls. These machines perform the following functions:
— flattening of the rounded dough pieces
— folding and overlapping of the flattened dough pieces
— extending the rolled pieces into desired lengths (*Fig. 173*)

In contrast to preparing buns/rolls manually, no intermediate proofing is required for shaping by means of specialized machines. Dough pieces must be adequately relaxed prior to rolling. This relaxation period depends on the length of the conveyor belts transporting the rounded pieces from the bun-rounder.

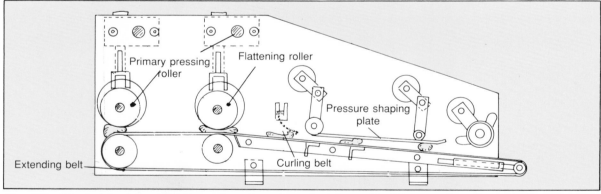

Primary pressing roller

Flattening roller

Pressure shaping plate

Extending belt

Curling belt

Fig. 173   **Work principle of folding rollers for wiener/hot dog rolls, Vienna rolls, submarine/hoagie rolls**

Fig. 174
Automated stamping machine (for Kaiser rolls)

Automated stamping machines give the Kaiser roll its distinctive pattern (*Fig. 174*). Stamping patterns are interchangeable with minimum effort and greatly reduce manual labor. Some systems are fully-automated and transport the stamped rolls directly into an overhead-proofer; others are still loaded manually by placing special insert trays, loaded with unstamped rolls, through the stamping machine.

A sufficient intermediate proof is required for satisfactory stamp designs on rolls.

74

Semi-Automated Make-up Equipment for Rolls

Machines for the make-up of doughs described so far can be used as individual machines in a bakery, regardless of whether supplementary equipment is available.

Through combining such machines with overhead-proofers and conveyor belts, semi-automated roll production in a continuous process is possible in almost any bakery.

Equipment for the Production of Bread

The *dough divider* for bread (as opposed to a divider for the roll production) is not equipped with a rounding device. It can be added separately or used individually for several purposes.

The divider scales the dough into identical sizes. The measuring chambers determining size are continuously adjustable for the usual bread weights. By checking for correct weights at random, adjustments can be made by either adding or subtracting dough weight. This prevents shortages of weight on the final product.

Additional Information

Work principles of dough dividers

Suction System:

The dough is sucked through the dough tunnel, pressed into a measuring chamber, cut by a rotary sliding device, and then ejected (Fig. 175). The dough is pressed from the pressure chamber into a measuring chamber, cut, then ejected.(Fig. 176).

Chamber Dividers:

The dough is transported in its natural direction of flow, via conveying rolls, through a measuring chamber. Without additional pressing, the dough filling the measuring chamber is cut, then ejected. This type of divider is most suitable for doughs containing rye flour, because of their "flowing" abilities.

Bread rounders have proved to be very useful machines for all types of doughs (rye-bread dough has to be very firm to prevent sticking). Spiral-shaped rounding devices are placed around a rotating, grooved cone or cylinder for upward dough movement. The dough pieces that enter the base of the rounder are drawn together in a rotary movement, stretched and then ejected at the top into a molding device or overhead proofer.

The cleanliness of this machine is important, as dough particles can fill the grooves and hinder its function to operate smoothly, as well as affect its sanitation.

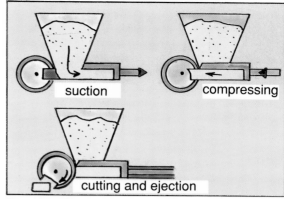

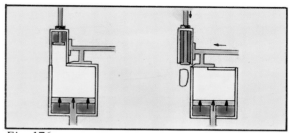

Fig. 175 **Work principle of the suction divider**

Fig. 176

Work principle of the pressurized divider

Fig. 177 **Cone-type bread rounder suitable for white, whole-wheat and variety breads**

Sheeters are used to shape the rounded dough pieces into oblong loaves which are extended to desired lengths.

The rounded dough pieces are initially flattened between two metal rollers, folded by a cloth or link chain and guided by metal or plastic parts. With most of the bread-molding sheeters, the desired length is achieved by two belts moving in opposite directions or through the pressure of a metal plate with two guides (metal/plastic) *(Fig. 173)*.

Equipment for use in commercial and industrial premises must be affixed with labels signifying appropriate regulatory approval.

Fig. 178
Official labels

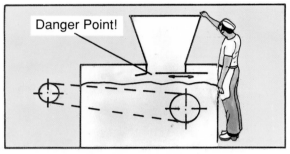

Danger Point!

Fig. 179 **Dough divider with hopper**

Caution!
New bakery equipment should be operated only after proper installation by certified experts. Safety and operating instructions should be carefully examined by potential operators. Safety standards are essential to prevent accidents.

Fig. 180 **Dough divider with disconnecting platform**

Hazards Connected with the Operation of Bakery Equipment

A local newspaper article reports an accident under the heading: "Baker Injured in Industrial Accident."
The article goes on to say that a baker fell off an empty milk-crate while controlling the flow of dough in a dough divider. As the hopper could not be reached without using the power-disconnecting platform, the milk-crate was used to avoid interrupting the operation. However, the baker broke his collarbone.
An accident?
Evaluate this scenario.

In spite of accident prevention regulations and safety standards, accidents happen frequently during the operation of bakery equipment.

The most frequent causes of accidents are:
— carelessness; and
— laziness.

In these cases, safety regulations are not respected or safety devices are made non-operational. The risk involved, as well as the prevention of accidents, can be best demonstrated on a dough divider with hopper or funnel feeding.

Most of the dough dividers have a funnel-shaped opening for feeding the dough into the machine.

Danger points include the feeder wings, the feeder screws and the pushing devices in the feeder funnel.

If a hand gets caught in these devices, injuries such as bruises, bone fractures, dislocations and even severing of the hand can occur.

To ensure the danger point is safer, the feeding funnel must be equipped with a ***protection device***. Protected funnels are designed so that the danger point within the funnel cannot be reached by a person of average height (*Fig. 179*).

The step-up platform attached to a divider must be designed so that when someone steps on it, the power supply is interrupted (*Fig. 180*).

More recent designs of dough dividers have the hopper/funnel inset partially protected with a safety bar. If dough is fed manually, a great deal of time and energy can be saved with this system. The machine stops if the safety bar is lifted.

The individual machine parts should be easily removable to provide ready access for cleaning. Protective covers must be connected to the driving mechanism of the machine in a way that makes it impossible to start when the device is not in place.

Fig. 181   **Dough divider with lowered and bar-protected hopper/funnel (left); Dough divider with protected hopper/funnel (right)**

* Make-up equipment, dangers and protection		
Machines:	Dangers:	Protection:
— Dough dividers and bun-rounding equipment.	➤ Bruising/crushing between pressing device and plate	➤ On newer machines, the activation can be performed only by using both hands, thus avoiding the danger
— Dough dividers with hopper/funnel attachment	➤ Bruising/crushing on the cutting devices	➤ Protected hopper/funnel; protection grid/bar above the cutting device
— Croissant roller, molders	➤ Contusion of fingers between the rollers	➤ Small opening between the rollers — 3 mm maximum
— Automated stamping machines	➤ Crushing between punching device and dough plate	➤ Protection bar which interrupts power supply if lifted
— Bread-molding sheeters, reversible sheeters	➤ Bruising/crushing of the fingers between the rollers	➤ Protective bar as emergency switch in front of rollers; feeder tray extension
	➤ Bruising on the belt system	➤ Cover over the belt supports

Preventive Maintenance of Dough Dividers

Bakery equipment requires constant care and maintenance to:
— avoid operational troubles;
— avoid unnecessary repair costs;
— increase the life expectancy of the machines; and
— ensure a sanitary production process.

The following maintenance work should be performed daily:
➤ Check the oil level in moving and cutting parts of dough dividers before starting up the operation.
An oil level which is too low leads to malfunctions and operational problems.
The maintenance instructions will indicate if the divider and overhead system must be flushed with oil after every production run.

Fig. 182

➤ Fill the dusting mechanism with flour.

The following maintenance work should be done on a weekly basis:

➤ Check the tension of drive belts and chain drives.
If the tension is insufficient, increase it according to operating instructions.

➤ Check the tension of conveyor and ejection belts.
Follow instructions for increasing tension!

➤ If necessary, lubricate parts in accordance with instructional manual.

Many machines require lubrication regularly, others only every three months.
Lubricating should be performed in accordance with a regular scheduled service (driving chains, guide rollers, spindles, stopping devices, etc.).
An oil change in the gears is performed normally after 5,000 to 10,000 operating hours, or at least once a year.

Caution!

Only edible oils (vegetable oils, etc.) should be used when oiling parts that make contact with dough and/or flour. This applies to the movable parts and cutting devices of a dough divider.

The oil should be resin-free as normal cooking oil resinates and causes operational problems.

* *For driving chains, etc., use only lubricating materials recommended by the manufacturer!*

Dough divider and bun-rounder machines must be cleaned daily and after each major stoppage in production, otherwise hardened dough can lead to operational trouble.

Fig. 183 **Removal of a drum of an automated divider/bun-rounder**

Cleaning Instructions:

— *Clean the dough hopper/funnel. Eliminate dough scraps with a plastic scraper (definitely not a metal scraper).*
— *Remove main piston, measuring/portioning piston, drum, cutting and shaping device, and clean in warm water.*
— *Clean the metal and plastic parts inside the machine with a plastic scraper.*
— *Clean the flour-duster and remove all old flour. In order to avoid lumps (from cleaning water) refill with flour only at start-up of production.*
— *Clean the pick-up and transport belt with a soft brush.*
— *Empty and clean the collected oil in the catcher.*
— *Wipe the outer case with a moist cloth and remove attached dough with a plastic scraper.*

Fig. 184 **Removal of the measuring pistons of an automated divider/bun-rounder**

Caution!

Important tips for cleaning dough divider/rounder:

— *Start cleaning from the top and work your way down.*
— *The use of water inside the machine should be prevented under all circumstances.*
— *The pick-up and transportation belts should not be scraped with a metal scraper or any other sharp object.*

78

Summary of the most important information on the make-up procedure of white-bread doughs

* *The size of the dough weight at the scaling stage depends on the desired product weight plus the baking loss.*
* *Scaling of the dough pieces for white-bread products is carried out by manual or mechanical means.*
* *Intermediate proof is the period of time during which dough relaxation occurs between rounding and shaping.*
* *Customary equipment used for the make-up of white-bread doughs includes:*
  — *Dough dividers/rounders*
  — *Overhead proofers*
  — *Semi-automated and fully-automated bun-rounders*
  — *Sheeters and molders*
  — *Bun-stamping machines (Kaiser roll machine)*
* *When operating dough make-up equipment, respect in particular:*
  — *the safety regulations; and*
  — *the sanitation codes.*

Proofing (Final Proof)

* *Proofing is the time period between the make-up and baking process.*

This period aims at obtaining maximum development of the dough.

During the final proof, the maturing process of the dough continues:

— *Swelling of the flour components continues.*	➤ *The dough becomes firmer and dryer.*
— *Fermentation of the sugars in the dough continues.*	➤ *The proportion of gas in the dough increases; the dough cells get larger and the cell walls extend further and get thinner.*
— *Decomposition of the flour components through enzymes of the flour and of the yeast continues.*	➤ *The proportion of substances contributing to formation of the aroma increases in the dough; the gluten loses some elasticity.*

The rate of speed can be influenced by the baker.

The following measures accelerate the final proofing:

➤ high yeast content
➤ development of a soft dough in a warm environment
➤ the use of baking additives containing sugar or enzymes
➤ optimum dough maturity
➤ ideal proofer conditions (appropriate temperature/humidity)

Proofing Maturity

The final proof is completed when the dough pieces (bread, rolls) have reached the desired proofing maturity (oven-ready).

* *Optimum proofing maturity is the degree of aeration of dough which produces the desired product quality.*

If the proofing maturity is exceeded, the product becomes deficient. Causes for deficiencies are:

— the gluten network is expanded by too many fermentation gases; this leads to over-extension of the gluten
— the cell walls break and the cells collapse
— the fine cells are destroyed and large cells with thick walls are formed
— the fermentation gases leave the dough

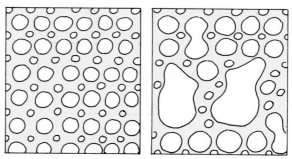

Fig. 185 **Cell picture showing optimum proofing maturity (left) and over-proofing (right)**

Evaluate the cell size and the thickness of the cell walls!

Food for Thought:

Cake batters and doughs prepared with baking powder are baked without a resting period, immediately after make-up. The leavening occurs during baking. Yeast dough must go through several stages prior to baking. Why?

A useful instrument to establish proofing maturity has not yet been developed. Instead, bakers must rely on their experience. Evaluations on proofing maturity are based on typical characteristics, such as:
— appearance of the dough surface;
— change in shape of the dough pieces;
— volume; and
— resistance of the dough when touched.

An erroneous evaluation of the final proofing maturity leads to product deficiencies.

Product deficiencies	
caused by under-proofing:	*caused by over-proofing:*
• *poor volume, dark crust, dense cells*	• *pale crust, large cells with thick walls, excessive volume*
• *breaking-up of the crust*	• *flat shape for tray-baked products (collapsed products)*
• *poor symmetry of product, due to changing of shape during baking.*	• *bark-like crust with small cracks*

Fig. 186
Controlling touch to check proofing maturity

Fig. 187 **Baked rolls which have been under-proofed**

Fig. 188 **Overproofed baked roll**

The optimum proofing maturity is different for each bakery product. Stamped rolls (Kaiser rolls) are considered at optimum proof when they are three-quarters proofed, whereas crusty rolls or any other round type of roll needs full proof.

Proofing Stability
Most yeast doughs retain gas to various degrees. Of the total gas quantity produced by the yeast in the dough, a portion leaves the dough (depending on the capacity of the dough to retain gas) and is lost.
Therefore, doughs made of flours of different quality show a different dough volume, although the production conditions and the gas development are identical. As a consequence, the product volume varies.

The following conclusion applies:

> *Doughs with a low ability to retain gas have a lower proofing stability. Doughs with a high ability to retain gas therefore have a high proofing stability.*

> * *Proofing stability is the ability of doughs to retain gas in proportion to gas development.*

The more stable the dough at the proofing stage, the better it will hold its shape and maintain its volume.

Proofing Tolerance
Loading fully-proofed dough pieces into the oven may be delayed by other products still baking (oven still occupied). Sometimes this delay will result in deficiencies and, in other cases, the quality of the product is not adversely affected.
Fully-proofed doughs show a varying degree of sensitivity:
— to an increase of the internal gas pressure (fermentation gases); and
— to external stress, such as placing or moving the dough pieces.
Doughs that can endure an extended period of overdevelopment (overproofing), without affecting the quality, have a high proofing tolerance.

The extent of the proofing tolerance is the time during which a dough can continue to mature after achieving proofing maturity, without loss of volume to the product.

Just as the proofing stability, the proofing tolerance of dough is largely determined by the quality of the flour used.

Measures contributing to the improvement of the proofing stability also increase the proofing tolerance.

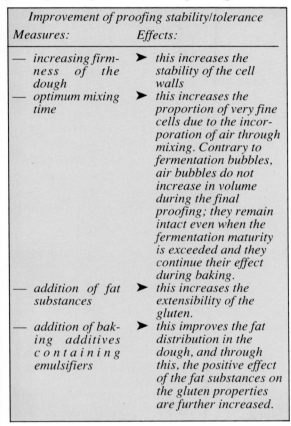

Improvement of proofing stability/tolerance	
Measures:	*Effects:*
— *increasing firmness of the dough*	➤ *this increases the stability of the cell walls*
— *optimum mixing time*	➤ *this increases the proportion of very fine cells due to the incorporation of air through mixing. Contrary to fermentation bubbles, air bubbles do not increase in volume during the final proofing; they remain intact even when the fermentation maturity is exceeded and they continue their effect during baking.*
— *addition of fat substances*	➤ *this increases the extensibility of the gluten.*
— *addition of baking additives containing emulsifiers*	➤ *this improves the fat distribution in the dough, and through this, the positive effect of the fat substances on the gluten properties are further increased.*

Proofer Temperatures

The following variances must be taken into consideration when products are placed in the proofer for final proofing:
➤ heat and moisture loss due to opening the doors excessively
➤ improper temperature and humidity values

These consequences can lead to deficiencies in the development of the product by:
➤ the dough pieces cooling down too much and possibly loaded into the oven too early, resulting in products being too small and compact. The cells of the crumb of such products will be dense.
➤ the dough pieces could form a skin, which would cause the crust to be pale, dull and thick. The product volume would remain small.

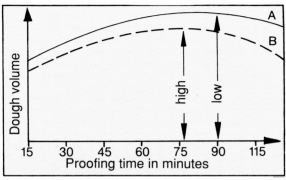

Fig. 189 **Schematic representation of the proofing stability of two doughs**

Evaluate and explain the curve development of doughs A and B.

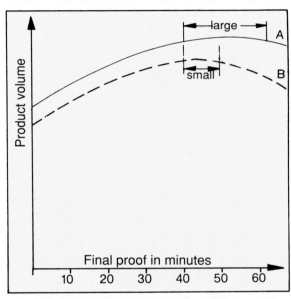

Fig. 190 **Schematic representation of the proofing tolerance of two doughs**

Explain the curve development of doughs A and B.

Reference:
Compare the proofing tolerance with the mixing tolerance and fermentation tolerance.

If products are not placed into a proofer for the final proof, they should be covered with a cloth or sheet (or plastic). This helps to prevent cooling and possible skin formation. A proofing chamber/room must be used to ensure continuous operation and to obtain consistent products. The prerequisite for perfect and rapid development of products is the regulated climate of the proofer.

Fig. 191 **Crust faults of a pan-baked loaf due to drafty, dry final proofing**

Fig. 192 **Uneven, rough crust, also noticeable on the bloom due to a dry intermediate proof**

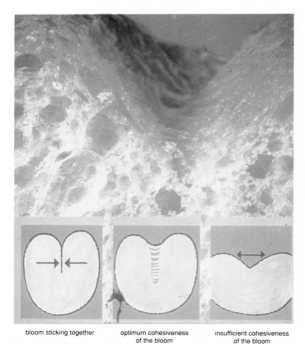

bloom sticking together   optimum cohesiveness of the bloom   insufficient cohesiveness of the bloom

Fig. 193 **Effect of the proofer humidity on the development of the bloom**

82

Values for the proofer climate		
Temperature		Relative Humidity
at 30°C	→	about 80%
at 35°C	→	about 70%
at 40°C	→	about 60%

Table 18

Proofer temperatures should not exceed 40°C for the proofing of buns and rolls and 35°C for white breads. High temperature differentials between dough pieces and proofer temperature should be avoided. Never place frozen or semi-frozen products in the proofer as this will lead, after a short time, to overdevelopment of the outer layers, while fermentation maturity will not yet be achieved in the center of the product.

Additional Information

Depending on the temperature, the air can absorb a certain amount of steam. Cool air absorbs little steam, while warm air absorbs a lot of steam. Therefore, in order to establish the air humidity, relative air humidity should be measured, not the absolute humidity (quantity of water in grams). The relative air humidity is the percentage of water the air can absorb.

1 m³ of air can absorb a maximum of:		
about 17 g of water	→	at 20°C
about 30 g of water	→	at 30°C
about 40 g of water	→	at 35°C

Table 19

The relative air humidity in the proofer should be between 60% and 80%. The steam contained in the air of the proofer precipitates into the products to be proofed. The steam condenses because the products are cooler than the air of the proofer. This is how the formation of skin is avoided.

Fig. 194
Rolls on a overhead/intermediate proofer system

The cooler the products that are placed into a proofer, the lower the initial air humidity must be. Otherwise, the dough skin becomes too humid (moist) and dough pieces stick together if they come in contact with each other.

Modern proofers are equipped with automated regulating devices for maintaining the pre-determined temperature development, taking into account the corresponding air humidity.

Summary of the Most Important Information on Proofing

* *Final proofing is the fermentation time of products prior to the baking process.*
  The final proof is accelerated through:
  — *a higher proportion of yeast in the dough;*
  — *keeping the dough soft during preparation;*
  — *the use of baking additives rich in sugar and enzymes;*
  — *preparing the dough in a warm environment; and*
  — *a controlled humid-warm climate in the proofer.*
* *Proofing maturity (oven-ready) is the best possible state of aeration of the dough in order to achieve the desired quality characteristics.*
* *Proofing stability is the gas retention capacity of dough pieces in proportion to gas development.*
* *Proofing tolerance is the ability of made-up dough to withstand waiting time after the final proof stage, without affecting product quality.*
  Proofing stability and proofing tolerance are enhanced through:
  — *keeping the dough firm during preparation;*
  — *optimum mixing time;*
  — *addition of shortening, fats; and*
  — *addition of emulsifiers.*
* *Underproofing and overproofing at the beginning of the baking process leads to deficiencies of the product.*

Retardation of Fermentation — Interruption of Fermentation

Bread, rolls and buns lose their freshness very rapidly. Consumers prefer baked goods fresh from the oven, but with conventional methods this cannot always be fully achieved.

Today bakers have the opportunity, through retardation of made-up products, to interrupt the fermentation process. This enables the baker to offer fresh-baked goods even outside the normal production period.

Through *retardation* and *interruption* of the fermentation process, fresh-baked goods are available on short notice.

Retardation of the Fermentation Process

* ***Retardation*** *of the fermentation process is defined as slowing down intermediate proofing without freezing the products, until it has almost come to a stop (at temperatures between 8°C and -5°C).*

The speed of the fermentation rate of the yeast, flour decomposition through enzymes, and the swelling of the flour components are delayed, but not interrupted. Therefore, the storability of the made-up products is limited.

Retardation of the fermentation process is possible for up to five hours with few deficiencies and up to 24 hours with small deficiencies in the product quality. A longer retardation of the fermentation process leads to large deficiencies in the quality of baked goods.

For retarding the fermentation process in the production of white-flour products, the following precautions should be taken to avoid faults in the finished goods:
➤ *prepare a firmer dough*
➤ *avoid baking additives containing enzymes and lecithin*
➤ *cool the products immediately after they have been made up*
➤ *make up doughs without resting time, or after a short resting time*
➤ *provide sufficient air humidity during cooling and storing*

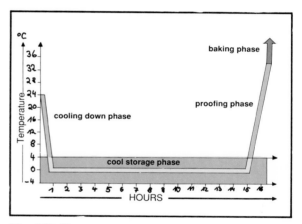

Fig. 195 **Temperature development during retardation of the fermentation process**

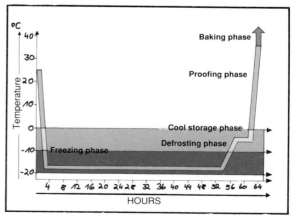

Fig. 196 **Temperature development during interruption of the fermentation process through freezing and defrosting**

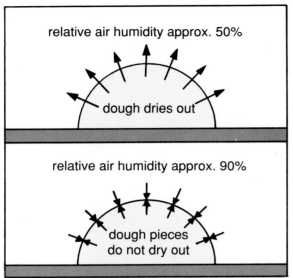

Fig. 197 **During retardation and interruption of the fermentation process, sufficient air humidity must be provided**

Explain the schematic representation.

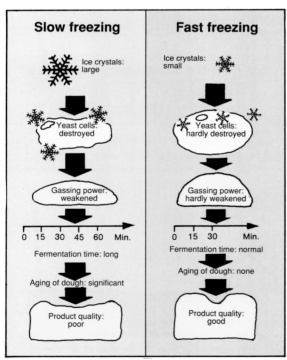

Fig. 198 **Effect of the speed of freezing on the dough and the product**

Explain the schematic representation.

Interruption of the Fermentation Process

* ***Interruption*** *of the fermentation process is achieved when all maturing processes — including fermentation — have come to a stop in the dough pieces through freezing at temperatures between -7°C to -18°C.*

Initial freezing temperatures normally lie between -15°C and -18°C. The storage temperature is adjusted at -7°C to -10°C.
No major deficiencies in the product quality are caused by a storage time of up to 24 hours.
Longer storage times of between 48 and 72 hours, which are quite usual, lead to distinct deficiencies in the quality of white-flour products.

Fully-automated chambers for interruption of the fermentation process work on the same principle as chambers for retardation of the fermentation process (see *Fig. 199*).
The only difference lies in the higher temperature decline.
For rolls, the temperature is reduced from 25°C to -15°C over a period of three hours. A faster temperature reduction has a positive effect on the quality of the final product. Defrosting and warming up the center of the dough pieces from -10°C to 25°C also takes about three hours. A faster temperature increase leads to deficiencies in the development of the product. The dough center is still almost frozen, whereas the outer layer shows signs of fermentation maturity.

Fig. 199 **Fully-automated chamber for interruption of the fermentation process**

Advantages and Disadvantages of Retardation and Interruption of the Fermentation Process

Retardation and interruption of the fermentation process differ:
— with regard to magnitude of reduction of the temperature;
— in the storability of the product; and
— in the energy consumption.

If made-up rolls are to be stored for a longer period of time (for more than five hours), it is recommended that interruption chambers be used rather than retardation chambers during the fermentation process.

Retardation/interruption of fermentation process	
Advantages:	*Disadvantages:*
• *oven-fresh rolls at any time*	• *smaller product volume* • *somewhat small bloom*
• *more economical use of the baking oven*	• *slight irregular browning of the crust* • *formation of crust bubbles (due to excessively high air humidity during the warming phase)*
• *avoidance of peak production times*	
• *better flavor*	• *crumb with larger cells*
• *better fresh-keeping properties (in the case of bread)*	• *higher costs (which can be absorbed through more efficient production)*

Fig. 200　Loading of products into a special fermentation-interruption chamber

Important information on rooms/chambers for retardation and interruption of fermentation process

* *Retardation: slowing down the intermediate proof through temperature reduction, without freezing the dough.*
* *Interruption: stopping all maturing processes through freezing the dough.*
* *Retardation of the fermentation process is possible for up to five hours without any noticeable deterioration of quality, whereas interruption is possible for up to 24 hours without noticeable loss of quality.*

Baking of Wheat-flour Products

Baking methods and processes are basically mentioned in the chapters entitled **Baking Processes and Baking Methods**. This chapter is concerned only with differing processes and methods, which are typical only for wheat-flour products.

Preparation of Products to be Baked

Preparation of the dough pieces for baking begins when the baker has established that the desired fermentation maturity (oven maturity) has been achieved.

In the case of white-flour products with a strong bloom, the time of optimum fermentation maturity lies prior to full maturity. This applies to almost all white bread and roll varieties. They are inserted into the oven at three-quarter proof.

Fully-proofed products show a small increase in volume during baking relative to the outer dough surface. Cuts and folds can therefore not develop a sufficient bloom.

Dough pieces for products without bloom (for example, hamburger buns) are placed in the oven upon reaching full proof.

Reference: *The principles of baking are mentioned in the chapter entitled **Baking Processes and Baking Methods**.*

Fig. 201　Cutting of French breads

Preparation of dough pieces for loading into the oven includes:
— egg-washing or water-washing;
— cutting or stamping; and
— turning of products (in proofing baskets).

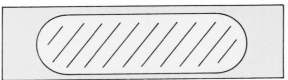

Large French bread

Pan-baked white bread

Caviar sticks (French sticks)

Baguettes

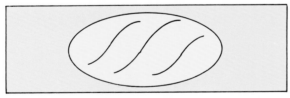

Small French loaf

Fig. 202 **Various cut designs**

Fig. 203 **Positioning of rolls on a turn-over plate using a turning apparatus**

The loaves to be baked are cut on their surface to obtain the appropriate pattern for the type of product. The depth of the cut must be increased:
— the lower the number of cuts,
— the shorter the time of proofing.

Bread baked without a pan is usually cut six times diagonally across the surface.

White bread baked in pans can be given a deep longitudinal cut across the center line of the surface, if cut at all.

Caviar or French sticks receive a large number of diagonal cuts of uniform length.

Baguettes receive three to four long, curved, diagonal cuts.

Small French breads can be given one long cut or three curved, nearly parallel-running, diagonal cuts. The blade of the cutting knife must be held at an angle while cutting small French breads and baguettes to increase the proportion of the crust.

White bread without a bloom can be slightly indented with a nail board to avoid fermentation bubbles on the surface.

For white-flour products not requiring any preparation (this applies to all small products like rolls) pans are placed into the oven immediately following the final proof.
Producers of large volumes of rolls use specialized equipment, as described below.

In this type of production, the rolls are placed upside-down on proofer trays and merely turned around prior to baking.
Turning is done:
— by hand;
— by the use of a turning device; and
— by flipping the product on to a oven-peel.
When using turning devices, a whole set of proofer trays is turned in one operation on to the perforated baking sheet. (*Fig. 204*)
When using a basculating device, the replacing and turning operation is not required.
The dough surface of rolls covered with seeds, (sesame seeds, poppy seeds, caraway seeds) coarse ground grain or coarse salt, is brushed with water to increase adhesion of the particles.
Loaves for baking directly on the hearth are placed on a peel, sprayed with water, cut, and then placed into the oven.
Where a random crack formation, a low-gloss or floury surface is desired (as in baguettes), white-flour products should not be wetted.

In some cases, weight markers are pressed into the moist surface to indicate the weight of the product. For white bread, markers for weight indication are not suitable. The contours of the dough surface shift and the weight indicators become illegible.

Loading the Oven

The procedure for loading the oven depends on the type of oven.

The most common type of oven in North America is the rotisserie oven, where four to 10 shelves rotate in a large enclosed heated chamber.

Other types include the old-fashioned brick oven and the deck oven, where one to six shelves are used (similar to a pizza oven). Products are often baked directly on the hearth in convection ovens (where heat is circulated by an internal fan), in a rack oven (where an entire rack of buns or bread can be placed into the oven), or in conveyor-type and tunnel ovens.

The oldest method of placing products into the oven is by the use of a **wooden peel,** a flat piece of wood attached to a long handle. They are still used in some bakeries, especially for baking products directly on the hearth or where the opening portion of the oven is too small to accommodate baking sheets and baking pans.

A **bascule** (an apparatus on the principle of a seesaw or teeter-totter) is used on deck-ovens of the same width and has the capacity to load many dozens of rolls or bread at once (*Fig. 206*).

Other oven-loading devices include a system where products are placed on a cloth or plastic tray which is hooked on a catch at the oven-opening. Products are pushed all the way into the oven, and, as the cloth/ plastic tray is pulled out, the catch revolves and the products are deposited on the oven hearth.

This system is very efficient, but can be used on deck ovens only.

For loading ovens with moving trays, like conveyor-type ovens, **fully-automated loading devices** can be used.

Fig. 204
Loading the oven with the use of a turning device (turning the rolls on to a baking sheet)

Fig. 205
Manual loading, with the use of an oven-peel

Fig. 206 **Loading with the use of a cloth/plastic flip-action apparatus**

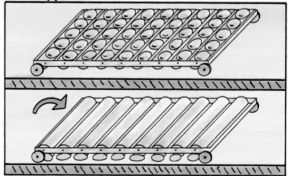

Fig. 207 **Function of the bascule apparatus**

When loading "rack" ovens, the entire proofing rack is placed into the oven by pushing it on wheels directly into the oven chamber. A rotating motion is triggered by closing the oven door and stops automatically when the door is opened again (*Fig. 208*).

Fig. 208
Unloading and loading of the rack oven

Baking sheets or bread pans are loaded into rotating or rotisserie-type ovens by filling each shelf one at a time, and forwarding or reversing the oven-tray movement by a control switch located at the front of the oven.

The rule of thumb for the spacing of bread loaves is as follows:

— *The distance between rolls on a baking pan or hearth should be 15 mm (one finger width).*

— *The distance between bread loaves, depending on their size, should be 60 mm (four finger widths).*

Spacing between bread pans placed in the oven, or in the case of baking on the hearth, between the dough pieces, is important. If the pans are too close together, products will bake unevenly and concave sidewalls can develop. Products placed too close to one another will tear on the sides that are touching.

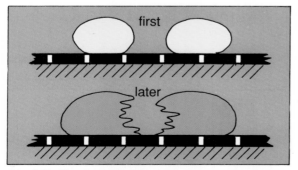

Fig. 209 **Products that have been placed too close together on the oven trays**

Generalized capacity of the baking area	
Product type:	Units per m² of baking area:
rolls	100 to 110
white bread or French bread	about 15
sandwich bread or large French bread	about 10

Table 20

The Effects of Steam on the Baking Process

The following factors determine if, during the baking of wheat-flour products, the desired product quality can be achieved:
— the baking temperature
— the baking time in relation to the size of the product
— the supply of steam

The baking temperature for these products is between 220°C and 240°C.
Crusty rolls and Vienna rolls are baked at temperatures between 230°C to 240°C. French breads are baked at decreasing temperatures between 240°C to 220°C.
Higher initial temperatures provide for fast crust development prior to maximum expansion. Baking at decreasing temperatures prevents premature browning of the crust. A longer baking time promotes the readiness of the crumb and a stronger crust formation. For small products, the baking time is between 18 to 22 minutes, for white breads about 40 to 45 minutes, and for French breads, 30 to 35 minutes.

Product	Baking temperature	Baking time
Crusty rolls, Vienna rolls	230°C - 240°C	18 - 22 min.
French breads, baguettes	240°C decreasing to 220°C	30 - 35 min.
White and brown breads	240°C decreasing to 220°C	40 - 45 min.

Table 21

Joe thinks:
The steam first applies pressure on the dough pieces, then it penetrates the dough and pushes the product outward. This is called "oven-spring." Is this true?

Food for Thought:
Does steam used in the oven cool the dough pieces or does it accelerate heat transmission?
Can the flattening of a loaf of bread be attributed to the application of steam pressure, or to the improved extensibility of the dough-skin, combined with expansion of the dough?

When crusty or hearth doughs are being baked, the hot air in the oven should be enriched with steam prior to commencement of the baking process. This will improve the product quality and taste.

Steam applied too late in the baking process has no effect on the product.

Once the outer dough skin has heated up, the steam can no longer build condensation. In contrast, if steam remains in the oven for too long, products containing rye flour could develop cracks. Wheat-flour products are not subject to cracking if steam remains in the oven over a period of time.

Remember: *First inject steam, then load products.*

Reference: *The effects of steam on the baking of bread are discussed in more detail in the chapter entitled* **Baking Processes***.*

---

* *Importance of the use of steam in baking*	
Processes:	*Effect on the product quality:*
— *Steam forms condensation on the dough surfaces.*	➤ *Therefore the outer dough/product skin remains extendible for a longer period of time;* • *this prevents breaking of the crust skin;* • *this makes a larger increase in the volume of the product possible;* • *this improves development of the bloom.*
— *Steam contains a considerably higher quantity of heat than air of the same temperature. The water condensing on the dough surface transmits heat better than air.*	➤ *The heat penetration of the dough pieces is accelerated. A strong, but very elastic crust is formed.*
— *Steam enhances the formation and distribution of dextrine on the dough surface.*	➤ *The browning of the crust is improved. The dextrines which are first dissolved, then dried again, form a shiny brown gloss on the crust.*

Summary of the most important information on baking wheats-flour products		
* *Baking*	*French and white breads*	*Crusty and Vienna rolls*
— *Baking temperature:*	➤ *240°C decreasing to 220° C*	➤ *230°C to 250°C*
— *Baking time:*	➤ *depending on size; 30 to 45 minutes*	➤ *18 to 22 min.*

* Wheat-flour products must be exposed to steam from the beginning to the end of the baking process:
— in order to avoid undesirable cracks in the crust;
— in order to enhance bloom development in the desired areas of cracking;
— in order to obtain a larger volume for the product; and
— in order to give the crust a better shine.

Evaluation of Wheat-flour Products

Every product has characteristics determining its quality. Wheat-flour products have general quality characteristics which apply to all varieties, and specific quality characteristics which apply to only one product type.

While the texture of a white bread is an essential characteristic, the crust for crusty rolls and baguettes determines the quality of these products.

Joe maintains:
"Customers demand large rolls. Therefore, we produce giant rolls with the aid of appropriate baking additives. The customer is happy, and it is easier for us to scale the dough for the rolls."
What do you think?

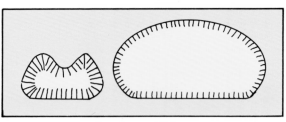

Fig. 210

Small product:	= **large area of crust**
	= **small amount of crumb**
Large product:	= **small amount of crust**
	= **higher crumb portion**

Fig. 211 **Vienna roll with well-developed bloom**

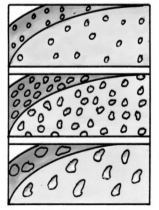

Fig. 212 **Evaluation of crispness**

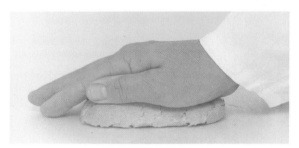

soft, brittle crust

tender-brittle crust

hard, splintery crust

Fig. 213 **Crispness in relation to cell development**

Quality Characteristics of Rolls

Volume

Product volume has an effect on almost all other quality characteristics. As the volume increases, other quality characteristics also increase up to a certain maximum volume.

High volume, blown-up rolls are rejected by many consumers because:
— the cells of the crumb are often inadequate;
— the crumb sticks together when the roll is cut or when a spread is applied;
— the flavor is less distinct; and
— when taking a bite, the blown-up crumb compresses too easily.

Crust

The crust of the product is of particular importance when evaluating the quality of smaller products due to their high proportion of crust. The crust has a high significance on the quality of the overall product. A high proportion of crust is desirable for such products.

> *As the portion and the volume of the crust increases:*
> — *the smaller the weight of the individual product;*
> — *the lighter the crumb;*
> — *the better the bloom is developed; and*
> — *the longer the baking time.*

The ***color of the crust*** should be golden-yellow and show a slight gloss. The bloom should show a strong curve and account for a large portion of the roll surface.

> * *The **bloom** is the desired, marked crack formation in the crust where the cut has been made.*

A strong relationship exists between product volume, crust proportion and bloom development. The quality of these characteristics, in combination with the aeration of the crumb, also determines the most important quality characteristic of a roll: the crispness of the crust.

> * *The **crispness** is the crisp, tender-brittle condition of the crust.*

Two factors are taken into account when crispness is evaluated:
— its specific conditions (what is the quality of the crispness?); and
— its duration (for how many hours is it maintained?).

The thinner the crust, the shorter the time it will remain crisp. In the extreme case, a crust can turn soft one hour after baking.

A thin crust rapidly absorbs moisture from the crumb and humidity from the air (*Fig. 214*).

The longer the baking time, the more the water content in the crust (and also in the crumb) decreases.

Therefore, the crust becomes stronger. A thick crust remains crisp longer. The moisture exchange between the crust and the crumb proceeds slower because of the thicker crust and the lower water content.

As the humidity in the air increases, the duration of the crispness decreases.

A long-lasting, tender-brittle crispness is achieved through:

— *good aeration of the crumb by means of cells with thin walls;*
— *a high proportion of crust; and*
— *a strong crust (achieved by means of slightly extending the baking time).*

* Characteristics of the crispness of rolls (five hours after baking):	
➤ slightly brittle, almost tough, soft crust	➤ typical for an insufficiently aerated and excessively dense crumb or for an insufficient baking time (under-baked)
➤ tender-brittle crust	➤ ideal state of aeration of the crumb, showing a large number of fine cells with thin walls
➤ hard, very brittle crust	➤ typical for insufficiently-aerated crumb showing cells with thick walls, for an excessively long baking time, or for doughs prepared in too warm an environment, or for exceeding the dough maturity

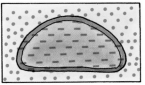

high air humidity

high water content in the crumb

thin crust

short-lasting crispness

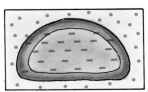

low air humidity

low water content in the crumb

thick crust

long-lasting crispness

Fig. 214

Explain the influence of the above factors on the duration of the crispness.

Fig. 215   **Roll with a sticky crumb**

Crumb

Food for Thought:
At the breakfast table, in hotels, for example, guests will often take the crumb out of the rolls and eat the crust only. What could be a reason for this kind of behavior?

The consumer evaluates the crumb of the roll on the ease with which a spread or firm butter can be applied, and the ease with which it can be chewed. These characteristics are determined by the degree of elasticity of the crumb.

The desired elasticity is achieved:

— through good aeration of the crumb; and
— through a sufficiently long baking time of the rolls (20 to 22 minutes).

Deficiencies in the elasticity of the crumb of rolls can be caused through an excessively high activity of the enzymes in the dough. In such a case it is recommended to use baking additives that do not contain any enzymes.

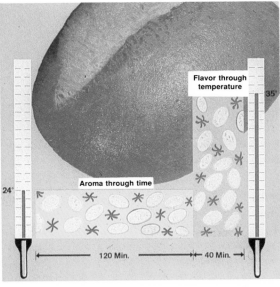

Fig. 216   **Dough temperature and product flavor**

Why is a long fermentation process in a cool environment still preferred to achieve aroma development?

The flavor should be rounded and distinct. Rolls with a large volume typically taste bland and flat.

Products made with excessively-aged and fermented dough have a strong yeasty taste.

Rolls that have a long fermentation time in a cool environment have a better taste than rolls that have had a short and warm fermentation process. Take these facts into account when evaluating *Fig. 216.*

Characteristics of Specialty Rolls

Rolls Containing Rye and Coarse Wheat Flours

Fig. 217 **Types of wheat-flour products, with portions of rye and coarse wheat flours**

Bakeries offer a great variety of buns and rolls, some containing rye flour, for a distinct flavor difference. The amount of rye flour used depends on consumer preferences, but generally amounts to 30% of the total amount of flour used.

Rolls with higher proportions of rye flour have a firm, almost hard crust and dense crumb structure with small cells. The volume of the products is visibly smaller.

Consumers prefer rye-flour rolls with only small portions of rye flour content.

Fig. 218 **Roll containing rye flour**

> **Reference:** *Examples for preparing doughs used to produce small products containing rye flour are given in the chapter entitled* **Specialty Bread***.*
> *Rolls containing 30% rye flour have the following quality characteristics in comparison to the usual roll:*
> ➤ *they are more compact*
> ➤ *the product volume is somewhat smaller*
> ➤ *the crust is slightly firmer*
> ➤ *the crumb is somewhat denser*
> ➤ *the flavor is heartier and more distinct*
> ➤ *the rolls keep fresh longer*

Soft Pretzels

Soft pretzels and rolls are unique in their characteristics, both by shape, flavor and handling.

After pretzels have been rolled into their well-known shape, a short proofing time follows, and cooling or a brief refrigeration period is required. As these pretzels cool, they become firm and can be handled without losing their shape.

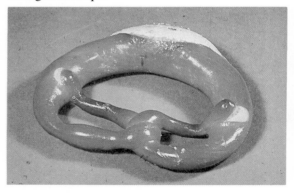

Their distinctive flavor comes from the "dip," a solution of water and sodium hydroxide (maximum ratio 4%). The firm pretzels are dipped into the solution, taken out by a perforated tray (do not touch the highly-corrosive solution) and placed on a baking sheet or oven-peel for loading into the oven. A sprinkle of salt and a cut with a sharp knife are traditional to the pretzel, whereas the roll is cut crisscross on the surface.

The "dip" solution gives a copper-tone color and shine to the pretzel. When freshly baked, soft pretzels have a slight caustic effect. This does, however, disappear and creates no known health hazards.

Be cautious with the "dip" (solution). The solution used for pretzels can cause skin burns. The use of rubber gloves is highly recommended when handling this product. Do not store this solution in containers that could be mistaken for drinking bottles.

Characteristics of White and French Bread

Large white bread loaves are evaluated according to the same principles as bread containing rye flour.

Baguettes

Typical for this French white bread variety is the high proportion of crust.
It is obtained:
— through the slim shape;
— through the strongly-developed bloom;
— through baking in decreasing heat; and
— through a correspondingly long baking time.

Fig. 220 **Baguettes: strong bloom and high proportion of crust**

Baguettes keep crisp and fresh for a long time and are normally broken when consumed. Breaking should occur with ease and should be "short" and tender-brittle.

Fig. 221 **Baguettes: typical uneven crumb with large cells**

The taste is particularly aromatic and characteristic.

To obtain the characteristics typical for baguettes, the dough should be prepared in a special way:
— *preparation in a cool environment*
— *soft dough preparation*
— *small amounts of yeast*
— *dough resting time of one to two hours. When preparing a sponge dough over two to three hours, the dough resting time can be considerably reduced.*

Sandwich Bread

Fig. 222

Sandwich bread does not require a crisp crust, but rather good toasting properties, a distinct, mild taste and long-lasting freshness.

Reference: *Characteristics determining the quality of bread and a control diagram for the evaluation of bread are found in the chapter* **Bread Evaluation**.

Fig. 223 **Quality characteristics of toast slices: "short," easy break**

Quality characteristics of sandwich bread:	Measures for obtaining the characteristics:
— slight crust formation, square slices	➤ baking in sandwich bread pans (closed baking pan)
— crumb with fine cells	➤ addition of milk and shortening; special make-up process
— good toasting properties; short breaking surface, tender crumb	➤ addition of milk, fat and sugar (tenderizers)
— long-lasting freshness	➤ addition of shortening and milk

Formula for Sandwich Bread		
1000 g	Bread-flour	
620 g	Water	
50 g	Fat	or appropriate baking additive
20 g	Sugar	
30 g	Milk powder	
20 g	Salt	
50 g	Yeast	

Table 22

While the addition of sugar, fat and milk powder is not typical in French bread types, white bread or sandwich breads contain between 3-5% sugar and fat, and about 2% milk powder.

Prepackaged Products

Food Regulatory Guidelines

Ingredients found in prepackaged products, such as white and sandwich bread, may need to be listed on the plastic bag. Check for local and federal labelling requirements.

Generally, prepackaged products sold on the bakery premises must comply with the same regulations, as if they were sold wholesale (for resale).

* *Prepackaged products are products packaged in the absence of the purchaser, whereby the quantity of the product contained in the package cannot be changed without opening or modifying the package.*

Labelling Guidelines

Self serve bakery products:
— *not prepackaged until time of sale, no labelling required.*

In-store prepackaged products:
— *either manufactured and prepackaged or delivered in bulk and prepackaged before time of sale, labelling required (bilingual where applicable)*
   — *common name,*
   — *net contents (in order of weight),*
   — *count (rolls, pastries),*
   — *weight (bread, cookies, fruit cake),*
   — *name and address of legal agent,*
   — *durable life date (except doughnuts)*

Reference: *Special information on how to list ingredients on a plastic bag is given in the chapter entitled* **Production of Sliced Bread**. *Additional information on the shelf life of baked products, such as "best before" date, is contained in the chapter entitled* **The Shelf Life of Bread**.

A guideline in establishing the optimum freshness date is the period of time during which the merchandise still possesses its quality characteristics.

Products which are not prepackaged do not require a "best before." Products sold over the counter usually fall into this category.

Labelling of packaged white bread:
1. Trade name - e.g. white bread
2. Name and address of producer or agent e.g. City Bread Ltd. Parkerhouse Lane Any Town
3. Declaration of ingredients (in order of weight) e.g. Flour Water Fat Sugar Yeast Salt
4. Best-before date e.g. best before June 8
5. Weight e.g. 20 oz. (567 g) net weight

Crusty Roll Faults and Their Causes

The following table gives an overview on deficiencies occurring in rolls and their causes. The origin of faults, their development, their causes, and measures to prevent such deficiencies are dealt with in the preceding chapter.

A single deficiency in flour quality, or a single deficiency in the production process often causes a multitude of problems during dough development and baking.

However, it is also possible that an individual roll deficiency is caused by various underlying shortcomings.

Only consideration of all deficiencies will determine the causes with a higher degree of certainty.

Crusty Roll Problems

Roll deficiencies:	Effect:	Causes:
Deficiencies in regard to the volume		
small volume (Fig. 224)	• dull color of the crust • hard crust • large, rough bloom • large cells with thick walls	➤ dough prepared in an excessively warm environment ➤ dough too firm; old
excessively small volume (Fig. 225)	• sticky crust • dense crumb with small cells	➤ dough prepared in an excessively cool environment ➤ dough too young ➤ insufficient intermediate proofing
excessively small volume (Fig. 226)	• somewhat dense crumb • rapidly diminishing crispness	➤ flour too low in gluten ➤ dough too firm ➤ mixing time too short
small volume (Fig. 227)	• pale, hard crust • small bloom • large cells	➤ too much floor time (intermediate proof too long) ➤ overproofing

Fig. 224 **Rolls made from "old" dough**

Fig. 225 **Rolls made from extremely young dough**

95

Fig. 226
Rolls made from a firm and undermixed dough

Fig. 227   Rolls made from dough with a prolonged intermediate proof

Crusty Roll Problems

Roll deficiencies:	Effect:	Causes:
Deficiencies in the Crust		
— Crust too light in color, too pale (Fig. 228)	• small volume • hard crust • large, rough bloom	➤ dough prepared too warm ➤ dough too old
— Crust too light in color, too pale (Fig. 229)	• somewhat hard crust • indented bloom	➤ fresh flour, insufficient amount of enzymes ➤ baking additives containing an insufficient amount of enzymes and sugar ➤ low baking temperature
— Crust pale, without shine, irregular brown color	• rough bloom	➤ intermediate and final proofing in too dry an environment ➤ lack of steam
— Crust softening rapidly (Fig. 230)	• small volume • weak bloom • irregular cells • rapidly diminishing crispness	➤ dough prepared in an excessively cool environment ➤ dough too young ➤ flour rich in enzymes in combination with enzymatic baking additives ➤ baking temperature too high
— Crust too hard, rough-brittle (Fig. 231)	• small volume • large cells with thick walls • pale crust • indented bloom	➤ dough prepared too warm ➤ dough too old ➤ too much proofing (overproofing)
— Insufficient, non-distinct bloom (Fig. 232)	• small volume	➤ dough overmixed
— Faded, sticky bloom (Fig. 233)	• small volume • rapidly diminishing crispness	➤ dough mixed too cool ➤ dough too young ➤ excessively soft dough ➤ protein in flour very strong

Fig. 228   Roll made with excessively warm dough and too dry an intermediate proof

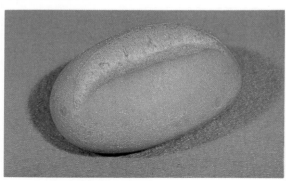

Fig. 229   Roll made from flour containing an insufficient amount of enzymes

Fig. 230   **Rolls made with flour rich in enzymes**

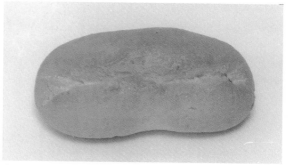

Fig. 231   **Roll made from overmatured and over-proofed dough**

Fig. 232   **Roll made from overmixed dough**

Fig. 233   **Rolls made from high-gluten flour with a short fermentation time**

Crusty roll problems		
Roll deficiencies:	*Effects:*	*Causes:*
— Sticky bloom	● *small volume* ● *pale crust* ● *hard crust*	➤ *dough too soft* ➤ *wet and sticky intermediate proof* ➤ *overproofing*
— Rough, large bloom (Fig. 224)	● *dull crust* ● *hard, rough-splintery crust*	➤ *dough was prepared too warm* ➤ *dough too old*
— Splintery crust (Fig. 234)	● *otherwise no deficiencies*	➤ *dough very soft* ➤ *proofer too wet (too much humidity)* ➤ *inappropriate freezing technique*
Faults in the Crumb Structure		
— Dense crumb with small cells (Fig. 235)	● *small volume* ● *slightly brittle, fast-softening crust*	➤ *dough prepared too cool* ➤ *dough too firm* ➤ *underdeveloped dough, too young* ➤ *undermixed*
— Uneven, large cells (Fig. 236)	● *underdeveloped bloom*	➤ *dough excessively soft*
— Deficiencies in the crumb elasticity (Fig. 238)	● *otherwise no deficiencies*	➤ *flour rich in enzymes in conjunction with enzymatic baking additives* ➤ *underbaked, baking time too short*
— Air pockets, holes in the crumb (Fig. 237)	● *somewhat small volume*	➤ *dough too soft* ➤ *dough too young* ➤ *insufficient intermediate proofing* ➤ *baking temperature too high*

Fig. 234 **Rolls kept frozen too long**

Fig. 235 **Roll with dense cells caused by young and firm dough (left); roll with large cells and holes, caused by dough being too soft**

Fig. 236 **Uneven, large cells caused by excessively soft dough**

Fig. 237 **Hollow spaces caused by insufficient proofing and baking at excessively high temperatures**

98

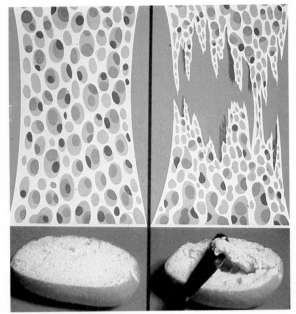

Fig. 238 **Deficiencies in the elasticity of the crumb**

Rope as a Bread Disease

A customer returns a loaf of white bread to the bakery with the claim that the bread is not thoroughly baked. It is, apparently, moldy inside.

The baker examines the complaint. The bread looks all right on the outside, but when broken into pieces, the bread is stringy inside. The crumb has a bad odor and is slimy in appearance.

The diagnosis would be that this bread has the dreaded bread disease called "rope."

Fig. 239

Cause of Rope

Rope is a direct cause of the hay bacilli (bacillus mesentericus).

This bacilli lives in the earth and dust and gets into the flour through the grain. Its spores survive the baking process and are not killed. The bacilli germinates in the crumb of the product and multiplies. To feed itself, it decomposes starch and other product components.

Development of the Disease

Spores require 12 to 24 hours to germinate and only then does the infection become obvious.

> *Characteristics of infected bakery products:*
>
> — *the crumb loses its elasticity*
> — *very fruity smell*
> — *the crumb later takes on a brown color and turns slimy*
> — *the fruity smell becomes disgusting*
> — *when broken into pieces, the crumb shows long, slimy strings*
> — *finally, the crumb collapses*
> — *even in the advanced stage of the disease, the crust shows no signs of the infection*

Fig. 240   **Rope in the advanced stage**

Endangered Bakery Products

The living conditions of the hay bacilli indicate the kind of products that may be endangered.

Living conditions:	Endangered products:
— The bacilli requires a minimum amount of moisture.	➤ Small products lose a lot of water during baking and storage; therefore mainly large-sized products with a high water content are endangered.
— The bacilli is sensitive to acid.	➤ Only non-sour (non-acid) bakery products are exposed. White bread is such a non-acid or low-acid product, with a correspondingly high water content.
— The spores must be exposed for a long period of time to temperatures between 35°C and 50°C to germinate.	➤ Only products cooling down slowly are endangered.
— The bacilli infects the outer shell of the grain.	➤ Bakery products made with flour rich in fibre are particularly endangered.

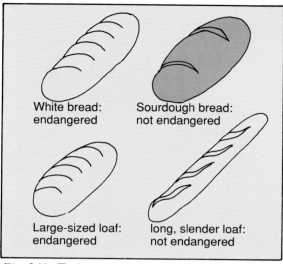

Fig. 241   **Endangered products**

Measures to Prevent Rope

The occurrence of rope in bakery products is normally limited to the warmer months of the year. But, under favorable conditions, rope can also occur at any other time.

> ** Preventive measures:*
>
> — *the addition of sourdough or baking additives containing acids to the dough*
> — *adding special agents for the prevention of rope*
> — *bake products thoroughly*
> — *cool products rapidly*
> — *remove infected bakery products from the premises; they are contagious*
> — *when the disease occurs, clean the premises and the equipment with a vinegar solution*

If infected bakery products are consumed, vomiting and diarrhea can occur.
Products infected with rope are adulterated food and therefore spoiled, and are definitely not to be sold.

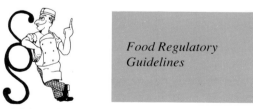

Food Regulatory Guidelines

The addition of protective agents to a dough may not be permitted in your area and it is recommended to consult local authorities.

> **Caution!**
> *Do not store rope-infected bread on the premises. Remove such bread from the premises and burn it!*

How to Maintain the Quality of Wheat-Flour Products

Fig. 242

Information on how to maintain the quality of wheat-flour products is covered in more detail in the chapter entitled **The Shelf Life of Bread**.

This chapter describes the typical characteristics of aging products and outlines steps to maintain the quality of wheat-flour products.

Wheat-flour products lose their freshness much faster than products containing rye flour:

— *because the wheat starch breaks down faster. The break down of starch is the main cause for the stale taste of bakery products;*

— *because wheat flour has an unfavorable influence on the water balance in bakery products due to its low content of swelling materials (e.g. pentosan);*

— *because wheat-flour products are made primarily with very light-colored flour containing a small amount of fibre. Flour rich in fibre improves the freshness characteristics;*

— *because wheat-flour products dry out faster due to their well-aerated texture; and*

— *because the quality characteristic determining the value of many wheat-flour products — the crispness — disappears after a few hours.*

Bakery products are called "fresh from the oven" only on the day of their production, as long as they are still warm. Properly frozen and defrosted rolls can by no means be called "fresh from the oven," but they can be called "fresh," provided they have the quality characteristics of fresh rolls.

Bakery products can be called fresh for as long as no distinct quality losses, compared with the initial freshness, have occurred. White bread is considered fresh only on the day of production. Bakery products are considered old when they have lost their typical freshness characteristics.

Steps for Maintaining Quality

Independent from the measures taken to obtain quality, there are, at the time of production, steps that can be taken to maintain the freshness of products for a longer period of time.

Preventive Measures

Measures:	Effects:
— *Aerate the products to obtain fine cells.*	➤ *In well-aerated products, starch forms a more durable paste.* **Retrogradation** *(re-composition of starch crystals) is delayed. The crust becomes stronger and therefore maintains its crispness for a longer period of time.*
— *Add some rye flour to the wheat-flour dough.*	➤ *Rye starch is partially broken down during baking through flour and baking agent amylase. Wheat starch absorbs a higher proportion of water for crumb formation, so adding rye flour makes for a moist crumb.*
— *Add preservatives, such as amylases and emulsifiers.*	➤ *Amylases improve freshness due to the breakdown of the starch, thereby reducing water absorption. Bran particles absorb, during incorporation into the dough, a multiple quantity of their own weight in water. The starch absorbs more water for paste formation during baking. Crumbs with sufficiently swelled starch maintain their freshness characteristics for a longer period of time. Some emulsifiers form compounds with starch that delay its breakdown.*
— *Bake products thoroughly.*	➤ *A strong crust remains crisp longer. The pasty starch of the crumb breaks down slower.*

Mold Prevention

The use of mold-preventing substances is not critical to maintaining the freshness of wheat-flour products. Wheat-flour products dry out quickly because they are heavily aerated, and mold requires a minimum amount of moisture for its own development.

Reference: *The chapter entitled **Mold as a Bread Disease** describes, in detail, the measures for mold prevention.*

Requirements for Short-term Storage

Rolls are usually sold and consumed while they are fresh. Loaves of white bread are still consumed days after they have been produced.

Rolls lose their crispness before their quality is diminished through the breakdown of starch or through drying out of the crumb.

Storage conditions for rolls, therefore, are exclusively oriented toward maintaining the quality of the crust, whereas storage for white bread aims at preserving the quality of the crumb.

Storage Requirements of Wheat-Flour Products:	
— *Rolls and white bread should be cooled quickly and vapors should be allowed to evaporate rapidly.* ➤	*Rolls fresh from the oven should be stored in baskets made of synthetic materials, wire mesh or wood. Let the steam from white bread evaporate by placing the loaves, well spaced, on bread racks.*
— *Rolls should be stored at room temperature and at an average air humidity.* ➤	*Avoid cool storage rooms due to their frequently high air humidity.*
— *White bread should be stored at a temperature of 15°C in a room that is not too dry.* ➤	*At room temperature, the crumb dries out too fast.*

Fig. 243 **Cooling fresh wheat-flour products**

Maintaining Quality Through Storage in Deep Freezers

The general perception is that frozen rolls are not quite as good as freshly-baked rolls.

However, when rolls are properly "shock-frozen" in high-performance freezers, they have, after defrosting, the same quality characteristics as freshly-baked rolls.

However, mistakes are frequently made during freezing, storage and defrosting. Therefore, in many cases, the quality of defrosted rolls is lower than that of rolls fresh from the oven.

Rolls that are frozen in traditional deep freezers take up to three hours to reach a freezing temperature of -7°C in the center of the crumb. Because the aging processes accelerate as the temperature decreases (to -7°C), the rolls are already "old" at the time of freezing.

Another typical characteristic of slowly-frozen rolls is the detachment of the crust from the crumb. This is caused by the drying-out processes occurring during freezing, and during storage in deep freezers.

Fig. 244 **Frozen rolls after two days of storage Left: shock-frozen; right: slowly frozen (in a traditional deep freezer)**

Compare the two rolls and give reasons for the differences.

High-performance Shock Freezing

In high-performance freezers, rolls freeze at temperatures between -25°C and -30°C under strong air movement. High-performance freezers must achieve the critical temperature of -7°C in the core of the rolls after about 45 minutes. The aging process taking place in this short period of time is insignificant.

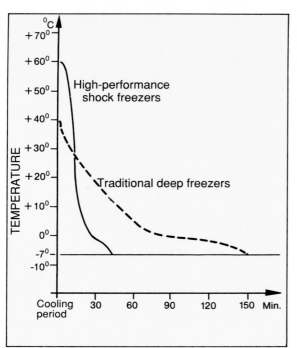

Fig. 245 **Temperature development during freez-ing of rolls**

Fig. 246 **Bread faults caused by an excessively long freezing time**

Fig. 247 **High-performance shock freezer**

102

Properly frozen rolls experience a loss in quality during storage, even if this loss occurs slowly:

➤ Loss in aroma
➤ Drying out of the crumb
➤ Breakdown of starch (retrogradation)

Frozen wheat-flour products should not be stored in a freezer for more than one to four days.

Approximate values for the storage time of wheat-flour products:
Large volume rolls .... 1 day (eg. hamburger rolls)
Rolls with a bloom .... 2 days (eg. Vienna rolls)
Rolls containing milk or fat .... 3 days (eg. Kaiser rolls)
White-bread loaves .... 3 to 4 days

Table No. 23

Economy of Operation

The costs of acquiring and maintaining a high-performance shock freezer are so high it is difficult to justify its purchase.

> *Advantages of freezing bakery products:*
>
> ➤ *Elimination of production peaks (on the weekend)*
> ➤ *More efficient production by means of making larger weekly batches of products that require lower daily quantities*
> ➤ *Production of an extra supply (for the sixth day in a five-day work week)*
> ➤ *Earlier availability for dispatching to branch outlets*
> ➤ *Availability of fresh bakery products during the whole day*

An important prerequisite for efficient, cost-effective use of a high-performance freezer is rigid adherence to shock-freezing procedures.

Refrigerators and freezers have various dimensions (depths x width) and should be large enough to suit the purpose for which they are intended.

Fig. 248 **Freezing cell with intermediate cooling room**

With rising energy costs, heat recycling plays an ever-increasing role. Some manufacturers of high-performance freezers offer units with heat recycling capability.

Functioning of Refrigerators

Pour a few drops of alcohol on the back of your hand. You will notice a strong cooling effect on your skin.

Cause: Alcohol withdraws warmth from its environment and uses it for the evaporation process.

> *Liquids require warmth to evaporate.*

This basic principle also applies to refrigerators.

> **Remember:** *Cold cannot be produced!*

For cooling, warmth must be withdrawn. In refrigerators, warmth is withdrawn from the place to be cooled, and the withdrawn warmth is supplied to another place. The vehicle in this process is the cooling agent. Cooling agents are gases which liquefy only at temperatures that are considerably below the freezing point of water. In high-performance freezers, cooling agents pass from the gaseous state to the liquid state (and vice versa) at temperatures of approximately -40°C. Cooling agents require a lot of energy for evaporation to maintain their low temperature. On the other hand, a lot of energy must be withdrawn from the gas in order to make it liquid.

The average cooling and freezing units are almost exclusively operated with compressor cooling machines. Heat absorption occurs in a closed cycle.

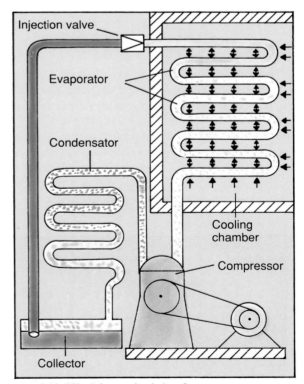

Fig. 249 **Working principle of a compressor**

Working principle of compressors:	
Process:	**Consequence:**
1) The gaseous cooling agent is condensed outside the cooling chamber by means of a compressor and pressed into the condensator.	➤ The condensed cooling agent heats up.
2) The condensed, hot cooling agent is cooled. The cooling agent passes its heat to the outside air or to the cooling water.	➤ Through cooling, the condensed gas liquefies.
3) The liquefied cooling agent is abruptly relaxed by means of an expansion valve and injected into the evaporator. The evaporator is located in the cooling chamber.	➤ The liquid cooling agent turns into gas and thereby absorbs heat from the cooling chamber. The cooling chamber turns colder, and the cooling agent becomes rich in energy.
4) The gaseous cooling agent, rich in energy, is sucked in by the compressor. Outside the cooling chamber it is again condensed and pressed into the condensator. This process occurs in a closed cycle.	➤ The condensed cooling agent turns hot.

Freezing with Liquid Gas

In addition to traditional freezing plants, freezers based on the liquid gas method are used. Here, the cooling agent is injected directly into the cooling chamber or into the cooling tunnel, and evaporated.

When the cooling agent is injected into the freezing chamber, the liquid gas promptly absorbs heat from its environment in order to evaporate. This means that the cooling agent is used up in the process and must be continuously purchased in the form of liquid gas.

Fig. 250 **Frozen carbon dioxide (-78.9°C)**

Advantages and disadvantages of freezing with liquid gas compared to traditional processes:	
Advantages:	**Disadvantages:**
➤ High freezing speed. Bakery products do not age during freezing. ➤ Better use of the unit due to short freezing times. ➤ Lower costs of unit acquisition.	➤ Liquid gas is used up and must be constantly replenished.

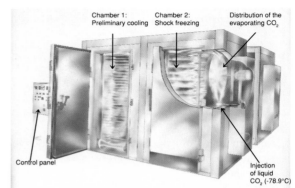

Fig. 251 **Shock freezer operating on the basis of liquid gas**

Additional Information
The cooling agent used is liquid nitrogen (N_2) or liquid carbon dioxide (CO_2). Nitrogen is cooled down so far by the manufacturer that it turns liquid. Liquid nitrogen passes back into the gaseous state during injection at -196°C.

Carbon dioxide passes from the gaseous state into the solid state during cooling at about -79°C. Under pressure, it liquefies during the cooling process.

Summary of the most important information on freezers and freezing units for wheat-flour products:

* Rules for freezing rolls:
— Freeze rolls almost immediately after they come out of the oven.
— In high-performance shock freezing the core temperature must reach -7°C after 45 minutes of freezing.
— Do not store rolls for more than two days at -20°C.
— First defrost rolls for 30 minutes at room temperature, then place them for a few minutes into the baking oven at 230°C, while adding a moderate amount of steam.
* Traditional cooling machines are:
— Compressor cooling machines: here, the heat is exchanged in a continuous cycle via a cooling agent.
— Cooling machines based on the liquid gas process: here, the liquid gas is injected as a cooling agent and the cooling agent is used up in the process.

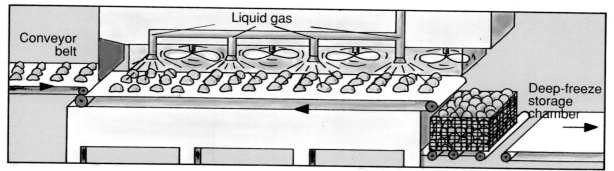

Fig. 252 **Working principle of a shock freezing plant operating with liquid gas and a conveyor belt system**

Weight Regulations for Wheat-Flour Products

Are there are any regulations regarding baked products?

In some countries, states or provinces, there are regulations governing baked goods.

For information about local weight and measurement regulations, contact the appropriate governing agency.

Joe claims: *"Buns have to weigh at least 50 g." Is this true?*

> *Here are some suggestions pertaining to the various weights:*
>
> White bread *454 g net weight*
> French bread *375 g net weight*
> Rye breads *500 g, 750 g, 1000 g, net weight*

For more information on the marking of prepackaged products refer to the chapter entitled Quality **Characteristics of Wheat-flour Products**.

Typical bread weights:
375 g, 454 g, 500 g, 675 g, 750 g, 910 g

Most regulations state:

— *Unsliced and unpackaged breads do not require a label, but their weight must be indicated.*
— *The net weight must be indicated on packaged bread.*

Exception:

• *Packaged rolls and buns*
• *Packaged bread produced on the premises with the net weight indicated on a sign near the product. It is not available in the self-serve area.*

Weight Labelling

The net weight of packaged bread must be indicated on the label. The weights listed above, and any other weights, are acceptable as long as the ***net weight*** is clearly indicated.

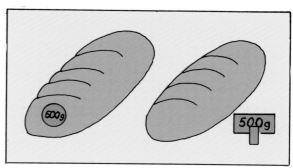

Fig. 253 **Placement of weight indication (left: European, right: North American)**

Reference: *For more details on the marking of prepackaged products, refer to the chapter entitled Quality Characteristics of White Bread.*

Weight Checks

An expert knows that it is sometimes very difficult to comply with weight regulations for bakery products:

— During scaling or make-up, a dough piece can fall off.
— Baking, cooling and storage losses are not always consistent.

Government agencies, such as the FDA in the United States and Consumer and Corporate Affairs in Canada, stipulate that bakery products of identical nominal weight shall not fall below the average nominal weight at the time of production.
What does this mean?

During weight checks, for example, 10 breads with a nominal weight of 0.5 kg must have a combined weight of 5 kg. The individual bread can, within certain limits, exceed or fall below the nominal weight.

If the weight of an individual bread loaf exceeds the allowed weight deviation, the bread cannot be sold according to the law (see *Table 25*).

Scales and measuring containers for the production of bakery products may fall under the regulation of standard calibration. However, an imprecise scale does not relieve the baker from his responsibility to adhere to weight regulations.

Legal weight deviations for bakery products	
Nominal weight:	Deviation:
500 g	up to 30 g
1000 g	up to 30 g
1000 g — 10,000 g	up to 3%

Table 25

Food for Thought: *What are the reasons for strict compliance with weight regulations?*

The Use and Application of Rye Flour

Fig. 254

Rye Flour Products

Because there are more than 200 different rye bread varieties it is impossible to know them all. Certain traditional bread varieties, and also some specialty breads, are covered in this chapter.

Bread can, for example, be classified:
— according to shape, or
— according to the flour mixture used.

Based on the shape, bread is classified into:
— bread baked without a pan in round or long shapes with a shiny or floury surface; and
— pan-baked breads with a smooth or shaped surface.

Depending on the flour mix used, bread is classified as follows:

— Wheat bread (white bread) containing more than 90% wheat;

— Mixed wheat bread containing more than 50%, but less than 90% wheat;

— Mixed bread containing 50% rye flour and 50% wheat;

— Mixed rye bread containing more than 50%, but less than 90% rye; and

— Rye bread containing more than 90% rye.

These categories apply to bread which is made with milled flour. The addition of meal is allowed, but it should not exceed 10% of the total content.

The composition of coarse and whole grains should also be identified.

Fig. 256 **Specialty bread made with dough containing rye flour**

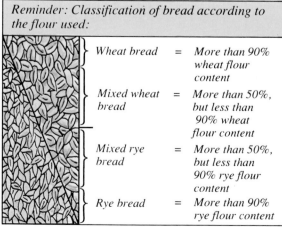

Reminder: Classification of bread according to the flour used:		
Wheat bread	=	More than 90% wheat flour content
Mixed wheat bread	=	More than 50%, but less than 90% wheat flour content
Mixed rye bread	=	More than 50%, but less than 90% rye flour content
Rye bread	=	More than 90% rye flour content

Table 26

107

Small Baked Products Containing Rye Flour

As the variety of small bakery products increases, those containing rye flour are increasingly becoming part of the daily baking program of North American bakeries. There is a large variety of small products, differing in shape, size and ingredients used. A content of less than 50% rye flour is usually necessary in order to obtain an adequate volume. In these cases, the designation "rye buns" should not be used. Therefore, frequent other designations are used for small products containing rye, for example:

— Swiss rye buns
— Farmer rolls
— Onion rolls
— Bacon 'n rye buns
— Party rolls

In principle, small bakery products containing rye differ from bread loaves through their weight.

No weight regulations apply to small products less than 250 g. Bread loaves however, must have the weight stated on the label.

(Refer to *Table 24* in the chapter entitled **Weight Regulations for Wheat-flour Products**).

Fig. 257
Several bread varieties from the same dough

Bread Varieties

It is possible to use the same dough to make different varieties of bread, depending on the shapes, makeup methods and baking methods.

But the consumer expects specific bread varieties to have certain characteristics. Bread varieties which are not restricted to a particular region are given generic names. These generic names are not protected. But for a specific bread variety, one expects universal quality characteristics.

Let's use an example:

Additional Information

The classification of bread must be in accordance with the type of milled product used. This rule applies to coarse grain, whole grain and white breads. Accordingly, a coarse rye bread must contain at least 90% coarse rye material; other rye or wheat products can amount up to 10%.

If the proportion of coarse rye is lower (but higher than 10%), the bread name should include the addition "with coarse-milled material." For example: A mixed wheat bread contains half of its wheat or rye content in the form of coarse-milled material: "Mixed wheat bread with coarse-milled material."

Whole-grain bread can be produced with only whole-grain materials, water/milk products, yeast, salt and, if applicable, sourdough. Whole-grain products must contain all the components of the grain. Only whole-grain products can be used for a whole-grain sourdough. Up to 10% of other bread grain products and/or additives can be added to the bread dough.

When using mixes of whole-grain rye and wheat products, the bread should be named in accordance with the predominant grain product, i.e. "Rye-Wheat Whole-Grain Bread" or "Wheat-Rye Whole-Grain Bread."

The above-mentioned types of grain product combinations apply also to white bread.

Joe thinks: *"It takes much too long to make a dough for each bread variety. One can make all kinds of different bread with the same dough without the customer noticing!"*

Fig. 258 **Kommissbrot**

Kommissbrot

This type of bread is made with dark rye flour, and its characteristic shape is formed by the shape of the pan.

Fig. 259 Berliner Country Bread

This type of bread is a long-shaped rye bread or mixed rye bread, baked without a pan, and with flour sprinkled over its surface. Its strong cracked surface is achieved by means of dry proofing, full fermentation maturity and especially high initial baking temperatures (preliminary baking method).

Fig. 260 Land Bread (Country-style Bread)

This bread variety is made mostly with dark flours of various mixes. Characteristic for this bread type is the aromatic, hearty flavor (sponge dough method), the floury and slightly uneven surface, a strong crust and large cells.

Fig. 261 Prairie Bread

This is a strongly leavened mixed rye bread. Typical is its smooth surface, showing cells. This is achieved by cutting the dough pieces in half, lengthwise, during the intermediate proof. The two bread loaves are baked with the cut surface turned up; the sides remain floury.

Fig. 262 Paderborner Bread

This bread variety is a mixed rye bread baked in a pan and made with light-colored wheat flour. In the region where it originated (in the German city of Paderborn), bakers use a rye-wheat-flour mixture, using mainly first clear flour as the wheat flour portion.

Fig. 263 Black Forest Rye Bread

This a mixed wheat bread in long and round shapes. Typical is its very loose crumb, its strong crust and its mildly-aromatic flavor.

Fig. 264 Westphalia Rye Bread

This mixed wheat bread receives a long cut on the floury surface at the time of full proof. Its somewhat rectangular shape is achieved in the baking pan. The crust on the sides is soft, and the crumb is moist and fresh.

Fig. 265 **Kasseler Basket Bread**

Kasseler Bread

This is a mixed rye bread made with light-colored flour. It is named after the German town of Kassel where it originated.

This bread is characterized by its shiny surface and the crust on each end. It is baked without a pan.

Basket Bread

This variety is a mixed wheat or rye bread that is placed in baskets during the final proof. The surface of the bread can be sprinkled with flour, or it can be shiny. The bread surface is imprinted with the basket pattern.

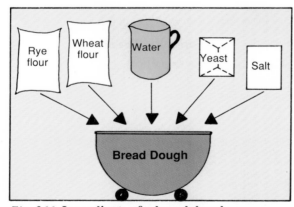

Fig. 266 **Ingredients of a bread dough**

Types of Rye Flours
White (Light) Rye Flour: The patent flour from the rye kernel. It is well suited to mildly-flavored, light-colored types of rye bread.
Medium Rye Flour: Consists of the whole rye kernel with the bran removed. Flour color is light gray and gives bread a pronounced rye flavor.
Dark Rye Flour: The product represents 100% of the grain. It is dark in color, possesses a pronounced flavor, and lacks the smooth texture of the other grades.
Rye Meal: Whole-grain, available in many particle sizes.

Table 27

Summary of information on bread varieties

Classification based on the shape:

e.g.—rough bread, loaf bread, pan-baked bread, bread baked without a pan

Classification based on bread makeup:

e.g.—crust sprinkled with flour, shiny crust, cut surface

Classification based on the mix of ground product used:

— *Bread with a wheat content of at least 90% (example: wheat bread)*
— *Bread with a wheat content of at least 50%, but less than 90% (example: mixed wheat bread)*
— *Bread with a rye content of at least 50%, but less than 90% (example: mixed rye bread)*
— *Bread with a rye content of at least 90% (example: rye bread)*

Bread varieties with generic names must have universal characteristics (e.g. Kommissbrot as a pan-baked bread).

Small bakery products containing rye weigh less than 250 g. They can be called rye rolls, mixed rye rolls, or mixed wheat rolls when they contain the corresponding flour mixes.

Rye Flour

The basic ingredients of bread and small bakery products containing rye are:

— rye flour/coarse rye;
— wheat flour/coarse wheat;
— water;
— yeast; and
— salt.

Bread varieties are primarily determined by the properties of the milled rye products used. The specific properties of milled rye products are listed below.

For bread containing rye, light, medium or dark rye flours are generally used. Coarse materials found in rye meal are used in coarse product bread varieties. A complete list of ground rye products is given in *Table 27*.

Additional Information
For large volume producers, specialty flours containing wheat and rye flours can be milled to serve specific needs.

Sometimes identical rye flour types show important differences in their baking behaviors. What could be the reasons?

> Differences in the baking behaviors of identical rye flour types are due to:
>
> — *different varieties of rye grains from which the flour is produced;*
> — *different growing regions of the rye;*
> — *different harvesting and climatic conditions which have an influence on the formation of the grain; and*
> — *different storage periods and conditions of the flour.*

It is important, therefore, that a baker checks the quality of supplied rye products prior to use.

Evaluation of Rye Flour

Evaluation by Means of Simple Tests

First of all, bakers can perform a sensory evaluation through;
— touch;
— smell;
— taste; and
— color.

Rye flour and wheat flour differ in color. Wheat flour is white with a yellowish shade and rye flour is bluish-gray.

Essential differences in the baking behavior of rye and wheat flour can be recognized when mixing flour into the dough and during baking.

Fig. 267 **Rye dough in a mixing bowl**

> **Reference:** *A detailed description of how to evaluate flour is given in the chapter entitled* **Evaluation of Wheat Flour.**

Test 19:
Prepare two doughs, one with 100 g of Baker's flour, the other one with 100 g of light rye flour. Evaluate the color and properties of both doughs.

a) 100 g wheat flour
             (Baker's flour)
   +60 g water
   + 2 g salt
   _____
   =162 g dough

b) 100 g light rye
             flour
   +70 g water
   + 2 g salt
   _____
   =172 g dough

Observations:
Both doughs are equally firm.
The rye dough is bluish/gray, the wheat dough is yellowish/white.
The rye dough is not as elastic as the wheat dough; it is short and moist.

Test 20:
Divide the doughs from *Test 19* in two halves and wash the gluten out of one half of each.

Observation:
The gluten from the wheat flour dough is soft. No cohesive gluten can be washed out from the rye flour dough.

> **Reference:** *The process of washing out the gluten is described in more detail in the chapter entitled* **Evaluation of Wheat Flour.**

Evaluation by Means of Baking Tests

Baking tests ensure a comprehensive evaluation of rye flour properties.

Test 21:

The **yeast baking test** is a standardized, simple method allowing the baker to establish the baking value of a rye flour.

The test data for light rye flour is as follows:

Rye flour	= 1000 g	Dough temp.	= 29°C
Water	= 700 g	Dough rest time	= 60 min.
Yeast	= 10 g	Baking time	= 60 min.
Salt	= 15 g		at 230°C.

In the yeast baking test, the baking value of the flour is determined by means of the crumb picture of the bread (refer to *Fig. 268* on page 112).

Baking value 1 identifies insufficient baking ability. The higher the baking value, the better the baking ability.

Fig. 268 **Results of the yeast baking test**

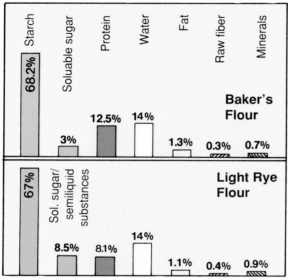

Table 28
Difference in composition of rye and wheat flours

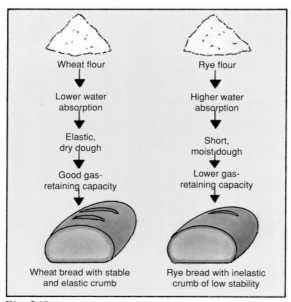

Fig. 269

112

In order to make the differences between rye and wheat flour more evident, a yeast baking test with baker's flour is performed.

Test 22:

Prepare a dough using Baker's flour based on the recipe for the yeast baking test. Observe the fermentation behavior and compare the bread produced with that obtained in the rye flour yeast baking test.

Observations:
— Rye doughs ferment faster than comparable wheat doughs.
— Non-sour rye doughs yield, in general, a less firm crumb structure than wheat doughs.

What is the reason for this?

Here are some reasons for the different baking behavior of rye and wheat flours

Rye and wheat flours at comparable degrees of milling differ in their composition.
Rye flour contains
— *less starch;*
— *less swollen protein;*
— *more soluble sugar;*
— *more water-binding semiliquid substances;*
— *more starch-digesting enzymes.*

The average values for flour made from rye and wheat grains indicated in *Table 28* are, of course, subject to large fluctuations, according to the variety, the year of harvest, milling, etc. Based on the observations made during the tests, we can now explain the following phenomena:

— the bluish/white color of the rye flour and of the rye dough (shell material and mineral content);
— the higher water absorption power of the rye during dough preparation (pentosan content);
— the moist and short dough condition of the rye dough (pentosan content);
— the lower gas-retaining capacity of the rye dough (lower protein content).

No explanation has as yet been found for the unstable bread crumb in the yeast baking test using rye flour. For that purpose, we must examine the combined effect of water absorption in the rye dough, enzyme activity and baking behavior.

Enzyme activities in rye dough are primarily governed by the starch-digesting amylases. They decompose the starch into soluble sugar. Pasty starch is most easily decomposed.

The **condition of rye starch** changes through the enzymatic digesting process occurring in the flour. This process continues during dough preparation and baking. Rye starch turns pasty between 53°C and 73°C. In this temperature range, the amylases are still active and decompose the starch.

The **water-absorbing substances** of rye flour increase the dough yield. Therefore, a larger quantity of water is available during baking to make the starch pasty. When starch is decomposed into soluble sugar by enzymes, it cannot absorb enough water. The "excess" water makes the bread crumb moist and inelastic. When starch is deteriorated to a great degree, the crumb is slack.

The enzyme activity in rye flour is also made evident through the results of flour analysis. In addition to the maltose number and the fall number, the **amylogram** is of particular interest. It measures the paste-forming ability of starch in measuring units (amylogram units), and the temperature at the beginning and end of the paste formation process.

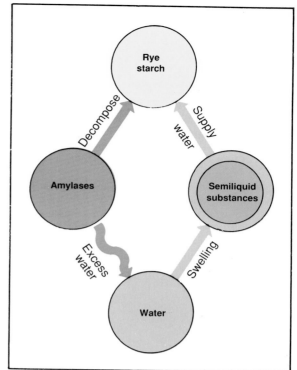

Fig. 270

Additional Information

In the amylograph, a flour-water slurry is heated up slowly from 25°C to 75°C. In the process, the starch in the flour turns into a paste (just as during the baking process).
A sensing device is used to translate the values measured into curves (Fig. 271), which are represented in the amylogram.

The data on the condition of rye starch is based on the following values:
— *Start of the paste formation process*
— *Paste formation maximum in amylogram units (AU)*
— *Paste formation end temperature*
The baker can expect a good baking ability of a rye flour:
— *at amylogram values between 250 and 400 AU; and*
— *at paste formation end temperatures between 65°C and 70°C.*

Maltose number	Amylogram	Fall number
Soluble sugar content	Condition of flour starch	Firmness of starch paste

Table 29 **Interpretation of flour analysis data**

Remember:
Ground rye products have a good baking ability at:

Maltose	Amylogram	Fall number
2 to 3%	*250 to 400 AU*	*over 150*

Reference: *For additional information on laboratory tests with flour, read the chapter entitled **Evaluation of Wheat Flour**.*

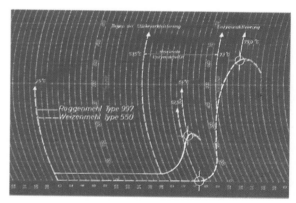

Fig. 271 **Amylogram**
By comparing the amylograms of wheat flour (dotted curve) and of rye flour (solid curve), the differing paste formation properties of rye and wheat flour become evident.

For the wheat flour shown:
— Temperatures range from 62.5°C to 79°C for paste formation
— Firmness = 620 AU
For the rye flour shown:
— Temperatures range from 53.5°C to 64°C for paste formation
— Firmness = 240 AU

113

Factors Influencing the Baking Ability of Rye Flour

Baking tests are a more thorough determination of the baking behavior of rye flour than the methods described so far.

The crumb of the bread and the flavor of the end product can be evaluated by means of the ***lactic-acid baking test***.

The ***sourdough baking test**** can establish an index number for the workability of rye flour through evaluation of the dough yield, the volume obtained, and the elasticity of the crumb.

The evaluation of the quality of various kinds of flour is not important to the daily operation of a bakery. But the baker must determine the quality of bread he can obtain in terms of crumb conditions, flavor and duration of freshness. The following test shows how this can be done (refer to *Table 30*).

*Reference: *A detailed description of sourdough and its influence on the baking process is found in the following pages.*

Sourdough Content

> ***Test 23:***
> Prepare six bread doughs, each made of 1,000 g rye flour (using the methods of preparation given in Table 30).
> A part of the rye flour is made sour in the following order:
>
> | No. 1 | No. 2 | No. 3 | No. 4 | No. 5 | No. 6 |
> |-------|-------|-------|-------|-------|-------|
> | 0 g | 100 g | 200 g | 300 g | 400 g | 500 g |
>
> The quantity of flour made sour can be expressed in terms of ***sour content*** (in % of the total rye quantity).
> The sour content in this test would then be:
>
> | No. 1 | No. 2 | No. 3 | No. 4 | No. 5 | No. 6 |
> |-------|-------|-------|-------|-------|-------|
> | 0% | 10% | 20% | 30% | 40% | 50% |
>
> The applications, test values and results should be summarized as in *Table 30* below.

Dough	1 0% sour	2 10% sour	3 20% sour	4 30% sour	5 40% sour	6 50% sour
Total flour quantity in grams	1,000	1,000	1,000	1,000	1,000	1,000
Total amount of liquid	710	700	690	680	670	660
Yeast (1.6%) in grams	16	16	16	16	16	16
Salt (1.8%) in grams	18	18	18	18	18	18
Dough condition	normal	normal	normal	normal	normal	166
Dough yield	171	170	169	168	167	10
Dough resting time in minutes	10	10	10	10	10	1,690
Dough weight immediately	1,750	1,735	1,730	1,725	1,705	1,690
Dough input in grams	1,750	1,735	1,730	1,725	1,705	50
Intermediate proof in minutes	50	50	50	50	50	28
Dough temperature in °C	28	28	28	27	29	32
Proofer temperature in °C	32	32	32	32	32	220
Oven temperature in °C	220	220	220	220	220	60
Baking time in minutes	60	60	60	60	60	
Product	1	2	3	4	5	6
Product weight after 1 hour	1,535	1,515	1,510	1,500	1,490	1,500
Product volume in cm³	2,980	3,020	2,680	2,700	2,980	2,760
Bread yield	153.5	151.5	151	150	149	150
Volume yield	298	302	268	270	298	276
Baking loss in %	12.3	12.7	12.7	13	12.6	11.2
Shape	somewhat flat	good	good	good	good	somewhat round
Browning	normal	normal	normal	normal	normal	normal
Condition of the crumb	sticky	moist	normal	normal	normal	normal
Evenness of cells	rather even	rather even	rather even	rather even	normal	rather even
Elasticity of the crumb	inelastic	almost good	good	good	good	good
Flavor	very flat	flat	somewhat aromatic	aromatic	aromatic	sour
Acid number	5	7.6	9.3	11	12.4	13.6

Table 30 **Conduction of sourdough baking test and results with varying sourdough contents**

Test results:

➤ Without sourdough, the crumb of the bread is unstable and the flavor is flat.

➤ With increasing sour content, the crumb becomes more stable and elastic; the flavor turns somewhat sour to aromatic.

➤ With a high sour content, the crumb turns rubbery-firm and the flavor is too sour.

➤ The measured pH number increases with increasing sour content.

➤ The highest quality of rye bread is achieved at a sour content between 30% and 40%.

The results of baking *Test 23* apply to rye flour with a normal baking ability. However, the baking ability of rye flour is often changed due to the activity of enzymes. Such flour is produced from years of harvest preceded by a moist-warm summer. In this case, the grain starts to germinate (grow) at the time of harvesting. The enzymes contained in the grain, start, at the same time, to decompose the starch into soluble sugar. The baker calls the rye flour obtained under such conditions **growth-impaired**.

This type of flour is flour with a high enzyme activity. We can produce such flour for test purposes by adding malt flour.

Test 24:

Prepare six bread doughs, each with 1,000 g of rye flour. Use the recipes from *Test 23*. In order to obtain a flour deteriorated through enzymes, add malt flour prior to dough preparation (even in the case of preparation of sourdough).

Adding 4 g of malt flour per 100 g of rye flour has a significant effect on the baking ability of rye flour.

Test results:

➤ Blisters and color discrepancies occur on the crust of bread made with a small sour content. The higher the sour content, the darker the color of the crust.

➤ Without sourdough, the crumb of the bread does not turn firm and is sticky. The higher the sour content, the more the stability and elasticity of the crumb increase.

➤ Good results with flour that has been affected by a high enzyme activity can be achieved with a sour content of 40%.

Remember:
Rye bread made with rye flour of normal baking ability has a sour content of about 30% to 40%. Rye flour that has been affected by high enzymatic activity should have a sour content between 40% and 45% in order to obtain good results.

Fig. 272
Rye bread with a sour content between 0 and 50%. Cells can be seen in the cross section. The inelasticity of the crumb of breads with a sour content of 0%, 10% and 20% are not shown in the picture. At an excessively high sour content of 50%, a round shape and uneven cells become evident.

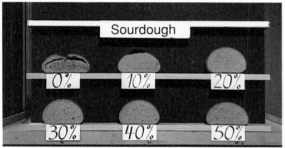

Fig. 273 Rye breads made with flour deteriorated through enzymatic activity and with sour contents varying between 0% and 50%. At a sour content of 0% and 10%, the crumb deficiencies are clearly recognizable.

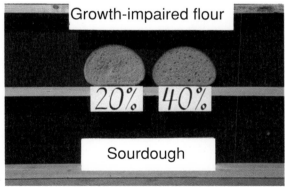

Fig. 274 Comparison of crumb elasticity of bread made with flour deteriorated through enzymatic activity and with sour contents of 20% and 40%. When the thumb is pushed into dough with a sour content of 20%, the inelasticity of the crumb is obvious. Bread with a sour content of 40% doesn't show the thumb imprint; the crumb is of the desired elasticity.

Reference: *The chapter entitled* **Baking Agents for Wheat-Flour Products** *introduced baking malt as a wheat bread baking agent.*
The activity of the enzymatic/diastatic malt is desirable for wheat-flour products. Make a comparison between this and the effect of the starch-decomposing enzymes on rye flour.

Fig. 275 **Starch paste prior to cooling**

Fig. 276 **Overturning test with cooled starch paste from** *Test 25*

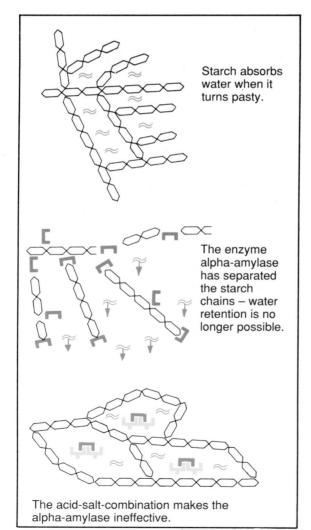

Starch absorbs water when it turns pasty.

The enzyme alpha-amylase has separated the starch chains – water retention is no longer possible.

The acid-salt-combination makes the alpha-amylase ineffective.

Fig. 277

116

Effect of Acid and Salt

In *Tests 23* and *24*, the effect of varying sour contents for rye bread was evaluated. However, the salt content of the dough should not be ignored. The normal dosage is 1.8% of salt (18 g per 1,000 g of flour).

The interrelationship between dough acidification and the effect of salt becomes evident in the following test:

Test 25:
Cook 1 litre of water and 100 g of wheat starch until a paste is formed. Put the paste into four beakers. Prepare the samples as follows:

No. 1	No. 2	No. 3	No. 4
without additive	+ 1 g malt flour	+ 1 g malt flour + 3 g of acid	+ 1 g malt flour + 3 g acid + 3 g salt

Turn the paste over once it has cooled.

Observations:
— The untreated starch paste solidifies to the point that the beaker can be inverted.
— The starch paste with malt flour addition liquefies.
— The starch paste with malt flour and acid additions turns into a mush.
— The starch paste with malt flour, acid and salt additions solidifies to the point that the beaker can be inverted.

Conclusions:
— Malt flour contains starch-digesting enzymes (amylases). The amylases decompose the starch into soluble sugar. Therefore, the water can no longer be retained.
— A combination of acid and salt prevents the amylases from being active. The amylases can no longer decompose the starch and the water can be retained by the starch.

Application to Rye Flour:

Rye flour rich in enzymes (growth-impaired rye flour) contains a large number of amylases. These weaken the baking ability through decomposition of the starch. Therefore, the water retention capacity during baking is limited. In order to maintain the water-retention capacity of the rye starch during baking, the rye dough is made sour. The addition of salt also slows down the activity of the enzymes. The combination of acid and salt has the highest stabilizing effect on the baking ability.

Test 26:

Prepare two bread doughs, each with 1,000 g of rye flour. Add four g of malt flour to each batch of rye flour.

Recipe:

A		B	
1000 g	rye flour	1000 g	rye flour
+ 650 g	water	+ 650 g	water
+ 10 g	yeast	+ 10 g	yeast
		+ 18 g	salt
		+ 12.5 g	lactic acid

Bake the bread under the conditions described in the yeast baking test. However, interrupt the baking process after 10 minutes and cut the bread into halves (see *Fig. 278*).

Observation:
— The bread without the addition of acid and salt has not formed a cohesive crumb.
— The bread with acid and salt additions has already formed a crumb.

Conclusion:
Rye flour requires the addition of acid and salt to stabilize its baking ability.

Additional Information
The firmness of the crumb structure containing rye depends primarily on starch. Its condition in connection with the enzymes acting in the rye flour is called the diastatic condition of the rye. Compared to wheat, harvesting conditions have an unfavorable effect on rye grains which are rich in enzymes, but lacking in starch. In a moist harvest climate, rapidly ripened crops experience a softening of the cellulose shells through enzymes in the rye kernel and the simultaneous effect of micro-organisms and their enzymes. Proteases and similar enzymes cause the albumen in the relatively large rye starch grains to dissolve so the starch-digesting enzymes (five different alpha-amylases) can now attack the starch grains and decompose them into soluble sugars.

The enzymatic activity in the rye continues during dough processing. Paste formation of rye starch during baking coincides with the optimum temperature of the enzymes (between 53°C and 73°C). Because the rye dough also contains more water, it is important to inhibit the enzyme activity through reduction of the pH value (below pH value 4.5 to 5.5) through the addition of the acid and salt, and thus obtain a good water retention in the crumb.

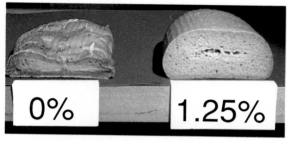

Fig. 278 Bread made with growth-impaired flour without acidification (left) and with lactic acid (right) after 10 minutes of baking

Summary of Important Information on the Baking Ability of Rye Flour
— *Rye flour has a better water absorption capacity than comparable wheat flour. Therefore, rye doughs produce a higher dough yield.* — *Rye flour is not able to retain enough dough water during baking to form an elastic crumb.* — *Starch-decomposing enzymes (amylases) have a negative effect on the water-retention capacity of rye flour. They decompose the starch into soluble sugar.* — *The activity of the starch-decomposing enzymes is slowed down when acid and salt are added to rye flour dough.* — *Rye flour must be acidified to stabilize its baking ability.*

Acidification of Doughs Containing Rye

To stabilize the baking ability of rye flour, doughs containing rye must be acidified when they are prepared.

This can be done in several ways:
— by preparing a fermenting sourdough;
— by adding baking additives with an acidifying effect; and
— by using a sourdough in combination with baking additives that have an acidifying effect on the dough.

What method of dough acidification is used in your local bakery?

Fermentation by means of a sourdough is certainly the oldest method used to acidify bread doughs. However, this does not mean that the method is outdated. On the contrary: the sourdough method has continuously been developed throughout the history of baking. Today there are a large number of modern methods available enabling bakers to use a sourdough for bread production in a safe and economical way. The most important methods are described on the following pages.

Compare the various methods for acidification of doughs containing rye. What do you think about Joe's statement?

Fig. 279 Egyptian woman forms bread (about 2000 years B.C.)

Objectives of the Use of Sourdough

Fermentation products of sourdough have various favorable effects on bread dough:

— they stabilize the baking ability of rye;
— they give the bread an aromatic flavor;
— they tenderize the bread crumb;
— they make the bread crumb firm and elastic;
— they improve fresh-keeping properties and the durable life of the bread.

Remember: *Objectives of the use of sourdough = improvement of the baking ability of rye*

Looseness of the crumb	+	Bread flavor	+	Tenderizing

Wheat flours are not normally acidified. Therefore, a sourdough is a fermenting dough made of rye flour or coarse rye and water.

Additional Information

Sourdough has a long history and originated thousands of years ago. In ancient Egypt, bread was an important staple, therefore a large number of bread varieties were available.

The Egyptians discovered fermenting sourdough by coincidence, when the remainder of a dough started fermenting in the warm environment. This is how they found the sour starter for preparation of a sourdough.

In biblical texts relating the 430-year-long imprisonment of the Jewish people in Egypt, something can be learned about sourdough. Moses is said to have prohibited his Jewish people from eating sour bread at the time of the Easter Lamb: "For seven days let your food be unleavened bread; from the first day no leaven is to be seen in your houses; whoever takes bread with leaven in it, from the first till the seventh day, will be cut off from Israel." (Exodus 12:15)

Micro-organisms of Sourdough

Fermentation of sourdough is caused by micro-organisms in flour and air. The baker is responsible for preparing sourdough under the most favorable living conditions for the desirable micro-organisms.

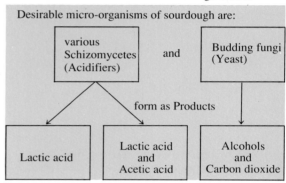

Desirable micro-organisms of sourdough are:

various Schizomycetes (Acidifiers)	and	Budding fungi (Yeast)

form as Products

Lactic acid	Lactic acid and Acetic acid	Alcohols and Carbon dioxide

Micro-organisms causing foreign fermentation processes and developing unpleasant flavors and odors (e.g. butyric acid bacteria) are undesirable in sourdough. Such micro-organisms get into sourdough naturally through flour and air. But if the baker sufficiently nurtures the growth of the desired micro-organisms, the undesirable ones will be naturally eliminated.

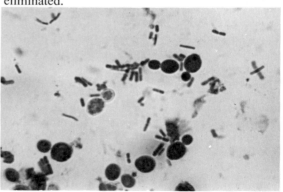

Fig. 280 **Micro-photograph of a sourdough (enlarged 1,200 times).** (In addition to the growth colonies of the sourdough yeast, rod-shaped acidifiers can also be seen.)

The fermentation products of acidifiers are poison for undesirable micro-organisms. But the activity of desirable micro-organisms is also limited through their own products of fermentation. Therefore, the sourdough takes care of its own preservation.

The micro-organisms of the sourdough ferment the flour substance and use it to form the desired products. The baker provides the micro-organisms in the sourdough with nutrients and moisture. By using proper techniques, a baker can also control the production of individual fermentation products.

→ Lactic acid forms in a soft dough at temperatures between 35°C and 40°C.

→ Acetic acid forms in a firm dough at temperatures around 20°C.

→ Formation of sourdough yeast is furthered in a soft dough that is rich in oxygen and at temperatures between 24°C and 26°C, where the yeast cells can multiply.

Processing Conditions

Because micro-organisms have varying needs, they cannot all be given ideal conditions for their development in the sourdough.

Therefore bakers consider various living conditions of micro-organisms in sourdough. When the sourdough is prepared in several phases, each phase fulfills a special purpose (e.g. furthering of lactic acid formation).

Specific sourdough methods are geared solely toward special living conditions of individual micro-organisms.

Example: Lactic Acid Formation

A one-phase sourdough preparation method, the **Berliner Short Sour Method**, serves primarily to form lactic acid. Therefore, it is especially geared toward meeting the conditions for lactic acid production = soft dough with a dough yield of 190 and a warm environment with a sourdough temperature of 35°C.

Example: Yeast Multiplication

With the **Whipped or Foam Sour Method**, the multiplication of yeast cells is furthered in two to five fermentation phases. The dough yield is about 250, the sour dough temperature about 26°C, and the dough is whipped to achieve air incorporation.

A baker can thereby change the processing condition to suit the needs of the desired fermentation products. This also allows bakers to control the quality of their bread by means of sourdough.

Flavor development in the bread is primarily due to the quantity of acid used and the ratio of lactic and acetic acid. A ratio of 75% to 80% lactic acid and 20% to 25% acetic acid (for a total acid content of a sourdough of 100%) is favorable. The acid quantity is measured in the acid value, by determining the quantity of soda lye required to neutralize the sourdough acids. But the acid value does not give any indication of the type and strength of the acids.

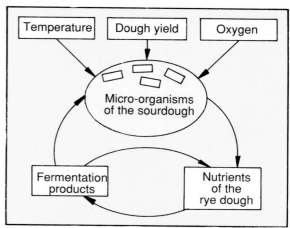

Fig. 281 **Interaction between the various processing conditions of the sourdough**

Additional Information
In years of research work, more than 100 different micro-organisms have been found in sourdough. Among these, eight groups of acidifiers of the lactobacillus type are very important.
Lactobacillus platarum (homofermentative) forms only lactic acid.
Lactobacillus fermenti and Lactobacillus brevis (heterofermentative) form other acids, besides lactic acid.

Explanation of terms:
homo = a term from the Greek language, means "equal" = of equal materials;
hetero = a term from the Greek language, means "different" = unequal.

Conditions for the acidifiers		
	homofermentative acidifiers	heterofermentative acidifiers
Soft dough	+	–
Firm dough	–	+
Sour temp. above 30°C	+	–
Sour temp. below 30°C	–	+
Long resting times	+	–
Presence of yeasts & CO_2	+	–

+ = furthers activity
– = furthers activity somewhat or not at all

Table 31 **Dependency of the acidifiers in the sourdough on dough processing conditions**

Reference: *The acid value determination is described in the chapter entitled* **Bread Evaluation.**

Remember:

Acetic acid formation = preparation of a firm, cool dough
Lactic acid formation = preparation of a soft, warm dough
Desired ratio of lactic acid to acetic acid =
75 to 80% lactic acid
20 to 25% acetic acid
The acid value measures the quantity of acids present in the sourdough; the pH value measures the strength of acids in the sourdough.

Thomas says: *"For a healthy sourdough, I also need an appropriate starter. A piece of bread dough is no good! It is best to take a piece from a mature sourdough. But what do I do when the sourdough starter must be stored for a few days? Or what should be done when the sourdough is unhealthy?"*

How does a bakery ensure that it always has a healthy sourdough starter? Ask your bakery how it deals with this type of problem.

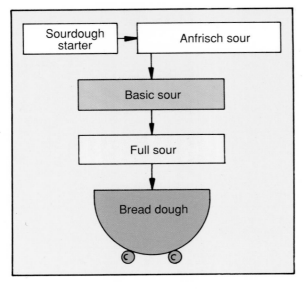

Fig. 282 **The effect of acids on the baking process depends primarily on their strength**

The acid strength is measured by means of the pH value (hydrogen-ion-concentration). On a scale of pH values from 0 to 14, a mature sourdough reaches the range between 3.4 and 4.2.

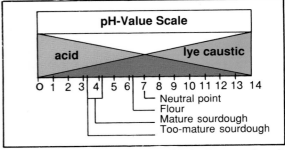

Fig. 283 **The strength of the acids in the sour dough is measured by means of the pH value**

Sourdough Starter, Starter Culture

Micro-organisms required for preparation of a sourdough are incorporated into the dough through a starter culture.

This can be achieved in the following ways:
→ spontaneous fermentation = a rye flour dough is refreshed in several phases until it ferments and turns sour;
→ use of sourdough in the last phase of maturity;
→ pure cultured sour = specific starter cultures for various types of sourdough preparations are purchased.

Spontaneous fermentation was the original method used, but it is not recommended for cultivation of a desired micro-organism culture.

Normally, the starter is taken from a mature full sour and renewed from time to time with pure cultured sour.

When starter cultures must be stored for several days, preferably at cool temperatures (9°C), measures must also be taken to prevent the starter from drying out.

Sourdough preparation aims at the formation of desired fermentation products in several phases commencing with a starter culture.

The mature sourdough is then used as the sole acidifier for preparation of the bread dough.

This method of bread dough preparation is called the ***indirect method*** (use of a preliminary sponge dough).

Three-phase Method

The various living conditions of micro-organisms in the sourdough are furthered by preparing dough in phases. Moreover, the maturing process of the sourdough is adjusted according to bakery operations (e.g. the timing of bread dough make-up).

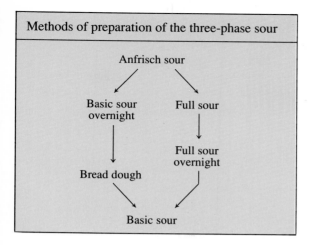

Methods of preparation of the three-phase sour

Anfrisch sour

→ Basic sour overnight   → Full sour

Basic sour overnight → Bread dough

Full sour → Full sour overnight

Bread dough → Basic sour

Full sour overnight → Basic sour

Objectives of Sourdough Preparation Phases

The following conditions are required for the ***three-phase-method:***

Phase	Objective	Conditions
Anfrisch sour	— Yeast multiplication — Development of the lactic acid formers	— soft (dough yield = 200) — Dough temperature 26°C – 28°C — Ventilation — Resting time 2 to 4 hours
Basic sour	— Acid formation	— medium firm (dough yield = 170) — Dough temperature 24°C – 26°C — Resting time 5 to 8 hours
Full sour	— Development of all micro-organisms (maturing phase)	— soft (dough yield = 200) — Dough temperature 28°C – 30°C — Ventilation — Resting time 2 to 3 hours

Basic Sour or Full Sour Overnight

If bakery operations require that a mature sourdough, prepared in three phases, must be available in the morning, a long maturing period is used (full sour or the full sour overnight).

Otherwise, the full sour is prepared in the morning (basic sour overnight). In both cases, the processing conditions must be as follows (example values):

Conditions: Basic Sour Overnight		**Conditions: Full Sour Overnight**
Dough yield = 200, Temperature = 26°C Resting time: 2 p.m. – 7 p.m.	→ Anfrisch sour ←	Dough yield = 220, Temperature = 26°C Resting time: noon – 3 p.m.
Dough yield = 160, Temperature = 25°C Resting time: 7 p.m. – 4 a.m.	→ Basic Sour ←	Dough yield = 170, Temperature = 28°C Resting time: 3 p.m. – 7 p.m.
Dough yield = 200, Temperature = 30°C Resting time: 4 a.m. – 7 a.m.	→ Full Sour ←	Dough yield = 180, temperature = 26°C Resting time: 7 p.m. – 4 a.m.

If bakery operations require availability of mature full sours at different times during the day (e.g. for several subsequent batches of bread doughs) the following can be done:

a) a mature full sour is used for several bread doughs:
   Advantage: less work
   Disadvantage: remaining quantities of full sour can become excessively mature, consequently resulting in bread deficiencies

b) the mature full sour is partly refreshed and used after a resting time of three hours:
   Advantage: availability of several mature full sours
   Disadvantage: more work; the last full sour may be insufficient, consequently resulting in bread deficiencies

c) the basic sour is used for several full sours which mature at different times due to the adaptation of the processing conditions:
   Advantage: availability of several mature full sours
   Disadvantage: more work

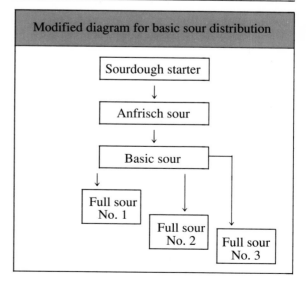

Modified diagram for basic sour distribution

Sourdough starter → Anfrisch sour → Basic sour → Full sour No. 1 / Full sour No. 2 / Full sour No. 3

Fig. 284

121

Phase Calculation of Flour and Water Quantities

When modifying the processing conditions, not only dough yield, temperature and resting time must be taken into account, but also the maturing time of a sourdough phase. This is significantly dependent on the flour quantity.

In the three-phase-method, flour quantities to be acidified per sourdough phase can be determined using the **Arkady-Multiplication Rule**.

According to this rule, the quantity of flour to be acidified per phase is calculated by multiplying the flour quantity of the preceding phase with the resting time in hours of the phase to be prepared (minus the flour quantity that has already been acidified).

The Arkady-Multiplication rule determines the respective flour quantity for a sourdough phase by means of back-calculating (starting with the total flour quantity for a dough).

Example for the calculation of the flour quantity per sourdough phase:

Existing flour quantity in a sourdough phase x resting time in hours of the phase to be prepared

= flour quantity to be acidified (minus existent flour quantity)

Example:

10 kg of flour in the Anfrisch sour
x 4 hours resting time of the basic sour

= 40 kg of flour for basic sour
−10 kg of flour (in the Anfrisch sour)

30 kg of flour to be acidified

Example for rye bread made with 100 kg of flour
Sour content = flour quantity to be acidified = 33 kg

Dough contains	= 100 kg flour
↓	
Full sour contains	= 33 kg flour
33 kg : 3 hours resting time	= 11 kg
↓	
Basic sour contains	= 11 kg flour
11 kg : 7 hrs. resting time	= 1.6 kg
↓	
Anfrisch sour contains	= 1.6 kg flour
1.6 kg : 4 hrs. resting time	= 0.4 kg
↓	
Starter contains	= 0.4 kg flour
0.4 kg flour + 0.4 kg water	= 0.8 kg
↓	
Starter weighs	= 0.8 kg

Dough = 67 kg of flour added
100 kg - 33 kg = 67 kg
↑
Full sour = 22 kg of flour added
↑ 33 kg - 11 kg = 22 kg
↑
Basic sour = 9.4 kg of flour added
↑ 11 kg - 1.6 kg = 9.4 kg
↑
Anfrisch sour = 1.6 kg of flour added
↑
Starter *)

*) The quantity of the starter is not included in the calculation, as it is again subtracted from the mature full sour prior to dough preparation.

Table 32

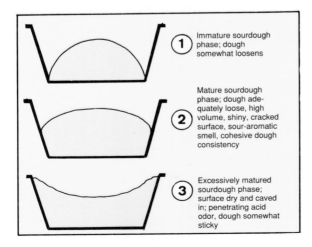

1. Immature sourdough phase; dough somewhat loosens

2. Mature sourdough phase; dough adequately loose, high volume, shiny, cracked surface, sour-aromatic smell, cohesive dough consistency

3. Excessively matured sourdough phase; surface dry and caved in; penetrating acid odor, dough somewhat sticky

The flour quantity per sourdough phase thus calculated can be incorporated into a schematic representation showing all processing conditions:

— Flour quantity per phase ⎱
— Water quantity per phase ⎰ =Dough yield

— Sourdough temperature
— Resting time

These conditions for processing of the sour must be combined by the baker in such a way that the sourdough phases can mature. How is it possible to determine when one of the phases of the three-phase method is mature?

The baker recognizes a mature three-phase-sour based on the following characteristics:
— very large volume (indication for appropriate yeast multiplication),
— the surface is slightly curved,

— the flour coating is distributed like islands on the shiny-moist sourdough surface,
— the smell is sour-aromatic when the surface is torn open,
— the dough is cohesive and loose.

Reference: *Consequences of excessively mature or young sourdoughs are discussed in the chapter entitled **Bread Deficiencies**.*

How to Control the Sourdough Maturing Process

How can the maturing process of the sourdough be accelerated or slowed down?
The baker has at his disposal three principal means of controlling the maturing process:

— the multiplication factor
— the dough temperature
— the dough yield

The ***multiplication factor*** is the rate at which the flour quantity increases from phase to phase.

Example:

In the Anfrisch sour, 1 kg of flour is acidified;
in the basic sour, 10 kg of flour is acidified.
The multiplication factor is therefore 10-fold.
Under a lower multiplication factor, the cultivated micro-organisms can rapidly acidify the freshly-added flour. Under a higher multiplication factor, however, it takes longer for the micro-organisms to ferment the flour into a mature sourdough.
The ***dough yield*** indicates the flour/water ratio in each phase.

Example:

When 8 litres of water are added to 10 kg of rye flour, the sour dough phase has a dough yield of 180.
In a soft dough (high dough yield), the micro-organisms can acidify the dough more rapidly. In a firm dough (low dough yield), the acidification process takes longer. In addition, the firmness of the sourdough has an influence on the type of sourdough acids formed. While lactic acid forms easily in a soft dough, a firm dough furthers the production of acetic acid.
The ***sourdough temperature*** determines the working speed of the micro-organisms.

Example:

A basic sour is prepared at a dough temperature of 27°C; a full sour is prepared at a dough temperature of 29°C.
In a basic sour, acid production is slow because the micro-organisms work slowly.
In a full sour, however, the micro-organisms can work faster.

The dough temperature has, moreover, an influence on the type of acids formed. A warm dough favors the formation of lactic acid; a cool dough favors the formation of acetic acid. Thus, temperature and firmness of the sourdough phases also determine the bread aroma.

Influence of the processing conditions of the three-phase method on the maturing process	
accelerated	slowed down
— low multiplication factor	— high multiplication factor
— soft dough	— firm dough
— warm dough	— cool dough

Table 33

Remember: *The multiplication factor, the sourdough temperature and the dough yield control the maturing process of the sourdough.*
But they also determine the type of acids formed and thus the aroma of the bread.

Model of the Three-Phase Method

Based on the flour quantities calculated in *Table 32*, a model for the three-phase sour can be developed, taking into account all processing conditions (see *Table 34*).

Just as the flour quantities per phase are deducted, so are the water quantities already incorporated in the preceding phases.

In our example, a dough yield of 200 for the Anfrisch sour requires per 1.6 kg of flour, an equal amount of water (1.6 kg).

In the basic sour, the flour quantity totalling (Anfrisch sour and basic sour) 11 kg is supposed to be acidified at a dough yield of 170.

Requirement per 11 kg of flour	= 7.700 litres
Less water from the Anfrisch sour	= 1.600 litres
= Water quantity of the basic sour	= 6.100 litres

In the full sour, the total flour quantity of the sourdough of 33 kg must be used with a dough yield of 200.

Requirement per 33 kg of flour	= 33.000 litres
Less water from the Anfrisch sour and the basic sour	= 7.700 litres
= Water quantity of the full sour	= 25.300 litres

A bread dough (or several bread doughs) can be prepared with the mature full sour. But first a starter is taken off for the next sourdough. Therefore, the starter quantity is not included into the calculation (*Table 34*). The remaining flour (in our example = 67 kg), the sourdough, the water, the salt, and perhaps the yeast, are combined into a bread dough.

Model for the production of rye bread with 100 kg of rye flour, using the three-phase method — sour content = 33%

Starter = 0.8 kg (do not incorporate this quantity in the calculation)

Anfrisch sour

Rye flour	=1.600 kg	}	Dough yield = 200
+Water	=1.600 kg		Dough temp. = 27°C
=Sourdough	=3.200 kg		Resting time = 4 hrs.

Basic sour

Anfrisch sour	=3.200 kg	}	Dough yield = 170
+Rye flour	=9.400 kg		Dough temp. = 26°C
+Water	=6.100 kg		Resting time = 7 hrs.
=Sourdough	=18.700 kg		

Full sour

Basic sour	=18.700 kg	}	Dough yield = 200
+Rye flour	=22.000 kg		Dough temp. = 29°C
+Water	=25.300 kg		Resting time = 3 hrs.
=Sourdough	=66.000 kg		

Table 34

Advantages and Disadvantages of the Three-phase Method

Advantages:
— good aroma formation through the acids and aromatic substances in the sourdough
— good leavening through sourdough yeasts
— good possibilities of process control due to short resting times of the sourdough phases

Disadvantages:
— very labor-intensive
— fermentation losses

Fig. 286 **Healthy sourdough — healthy bread**

Summary of bread dough preparation using the three-phase method

Type of activity	**Objective**	**Reason**
Establish sour content	➤ Acidify the appropriate portion of the rye flour to obtain the desired elasticity and flavor	➤ To avoid deficiencies in the crumb and in the flavor
Prepare a sourdough with rye flour	➤ Improve the baking ability of the rye flour	➤ To make the mucic substances and the albumen of the rye flour firm; to slow down the enzymatic decomposition of the rye starch
Process the sourdough in phases until the bread dough is ready	➤ Mature Anfrisch sour, basic sour, full sour	➤ To further the micro-organisms by modifying dough firmness, dough temperature and resting times

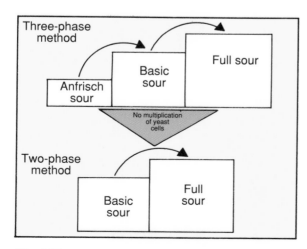

Fig. 287

Two-Phase Method

During the individual phases of the three-phase-method, micro-organisms in the sourdough should be furthered in specific ways. The mature sourdough can then achieve the following through the fermentation products of the micro-organisms:

— Leavening of the dough
— Stabilization of the baking ability of the rye
— Flavor development

When the bread is leavened by adding baker's yeast directly to the bread dough, the leavening effect of the sourdough is reduced. Therefore multiplication of the yeast cells in the sourdough is not required. The phase of the Anfrisch sour that furthers yeast multiplication can be omitted.

Therefore the sourdough can be prepared in two phases: basic sour + full sour.

Although dough preparation is simplified, the two-phase method yields a bread of good quality with an aromatic flavor.

Advantages over the Three-Phase Method:
— *less labor intensive*
— *simple calculation of water and flour quantities*
— *long storage tolerance of the basic sour (elimination of the risk of "autolysis")*

The two-phase method enables a baker to prepare the basic sour overnight, but the full sour can also be prepared overnight.

Processing Conditions of the Two-Phase Method

Because the basic sour requires a long time to mature, it can be prepared during the bakery's normal operating hours. The required process is as follows:

→ *Starter: normally 2.5% of the quantity of flour to be acidified.*
→ *Basic sour: Flour quantity = 16 x the starter quantity, resting time is 15 to 24 hours.*
→ *Full sour: Flour quantity = 2.5 x the flour quantity used for the basic sour; resting time is 2.5 to 3.5 hours.*

Model for the Two-Phase Method

When 100 kg of flour is used to make bread (with a sour content of 40%), the following model applies:

Quantity of flour to be acidified	= 40.000 kg
2.5% of which consists of starter	= 1.000 kg
(not to be taken into account for quantity calculation)	

Basic sour flour content	
= 1.0 kg x 16	= 16.000 kg
Full sour flour = 16 kg x 2.5	= 40.000 kg
minus basic sour flour content	= 16.000 kg
Full sour flour content	= 24.000 kg

The model on the right hand side can also be used for mixed rye breads with ratios of 80/20 and 70/30 respectively.

The respective wheat content is taken into account in the dough preparation by reducing the rye content of the dough, e.g. in the case of mixed rye breads with a ratio of 80/20, only 48 kg of rye flour (40% = 32 kg of rye flour has been acidified), and 20 kg of wheat flour would be added during dough preparation.

Summary of Important Information on the Two-Phase Method

➤ No multiplication of yeast in the sour dough	➤ No preparation of Anfrisch sour	➤ Addition of yeast to the breaddough
➤ Acid formation in only two phases	➤ Primarily in the basic sour	➤ Cool, firm basic sour, long resting times

Tips for further processing: *Compare the processing conditions of the two-phase method with those of the three-phase method. Which conditions allow the basic sour of the two-phase-method to mature in 15 to 24 hours?*

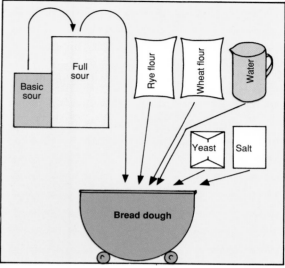

Fig. 288

Preparation of a bread dough with sourdough, using the two-phase method

Model for Rye Bread Production with 100 kg Flour (Two-Phase Method)

Basic sour (do not include starter quantity in your calculation)
Starter	= 1.0 kg		Dough yield =	150
Rye flour	= 16.0 kg		Temperature =	22 – 26°C
+ Water	= 8.0 kg		Resting time =	15 – 24 hrs.
= Basic sour =	24.0 kg			

Full sour
Basic sour =	24.0 kg		Dough yield =	180
+ Rye flour	= 24.0 kg		Temperature =	28 – 32°C
+ Water	= 24.0 kg		Resting time =	2.5 – 3.5 hrs.
= Full sour	= 72.0 kg			

Dough
Full sour	= 72.0 kg		Dough yield = 165
+ Flour	= 60.0 kg		Temperature = 27°C
+ Water	= 33.0 kg		
= Dough	= 165.0 kg		

*)	Salt added	= 1.8 kg	to the dough
	Yeast added	= 1.4 kg	

Table 35

Tips for further processing:
The model in Table 35 applies when 100 kg of flour is used to make bread.

Try to modify the model so it can be used to make mixed rye bread with 80% rye flour and 20% wheat flour, using a total flour quantity of 20 kg.

125

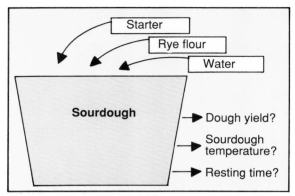

Fig. 289 **Sourdough preparation using the one-phase method**

Tips for further processing: *The maturing process, in the case of sourdough preparation using the one-phase-method, is essentially controlled by means of the processing conditions. Establish the processing conditions of the sourdoughs prepared here using the one-phase method. Compile the values in a table.*

Berliner Short Sour Method

The ***Berliner Short Sour Method*** achieves sourdough maturation with a resting time of three hours by means of:

— high starter quantity
(20% of the flour quantity to be acidified)

— soft dough
(dough yield: 190)

— high sourdough temperature
(35 – 36°C during the entire resting time)

Advantages:
— *less chance of spoilage*
— *mild flavor*
(primarily lactic acid formation)

Disadvantages:
— *sourdough must be stored in a temperature-controlled container*

Model for Rye Bread Production with 100 kg of Flour (Berliner Short Sour Method)

1. Sour dough
    Starter*)   = 8.0 kg
    + Rye flour   = 40.0 kg ⎫ Dough yield   = 190
    + Water   = 36.0 kg ⎬ Temperature = 36°C
    = Short sour = 76.0 kg ⎭ Resting time = 3 hrs.

2. Dough
    Short sour   = 76.0 kg ⎫ Dough yield   = 160
    + Rye flour   = 60.0 kg ⎬ Temperature = 27°C
    + Water   = 24.0 kg ⎭
    = Dough**)   = 160.0 kg

*) Do not include starter quantity in the calculation!
**) Salt added = 1.8 kg ⎫ to the dough
     Yeast added = 1.8 kg ⎭

Sourdough Preparation Using the One-Phase-Method

Sourdough preparation in one single phase significantly simplifies the process for the baker. Why?

— The need for multiplication of yeast cells in the sourdough is eliminated. Leavening occurs exclusively at the dough stage through the addition of yeast.

— The process conditions are adjusted in such a way that the micro-organisms find appropriate living conditions in the sourdough and are able to form the desired lactic acid and acetic acid ratio.

— Due to the absence of yeast, the sour cannot ferment. Therefore, the maturity level of the sour cannot be established based on the increase in volume, but only by means of measuring the acid values.

— The mature sourdough can be stored for a longer period of time without showing symptoms of excessive maturity.

There are various types of one-phase-methods requiring totally different processing conditions. The following typical examples are studied in detail:

— Berliner short sour,
— Detmolder one-phase sour,
— Weinheimer one-phase sour,
— Salt sour.

Detmolder One-Phase Method

The ***Detmolder One-Phase Method*** is a long-term method with resting times between 15 and 20 hours without the sour dough turning excessively mature. This is possible through:

— varying quantities of starter (depending on the sour temperature to be observed);
— uniform dough yield of 180 for the sourdough phase; and
— a somewhat lower sour content.

Sour content and starter quantities for the Detmolder One-Phase Method using various flour mixes are listed in *Table 37*.

Flour mix	Sour content		Starter quantity at sour temperature			
			20 - 23°C	24 - 26°C	26 - 27°C	27 - 28°C
Rye : Wheat	kg	%	(20%)	(10%)	(5%)	(2%)
100:00	35	35	7.0	3.5	1.75	0.70
90:10	35	38.8	7.0	3.5	1.75	0.70
80:20	32	40	6.4	3.2	1.60	0.64
70:30	28	40	5.6	2.8	1.40	0.56
60:40	24	40	4.8	2.4	1.20	0.48
50:50	20	40	4.0	2.0	1.00	0.40
40:60	16	40	3.2	1.6	0.80	0.32
30:70	16	53.3	3.2	1.6	0.80	0.32
20:80	12	60	2.4	1.2	0.60	0.24

Table 37

Based on this, the model for preparation of mixed rye bread (70:30) is as follows:

Model for the production of mixed rye bread (70:30) with 100 kg of flour using the Detmolder One-Phase Method, at sourdough temperatures between 20 and 23°C.		

```
1. Sourdough
   Starter*)      =   5.6 kg
 + Rye flour      =  28.0 kg  ⎫  Dough yield = 180
 + Water          =  22.4 kg  ⎬  Temperature = 23°C
 = Sourdough      =  50.4 kg  ⎭  Resting time = 15 to 20 hrs.

2. Dough
   Sour dough     =  50.4 kg  ⎫  Dough yield = 165
 + Rye flour      =  42.0 kg  ⎪  Temperature = 28°C
 + Wheat flour    =  30.0 kg  ⎬  Resting time = none
 + Water          =  42.6 kg  ⎭
 = Dough **)      = 165.0 kg

 *)  Do not include starter quantity in the calculation.
 **) Salt added   =   1.8 kg  ⎫  to the dough
     Yeast added  =   1.8 kg  ⎭
```

Table 38

When preparing the dough, the remainder of the rye flour, the wheat flour and the quantity of water to be added are taken into account for the dough yield of 165.

The quantities given for the dough can, of course, be distributed among several doughs (within a resting time of about 15 to 20 hours), without considerable changes in flavor occurring in the bread.

To further aroma formation, it is generally recommended to use higher sourdough temperatures and smaller quantities of starter.

Weinheimer One-Phase Method

The Weinheimer One-Phase Method is based on higher sourdough temperatures. Therefore, the sourdough can be prepared with a smaller quantity of starter:
— Starter = normally 2% of the quantity of flour to be acidified;
— Sourdough temperature: starting with 28°C, decreasing to 23°C;
— Resting period = 15 to 30 hours;
— Sour contents = approximately the same as for the Detmolder One-Phase Method, depending on the flour mix.

Advantages:
— *It is possible to let the sourdough rest for long periods of time without the risk of excessive acidification.*
— *No special containers are required for temperature control of the sourdough.*
Disadvantages:
— *Little flexibility with regard to quantities when a sudden need arises.*

Salt-Sour Method

The patented Monheimer Salt-Sour Method achieves excellent results in terms of baking technique and flavor using a one-phase sourdough method.

As the name indicates, 2% of salt is added to the flour quantity to be acidified. The effect is as follows:
— The activity of the sourdough yeast cells is slowed down.
— The acid formation is delayed (and by this, also the maturing process).
— A positive influence on the flour albumen is achieved (it is strengthened).
— The enzyme activity is reduced; the sourdough has a lesser tendency to take on a brown color.

Due to the addition of salt, the sour dough must be prepared under the following conditions, in spite of long resting times of at least 22 to 24 hours:
— a comparatively high amount of starter (30% of the quantity of flour to be acidified)
— dough yield of 200
— high sourdough temperatures, starting with 35°C, then decreasing to about 20°C.

The following model indicates the other process characteristics of the Salt-Sour Method, using, as an example, a mixed rye bread (70:30).

Model for production of mixed rye bread (70:30) with 100 kg of flour, using the Salt-Sour Method		

```
1. Sourdough
   Starter*)      =   9.0 kg*)
 + Rye flour      =  30.0 kg  ⎫  Temperature     35 → 20°C
 + Water          =  30.0 kg  ⎬  Dough yield   = 200
 + Salt           =   0.6 kg  ⎭  Resting time  = 18 to 24 hrs.
 = Sour dough     =  60.6 kg

2. Dough
   Sourdough      =  60.6 kg  ⎫
 + Rye flour      =  40.0 kg  ⎪  Temperature   = 27°C
 + Wheat flour    =  30.0 kg  ⎬  Dough yield   = 167
 + Water          =  37.0 kg  ⎭  Resting time  = 10 minutes
 = Dough**)       = 167.0 kg

 *)  Do not include the starter quantity in the calculation.
 **) Salt added   =   1.2 kg  ⎫  to the dough
     Yeast added  =   1.8 kg  ⎭
```

Table 39

Due to the specific temperature development during the process, the acid formation achieved is the same as in the case of the multi-phase methods. After about 18 to 24 hours, self-preservation of the sour occurs. At that time, the starter for a new salt sour must be removed and stored in the refrigerator until preparation of a new batch. The mature salt sour can be stored for about three days at 5 to 15°C. In this case, however, the addition of sour to the dough should be reduced by 3 to 5%.

Advantages of the Salt Sour:

— *simple processing, high maturity tolerance*
— *good aroma formation*
— *good firmness of the dough*
— *bread can be sliced with ease*

Disadvantages of the Salt Sour:

— *special containers for sour storage are required*

Through the digestive activity of the enzymes, sourdoughs exposed to a long resting time (e.g. the salt sour) turn nearly liquid during the resting time. Consequently, they can be portioned with ease, but they require special containers made of synthetic material for storage.

For further simplification, some sourdough containers come with mixing and metering devices.

Summary of important features of the one-phase method of sourdough preparation			
Berliner Short Sour	➤ Maturing time 3 hrs.	➤ Dough yield = 190 Sourdough temperatures: 35 – 36°C	➤ heatable storage container required
Detmolder One-Phase Sour	➤ Maturing time 15 – 20 hrs.	➤ Dough yield = 180 Various sourdough temperatures possible; starter quantity depending on sourdough temperature	➤ no special storage container required
Weinheimer One-Phase Sour	➤ Maturing time 15 – 30 hrs.	➤ Dough yield = 180 Sourdough temperatures starting at 28°C, decreasing to 23°C; starter quantity: 2% of the flour quantity of the sour	➤ no special storage container required
Salt-Sour Method	➤ Maturing time 22 – 24 hours	➤ Dough yield = 200 Salt added: 2% of the flour quantity of the sour; Sour temperature starting at 35°C, decreasing to 20°C; Starter = 30% of the flour quantity of the sour	➤ storage container desirable; required for cool storage of the mature sour

Dough Acidification Machines

Medium to large bakeries should consider sourdough processing in a dough-acidification machine. The following sketch shows, as an example, a sour dough preparator (A) combined with a storage container (B) for storage of the mature sourdough. In these machines, a salt sour is brought to maturity in a temperature-controlled environment (Part A) and stored in a cool environment up to the time of further processing (Part B).

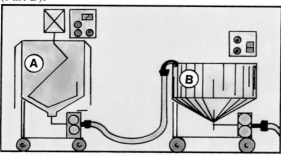

Fig. 290 **Dough acidification machine**
A = Sourdough preparator with automatic temperature control and agitator
B = Sourdough storage container (cool storage) for mature sourdoughs with automatic metering device

Other methods use a selected starter culture (without yeasts) to mature a sourdough in an automated sourdough preparator through heating and natural cooling. During the resting time, the sourdough goes through all temperature ranges favorable for a multi-phase sour. Through self-preservation, this sour is maintained for several days in a processable condition.

A continuous and automated production of sourdoughs (with yeasts) can be achieved in large-scale bakeries by using special fermentation phases in a closed system. Through adjustment of the sourdough temperatures, of dough yields and of duration of fermentation, yeast multiplication and acid production can be controlled. The mature sour is metered in a fully-automated process in a tank for dough preparation. At the same time, a new sour dough matures in the fermentation chambers.

Therefore, this type of sourdough preparation is called ***continuous***.

Cool Storage of Sourdoughs
Salt sour is suited for longer-term storage of a mature sourdough. But other sourdoughs can also be stored in mature condition in a cool environment. However, the storage temperature should be so low that the acidification process is stopped.

Satisfactory results have been achieved with storage temperatures of 5°C. It is possible to store a sourdough for four days without quality deficiencies occurring in the bread.
Storage conditions for cool storage of sourdough:
— *Make the sourdough somewhat firmer than normal;*
— *Let the sourdough mature for about 8 hours at temperatures between 30 and 32°C;*
— *Renew the sourdough starter more often than normal;*
— *Reduce the sour content somewhat;*
— *The liquid added to the dough should be warmer in order to compensate for the cool sourdough content.*

Acidifying Baking Agents

Fig. 291 **Chemicals in the bread?**

Chemicals in the bread? This question is often asked by the layman when baking agents are discussed. This question must be properly evaluated:

— Baking agents should not be dismissed simply on the grounds that they are "chemicals." After all, bread dough is teeming with "micro-organisms" including yeast, without which most breads would not exist!
— Acidifying baking agents contain ingredients for the bread dough in concentrated form. Above all, they contain organic acids such as lactic acid, acetic acid, citric acid or their salts.
— Acidifying baking agents are offered in various forms, such as powders, acidified flours, dried sourdough extracts, paste and liquid acid concentrates, and sourdough concentrates.

The acid value of acidifying baking agents varies depending on the composition of the product. Acidifiers offered for mixed wheat flour have, for example, an acid value of 70 or greater and a pH value around 4.6. Acidifiers suited for rye and mixed rye bread have, for example, an acid value between 300 and 400 and pH values around 3.2. A pure acid salt has an acid value of 1,080 with a pH value of 2.7.

Correspondingly, the quantities to be added (between 0.8 and 5% of the flour quantity) and the effects of these baking agents vary.

Basic types of acidifying baking agents
1. Acidified flours *2. Sour salts* *3. Dried sourdough extracts* *4. Sour concentrates*

Direct Method

Without preparation of a sourdough, doughs containing rye can only be acidified with acidifying baking agents. This type of bread dough preparation is called "direct method."

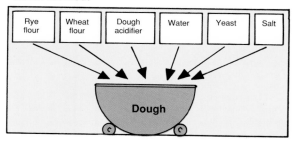

Fig. 292

When using acidifying baking agents, the manufacturer's instructions should be followed. Larger deviations from the quantities to be added or mixing with products of other manufacturers can lead to deficiencies in the quality of the bread.

Acidifiers in powder form should be mixed with the flour in dry condition. They should not be used together with yeast.

To allow the dough components to swell and to let the acid take effect, a dough resting time of between 20 and 50 minutes is required for doughs prepared by this direct method.

When the acidifying baking agents are used appropriately, dough acidification can be free from risks. The bread crumb is sufficiently elastic and can be easily cut. When using acidifying baking agents, a noticeable increase in the dough yield (compared to the indirect method) can be observed, especially when the baking agent contains water-absorbing flour components or dried sourdough components.

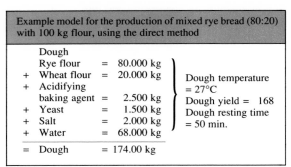

Table 40

Food for Thought: *Is it right to indicate the theoretical dough yield in the model for the direct method without the water-absorbing flour content of the dough acidifier?*

Liquid sours and sour concentrates contain products of fully mature sourdoughs. An aromatic, unchanging bread flavor and a longer durable life are ensured. These concentrates are suited equally well for mixed rye and mixed wheat bread; the quantity to be added must be adjusted to the quantity of rye flour used.

Use of Sour Concentrate for			
Mixed Rye Bread		Mixed Wheat Bread	
Dark Rye Flour	8.000 kg	Bread Flour	7.000 kg
Medium Rye Flour	2.000 kg	Medium Rye Flour	3.000 kg
Sour concentrate	0.800 kg	Sour concentrate	0.300 kg
Salt	0.200 kg	Salt	0.200 kg
Yeast	0.150 kg	Yeast	0.275 kg
Water	about 7.000 kg	Water	about 6.800 kg
Total dough	about 18.150 kg	Total dough	about 17.575 kg

Table 41

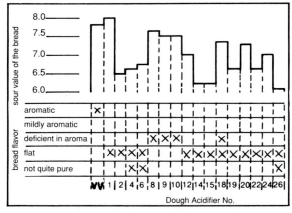

Table 42 **Influence of acidifying baking agents on the acid value of the bread and on the bread flavor (mixed rye bread)**

The values obtained are derived from a comparison test using the direct method of 16 different acidifying baking agents and the indirect method (for one bread) with a sour content of 30%. The tests were performed at the Technological Institute of Grain and Flour Science in Detmold, West Germany.

As *Table 42* indicates, various acidifying baking agents yield very different results. Therefore, it is important to choose, for each bread type, the suitable dough acidifier and the most appropriate quantity to be added.

It should be noted that the direct method produces mixed rye, mixed wheat and rye bread without requiring sourdough processes.

The aroma of the bread is, however, not comparable with that of a bread made with sourdough. Fresh-keeping and shelf life features are also less favorable than in bread made with sourdough.

Additional Information

The reduced shelf life of bread made using the direct method is not due to the acid value, but to the type of acids used. Citric, acetic and lactic acids and their salts, as components of acidifying baking agents, do not impair the growth of the mold. However, the low-molecular fat acids, acetic acids and propionic acids found in sour-doughs are able to penetrate into the mold fungus and to eliminate the enzymatic effect of the mold.

Acetic acid, which evaporates easily, cannot be retained in a baking agent in powder form. In the sourdough, however, acetic acid is formed (1/4 to 1/5 of the total amount of acid).

Combined Method

In order to achieve the flavor of a sourdough while using acidifying baking agents, many baking agent manufacturers recommend preparing a basic sour and combining it with an acidifying baking agent (***combined method***).

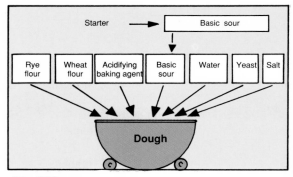

Fig. 293

Model for the production of mixed rye bread (80/20) using the combined method			
1. Sour			
Starter*)	= 2.000 kg	}	Temperature = 25°C
+ Rye flour	= 10.000 kg	}	Dough yield = 170
+ Water	= 7.000 kg	}	Resting time
= Sourdough	= 17.000 kg		= 12 – 18 hrs.
2. Dough			
Sourdough	= 17.000 kg	}	
+ Rye flour	= 70.000 kg	}	Dough temp. = 27°C
+ Wheat flour	= 20.000 kg	}	
+ Dough acidifying			
baking agent	= 2.000 kg	}	Dough yield = 168
+ Yeast	= 1.500 kg	}	Dough resting time
+ Salt	= 2.000 kg	}	= 40 min.
+ Water	= 61.000 kg	}	
= Dough	=173.500 kg		

*) Do not include the starter quantity in the calculation.

Table 43

Food for Thought: *In your opinion, what are the advantages of the indirect, direct and combined processing methods for bread production?*

Complete Bakery Mixes for Bread

For the production of rye bread and mixed bread, the baker uses not only the sourdough and dough acidification methods, but he also uses **complete bakery mixes**.

These mixes contain all the ingredients required for a specific type of bread or small bakery product. Water and yeast are added at the time of dough preparation.

In addition to complete mixes, **concentrates** are available that can be added to flour. These concentrates contain all the other ingredients for the type of product desired.

Are these mixes raw materials for use by the baker, or have they been developed exclusively for the "home bakery?" These questions cannot be answered solely with technological arguments (e.g. ease of putting together the ingredients for a recipe). Economic factors must also be taken into consideration. The use of mixes for bread production is particularly advantageous for:
— bread and small bakery products produced in small quantities;
— specialty breads and special types of small bakery products using various kinds of raw materials;
— specialty bakery products subjected to legal regulations with regard to minimum and maximum quantities of ingredients (e.g. bread made especially for diabetics).

For these types of products, it may be advantageous for the baker to use mixes or concentrates.

If the intent is, however, to change the recipe given for the mix or the concentrate in order to obtain a special product, the effort required would not justify the extra cost. Such changes may also cause problems with regard to baking technique and food regulations (e.g. in the case of specialty bread recipes).

Preparation of Doughs Containing Rye

Fig. 294

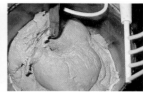

Fig. 295

Ingredients of Bread Doughs

The kind of ingredients required for a bread dough depend, of course, on the type of bread to be produced. For three-grain bread, for example, the baker needs three different kinds of grain products; for butter milk bread, he adds butter milk to the dough instead of water.

Essential differences in the composition of the dough also result from the processing method used:
— When using the three-phase sour of the indirect method, the addition of yeast to the dough can be reduced considerably.
— When using the direct method, a dough acidifying baking agent is required.
— When using the combined method, a dough acidifying baking agent must be used in addition to the sour content.

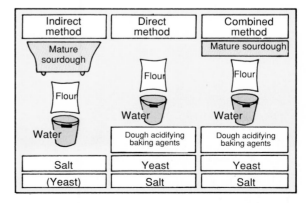

Fig. 296 **Ingredients of bread depending on the processing method used**

131

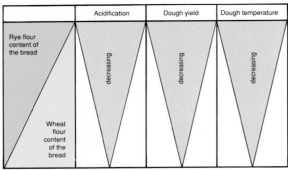

	Acidification	Dough yield	Dough temperature
Rye flour content of the bread	decreasing	decreasing	decreasing
Wheat flour content of the bread			

Fig. 297 **Inter-relationship between flour mixes and processing methods for doughs containing rye**

Remember
→ Sour content of mixed flour is determined as a percentage of the rye flour content that is acidified

Application

Total flour quantity = 100 kg
Proportion of rye flour = 60 kg
Proportion of rye
flour that is acidified = 24 kg

→ Calculate sour content

60 kg of rye flour ≅ 100%
1 kg of rye flour ≅ 100%/60
24 kg of rye flour ≅ 100 x 24/60 = 40%

→ To achieve a sour content of 40% remove 24 kg of rye flour from 60 kg of rye flour and acidify it

Fig. 298

Joe thinks: *"I don't need a recipe to make a bread dough. I know what the ingredients are. I also know the correct quantities. I'm a hands-on baker!"*
What are, in your opinion, the advantages of having a working recipe for bread dough preparation.

The quantity of liquid added and the processing methods depend on the flour mix used for the bread variety to be produced:

Bread with a higher rye content	Bread with a higher wheat content
– higher degree of acidification – higher water content – higher dough temperature	– lower degree of acidification – lower water content – lower dough temperature

Mixed wheat bread is not acidified to the same extent as rye bread and mixed rye bread. To obtain a better flavor, the baker often acidifies more than half of the rye flour content of mixed wheat bread.

Take a look at one example each for mixed rye and mixed wheat bread:

— When making mixed rye bread containing 70 kg of rye flour and 30 kg of wheat flour, the baker acidifies 28 kg of the rye flour = 40% of the rye flour;
— When making mixed wheat bread containing 60 kg of wheat flour and 40 kg of rye flour, the baker acidifies 20 kg of the rye flour = 50% of the rye flour.

The acidified portion of the rye flour is called the sour content. Therefore, in our example, the sour content is proportionately higher in the mixed wheat flour than in the mixed rye flour.

Even an experienced baker requires a precise recipe to produce bread of uniform quality. Food regulatory bodies also require a precise recipe.

How can the baker do this?

Working Recipe for Bread Doughs
We have examined models for the individual methods of acidification. For the purpose of simplicity and ease of comparison, these models are based on 100 kg of flour. However, this amount is not typical for a bakery operation. In a bakery operation, the ingredients of a dough are represented in a working recipe that can be related:

— to a certain amount of total flour, e.g. 40 kg of rye flour and 20 kg of wheat flour;
— to a certain amount of liquid added, e.g. 20 litres of water;
— to a certain amount of bread dough, e.g. 75 pieces of bread of 1 kg each.

How to Put Together a Working Recipe
All ingredients and processing methods are listed in a working recipe.

<table>
<tbody>
<tr><td colspan="3">Tips for working recipes for doughs containing rye:</td></tr>
</tbody>
</table>

Tips for working recipes for doughs containing rye:
— *Make up a recipe card for each bread variety.*
— *List the ingredients in the order in which they are to be incorporated into the dough.*
— *List in the recipe the quantities usually used in your bakery (bakery recipe).*
— *Include additional conversion factors for larger quantities (e.g. 1.5-fold quantity).*
— *List all the processing, fermentation and baking conditions (including cost & yields).*

The working recipe is an important tool for the baker. He or she uses it to improve precision of production.

Requirements are different with regard to food regulations, where the ingredients must be listed for the consumer.

List of Ingredients

When bread is to be sold in a prepackaged format, the package must show a list of ingredients. This list is meant to inform the consumer about the composition of the bread. It is, however, not a recipe indicating the quantities in grams. The purpose is to list all the ingredients used in the production and those found in the finished product. Therefore, the recipe is the basis for the list of ingredients. Substances that get into the finished bread product, but are not a part of the recipe (i.e. unintentional substances) are not considered to be ingredients.

What is the baker's task in compiling the list of ingredients?

The ingredients must be organized according to their weight proportions. Water is to be included in the list of ingredients only if the end product contains more than 5% water. Therefore, we determine, in our example, the water content of the end product. First, all the "dry" ingredients are added together. Their weight is deducted from the weight of the bakery product to obtain the amount of water remaining in the dough (see *Table 44*). This proportional weight of the water is included in the list of ingredients.

Example:

Based on the quantities of ingredients listed in *Table 44*, the following order applies: Rye flour, wheat flour, water, sourdough, yeast, baking additive, salt.

Recipe for mixed rye bread (60/40), made with a total flour content of 10 kg, and using the combined method
5.200 kg of rye flour
+ 4.000 kg of wheat flour
+ 1.615 kg of salt sour
+ 0.400 kg of yeast
+ 0.200 kg of baking agent
+ 0.150 kg of salt
= 11.565 kg of recipe components
+ 6.500 kg of water added to the dough
15.300 kg of baked product weight (established by scaling)
− 11.565 kg of recipe components
= 3.735 kg of remaining water in the finished bread

Table 44 **Recipe to establish the list of ingredients of bread**

Examples of a conversion of this recipe into possible lists of ingredients are shown in the following table.

Examples of possible lists of ingredients		
Example 1:	**Example 2:**	**Example 3:**
Rye flour	Flour	Flour
Wheat flour	(Rye,	(Rye,
Water	Wheat)	Wheat)
Sourdough	Water	Water
Yeast	Yeast	Sourdough
Baking additive	Baking additive	with baking agent
(Acidifying	(Acidifying	(Acidifying
agent)	agent)	agent)
Salt	Salt	Yeast
		Salt

Table 45 **List of ingredients for mixed rye bread, using the combined processing method**

Remember:
In order to be able to establish the correct order of ingredients used, the following principles must be observed:
— *Organize the recipe according to the quantities of ingredients and categorize the water according to the amount of water remaining in the product.*
— *Establish lists of ingredients in such a way that they can be used as a basis for labelling of the end product.*
— *Do not change the quantities of ingredients of the recipe or during production, so that the printed list of ingredients remains valid.*

What are the requirements regarding the listing of ingredients? The ingredients must be listed with their usual trade names. Rye and wheat flour, water, yeast and salt are listed as such (see *Table 45*).

But the sourdough itself is composed of rye flour and water. It contains several ingredients — it is itself a composite ingredient.

Other composite ingredients of bread are, for example, baking agents, mixes, remaining bread, and baking concentrates. These are identified solely by means of their generic name (e.g. baking agent) when they represent less than 25% of the end product. If they make up more than 25% of the end product, the individual components of the composite ingredient should be listed.

> **Reference:** *For listing of added substances (e.g. preservatives), refer to the chapter entitled* **Production of Sliced Bread**. *Other examples for lists of ingredients are given in the chapters entitled* **Quality Characteristics of Sandwich Bread** *and* **Dietary Bakery Products**.

> **Remember:**
>
> *The list of ingredients*
> — *must be easily recognizable by the consumer on the package;*
> — *must be identified by the word "ingredients;"*
> — *must list the ingredients according to the quantities contained in the end product;*
> — *must list all the substances added that have an effect on the end product.*

> **Food for Thought:**
> *In the chapter entitled* **Processing of Wheat Dough**, *the direct processing method is represented as being the method most frequently used today for production of wheat-flour products.*
> *Make a comparison of the processing methods for doughs containing rye.*

Example:

A bread is prepared with a sour content of 40%. In this case, it must be labelled as follows: Sourdough (rye flour, water).

It is also possible, however, to group together the composite ingredients and other ingredients. You can, for example, group the quantities of rye flour and water used for the sourdough and the quantities of rye flour and water used for the bread dough. In this case, the term "sourdough" is not used in the list of ingredients (see Example 2 in *Table 45*).

Composite ingredients can be listed as mixes. When using the combined method, it is possible to list, for example, dough acidifying baking agents and sourdough together (see Example 3 in *Table 45*).

But when the composite ingredients amount to more than 25% of the end product, all the individual components must be listed separately.

As our example shows, the list of ingredients can be made up in various ways, even if the recipes are identical. The producer of bakery products decides which form the information will be presented to the consumer.

Preparation of Dough Ingredients

The ingredients for dough containing rye flour are prepared in the same way as for wheat doughs. However, different bread doughs have special features.

> **Reference:**
> *The chapter entitled* **Processing of Wheat Dough** *gives detailed information on the preparation of dough.*

Preparation of Sourdough

Sourdough must be mature before a bread dough can be prepared.

When using the multi-phase method, the degree of maturity of the sour is recognizable by its curvature, its large volume and its cracked, shiny surface.

In the case of sourdoughs that are to be used exclusively for acidification purposes, the degree of maturity can be established by measuring the acid value and the pH value.

The baker can compensate, to a certain extent, for insufficient maturity of the sourdough by taking the following measures during dough preparation:

Problem	Consequences	Corrective Measures	Reasons
Excessively young sourdough	— round-shaped bread — small volume — flat flavor — inelastic, dense crumb	— warm dough — add yeast supplement — add acidifier supplement	— better proof — acid for stabilization of the crumb
Excessively old sourdough	— very flat-shaped bread — blistering — crumb with large cells — uneven cells — excessively sour flavor	— further "freshening" of the sour — small amount of excessively mature sour and addition of acidifying baking agents	— to rejuvenate the sour — to adjust the degree of acidification

Preparation of the Flour

As in the case of wheat doughs, the flour for doughs containing rye must be sifted and its temperature must be appropriate.

When producing mixed bread, it is important to use the proper ratio of rye and wheat. The rye or wheat flour can be composed of various bread flour types.

Examples of usual flour mixes for bread	
Mixed rye bread (80/20)	= 80% of Light Rye Flour 20% of First Clear Flour
Mixed rye bread (70/30)	= 70% of Medium Rye Flour 30% of Baker's Flour
Mixed wheat bread (80/20)	= 80% of First Clear Flour 20% of Medium Rye Flour
Mixed wheat bread (70/30)	= 70% of First Clear Flour 30% of Medium Rye Flour

Table 46

The type of flour mix used not only determines the color of the bread crumb, but bread volume, bread shape, flavor and fresh-keeping properties. Therefore, the flour to be mixed is chosen from various types (e.g. the 20% of wheat flour used for a mixed rye bread can be composed of Patent or First Clear flours).

Effect of the bread flour mix on the dough and on the product	
(Patent Flour)	(First Clear Flour)
— smooth doughs — higher fermentation stability when a large proportion of wheat flour is used — lower fresh-keeping properties — lighter-colored crumb	— softer doughs — lower fermentation stability — lower volume when a large proportion of wheat flour is used — longer fresh-keeping properties — yellowish crumb

Table 47

The effects are as follows:
— Patent Flour = lighter in color, rich in starch, strong gluten, less water retention in the dough;
— First Clear Flour = darker in color, richer in enzymes, richer in protein, weaker gluten, higher water retention

When different wheat flours with a high rye content are used, the bread volume is very similar. When Patent Flour is used for bread with a high wheat flour content, a noticeably better fermentation stability and a higher bread volume can be achieved.

For rye flour and coarse rye, a larger fluctuation in the baking ability of the bread can be expected from year to year, but also within a year. The mills try to counteract this effect through blending. In spite of this, the flour quality fluctuates, causing problems in the quality of bread produced.

The baker can take the following measures to compensate for differing qualities of flour:

Flour quality	Measures
Dry flour, somewhat poor in enzymes ➤ *Consequences: slow fermentation, lesser degree of browning, dry crumb*	– *prepare a soft dough, allowing for subsequent swelling* – *add baking agents containing enzymes* – *add old dough (save leftover dough)* – *add darker-colored wheat flour of good quality*
Moist flour, of lower quality ➤ *Consequences: rapid fermentation, high degree of browning, moist crumb*	– *prepare a firmer dough* – *increase sour content or add dough acidifiers* – *bake thoroughly*

Reference:
Formulae for calcula-tion of the temperature of the liquid added are listed in the chapter entitled Processing Wheat Dough.

Fig. 299 **Water mixing and metering device**

Usual dough temperatures for bread doughs
Rye bread .... 28 – 30°C
Mixed rye bread .... 26 – 28°C
Mixed wheat bread .... 24 – 26°C

Table 48

Reference:
For calculation of the dough yield, refer to the chapter entitled Proc-essing of Wheat Dough.

Average dough yield of various bread varieties
Coarse rye bread .... Dough yield 176 – 190
Rye bread .... Dough yield 175 – 178
Mixed rye bread .... Dough yield 172 – 176
Mixed wheat bread .... Dough yield 166 – 170

Table 49

Fig. 300
Sufficient or insufficient aeration depending on the firmness of the dough

Preparation of Liquid to be Added to the Dough

Bakers can influence dough firmness and dough temperature through the liquid added. A water mixing and metering device is useful.

The required temperature for the liquid to be added depends on:
— the desired dough temperature;
— the flour temperature; and
— the sourdough temperature (when using the indi-rect dough processing method).

Because doughs containing rye are mixed less inten-sively than others, its temperature does not signifi-cantly increase during mixing. Therefore, when meas-uring the temperature of the liquid added, it is not necessary to allow for an increase in dough tempera-ture.

Rye bread doughs are not sensitive to higher tempera-tures. Mixed bread doughs with increasing wheat content react to higher temperatures. The higher the dough temperature, the faster the dough ages, result-ing in an end product with a dry crumb and a flat flavor.

Rye Doughs: Factors Affecting Yields

The baker recognizes the appropriate dough firmness based on the processing qualities of the dough and on the quality of the end product.

Doughs containing rye should be kept as soft as possible. Softer rye doughs have a more tender crumb and a more aromatic flavor.

The correct flour/water ratio depends on the dough yield. Average values for dough yields on breads are shown in *Table 49*.

The dough yield depends on various factors:

Factors that can increase the dough yield	*Factors that can decrease the dough yield*
– *lower water content of the flour* – *darker-colored flours* – *warm doughs* – *direct dough proc-essing method* – *manual preparation*	– *moist flour* – *lighter-colored flours* – *cooler doughs* – *indirect dough processing method* – *fully-automated preparation*

Food for Thought:
Why does the direct dough processing method (acidification by means of baking agents) achieve a higher dough yield than the indirect processing method (with sourdough)?

Preparation of Salt, Yeast and Baking Agents

When using the indirect rye dough processing method, the yeast quantity must be partially reduced because the sourdough contributes to dough softening. When a salt sour is used, the quantity of salt added to the dough must be reduced in proportion to the salt content of the sourdough.

Precise scaling is required for those ingredients added in small quantities. Even small errors in the quantities added can cause significant bread deficiencies. Consider the effect not enough salt could have on bread dough.

The salt, yeast and baking agents can be added together with the liquid, using the direct method.

Mixing of Doughs Containing Rye

Normal bread doughs contain only a small number of ingredients that are rapidly distributed during mixing. Hydration of the dry dough components also proceeds rapidly, because the albumen and the mucic substances of the rye flour combine easily with water. Therefore, it is not necessary to mix rye doughs intensively. Intensive bread-dough mixers are not used for rye doughs.

Capacity and ease of operation are important factors when selecting mixers for rye doughs. Movable and lifting devices are required for large bread dough batches (see *Fig. 301*).

Fig. 301
Lifting device and movable container of a mixing machine

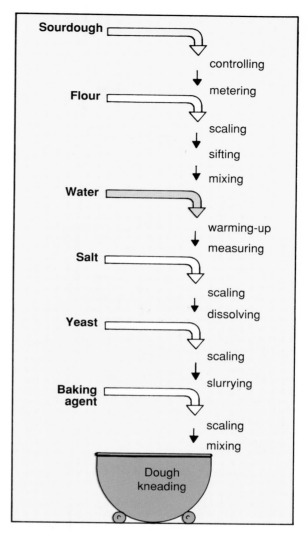

Fig. 302

Although the formation of doughs containing rye is not a problem, the dough-making device must guarantee optimum kneading in accordance with operational requirements.

Factors having an effect on the mixing time of bread doughs	
decreasing effect	**increasing effect**
– rapid mixing	– slow mixing
– higher rye content of the dough	– higher wheat content of the dough
– soft flour	– flour with a high bran content, coarse flour
– light-colored flour with a small bran content	
– sifted flour	– unsifted flour
– higher dough temperature	– lower dough temperature
– firm dough	– soft dough
– indirect method	– direct method

137

Summary of the most important information on the preparation of doughs containing rye

➤ *Use one recipe each for bread doughs normally prepared in your bakery.*

➤ *Make up a list of ingredients for labelling of bread varieties sold in prepackaged format.*

➤ *Scale the ingredients for bread doughs carefully, adjust their temperature and prepare them for dough make-up.*

➤ *Sourdough must be mature before it can be processed. Add acidifying baking agents to excessively young sourdough. Use a smaller amount of acidifying baking agents for excessively matured sourdough and adjust acidification by adding acidifying baking agents.*

➤ *Do not mix rye doughs intensively.*

Fig. 303 **Dark rye bread baked in a pan**

Fig. 304 **Light-colored mixed wheat bread loaf**

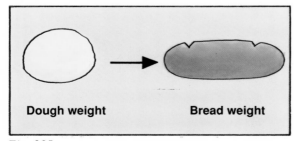

Dough weight   **Bread weight**

Fig. 305

Food for Thought: *The optimum degree of dough maturity for wheat-flour bakery products can be achieved through specific processing methods. Why is this less important for other bread doughs?*
Take into account that doughs for small wheat-flour products are not necessarily prepared for only one oven batch.

Preparation of Doughs Containing Rye

Dough preparation varies considerably between a light-colored mixed wheat bread dough or a dark-colored rye dough. Consider the different dough properties. Dough preparation is difficult in both cases.

— Dark-colored rye dough is moist and short.
— Light-colored mixed wheat bread dough is smooth-dry and elastic-tough.

The preparation of such doughs requires technical knowledge.

Apart from the specific processing conditions for individual bread doughs, special steps are required for the preparation of all bread doughs. These steps are discussed in detail in the following sections.

Dough Resting Time (Floor Time)

Rye doughs processed using the indirect method do not require a dough resting time after dough preparation.

Dough resting times between 20 to 50 minutes are recommended for doughs made using the direct method, and for mixed breads with a higher wheat content.

Scaling

Prior to shaping, dough pieces must be scaled so that the cooled end product has the proper weight.

For small bakery products containing rye, and for small wheat products like rolls, the baker usually uses a press weight (weight per dough-press or head).

When making bread, the baker normally weighs each loaf or portions each loaf by means of a machine.

* Remember:

Dough input =

Bread weight

+ Baking loss

138

Bread in European countries (i.e. Germany) can be produced only in specific units of weight, i.e.:
— a minimum weight of 500 g;
— in weights between 500 and 2,000 g which can be divided by 250;
— in weights between 2,000 and 10,000 g, which can be divided by 500.

The nominal weight of a bread, after it has cooled, is calculated as an average of the weight of 10 breads.

It is, therefore, important that weight losses during bread production are considered so that the correct dough quantity per bread can be scaled. This quantity of dough is called the **dough input**.

The dough input is the basic value used for percentage calculations of bread weight and baking loss.

Example: Dough input for a mixed wheat bread	= 0.625 kg (100%)
– Loss during baking	= 0.125 kg (20%)
= Bread weight	= 0.500 kg (80%)

Precise manual scaling and exact adjustment of dough portioning machines is required in order to achieve the proper bread weight based on the dough input calculated.

Shaping of Bread

Whether the shaping of bread is done by hand (manually) or by machines (mechanically) depends on the size of the bakery operation and the bread varieties to be produced.

Although small bakery products containing rye and small wheat products are shaped mechanically, the shaping of a large number of bread varieties is difficult to achieve by means of a specific machine.

It is not so much the different shapes of breads, such as loaves, bread baked in pans or baskets, that present a problem for mechanical shaping, but rather the differences in flour mixes.

A bread molder that is suited for rye bread, is, for example, not equally well suited for shaping mixed wheat bread.

Bread-molder machines cannot adapt to the dough. Rather, dough processing must be adapted to the dough-shaping machines used. The following measures improve the results achieved when mechanically shaping doughs containing rye:
— preparation of a somewhat firmer dough;
— round-shaping of dough pieces prior to giving them a long shape;
— reducing the intermediate proofing time by about 15%, when using the manual method.

A Controversy
Joe complains about his examination. He tells his colleague, Thomas, the following story: During the examination, he had to work the bread dough manually and give it a long shape. But he told the supervisor that in his bakery he was working with a modern bread-shaping machine and that manual shaping is outdated.

The supervisor then asked Joe what he would do if he worked in another bakery that did not have such a machine — or when the machine in his bakery was not operational.

After the examination, Joe's boss agreed that a bakery cannot work without a dough-shaping machine.

But Thomas felt that a baker should learn how to shape bread manually.

What do you think?

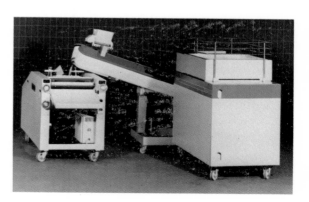

Fig. 306 **Bread-molding equipment**

Figs. 307 and 308 Bread deficiencies caused by the seam of the dough becoming unrolled (left) and air pockets in the crumb (right)

Reference:
The processing conditions during final proofing shown for small products apply also to bread. Go over that chapter again if you do not remember the conditions required for achievement of optimum fermentation maturity.

Fig. 309

Fig. 310

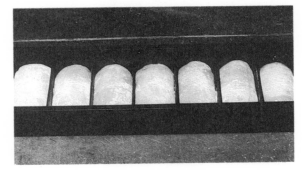

Fig. 311

140

When bread is shaped mechanically or manually, it is important to avoid using flour excessively.

Excessive use of flour during shaping can cause wrinkles in the crust, cracking of the seam and hollow spaces in the crumb.

Proofing of Bread

The shaped dough pieces for bread are placed onto various types of devices for the final proof. The following methods are used:

— Place the dough pieces on fermentation boards and cover them with cloth.
— Place the dough pieces into baskets made of peeled rattan reeds or synthetic materials (with the seam up).
— Place the dough pieces into bread pans or baking sheets.

For proofing, the dough pieces can be placed into roll-in devices in the baking room, into stationary fermentation chambers, or into continuous proofing chambers.

When the air movement in the proofer is low, the humidity values should be increased by 5 to 10% of relative air humidity.

A good bread volume can be achieved if the dough pieces are exposed to a longer proofing time at high air humidity. This promotes, at the same time, an increase of dough volume in the oven and a better shine on the crust.

Remember:	
Acceleration of final proofing	Deceleration of final proofing
— high temperature in the fermentation chamber (30 – 40°C) air humidity should not be too high (about 60%)	— low temperature in the fermentation chamber (20 – 30°C) air humidity should not be too low (about 80%)

Control of the Proofing Process
Measures to control the fermentation process are used to a lesser extent for large breads than for small wheat products because the production equipment required is usually unavailable. Interruption of the fermentation process is also difficult due to the size of the dough pieces. However, retardation of the fermentation process is possible under the following conditions:

— somewhat firmer, cooler doughs,
— lower amount of yeast added.

Preliminary cooling, storage and fermentation procedures can be adjusted to some degree to suit the bakery's operational requirements.

Fermentation Maturity

The optimum degree of fermentation maturity depends on the bread variety, the processing conditions of the dough and the baking method used. Critical faults in the shape of the bread are due to excessively low or excessively high proofing.

Fermentation Tolerance

Doughs containing rye have a lower fermentation tolerance than wheat doughs. This means that the fermentation tolerance decreases with an increasing content of rye. In other words, the time frame in which the optimum volume can be achieved is shorter.

This is, however, not of major importance, as rye bread and mixed rye bread significantly increase in volume in the oven. *Fig. 313* shows that the time frame for optimum development is short for mixed rye bread, but, on the whole, the deviations in volume are not very noticeable.

Summary of important information on the processing of dough containing rye

➤ *Milled rye products must be acidified to improve their baking ability.*

➤ *Acidification of doughs containing rye can be achieved through various sourdough processing methods, through acidifying baking agents or through a combination of sourdough and acidifying baking agents.*

➤ *Doughs containing rye require different processing conditions than wheat doughs:*
  — they are kept softer (higher dough yield),
  — they are kept warmer,
  — they are mixed less intensively.

➤ *The preparation and subsequent intermediate proof of doughs containing rye is largely dependent on the flour mix used for the dough. Bread doughs with a higher rye content can be formed in one working step. They require a shorter intermediate proofing time and they have a lower fermentation tolerance.*

Fig. 312 **Faults in volume and shape caused by an incorrect degree of fermentation; excessively round shape and small volume due to insufficient proofing (left) and excessively flat shape due to excessive proofing (right)**

Reference:
For more information on fermentation maturity and fermentation tolerance, refer to pages 80 and 81.

Additional Information

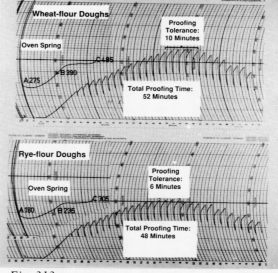

Fig. 313

A maturograph is a device developed in Germany that measures a combination of values to give an indication of the proofing tolerance of dough. The maturograms above illustrate that wheat-flour dough (top) has a greater proofing tolerance than rye dough (bottom). Wheat-flour doughs also have a greater increase in volume during the initial stages of the maturation process. Rye doughs exhibit a more stable, continuous increase in volume.

141

Baking Ovens

"The baking oven is the heart of the bakery" — this old saying is still valid today.

In the picture to the right, you can see that the oven is the focal point of the bakery. You can also see that doughs are brought to the oven for baking while other doughs are prepared for baking.

The baking oven determines the nature of a bakery operation.

Baking Oven Requirements

The baker needs... ▼	Baking oven manufacturers offer... ▼
— rapid heating and flexibility in temperature	— baking ovens with efficient heating systems;
— low space requirements, but large baking surface	— baking ovens requiring a minimum of space due to their steel-body design; baking hearths with several superimposed baking levels
— ease of loading	— baking ovens with various semi-automated loading devices
— ease of operation	— baking ovens with ergonomic operational devices; heat and steam evacuation devices
— operational safety	— baking ovens with safety devices for electrical and motor equipment
— ease of maintenance	— baking ovens requiring minimum maintenance
— low energy consumption	— baking ovens with easy-to-control heater elements; recycling of heat produced
— low environmental impact	— baking ovens with waste gas control; low-noise equipment

Fig. 314 **A bakery in Thuringia, West Germany**

This scene has not changed, except that today's baking ovens are more modern and could almost be called 'baking machines.' The baker has contributed to modern oven designs by expressing specific requirements.

Food for Thought:
How much does the nature of the baking oven in your bakery have an influence on the work pattern?

Multi-Deck Ovens

Multi-deck ovens suit many of the requirements of modern bakeries and are now available in many sizes and design configurations. Each hearth is independent of the others in terms of insulation and heating. Depending on the make and model, each crown height (the internal height of the hearth) may vary from 150 mm for cinnamon buns, muffins, pastries, etc. to 250 mm for pan bread, French bread or rye. The multi-deck unit may contain a mixture of "low" and "high" crowns with a maximum of four high or six low crowns per unit.

Heating can be either electric or gas, and units can be fitted with steam injection systems. Separate heating is available for the top and bottom of the hearth, thus giving control for products requiring bottom and top heat.

Advantages of multi-deck ovens:
— *minimum space requirement*
— *large flexibility with regard to temperature*
— *semi-automated system; easy loading*
— *lower cost of operation*
— *little heat loss*
— *easy cleaning and maintenance*

There are three basic types of oven heating systems:
— Conduction: heat transfer through a solid object
— Convection: transfer of heat by air/steam or gas
— Radiation: heat is radiated by oven walls, hearth and tubes

There are two types of hot air/gas heating systems:
→ *Agitated* ➤ *air circulated by fans*
→ *Non-agitated* ➤ *natural air currents*

Hot-Air Circulation (Convection) Ovens

The heating gas produced in *hot-air circulation ovens* is first routed through a heat exchanger. The hot air produced in the heat exchanger is then flushed into the baking hearths by means of circulation ventilators. It is also possible to introduce moisture (vapors) into the baking hearths at the same time.

Even though the hot plates of the hearth conduct the heat directly to the bottom of the bakery product, this type of baking process is based primarily on heat convection. The direct contact between the bakery product and a hot baking atmosphere ensures a uniform baking result.

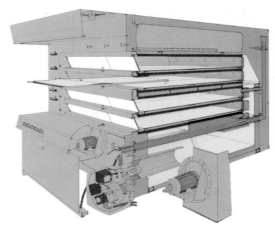

Fig. 316
Design and hot-gas flow of a modern four-level oven

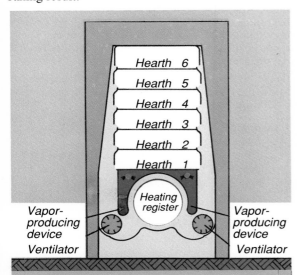

Fig. 315 **Working principle of a hot-air circulation oven**

We can also think of the hot-air circulation oven as being a uniform baking chamber which has various levels similar to a kitchen stove. Heat and vapors are introduced into all baking hearths of the oven simultaneously. To ensure central supply of all baking hearths, there are restrictions with regard to the dimensions of the oven. Heat distribution is poor after a certain optimum size of oven is reached. The larger plant ovens are no longer favored by bakers. For this reason, bakers are purchasing a number of smaller ovens to meet their needs.

Advantages of hot-air circulation ovens:
— less fuel consumption;
— intensive heat application to the product (agitated baking atmosphere);
— high degree of temperature flexibility throughout the entire oven.

Disadvantages of hot-air circulation ovens:
— the baking conditions are identical in all baking hearths (heat and vapors); therefore, only baking programs with generally uniform requirements can be used.

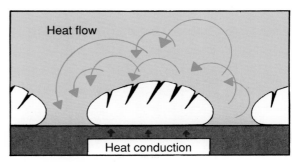

Fig. 317 **Baking through heat flow**

Hot Gas Circulation Ovens

In *hot gas circulation ovens*, the gas produced by combustion is first routed by circulation ventilators through heating channels located between the baking hearths. The heat is transferred to the bakery product from the top and bottom of the baking hearth. The hearth surface itself has a heat conducting effect. However, the primary principle is that of heat radiation. The large surfaces of the baking chamber walls ensure an intensive heat exchange so that the hot-air circulation oven and hot gas circulation oven have an equally good heat balance.

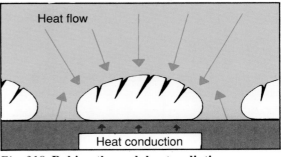

Fig. 318 **Baking through heat radiation**

143

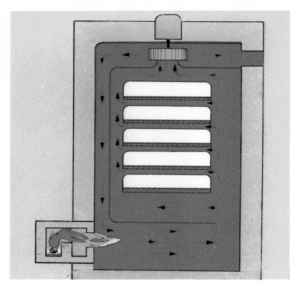

Fig. 319
Working principle of a hot gas circulation oven

Fig. 320
Heat transfer through heating channels in the hot gas circulation oven

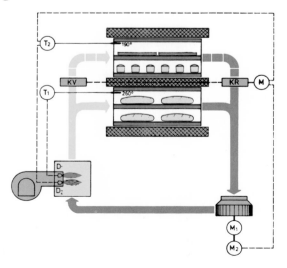

Fig. 321 **Oven with groups of hearths and two different temperature ranges**

144

In a hot gas circulation oven, all baking hearths are independent with regard to steam application and regulation of baking conditions (e.g. opening and closing of vents).

In some oven types, two different ranges of baking temperatures can be used in the individual hearths. It is also possible to switch off groups of hearths, thereby making it possible to save energy when there are fluctuations in production. On the other hand, the higher costs of acquisition must be taken into account. When purchasing an oven, a baker must understand that he or she is making a long-term commitment, and the oven should be able to meet both present and future needs.

Baking oven manufacturers also offer ovens combining hot gas circulation and hot air circulation. In this type of heating system, the hot air is flushed into the baking hearths, but it is possible to achieve a partly non-agitated baking atmosphere using shutters. These types of ovens also introduce steam into individual baking chambers.

Ovens with a hot gas circulation system have the following characteristics, as compared to ovens with a hot-air circulation system:

> *Advantages:*
> — fuel savings;
> — different baking conditions can be used in the individual baking hearths;
> — high degree of flexibility with regard to temperature;
> — use of hearth groups.
>
> *Disadvantages:*
> — impairment of heat transfer through soot buildup in the heating channels.

Rack Ovens

Rack ovens are similar to multi-deck ovens in that they both have a small space requirement combined with a large baking surface. However, the baking chamber is not subdivided into individual hearths. Rack ovens were developed in Scandinavia.

Baker Smith is convinced: *"Our new rack oven is great! But to make full use of it, we have to make some changes to our production process!"* What does he mean by that? *Evaluate the production process when using a rack oven.*

Using Rack Ovens

The following procedures apply to rack ovens:

— *the dough pieces are placed onto trays in a movable frame or rack*
— *the loaded racks are then placed in the proofer*
— *after proofing, the racks are wheeled from the proofer straight into the oven*
— *the racks are then wheeled into the cooling area or sales room*

The rack oven not only introduces a new loading method, but it requires a different production process.

Fig. 323
Rack oven with 12 bread trays

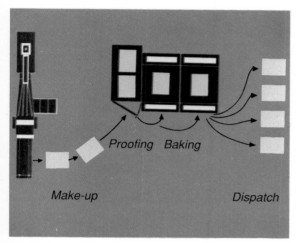

Fig. 322

The rack oven has not only the advantage already mentioned of "rack production," which has given this oven its name, but it also allows optimum use of its large surface. Because the spacing between rack oven trays can be adjusted depending on the type of product introduced, (the spacing for fine bakery products is, for example, 6 cm; for rolls about 8 cm; and for bread between 12 and 17 cm), a smaller or larger number of standardized trays can be introduced into this type of oven.

In the most favorable case, i.e. for fine bakery products, the available baking surface is enormous.

On a basic surface of about 3 m², using 20 trays, about 1,000 rolls can be baked simultaneously. This corresponds to a baking surface of 12 m² of a normal oven type. In double rack ovens, for example, a combined baking surface of 32 m² is available. This is equivalent to the baking performance of a continuous oven with a surface area of about 53 m².

Heating the Rack Oven

The high baking performance of the rack oven is primarily due to a very efficient heating system. Depending on the heating system, the heating chambers are located on the side, on the back, or above the baking chambers. The heating system can operate with any type of fuel.

Heat convection is primarily used to heat a cupboard-like baking chamber. But in some oven types, the frames turn around their own axis (rotary ovens) during baking to obtain a better heat flow. In other types of ovens, the same effect is achieved by means of a continuous change in the direction of the heat flow.

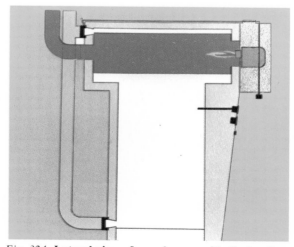

Fig. 324 **Lateral view of a rack oven with the heating chamber located in the upper part. This oven operates based on the principle of hot air circulation, but the frame does not move during the baking process.**

145

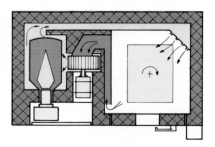

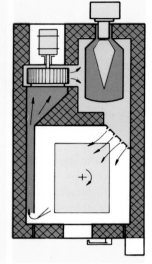

Fig. 325a
A rack oven with a com-
bustion chamber located
a) on the side; and
b) in the back.
During baking, the mov-
able frame turns in the direction of the arrows.

Fig. 325b

When the door of the rack oven is opened to load or
unload racks of bread or buns, the circulating or rotating movement stops. The heat loss occurring is significant, ranging between 20 and 30°C.
In order to achieve the desired rapid reheating, the
heating elements are located in a very high place. It is
also important to ensure a large supply of moist vapor,
by means of a high-performance steam generator.

Baking in the Rack Oven

Humidification of the dough pieces at the beginning of
the baking process in the rack oven occurs at moderate circulation or in a non-agitated baking atmosphere.

Since the baking trays initially have the same temperature as the dough pieces, the bottom crust formation is
typically low in the rack oven, compared with heat
conduction through the hearth surfaces in other baking ovens.

Perforation in some baking trays also presents a problem, as sweeter dough products may stick to them. But
baking products in rack ovens have such great advantages in quality, quantity, and efficiency that such
equipment is used in more bakeries.

Advantages of the Rack Oven:
— high baking performance combined with low
   space requirement,
— rolling production,
— easy adjustment of the oven capacity to the
   requirements of the bakery operations,
— good use of energy.

Disadvantages of the Rack Oven:
— less developed bottom crust of bread,
— basically suited for uniform baking programs.

In order to combine the advantages of various types of
baking ovens, and to obtain larger baking oven capacities with a high degree of adaptability to bakery operations, large bakeries use various different ovens as
shown in *Fig. 326.*

Fig. 326 **Combination of brick oven with steam, multi-deck and rack ovens**

146

Large-Scale Baking Ovens

In large commercial and industrial bakery operations, bread, small wheat products and certain fine bakery products of identical kinds are produced in large numbers. For this purpose, large baking surfaces (baking oven capacities) are required.

Larger baking oven capacities can be achieved as follows:
— multi-level arrangement of large baking surfaces (e.g. five hearths placed one upon another, each with a baking surface of 4 m²)
— combination of various types of baking ovens (as shown in *Fig. 326*)
— uniform baking ovens with movable baking surfaces

Net belts, stone plate belts, or conveyor belts are used in ovens with movable baking surfaces. The dough pieces can be introduced automatically so they pass through the oven during baking *(continuous oven and tunnel oven)*, and leave the hearth bottom when the baking process is finished.

Such ovens are 25 meters long or more. In the individual zones of the oven, moisture, temperature and moving speed are regulated depending on the type and size of the product. A new type of oven is the multi-deck steel mesh net belt oven, where up to four levels are placed one upon another. These ovens have a low space requirement.

In *auto-ovens*, suspended baking plates are moved in a loop and baking time is regulated by adjusting the rotational speed.

Fig. 327 **Baking in a continuous belt oven. The dough is fed from the front side of the oven, which cannot be seen here**

The *reversing oven*, of medium size, has movable baking trays that are loaded and unloaded from the front.

Obviously the dough pieces loaded first are exposed to a longer baking time. The temperature can be adjusted individually in the various zones for products requiring a shorter baking time.

It is also possible to unload the product at the back of the oven. However, this type of reversing oven cannot be placed against a wall. It differs from a continuous oven in that the baking trays do not move during baking.

Fig. 328 **Crusty rolls being unloaded from a reversing band oven**

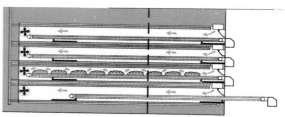

Fig. 329 **Working principle of a reversing oven**

Advantages of continuous and reversing ovens:
— high baking performance,
— continuous baking process combined with automated dough processing.

Disadvantages of continuous and reversing ovens:
— relatively high space requirement (in reversing ovens with several baking levels, this disadvantage can only be compensated for at the expense of the ease of operation),
— suited for uniform production programs (e.g. rolls or large loaves of bread),
— steel mesh belts with insufficient heat conduction.

When larger baking oven surfaces are required in commercial bakeries, various ovens are often combined. This has the following advantages:

— various types of bakery products can be baked simultaneously under differing baking conditions (e.g. bread and cake products);
— the required heated baking surface can be increased or reduced, depending on the operational requirements (e.g. seasonal business, weekends and holidays);
— for specific baking needs, the most appropriate feeding methods can be used (e.g. use of an extensible oven or of a placing device).

147

Oven Loading Systems

Although the peel is practical for batch feeding individual doughs, various other devices are also used for efficient and rapid loading.

Fig. 330 **Loading individual bread loaves with a peel is time-consuming**

It is customary to use the *extensible hearth* or the *extensible oven* for pan-baked bread.
The entire hot hearth can be moved out for the purpose of loading or baking. In this case, the product is primarily taken off the proofing trays and placed on the hearth by hand. This kind of operation must be performed quickly as the baker can be burned by the hot hearth surfaces.

Fig. 331 **Extensible oven**

Oven-Setters

Loading devices, in the form of trays carrying proofed products, are a quick and efficient way to load an oven. In order to reduce the lifting operation required in multi-deck ovens, a special loading device can be used. This also allows for a one-man operation.
Operations are made easier when the hearths are arranged side by side (rather than four or five levels on top of one another).

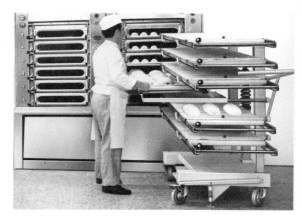

Fig. 332 **Loading in a one-man operation with a special loading device**

The loading device not only ensures faster loading of the dough pieces into the oven, but also makes the physical lifting operation easier.
The following principle applies: "Do not carry what you can roll."
Another important factor to be considered with baking ovens is the working level of the operation's elements. The hearths should be arranged so that a person can look inside while standing upright. The switch, lock and oven equipment should be easily accessible.
This reduces the physical work required for the operation of a baking oven.

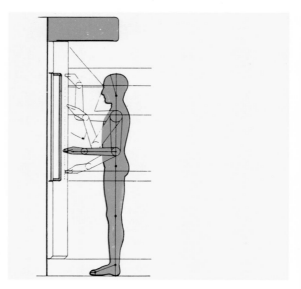

Fig. 333
Ease of operation when using a baking oven

Food for Thought: *The loading and special placement device, and the movable parts of a rack oven all ensure ease of operation. How is this achieved in each case?*

Heating Systems for Baking Ovens

So far, we have only looked at the design and feeding mechanisms of the baking oven. Based on this, the various types of baking ovens can be categorized, as shown in *Table 50*.

Energy conservation concerns have caused us to reconsider the various means of heating baking ovens.

Classification of Baking Ovens		
Design	Type of hearth surface	Loading
Brick ovens	stationary baking surface	Peel-loaded ovens
Steel-frame ovens	movable baking surface	Extensible ovens Rack ovens
Steel-body ovens	(e.g. reversing ovens) movable baking surface (e.g. net belt, auto-ovens)	Rotating or shelf oven Deck oven

Table 50

Direct and Indirect Heating

The type of fuel to be used for a baking oven depends primarily on economical aspects and on local conditions. Some changes have occurred over the years.

Solid-type fuels, such as wood and coal, were used primarily until about 1950, particularly for heating the old "brick" oven and the wood-fired oven. The combustion chamber in these types of ovens is located directly inside the baking hearth.

The ashes are removed immediately prior to baking. As an increase in temperature is not possible during baking with this type of ***direct-heated oven***, the initial temperatures are very high. This has a particularly favorable effect on the formation of the bread crust. This advantage can still be achieved today with bread baked in a wood-burning oven or in a stone oven.

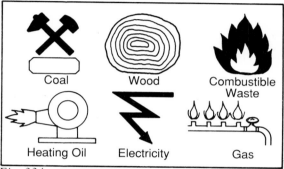

Coal　　Wood　　Combustible Waste

Heating Oil　　Electricity　　Gas

Fig. 334

Reference:
*Please refer to the chapter entitled **Specialty Bread** to learn more about special baking processes.*

The desire for more flexibility with regard to oven temperature and the necessity to increase the temperature during the baking process has led to the development of ***indirect-heated baking ovens***.

The first indirect-heated baking oven was the tunnel or underdraft oven, in which the heating gases were conducted through masonry tunnels, located below and above the baking hearths, into the chimney. This was not a very efficient oven because of the heat retention of the thick stone walls between the hearth and the heating tunnel and the insulating effect of the soot and ashes produced by the fire.

Today, the modern hot gas circulation oven still uses the principle of the tunnel oven.

Food for Thought: *Why do heated gas circulation ovens have a much better heat balance than the historic tunnel ovens?*

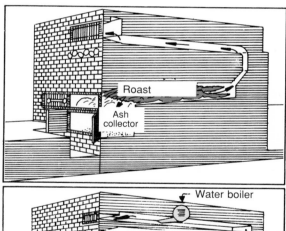

Roast

Ash collector

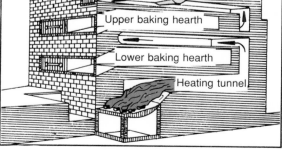

Water boiler

Upper baking hearth

Lower baking hearth

Heating tunnel

Fig. 335 **The old brick oven (above) is direct-heated. The tunnel oven (below) was the first indirect-heated baking oven.**

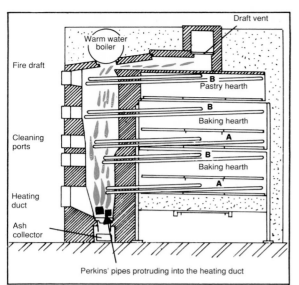

Fig. 336
Cross-section of a steel-body steam oven

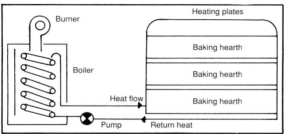

Fig. 337 **Working principle of the hot oil circulation oven**

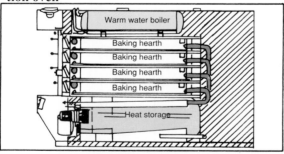

Fig. 338 **Cross-section of an electric baking oven with overnight heat storage**

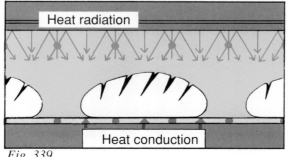

Fig. 339
Electric heating with resistance heating elements

150

Heat Transfer in Steam-Operated Baking Ovens

Heat transfer in a ***steam-operated baking oven*** occurs through a heat carrier system called "Perkins' pipes." Steam pressure pipes are partially filled with water or an aqueous solution. The pipes are arranged in a slight incline underneath the hearth bottom (for lower heat) and in the ceiling of the baking hearth (for upper heat). The ends of the pipes protrude into the heating duct of the oven, the upper pipes extending further into the heating duct than the lower ones (see *Fig. 336*). In this way, all pipes receive enough heat.

The steam-operated baking oven can be heated by means of solid fuels such as coal, wood, peat, oil or gas. The material in the pipes is heated, rises in the form of steam under increasing inner pressure in the pipes to the baking hearth, gives off heat and flows back to the heat source.

Today this system has been developed further, resulting in an oven with continuous pipes, arranged in loops around several baking hearths.

Heat Transfer in Hot Oil Circulation Ovens

This type of oven is heated by a heat transfer system. As the name indicates, heated thermo oil is used for heating in a circulation system. The working principle of this heating system is similar to that of a warm water central heating system.

The oil is heated in a separate boiler until it reaches about 300°C, then is conducted via a piping system around the individual baking hearths. Contrary to the steam-heated baking oven, the inside pressure in the heating pipes is not increased. It is possible to include the proofer, the hot water boiler, or the furnace for the room heating system into the return run of the steam pipes.

Heat Transfer in Electric Ovens

Electricity is suited for all types of heating systems. Therefore, ***electric ovens*** are offered in various designs. They are ideal baking ovens because they do not require a smoke ventilation system, nor a fuel supply; they are noise-free and clean. In Europe, the high cost of electricity has prohibited the common use of this type of baking oven. In North America, electric ovens, which are relatively small, are popular in areas where retail space is at a premium. Many bakery franchise operations use electric ovens for this reason.

This type of indirect heat generation by means of electric energy has the following disadvantages:
— less favorable heating balance through radiation losses;
— low degree of temperature flexibility.

In Europe, following the increase in price of fossil sources of energy (oil, coal, gas), electric heating of baking ovens has become more economical. The heat is produced by means of elements located in the baking hearths. Separate elements are used for upper and lower heat, and the hearths are individually adjustable. Hearth surfaces that are not required remain unheated.

The elements are often incorporated into the fireproof plates that retain heat, allowing the oven temperature to be easily adjusted to higher temperatures when needed. This is also favorable because the basic cost of electricity can be reduced.

Additional Information

Infrared and Microwave Baking Ovens

A special type of heat generation involves the use of infrared heat radiation which allows, for example, crust formation and browning. Cookies (flat products) can, for example, be baked using infrared radiation. However, crumb formation is not possible.

Food products containing water can be heated and baked by means of high frequency waves. In the microwave oven, the waves are distributed by means of a transmitter. The oven remains cold in the process. Only the particles of food products containing water are accelerated. The inner friction generated produces so much heat that the product is cooked in a very short time. However, crust formation is impossible.

Although equipment manufacturers offer a combination of infrared and microwave heating processes, this type of heating is not normally used in the baking industry.

Heat Transfer in Gas Ovens

Due to the very efficient combustion of gas, (natural gas and liquid gas), *gas heating systems* have a particularly small effect on the environment. Gas heating systems can be used for direct heating (convection heaters) or indirect heating (radiation heaters).
Rotating and rack ovens frequently operate with gas heating systems. For other oven types, variable burners (oil/gas) are used.

Maintenance of Baking Ovens

If regular maintenance work is performed on baking ovens, breakdowns can be avoided.
Part of the maintenance program for *baking oven heating systems* is the removal of soot and flue ashes. When these residues of combustion are allowed to deposit in the heating system, the heat transfer to the baking hearth is reduced.
The use of oil and gas burners requires regular cleaning of the ignition, the photo cells, the air slots, and the ventilation wheel. Other problem sources are primarily flour dust and humidity.
Steam hoses and steam pipes are subject to calcium deposits when the water is hard. The calcium deposits must be eliminated from time to time through flushing.
Electric oven equipment must always be checked by a licensed electrician.

Classification of baking ovens based on the type of heating used			
Type	Fuel	Heat transfer	Heat generation
Direct heating (wood-burning oven, old brick oven)	Coal	Heat convection	through a heating element outside the baking hearth (centralized)
	Wood	Heat radiation	
	Peat moss	Heat conduction	
Indirect heating (steam-operated baking ovens, hot gas circulation ovens)	Oil	Heat conduction	
	Gas	Heat conduction	
	Electricity	Friction heating (microwave)	direct heating in the baking hearth (decentralized)

Table 51

Summary of Important Information About Baking Ovens

➤ *Masonry stone ovens and steel-frame ovens store heat and the temperature is not easily adjusted. Steel-body ovens are more flexible with regard to temperature adjustments and they radiate less heat.*

➤ *Fuels normally used include electricity, gas and heating oil. Older baking oven systems are heated by coal, wood or peat. Electricity and gas have a minimal effect on the environment because they do not produce waste gases.*

➤ *Loading modern baking ovens is made easier through the use of loading conveyor belts, extensible ovens and roll-in compartments.*

➤ *The various types of baking ovens can be classified based on the following features:*
  — direct or indirect heating systems
  — masonry, steel-frame and steel-body baking ovens
  — the type of fuel used
  — the system of heat transfer used;
  — the type of oven feeding used.

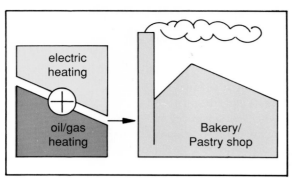

Fig.340

Environmental Protection and Energy Savings

The production of bakery products requires a large amount of energy for heat generation, equipment, power and lighting.

It has been established that on average 1,700 kw/h of energy is required per ton of flour used. Of this amount, the ovens consume about 1,500 kw/h (= 88%). Therefore, the oven consumes most of the energy required in a bakery operation.

Food for Thought: *What is the best kind of energy for a large-scale or a small-scale bakery in terms of environmental protection?*

Additional Information

Environmental Requirements for Ovens in Europe

Measuring Waste Gas
The direction of current North American regulatory reform is toward stricter emission standards in every industry. In Europe, when using baking ovens operated by means of fossil fuels, waste gas control is mandatory. Measured are:
— the waste gas temperature; and
— the carbon dioxide content (CO_2) in the waste gas.

Optimum values for waste gas temperatures in a heated gas circulation system are about 20 to 30°C above the baking oven temperature; when using hot air circulation systems, the temperature should be about 60 to 70°C above the baking oven temperature. These temperatures can be continuously measured by a thermometer built into the waste gas pipe. The CO_2 content is determined by the fuel/air ratio set at the burner. Well-adjusted oil burners should show values around 10%; natural gas burners, values of about 8%.
Soot in the chimney gas ducts has a negative effect on the heat transfer into the baking hearths. Thus, the heating process takes longer and more waste gas is produced.

Heat Production and Environmental Protection

Until now, cost was the most important factor when determining the type of fuel to be used. Energy crises and environmental concerns have focused attention on other factors as well, for example:
— safety of supply,
— economical use of energy,
— environmental problems related to heat generation.

When a bakery owner wants to purchase a new baking oven, the decision might be based on a profitability study. *Table 52* gives a summary of the various factors, such as electricity and natural gas supply, that must be taken into account when looking at the economics of a project. But environmental factors should also be considered.

When solid fuels and oil are burnt, ashes, soot and harmful residues of combustion (such as carbon monoxide and sulphur dioxide) are produced. Sulphur dioxide causes, for example, environmental damage due to "acid rain."

Through regular control and maintenance of the burners and of the heating tunnels of baking ovens, waste emission can be reduced. Waste control allows the baker to heat economically and, at the same time, to prevent environmental damage.

When baking ovens are heated by electricity, smoke gases are not produced. The heat loss is also smaller compared to other types of energy sources. However, power generating plants convert only about 1/3 of the energy used into electricity.

Costs (x) associated with various types of energy sources				
	Connection to electric main	Tank storage	Maintenance of chimney/burner	Stockpiling costs
Wood, coal, heating		×	×	×
Natural gas	×		×	
Liquid gas		×	×	×
Electricity	×			

Table 52

Economical Use of Energy

You might be surprised by the following statement: Only about 45% of the energy consumed by a baking oven reaches the product. The remainder is lost heat. *Fig. 341* shows how the energy produced in ovens with oil and gas heating systems is used.

What can the baker do to reduce the loss of energy?

New oven acquisitions or equipment for economical use of energy are expensive. The long-term capital investment can, however, result in considerable energy savings.

Examples:

— A masonry baking oven with a high energy consumption is replaced with a well-insulated multi-level steel-body oven.
— Purchase of a baking oven with hearth groups that can be disconnected.
— A coal-fired oven is equipped with a gas heating system.
— A warm water boiler is incorporated into the fume evacuating channel, in which the fume heat is used for room heating or for warm water supply.

Organizational measures for daily operations can also contribute toward saving energy.

Examples:

— Avoiding prolonged idle time of the heated baking oven;
— Avoiding production breaks during which the baking oven is not used;
— Avoiding frequent changes in baking temperatures with cooling-off and heating-up phases;
— Avoiding excessive cooling-off of the baking oven by keeping doors, vents and exhausts closed when possible;
— Avoiding steam generation when the steam has no technical effect on the product;
— Avoiding heat losses through poorly-adjusted burners, and excessive soot development in the exhaust system.

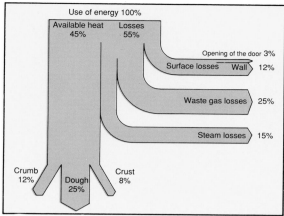

Fig. 341 Energy balance of baking ovens heated by oil and gas

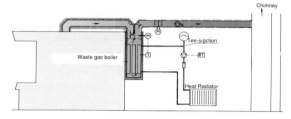

Fig. 342
Energy savings by using a waste gas boiler for room heating. Waste water heat can also be used to produce a warm water supply.

Think about daily measures for energy savings. This is a contribution toward environmental protection and energy savings.

Food for Thought: *What measures for energy savings are taken in your bakery, and what additional measures could be taken?*

The Baking Process

During the baking process, the raw dough turns into a digestible, good-tasting product. Moreover, the baking process has a significant influence on the quality of the product and slight changes in this process can make the difference between a good product and a mediocre product. It is important to know the individual processes taking place during baking and the measures that can have an influence on these processes.

The stages in the baking process include:
1) the formation and expansion of gases;
2) the trapping of gases in the gluten (protein) network;
3) paste formation of starches;
4) the coagulation of proteins; and
5) crust formation and browning.

Fig. 343 **Bread after a baking time of 10 minutes with a large, "doughy" center part**

Fig. 344 **Bread after a baking time of 20 minutes with a doughy center part**

Fig. 345 **Bread after a baking time of 30 minutes with a cohesive, but very moist crumb**

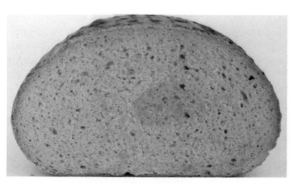

Fig. 346 **Bread after a baking time of 40 minutes with a still very inelastic crumb (thumb imprint !)**

Fig. 347 **Bread after a baking time of 60 minutes with a firm crumb and a strong crust**

To illustrate the processes occurring during baking, *Figs. 343 to 347* show a cross-section of a rye bread after 10, 20, 30, 40 and 60 minutes of baking. We can see the following:

— The heat penetrates the dough piece from the outside to the inside.
— The doughy center part of the bread is gradually transformed into a solid crumb.
— The surface of the bread is gradually transformed into a firm crust.
— Various transformation processes occur simultaneously, depending on the level of temperature reached. Although the center part is doughy, the crumb firms up and the crust is formed on the surface.

Crumb Formation

What are the processes responsible for transformation of the dough into a bread with a firm crumb?

➤ The bread is loaded into the oven at proofer temperature. The temperature in the center part of the dough pieces increases very slowly. In the temperature range between 35 and 50°C, the enzymes and the yeast cells become very active.
➤ The number and size of the dough cells depends on the shaping. During baking, the cells extend due to the expansion of gas.

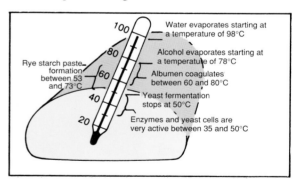

Fig. 348 **Crumb formation**

➤ Expansion of the dough cells causes curving and a strong increase in volume of the bread = increase of volume during baking.
➤ At 50°C, the activity of the yeast cells stop. Between 53 and 60°C, the acidifiers and the yeast die.
➤ The albumen coagulates between 50 and 70°C and releases the water it has absorbed during dough formation.
➤ The rye starch turns into a paste between 53 and 73°C. In the process, it absorbs the dough water and the released water during coagulation of the albumen. This process is necessary to achieve a firm crumb. The paste-forming ability of the rye starch is reduced through the activity of the starch-digesting enzymes.

154

➤ The fermentation alcohol evaporates starting at a temperature of 78°C. It partially combines with the dough acids to form aromatic compounds = esters.

➤ The water content of the crumb is reduced due to evaporation of water from the inside of the dough piece.

During baking of white-bread products, a soft-dry crumb is formed. Rye products have a wet-moist crumb.

What is the reason for the difference?

The wet-moist crumb of rye products is due to the following factors:

Conditions	Effect on the crumb
— higher water content in the dough	➤ improved swelling; complete paste formation of the starch
— higher proportion of mucic (semiliquid) substances	➤ more water available for paste formation; longer fresh-keeping properties due to a moist crumb
— higher proportion of soluble substances due to enzymatic decomposition of the starch	➤ larger amount of free water; better fresh-keeping properties
— higher degree of paste formation of the rye starch	➤ maximum water absorption by the starch; no starch residues in granular form
— lower degree of water evaporation from the firmer crumb during baking	➤ larger amount of free water; longer fresh-keeping properties

The differences between rye and wheat bread crumbs can be recognized in cell structure pictures. In *Figs. 349* and *350*, a wheat bread crumb and a rye bread crumb are greatly enlarged.

The wheat bread has:
— even cells;
— a very loose crumb;
— thin cell walls with gluten film; and
— pasty starch uniformly embedded into the gluten structure.

The rye bread has:
— uneven cells;
— a firmer crumb;
— thick cell walls with many uneven, pasty starch grains; and
— unevenly distributed gluten film in the starch paste.

Due to the structure of its crumb, bread containing rye keeps fresh longer than wheat bread. With an increasing wheat content, a mixed bread crumb loses its firmness and gradually takes on the characteristics of a wheat bread.

Additional Information
Electron Microscope
The standard optical microscope operates with magnifying lenses and light. The light is reflected from the object through the lenses. Thus, the object is magnified. It is possible to magnify an object 2,000 times.
Objects that are smaller than the wavelength of light cannot be viewed with an optical microscope. This is where the electron microscope is used. It operates with bundled electron rays (subatomic particles). The pattern that the electrons record from the object is not visible to the eye. It is projected onto a screen, making it possible to magnify an object 200,000 times.

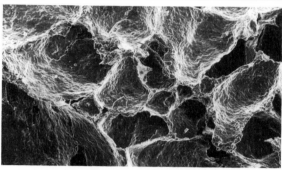

Fig. 349 **Wheat bread crumb (projected by an electron microscope)**

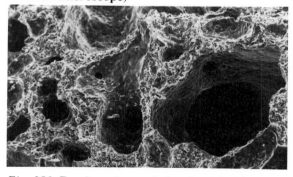

Fig. 350 **Rye bread crumb (projected by an electron microscope)**

Food for Thought:
When cooking a pastry cream, 100 g starch absorbs about 1,000 g liquid. Solidification of the bread crumb is also caused through water absorption by the starch.
Give reasons for solidification of the bread crumb by determining the liquid/starch ratio in the bread.

155

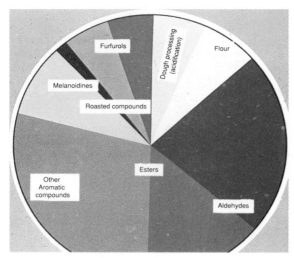

Fig. 451 **Bread aroma**

The crust is of significance for the bread for the following reasons:
— It gives the bread a solid outer support.
— It contains a large number of aromatic substances.
— It passes on a large number of aromatic substances to the spongy crumb structure.
— It acts as an insulating layer and delays the loss of aroma and moisture.
— It protects the crumb, which contains a larger amount of water, from attacks through micro-organisms in the air.

Crust Formation

Water on the surface of the dough pieces evaporates rapidly during exposure to intense oven temperatures. Only a small amount of residual water remains.

The boiling temperature of water (100°C) is the highest temperature that can be achieved when cooking or baking food products containing a large amount of water. However, it is possible to achieve temperatures of more than 100°C in the outer layers of the bread because they contain less water. A stronger crust can be obtained.

What are the processes leading to the formation of the bread crust?

➤ At temperatures of less than 100°C, compounds are formed in the outer layers of the bread between sugars and components of the albumen. These ***sugar-albumen-compounds*** (called melanoidines) take on a brown color.

The chemical reaction between sugar and albumen occurs without any enzymes being involved in the process. Therefore, this kind of browning is called "non-enzymatic browning," or, based on the name of the person who has discovered this reaction, "Maillard Reaction." The melanoidines generate a flavor while they form, and a large number of byproducts are produced which also have an influence on the aroma of the bread.

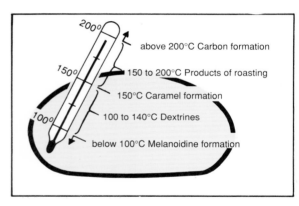

Fig. 352 **Crust formation**

➤ At temperatures between 100 and 115°C, the paste-like starch in the crust dries out. It can then be decomposed by means of heat into water-soluble ***dextrines***. These dextrines are initially light yellow, and take on a brown color as the heat increases.

➤ Between 140 and 150°C, the soluble sugars form a brown ***caramel sugar*** in the crust.

➤ Between 150 and 200°C, products of the ***roasting process*** form, which have a darker color.

At 200°C, the crust starts to burn. Black-brown, very bitter ***carbon products*** are formed.

Therefore, it is important to regulate the baking process so that no carbon products can be formed in the crust.

Summary of the processes occurring during baking	
Processes	**Effects**
➤ paste formation of the starch occurs	➤ digestible product
➤ albumen coagulates	
➤ dough liquid partly evaporates	➤ firm product
➤ heat expansion	➤ loose crumb
➤ micro-organisms die	➤ durable product
➤ enzymes become inactive	➤ storable product
➤ ester, melanoidine, caramel and roasted substances are formed	➤ aromatic product

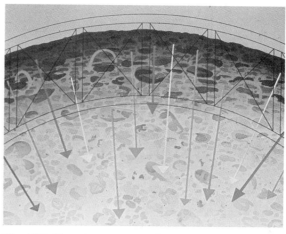

Fig. 353 **Crust as a protective layer of the bread**

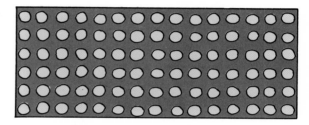

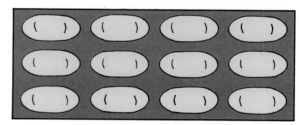

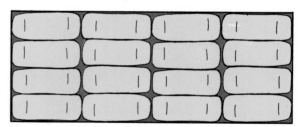

Fig. 354

Baking oven filled with rolls, with pan-baked bread, and with bread baked without a pan

Baking Procedure

Compare the baking time of 100 kg of rolls (= 2,000 to 2,500 pieces) with that of 100 kg of bread (= 100 pieces per 1 kg).

One would probably assume that rolls are baked within a considerably shorter period of time than bread. But it is not quite so simple.

The conditions of the baking oven must be considered when determining the overall baking procedures.

The baking procedure depends on:
→ *the baking time of the individual types of product;*
→ *the capacity of the baking oven; and*
→ *the time it takes to introduce the product and bake it.*

For comparison purposes, it is more appropriate to evaluate the baking performance in kg of product per m^2 of baking surface during a certain period of time. It is also important to consider the product weight and the number of pieces placed onto a baking surface (see *Fig. 354*). In our example, the baking time of pan-baked bread is about four times as long as that for rolls. But, in spite of this, the baking performance per kg of product is higher, because more kg of bread per m^2 of baking surface are baked.

The baker can use the baking performance per oven load as the basis for the quantity of dough to be produced. For planning purposes, he or she not only considers the production time, but also the time required for loading and baking the product.

Baking Temperatures and Baking Times

In order to be able to measure the correct baking times and baking temperatures, the following factors must be taken into consideration:
— product weight,
— product shape,
— dough composition,
— oven system,
— baking process.

Food for Thought:
Give reasons for the difference in baking performance when bread is baked in a pan and when it is baked without a pan. Consider not only the number of dough pieces that fit into the oven, but also the loading and baking methods.

157

Baking temperatures and baking times of various bread varieties			
	Bread Type	Temperature	Baking Time
0,500 kg	Mixed rye bread, baked without a pan	260–210 °C	35– 40 Min.
0,500 kg	Mixed wheat bread, baked without a pan	240–200 °C	30– 35 Min.
1,500 kg	Mixed rye bread, baked without a pan	270–220 °C	65– 75 Min.
1,500 kg	Mixed rye bread, baked in a pan	260–220 °C	75–120 Min.
1,000 kg	Rye bread, baked without a pan	270–220 °C	60– 65 Min.
1,000 kg	Coarse rye bread, baked in closed boxes	220–160 °C	240–300 Min.

Table 53

Reference: *Establish the baking temperatures and baking times used in your bakery! Compare the values shown in Table 53 with the values established for your bakery and with those indicated by your colleagues.*

Fig. 355 **Berliner country bread is a type of bread that normally undergoes a prebaking process**

Fig. 356 **Rupture in the side crust caused by the lack of steam application**

158

The values shown in *Table 53* are only approximate values.

Differences in the baking time under identical baking conditions can be caused, for example, by the processing methods used for the dough.

Influences on the baking time (at identical temperature)	
Shorter baking time	*Longer baking time*
— *higher wheat flour content in the dough*	— *higher rye content in the dough*
— *light-colored flour*	— *doughs containing coarse materials*
— *bread baked without a pan*	— *pan-baked bread*
— *bread with a loose crumb*	— *bread with a firm crumb*

In principle, most bread varieties are baked initially at high temperatures, then with decreasing heat.
Larger deviations in the baking temperatures are encountered with special baking methods, e.g. baking in the steam-operated oven. Larger deviations in the baking time also occur when using the interrupted baking method.

The Prebaking Process
When this special baking method is used, the bread is prebaked during the first 1 to 5 minutes at temperatures ranging between 330 and 430°C. The main baking process occurs at the usual baking temperatures and baking times. Industrial bakery operations use special ovens for the prebaking process. But the effect of the prebaking method can also be achieved in baking ovens with several hearths, where the temperature can be adjusted individually. First, the bread is baked in a hot hearth, then it is transferred into another hearth for the main baking process.
When the temperatures during prebaking are higher than 400°C, the addition of steam can be omitted. In this case, the crust forms even faster. But ruptures in the crust can easily occur (see *Fig. 356*).

What happens during the prebaking process?
➤ Rapid crust formation
➤ High increase in volume during prebaking.
➤ Some additional increase in volume after the dough pieces have been transferred to a lower baking temperature.

What are the advantages of using the prebaking process?
Rye bread and mixed bread with a high rye content have a low gas retention capacity. Therefore, they remain small in volume. Prebaking is a special method used to increase the volume and to obtain a special type of bread:

Measures taken during prebaking	Effects on the bread
— softer dough with full fermentation maturity	➤ good aeration
— dryer proof, floury surface	➤ country-style character of the bread crust
— high initial heat	➤ dough pieces do not flatten out; high increase in volume during baking
— interruption of the baking process between prebaking and main baking	➤ additional increase in volume of the doughy center part of the product causes the cells to become large and uneven (country bread effect)
— long baking time	➤ strong crust

Steam Baking Method

Coarse bread varieties and pumpernickel are baked in saturated steam at about 100°C in closed baking pans (sandwich bread pans). Because the temperature is low, the process resembles that of cooking and takes correspondingly longer (for pumpernickel: about 16 hours). The coarse components are steamed during the long baking time until they become soft and partly decomposed. Instead of the normal bread crust, bread baked in a vapor baking chamber has only a skin.

The entire baking procedure consists of placing the closed breadpans into the oven and controlling the steam application.

Interrupted Baking Method

When this method is used, the baking procedure is interrupted after about 75 to 80% of the normal baking time has elapsed. The prebaked bread can now be stored for up to 20 hours (at sufficient air humidity). It is baked again for a short period of time before it is offered for sale. Therefore the total baking time is somewhat longer. An example of 1 kg of mixed rye bread:

Normal baking time .... 60 minutes	
Interruption of the baking process after .... 48 minutes	
Storage for up to 20 hours	
Subsequent baking time of .... 12 minutes	
+ 12 minutes	
Total baking time of .... 72 minutes	

When this method is used, fresh rye bread is always available. When an additional layer of starch paste is applied to the bread, prior to additional baking, a double-crust effect can be achieved.

Food for Thought:
To what extent is prebaking possible in a bakery operation? What makes it difficult — what makes it easy?

Closed baking pan (sandwich breadpan)

Fig. 357 **Baking in sandwich bread pans (baking pans with lids to avoid strong crust formation)**

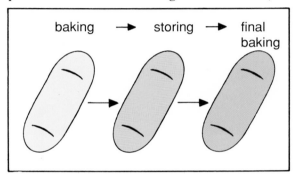

baking → storing → final baking

Fig. 358

Principle of the interrupted baking method

Advantages of the interrupted baking	*Disadvantages of the interrupted baking method*
— *fresh bread supply*	— *additional baking loss (due to storage and additional baking)*
— *the main baking process is performed when the work load is less intensive*	— *considerable decrease of the bread volume*
— *more thoroughly-baked bread with a better crust*	— *faster aging during intermediate storage*
	— *risk of obtaining an inelastic crumb when the initial baking time is too short*

Food for Thought: *By using the prebaking method, the baker wants to achieve a higher quality of bread for the consumer.*
Is it worth the additional effort?

Fig. 359 **Traditional bread stamps**

Fig. 360 **Loading an extensible oven**

Fig. 361 **Loading a reversing oven**

Reference:
The effects of steam application are treated in detail in the chapter entitled Baking of Wheat-flour Products. Read this chapter again if you require more information on this subject.

Oven Loading

The baker needs extensive experience in order to determine the optimum fermentation maturity of dough pieces, and must take into consideration not only the condition of the dough, but of the oven as well. The baker establishes this "moment" for wheat-flour products, and for bread, by looking at the volume and by touching the dough pieces.

Depending on the bread type, the dough pieces are treated immediately before they are placed into the oven. They are cut, marked, coated, etc. Very often the baker can compensate for minor fermentation mistakes by using the following methods:
— by brushing with water when a skin forms during intermediate proof; and
— by applying strong cuts when the dough pieces are not sufficiently developed.

The surface treatment of breads, and cuts or marks applied, depend on the bakery, the area, region or customs.
The oven must be loaded quickly. Manual loading can cause problems due to heat escaping from the baking oven.

Loading methods	Oven type
"by hand" — by using a "Peel"	→ Deck-oven (2-6 shelves)
— placed with or without pans	→ Extensible hearth
— by rolling the rack into the rack oven	→ Rack oven
"semi-automated" — by operating the load- ing/placing device	→ Multi-shelf deck oven
"fully-automated" — by way of a conveyor belt	→ Travelling tray oven

Steam Application

Steam provides a moist baking atmosphere in the baking oven.
Although wheat-flour products are exposed to a moist heat during the entire baking time, the vapor applied to mixed rye bread and rye bread must be removed after a short time by opening the vent.

What are the effects of steam on baking bread?
Steam has the following effects:

➤ distribution and conduction of the heat

➤ humidification of the product surface, causing delayed firming up of the crust

➤ dissolution and distribution of sugars, causing the crust to turn brown and shiny

The quantity of steam applied and the period of exposure of the dough pieces to the steam must be adjusted primarily:
— to the bread type;
— to the oven temperature; and
— to the degree of fermentation maturity of the dough pieces.

Even large deviations in the steam application have almost no influence on the volume of the product. But the shape of the product and even the cell structure vary depending on the amount and type of steam application.

No exact indications can be made with regard to the quantity of steam to be applied before and after loading of dough pieces into the oven (nor for the length of exposure up to the moment when the exhaust vent is opened). The interrelationship between fermentation maturity of the dough pieces, the oven temperature and the steam application is shown in *Fig. 362.*

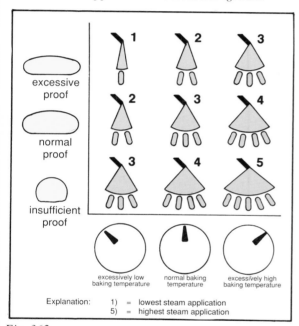

Fig. 362

> **Remember:**
>
> ➤ In case of insufficient proof, the steam application must be higher.
>
> ➤ This has a favorable effect on the extensibility of the product skin, which also retains its crispness.
> Round shaping of the bread is reduced. The product volume can develop better.
>
> ➤ In case of excessive proof, the steam application must be smaller.
>
> ➤ Crust formation starts earlier. The bread has less tendency to flatten out.

But even when the fermentation maturity is optimal and the oven temperature correct, it is important to apply the steam in an appropriate fashion to avoid bread deficiencies.

Steam application: high   average   low
(Rye bread, low proof)

Fig. 363

Effect of various steam application modes on the volume and cell structure of rye bread (baked at low proof)

Effect of the quantity of steam applied on the quality of the bread	
too little	*too much*
— *dull crust*	— *very shiny crust*
— *pale color of the bread crust*	— *transversal cracks in the crust*
— *longitudinal cracks in the crust*	— *very flat bread bottom*
— *low curvature of the bread*	

One must consider that steam generation consumes a lot of energy. Therefore, excessive steam application can have a negative effect on the cost of bread production.

Volume Changes During Baking

At the beginning of the baking process bread dough pieces flatten out when steam is first applied. However, after about two to three minutes, the dough rises and significantly increases in volume.

This increase in volume during baking and the curvature of the product are characteristic of the baking process. These phenomena are caused through the expansion of the fermentation gases and the steam pressure.

The crust of wheat-flour products rapidly turns rigid during baking. When this happens, no further increase in bread volume is possible. The crust of rye and mixed rye bread remains extensible during the entire baking time. Therefore, it can increase in volume until the end of the baking time.

What causes the increase in the volume of bread containing rye? The number of dough cells is determined by the makeup of the dough. Their size and the possible gas pressure inside the cells is determined by the proofing procedure.

161

The relationship between dough piece development and increase in volume in the oven (bread)			
Proofing time	*Cell structure*	*Effect on the increase in volume in the oven*	
too short	*small cells*	*round shape;* *a strong increase in volume in the oven compared to the original volume causes the bread to take a round shape and cracks to form in the crumb*	
normal	*normal size cells*	*adequate increase in volume in the oven*	
too long	*excessively large cells*	*excessively flat shape;* *the cells cannot resist the gas pressure; the cell walls break, large cells form and fermentation gases escape*	

In addition to correct proofing times, the following factors have a positive effect on the increase in bread volume in the oven:
— doughs with a good gas formation and gas retention capacity;
— dough additives enhancing the fermentation processes;
— preparation of a soft dough;
— higher air humidity during proofing;
— higher initial temperatures during baking;
— application of an optimum quantity of steam;
— wide spacing of the dough pieces in case of excessive proof, and narrow spacing in case of insufficient proof.

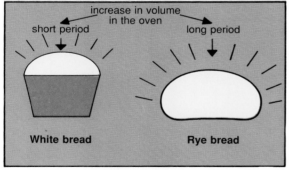

Fig. 364 Increase in volume of wheat-flour products and rye products in the oven

Fig. 365
Bread with a shiny and well-developed crust

162

How to Supervise and Control the Baking Process

Crumb and crust formation differ widely depending on the bread type, the size of the product, and the baking method used.
The baker can control baking:
— by adjusting the baking temperature;
— by adjusting the baking time; and
— by adjusting the steam application.

In addition, he can use a large number of measures in order to obtain the desired bread characteristics. Using light-colored basket bread and country-style bread as examples, we can demonstrate the effect of various measures.

Measures used for country-style bread	*Measures used for light-colored basket bread*
➤ *high initial baking temperature*	➤ *normal, decreasing baking temperature*
➤ *low steam application to maintain the floury surface*	➤ *sufficient steam application to obtain a closed, shiny crust*
➤ *stronger upper heat to obtain a strong crust*	➤ *uniform upper and lower heat application*
➤ *longer baking time*	➤ *normal baking time*
➤ *during the last quarter of the baking time, the temperature is again increased*	➤ *appropriate starch paste application after baking*

For technical reasons (e.g. when some areas in the baking oven are cooler than others or to accommodate new batches) it is sometimes necessary to move the bread during baking. In baking ovens with a high temperature prebaking hearth, the bread loaves are moved into another hearth during the baking process.

This type of operation must be carried out carefully, because the not-yet-stabilized crumb has a tendency to ring or band formation.

End of the Baking Phase

How does a baker determine the end of the baking phase for bread?

Although the end of the baking phase is established primarily based on the color of the crust for small wheat-flour products, there are several other ways to determine the end of the baking phase for bread:
— based on the baking time;
— based on the knocking method (by knocking against the product bottom, a "hollow" sound indicates completion of baking);
— based on weight samples;
— based on the color of the crust.

Bread loaves coming right out of the oven must be handled very carefully; they cannot be placed too close together or one on top of another.

When a shiny product is desired, the bread should be coated with water or a starch paste immediately after baking in order to dissolve the dextrines and the soluble sugar in the crust, and to distribute them evenly to increase the shininess of the crust.

A closed bread crust protects the moist inside part of the bread. It prevents the crumb from drying out and also protects against attacks by micro-organisms. Since all mold germs are destroyed during baking, bread coming out of the oven is free from mold spores.

After baking, the bread must be allowed to cool properly. Short-term storage until the bread is offered for sale should:
— be done under hygienic conditions; and
— ensure fresh-keeping properties of the bread.

Appropriate room temperatures range between 18 and 20°C at a relative air humidity of 70%.

Baking Loss and Bread Yield

Weigh several bread loaves from the same oven batch about one hour after they have cooled and compare:
— the weights of the various bread loaves;
— the weights of the bread loaves in relationship to their dough input; and
— the weights of the bread loaves with those of the same bread type baked on the previous day.

You will notice that a weight loss has occurred during baking, cooling and storage of the bread loaves.

Fig. 366 **Country-style bread varieties**

Fig. 367 **Establishing the end of the baking phase by knocking on the bottom of a bread loaf**

Fig. 368 **This is how a well-baked rye bread crust should look**

Fig. 369 **Check the weight of the bread loaves**

163

* *The weight differential between the dough input and the weight of the product on the day of production is called the baking loss.*

The baking loss is first determined in grams, then it is related to the dough weight (the dough input) as a percentage, for example:

Dough input .... 1,150 g
Bread weight .... 1,000 g
_____

Baking loss .... 150 g
Calculation: 1,150 g   =   100%
                     150 g   =   ? %
_____

$$\frac{100 \times 150}{1,150} = 13\%$$
(rounded up)

The amount of the baking loss depends on a large number of factors, such as:
— the firmness of the dough;
— the dough processing method;
— the degree of softness of the dough;
— the degree of fermentation maturity;
— the baking temperature and the baking time;
— the product size; and
— the product shape and the product type.

Therefore, the baking loss is determined in order to calculate the correct dough input. *Table 54* shows sample values for baking losses.
When the final bread weight is related to 100 parts by weight of flour, bread yield (BY) is obtained.

* *The bread yield is the quantity of product obtained with 100 parts by weight of flour.*

Example:
The baker uses 40 kg flour to make bread. He obtains 60 kg bread (end product).
How high is the bread yield?
Calculation:

40 kg flour yields .... 60 kg bread
100 kg flour yield .... ? kg bread

$$\frac{60 \times 100}{40} = 150 \text{ BY}$$

The bread yield is of practical importance to establish the quantity of flour required. It is also a basis for the calculation.

Like the baking loss, the bread yield depends on various factors, e.g.:
— the flour quality;
— the baking agents added;
— the dough firmness;
— the fermentation process; and
— the baking loss.

Reference:
In the chapter entitled **Makeup of Wheat Doughs**, *the factors having an effect on the baking loss are shown in detail. Read this chapter again if you need more information.*

Bread shape	Average baking losses	
	Bread weight	Baking loss
baked without a pan	500 g	16 – 22%
baked without a pan	1,000 g	9 – 15%
baked without a pan	1,500 g	8 – 12%
baked without a pan	2,000 g	7 – 11%
baked in a pan	1,000 g	8 – 12%
baked in an enclosed pan	1,000 g	8 – 10%

Table 54

Remember

Formula to calculate the baking loss (BL) in per cent

$$BL = \frac{(dough\ input - bread\ weight) \times 100}{dough\ input}$$

Examples for bread yields of 1-kg-bread loaves	
Bread type .... Bread yield	
Coarse rye bread .... 154 – 157	
Rye bread .... 152 – 155	
Mixed rye bread .... 149 – 153	
Mixed wheat bread .... 144 – 148	

Table 55

Remember

Formula to determine the bread yield

$$BY = \frac{product\ weight \times 100}{flour\ weight}$$

Bread Evaluation

Fig. 370 **Evaluation of bread by experts**

Are you able to accurately determine the quality of a bread?

Bread evaluation aims at determining the quality of a bread. This is done, for example, during official bread examinations by the bakery trade or by the bread industry.

But the baker should always check the bread himself to determine its quality.

What is the criteria for evaluation of the quality of bread?

Experts in the judging of bread base their evaluation on the following six criteria, which are designed specifically for hearth, wheat-flour, mixed rye, rye, coarse rye and whole-grain breads.

1. *Form and makeup of the bread*
2. *Crust, surface of the bread*
3. *Tenderness and cell structure*
4. *Elasticity of the bread crumb*
5. *Structure of the bread crumb*
6. *Smell and flavor of the bread*

Evaluation Based on Specific Criteria

The evaluation table showing the various criteria for bread evaluation indicates many deficiencies. The points deducted for each deficiency are also listed.

Example:

The crust at the bottom of a bread is burnt; therefore, only 4 of the 5 points available for the criteria "crust" are awarded.

Example:

If the crust shows two types of deficiencies (very thin crust, uneven color), then only 3 of the 5 points are awarded.

If two or more types of deficiencies are stated for one criteria, the lowest number of points for this criteria is awarded.

Judges who have received special training for official bread examinations evaluate all criteria through sensorial tests. Based on their evaluations, they establish a quality number for the bread (see *Table 57 on p. 166*).

Factors used for Bread Evaluation Criteria		
	Factor x 5 = maximum points	
1. Form/make-up	= 1 x 5 =	5
2. Crust/surface	= 1 x 5 =	5
3. Degree of tenderness/ cell structure	= 3 x 5 =	15
4. Elasticity	= 3 x 5 =	15
5. Structure	= 3 x 5 =	15
6. Smell/flavor	= 9 x 5 =	45
	= 20 ⟶	100

Table 56

As you can see by looking at the criteria, they do not all have the same weight in determining the quality. The bread flavor, for example, is assigned nine evaluation factors; thus it is rated three times as high as the criterion "elasticity of the crumb."

The importance of the bread flavor on the evaluation scale can be recognized by the fact that additional salt and acid value determinations are required when the criterion "flavor" receives only 2 or 3 points.

Additional Information

Example for bread evaluation

	Evaluation	x	Factors	=	Points
1. Form/makeup	5	x	1	=	5
2. Crust/surface	5	x	1	=	5
3. Tenderness/ cell structure	4	x	3	=	12
4. Elasticity	5	x	3	=	15
5. Structure	5	x	3	=	15
6. Smell/flavor	4	x	9	=	36
			20		88

Weighted rating : Number of Factors = Quality
88 : 20   = 4.4

Table 57

Fig. 371 **Acid value determination**

Acid values of various bread types	
Mixed wheat bread	6 – 8
Mixed rye bread	7 – 9
Rye bread	8 – 10
Coarse rye and whole grain bread	8 – 14

Table 58

Acid Value Determination and pH Value

The acid value indicates the total amount of acid (acid quantity) contained in the bread. It does not provide any information on the types of acids and the intensity of their flavor (strength). These are indicated by the pH value.

How is the acid value measured? For an exact determination, we must use the standard method (see *Fig. 371*) which includes a bowl, magnetic stirrer, pH value measuring device, burette for caustic soda, measuring beaker, measuring cylinder and a support stand.

Procedure for Determining the Acid Value

The procedure is as follows:
1. Take 10 grams of crumb from the center of the bread, crush it in the bowl and mix it with 5 ml of acetone.

2. Measure 95 ml of distilled water, of which 50 ml are gradually added to the crushed bread crumbs.

3. Pour this slurry into the 200 ml beaker; flush the bowl with the remainder of the water, and add it to the 200 ml beaker.

4. Dip the measuring chain of the pH measuring device into the slurry, then gradually add 0.1 ml of caustic soda with the burette (continuously stirring) until a pH value of 8.5 is reached.

5. After 5 more minutes of stirring, the pH value decreases again (due to subsequently dissolved acid from the crumb particles). Again add caustic soda until a pH value of 8.5 is reached and until this value is maintained for 1 minute.

6. The total amount of caustic soda consumed corresponds to the acid value of the bread. *Table 58* shows the normal acid values of various bread types.

The strength of the acids can be established by determining the pH value.

The following pH values are considered to be normal:

— Mixed wheat	= 5.6 – 5.8
— Mixed rye bread	= 4.6 – 4.8
— Rye bread	= 4.1 – 4.3
— Coarse rye and whole grain bread	= 4.1 – 4.3

Measuring is best performed by using the measuring chain of an electronic pH device, because paper tests and testing liquids are too imprecise.

To evaluate bread flavor, the acid value and the pH value can only be marginally used (e.g. to explain deficiencies). These values can by no means measure the intensity of the desired bread aroma. This can be done only through sensorial evaluation by an expert.

Bread Faults

Fig. 372 Deficient bread - inedible/indigestible bread

What is a deficiency?
A deficiency can only be established when we know exactly how something is supposed to be. This applies to bread as well.

Everybody can see that the bread shown in *Fig. 372* is deficient. But can you also recognize bread deficiencies that are not so obvious? Do you know the causes of bread deficiencies and the ways they can be avoided?

> * *Deficiencies are deviations from the desired quality characteristics of a bread, caused by deficient ingredients or mistakes in the production and storage of the bread.*

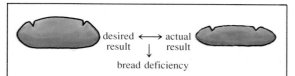

desired ⟷ actual
result   ↓   result
bread deficiency

e.g. caused by:
— deficiencies in the baking ability of the flour;
— error during acidification;
— errors in the recipe;
— errors in the preparation of the dough;
— errors during makeup and fermentation of the dough;
— errors during baking; and
— errors during bread storage.

Further information

On the evaluation sheets for bread examinations, each characteristic to be evaluated (deviation = bread deficiency) is attributed a specific point value.

Find out which bread characteristics are attributed a higher or lower value. Draw conclusions with regard to the evaluation of bread deficiencies.

Bread deficiencies are recognizable only when comparing the deficiency with the desired result. They also vary from bread type to bread type. A floury surface is, for example, considered a deficiency in bread which is supposed to have a shiny crust. However, such a crust is a typical quality characteristic of Berliner country bread and not a deficiency.

The expectations of consumers with regard to "their bread" also have an influence on the classification of deficiencies. Small breaks in the crust, flour particles on the bread crust, and an uneven cell structure are, for example, typical characteristics of country-style bread varieties and are not considered deficiencies.

Some bread deficiencies are considered minor, while others can considerably reduce the flavor and enjoyment value.

Examples of the effects of bread deficiencies on the wholesomeness of bread:

— flat bread aroma ➤ negative effect on the appetite

— excessively acid flavor ➤ indigestion

— inelastic bread crumb ➤ creates a heavy, bloated feeling in the stomach

**Bread Deficiencies
Reduce the Consumption Value**
The elasticity of the bread crumb is an important quality characteristic. The elasticity can be checked by pressing the thumb into the crumb. When the imprint of the thumb in the crumb does not disappear, the crumb is considered to be inelastic (see *Fig. 373*).

Fig. 373

Inelastic Crumb

The elasticity of the crumb varies widely from bread type to bread type. Compare, for example, a white bread, a rye bread, and a coarse grain bread, and you will notice crumbs with widely varying degrees of elasticity. It is the structure of the cell walls in the bread crumb that determines the elasticity. In bread containing rye, the structure of the cell walls depends on the degree of paste formation achieved. An insufficient degree of paste formation leads to a low stability of the cell walls and an inelastic crumb.

Fig. 374
Water bands indicative of an inelastic crumb

Water Bands

The large water band (pasty crumb) at the bottom of the bread occurs simultaneously with an inelastic crumb and often is accompanied by a hollow space under the upper crust.

The water band forms at the beginning of the baking process and is due to insufficient water retention in the crumb. The crumb is weakened; the starch paste forms a deposit. The pasty substance cannot retain the fermentation gases and settles at the bottom of the bread (*Fig. 374*).

Problems Slicing Bread

If bread cannot be sliced after it has cooled, it is also difficult to apply a spread to it. A moist crumb (see *Fig. 375*) or moist bread crumbs are indicative of insufficient water retention.

The causes could be varied:
— growth-impaired rye flour or a high enzymatic activity in the flour
— insufficient acidification of the dough
— excessively high dough yield
— insufficient quantity of salt added to the dough, or lack of salt
— insufficient baking time

Fig. 375 **Bread with a very moist crumb can be difficult to slice**

Fig. 376
Dry crumb and thin crust

When the crumb is too dry (see *Fig. 376*), the cell walls are so thin that they break when the bread is sliced. In our example, the dough contained a high amount of wheat flour and was too stiff. It was also overproofed and baked at too low a baking temperature.

Bread Deficiencies
Reduce the Flavor of the Bread
Deficient Bread Flavor

It is not possible to argue about flavor, and the expectations of consumers with regard to the flavor of bread depend also on the type of bread produced.

In consumer surveys, the majority of complaints are directed against deficiencies in the bread flavor.

Three common deficiencies regarding bread flavor:
— When the bread crumb is inelastic, the bread often tastes pasty. The crumb contracts when chewed. The aromatic substances are locked into the crumb paste. Therefore, the bread tastes flat.
— A flat bread flavor, when the structure of the crumb is otherwise stable, occurs when the dough has not been sufficiently acidified and when the baking time is too short. This deficiency becomes even more apparent when light-colored flour is used and when not enough salt is added.
— The bread tastes too sour when the sour content is too high, or when an excessive amount of acidifying agents are added to the dough. But often the reason is an excessively high acetic acid content in the sourdough. This is the case when the sourdough is prepared in an excessively cool environment, in which the production of acetic acid is furthered.

Excessively Small Volume

When the bread volume is too small, other quality deficiencies often occur at the same time: e.g., excessively dense crumb and dense cells. The expert can easily recognize that these deficiencies are caused when the dough is too firm or not sufficiently aerated.

Excessively Light or Dark-Colored Crust

These deficiencies are frequently caused by inadequate baking temperatures, but they can also be indicative of deficiencies in the dough.

The color of the crust is too light:
— when the flour is fresh and contains a low amount of enzymes; and
— when the dough is too warm, or when the dough is too old.

The color of the crust is too dark:
— when the flour is rich in enzymes; and
— when the dough is too cool, or when the dough is too young.

Fig. 377 **Excessively light-colored, thin crust vs. excessively dark crust**

Breaks Occurring in the Crust

When breaks occur on the entire bread surface, they are indicative of deficient steam application during baking. An excessive application of steam, e.g., an unopened vent, leads to transversal breaks (across the width of the bread) and produces a shiny surface (*Fig. 378*).

The crust breaks along the side of the bread loaf (*Fig. 379*) when the bread is baked without a pan and when the loaves are placed too close together. This deficiency is exaggerated at excessively high proofing, or when the oven is too cold. Similar breaks occur when the dough pieces have stuck to the proofing basket or to the cloth.

Fig. 378 **Breaks in the crust**

Fig. 379 **Break along the side of the bread loaf**

Sugar Blisters

A checkered crust with "sugar blisters" is often indicative of a weak crumb. Sugar blisters occur above hollow spaces between the crumb and the crust. This type of deficiency is prevalent in bread made with flour of a high enzyme content.

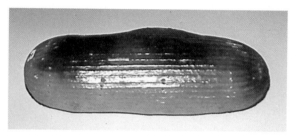

Fig. 380 **Sugar blisters**

Breaks Occurring in the Crumb

Breaks in the crumb can be due to a number of reasons:

— When the bread is exposed to very high prebaking temperatures, the excessive gas pressure causes breaks. The cells break and cracks form in the crumb (*Fig. 381*).
— When the bread is baked too long, the crumb dries out and breaks. This type of deficiency often occurs at the ends of bread loaves with a convex shape. The ends bake through too long, and cracks form (*Fig. 382*).
— Stress occurring in the bread during the cooling process can cause cracks in the crumb, especially when the crumb is not sufficiently cohesive. This often happens when the dough is too firm (*Fig. 383*).

Fig. 381 **Horizontal break in the crumb. Reason: excessively high bottom heat, or insufficient elasticity of the crumb**

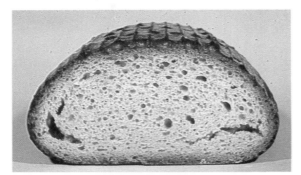

Fig. 382 **Side breaks in the crumb caused by high baking temperatures**

Fig. 383

Vertical break in the crumb caused by stress occurring in the crumb during the cooling phase

Fig. 384 **Water ring**

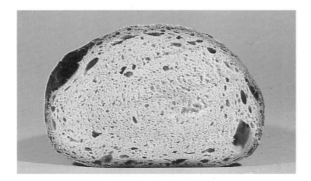

Fig. 385 **Air pockets occurring when the crumb is not sufficiently cohesive**

170

Water Ring

A water ring in the crumb forms:

— during baking at excessively high initial temperatures, when the increase in volume during baking causes the doughy center part to press against the firm outer layers; and

— during the cooling phase of bread with a very tender and inelastic crumb, when the cool outer layers press against the hot center part.

In both cases, a ring with denser cells forms. This deficiency is incorrectly called a "water ring." The water content is actually identical in the ring and in the remainder of the crumb.

The expert has no problem determining deficiencies in bread with a water ring.

— The ring formed during baking contains a very loose center crumb, making it difficult to apply a spread to this area.

— The water ring formed during the cooling phase contains an inelastic crumb.

Air Pockets in the Crumb

The hollow spaces (air pockets) in the crumb can also have widely differing causes.

— They can occur in an inelastic crumb with blisters between the crumb and the crust (*Fig. 385*).

— They can occur when the dough has been mixed too soft and too warm and is subjected to a high fermentation activity. In this case, air pockets occur simultaneously in many areas of the crumb (*Fig. 386*).

— They can occur when the dough pieces have been misshaped. In this case, the air pockets occur only in a few areas in the crumb. The inside surface of the pockets is smooth and shiny (*Fig. 387*).

— They can occur when the dough is too soft. In this case, the cells are very uneven (*Fig. 388*).

Fig. 386 **Air pockets in bread made with excessively soft and warm dough**

Fig. 387 **Air pockets due to inadequate shaping of the dough**

Fig. 388 **Air pockets and uneven cells due to excessively soft dough (right); for comparison purposes, a bread made of excessively firm dough (left)**

List of Major Bread Faults

Faults	➤ Possible Causes	Faults	➤ Possible Causes
Deficiencies in the shape of the bread		**Deficiencies in the bread crumb**	
1. Excessively small bread volume	➤ — flour low in enzymes — insufficient aeration — excessively firm dough — insufficient increase in volume in the oven	1. Inelastic, moist crumb	➤ — flour rich in enzymes — young dough — excessively soft dough — insufficient acidification of the dough — insufficient baking time
2. Excessively young bread	➤ — excessively firm dough — insufficient proofing	2. Dry crumb	➤ — excessively firm dough — high wheat content — excessive aeration — excessive volume increase during baking — initial temperature too low
3. Excessively flat bread	➤ — excessively soft dough — excessive proofing		
4. Irregular shape	➤ — excessively soft dough — sticks to pans	3. Water ring	➤ — excessive proof and baking temperature too high, or — excessive aeration
Deficiencies in the bread crust		4. Water band	➤ — flour rich in enzymes — insufficient acidification of the dough
1. Breaks in the crust	➤ — insufficient steam application, or lack thereof — excessive steam application	5. Dense cells	➤ — excessively firm dough — insufficiently matured dough — insufficient aeration
2. Breaks in the crust along the side of the bread loaf	➤ — dough pieces too close — flattened dough pieces — insufficiently heated oven — sticks to pans	6. Large cells	➤ — excessively aged dough — excessively soft dough — excessive aeration
3. Breaks in the seam	➤ — excessive use of flour during dough makeup — excessively firm dough	7. Uneven cells	➤ — excessively warm dough — excessively soft dough — excessively aged dough — excessive proof — excessively old sourdough
4. Excessive browning	➤ — flour rich in enzymes — moist, young dough — high baking temperatures		
5. Insufficient browning	➤ — fresh flour, few enzymes — warm, old dough — baking temperature too low	8. Dry cracks	➤ — excessively firm dough — flour with a low amount of enzymes
6. Sugar blisters	➤ — young dough — insufficient acidification — flour rich in enzymes	9. Air pockets	➤ — too much upper or lower heat — make-up deficiencies — excessively long baking time
Deficiencies in the bread flavor			
1. Flat flavor	➤ — insufficient acidification — insufficient amount of salt — insufficient aeration — insufficient baking time		
2. Acid flavor	➤ — excessive acidification — excessive acetic acid content		

How to Avoid Bread Deficiencies

It is difficult even for the expert to correctly establish the causes of bread deficiencies and to identify appropriate measures for avoiding them. The above list of major bread deficiencies shows us how manifold the causes of some bread deficiencies can be. The causes of known bread deficiencies and measures for avoiding them are shown in the table on the following page.

Cause of the deficiency	➤ Consequence: bread deficiencies	➤ Measures taken to avoid bread deficiencies
flour containing an insufficient amount of enzymes, rich in starch	➤ small bread volume, poor aeration, insufficient browning of the crust, limited shelf life, dry crumb	➤ addition of enzymatic baking agents ➤ preparation of a soft dough ➤ longer dough resting time
growth-impaired flour or high enzymatic activity	➤ inelastic crumb, strong browning of the crust, sugar blisters, water rings	➤ addition of flour with a better baking ability ➤ increase of sour content or addition of a larger amount of dough acidifying baking agents ➤ preparation of a firmer dough ➤ less proofing ➤ more thorough baking
immature sourdough (similar: insufficient sour content)	➤ round shape of the bread, uneven cells, moist crumb with water ring, flat taste	➤ addition of a larger amount of acidifying baking agents and yeast to the bread dough ➤ preparation of a warm dough ➤ changing sourdough preparation method
excessively mature sourdough	➤ broad shape, tough crust, unpleasant acid taste	➤ reduction of the sour content and replacement of a part of the sourdough with dough acidifying baking agents ➤ preparation of a new sourdough
excessively soft dough	➤ irregular shape, uneven cells, formation of bubbles underneath the crust	➤ less proofing time ➤ maintaining extensibility of the crust for as long as possible ➤ thorough baking
excessively firm dough	➤ small volume, dense cells, breaks in the crumb, dry crumb	➤ baking dough pieces at full proof
short intermediate proof	➤ small volume, round shape, dense cells in the crumb, tendency to form water rings	➤ higher steam application ➤ even better: prolonging proofing
long intermediate proof	➤ irregular shape, flat shape, large flat cells, risk of breaks in the crust along the side of the bread loaf	➤ hot oven ➤ reducing steam application ➤ ensuring wider spacing between bread baked without a pan
oven temperature too low	➤ broad shape, light color, hard crust, flat taste	➤ prolonging baking time slightly
oven temperature too high	➤ excessively strong browning of the crust, risk of insufficient baking of the center part	➤ higher steam application ➤ opening steam exhaust vent for a longer period of time
insufficient steam application	➤ small volume, dull crust with breaks	➤ adjusting steam application to the degree of proofing
excessive steam application	➤ flat shape, breaks in the crust, very shiny crust	➤ adjusting steam application to the degree of proofing
insufficient baking time	➤ leathery crust, insufficient browning, moist crumb, flat taste	➤ matching corresponding baking time and baking temperature
excessively long baking time	➤ hard, thick crust, possibly excessive browning of the crust, breaks in the crumb	➤ matching corresponding baking time and baking temperature
premature stacking of the baked bread	➤ increase of crumb density at the points of pressure, deformations, bread loaves sticking together	➤ adequately cooling the bread ➤ not stacking bread while warm or very fresh

Comparison Between Fresh and Stale Breads

When comparing the taste of fresh bread and old bread, you will clearly notice differences in the characteristics of the two.

In the picture opposite, it is easy to recognize one generally known difference between fresh and old bread — the condition of the crumb. The one-kg weight sinks into the fresh bread crumb; the crumb is soft and elastic. However, the old bread carries the weight; it is firm and rigid.

But this is not the only difference between old and fresh bread:

Characteristics	
fresh bread	*old bread*
— *crisp crust*	— *soft, leather-like crust, turning hard*
— *soft, elastic crumb*	— *firm, dry crumb*
— *fresh, aromatic smell*	— *flat smell*
— *pronounced flavor*	— *little flavor*
— *normal product weight*	— *smaller product weight*

Processes Occurring When Bread Ages

Based on the various changes in the quality of maturing bread, one can already see that it is not only the water loss that ages the bread. Various biochemical and physical processes occur. Let us explain these processes:

→ Immediately after baking, the bread crust contains about 5 to 10% water, and the crumb contains between 40 and 50% water.
During storage, the water content of the bread crumb and crust approaches the same percentage. The crust loses its crispness. First it becomes "softer," and the longer the bread is stored, the more the crust turns firm and dry.

→ The starch that has turned into a paste during baking forms a soft, moist and elastic crumb structure. When the bread is stored, the starch releases the retained water. This water can evaporate from the product.

Fig. 389

Additional Information
The freshness of the bread is established by measuring how far a penetrometer (see Fig. 390) can penetrate into a standard slice of bread. Fresh bread is easy to penetrate = high penetrometer units.

Fig. 390
Bread examination by means of a penetrometer

Remember	
Aging Bread	
Processes	*Effects*
► *migration of the liquid from the crumb to the crust*	► *loss of crispness, soft crust*
► *retrogradation of the pasty flour starch*	► *granular, solid flour starch*
► *evaporation of substances generating smell/flavor*	► *loss of smell and flavor*
► *evaporation of the water*	► *loss of weight, dry, hard bread*

173

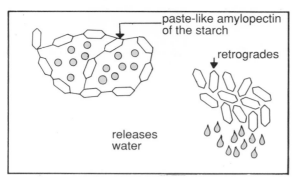

Fig. 391
Retrogradation of the starch

Definition: Minimum freshness period

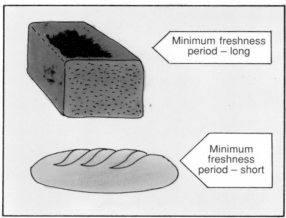

Minimum freshness period – long

Minimum freshness period – short

Fig. 392
Long minimum freshness period of coarse rye bread and short minimum freshness period of white bread

Food Regulatory Guidelines

Examples for the minimum freshness periods of various bread types	
Bread type	Minimum freshness period
Wheat bread	1 – 3 days
Mixed wheat bread	2 – 5 days
Mixed rye bread	5 – 7 days
Rye bread	6 – 10 days
Coarse rye bread	8 – 12 days

Table 59

The ***starch*** itself loses its ability to form a paste. The amylopectin of the starch turns solid and granular from the effect of retrogradation; the amylose leaves the starch and loses its ability to dissolve in water.

→ The ***substances generating the smell and the flavor*** partially evaporate. This causes the round, aromatic flavor of the product to turn flat.

→ The ***loss of water*** through evaporation leads to weight losses (= loss of weight during storage). But the flavor of the bread is also affected by the loss in moisture.

Minimum Freshness Period

The enjoyment value of various bakery products is maintained for different periods of time according to the type of product. This becomes very clear when we compare coarse rye bread and white bread. While coarse rye bread keeps fresh for a long time, white bread loses its freshness rapidly. It is difficult to arrive at a general rule for the minimum freshness period of bakery products.

Remember: *the minimum freshness period is the period of time for which bakery products retain their specific properties when stored under adequate conditions.*

The minimum freshness period can only be determined by the producer, who must consider the product quality based on the recipe. He or she does not have to take into account the storage conditions in the customer's home or the possibility that the customer may open the package.

Indication of the Minimum Freshness Period on Prepackaged Bread

When bakery products are offered for sale in a prepackaged format, the best-before date must be indicated on the package. The following information must be provided:
— name and location of the manufacturer
— trade name
— weight
— list of ingredients
— ***best-before date***
— bilingual description, where applicable

When establishing the ***best-before date***, the quality of the bread itself does not have to be considered. Bread ages whether it is of average or exceptional quality. The loss in freshness of bread is measured in comparison to the initial quality after baking. When the bread loses the quality of its crust and crumb as well as that of its smell and flavor, it also loses freshness. If bread is evaluated based on the five-point system, freshness is one of the criteria for evaluation of quality.

Therefore, the minimum freshness period can be determined as follows: Bread is considered fresh up to the time it has lost 0.5 of the initial five points.

Example: A bread receives 4.8 points during its evaluation. After a certain storage time, the same bread is evaluated again, and this time it only receives 4.3 points because it lost its freshness characteristics. However, the minimum freshness date has not been reached.

The differences in quality between fresh bread and old bread determine the minimum freshness period. The bread is, even after the minimum freshness date, totally acceptable according to general health standards. This means it can be sold and consumed after the minimum freshness date has passed.

If a bread is spoiled, e.g., through mold, within the minimum freshness period, a baker must check to see:
— if the storage conditions were adequate;
— if the packaging was damaged;
— if dirt or other pollutants caused it to spoil;
— if the minimum freshness date should be shortened in the future; and
— if the bread was packaged while it was still warm.

Additional Information

When bakery products are sold in a prepackaged format, the best-before date must be indicated.
The best-before date should be shown along with other pertinent information. A reference to other areas, e.g. "see closing tag for freshness date," is also allowed.

The label normally reads as follows:
"Best before ..."

When the best-before date is less than three months, it is sufficient to indicate the day and the month. This applies to almost all bread varieties.

When the best-before date ranges between three and 18 months, it is sufficient to indicate the month and the year (e.g., "Best before the end of September 19 ..."). This could apply, for example, to Swedish rye.

The date cannot be indicated in the form of a code.

Other dates (e.g., date of manufacture, date of packaging, etc.) are not required.

How to Prolong the Freshness of Bread

The baker can take measures to enhance the fresh-keeping properties of bread during dough preparation (see *Table 60*).

Preventive Measures During Dough Makeup

Flour Types and Flour Mixes used for bread have a large influence on the minimum freshness period. Darker flour containing a larger amount of fibre material and coarse grains improves the swelling capacity of the dough. It has a positive effect on the formation of starch paste, and the end product keeps fresh for a longer period of time.

Summary of conditions having an effect on the fresh-keeping qualities of the bread	
shorter	longer
— light-colored wheat flour in the dough	— dark-colored wheat flour in the dough
— light-colored rye flour in the dough	— dark-colored rye flour in the dough
— straight dough preparation method	— coarse rye in the dough
— preparation of a firm dough	— indirect dough preparation method
	— preparation of a soft dough
	— addition of sour milk products
	— addition of fats and baking agents enhancing fresh-keeping properties

Table 60

In addition to this, the baker can *improve paste formation of the starch by using dough additives*, or by adjusting the dough processing conditions:
— by using the indirect processing method;
— by preparing soft, cool doughs;
— by adding sour milk products; and
— by adding baking agents containing water-absorbing substances.

Pasty starch can make the bread crumb stay moist longer.
Fats and special fresh-keeping baking agents used as dough ingredients allow the formation of compounds with the pasty starch. The compounds later prevent the retrogradation of starch.
These measures are of special importance in years when the flour is dry.
When using anti-staling agents, it is mandatory to follow the quantities specified by the manufacturer. The quantity added must also be adjusted to the flour quantity because an excessive amount of anti-staling agents can make the crumb too moist and chewy.

Additional Information

A distinction must be made between fresh-keeping agents and food preservatives. Fresh-keeping agents are used to delay retrogradation and recrystallization of the starch that has formed a paste in the product. Preservatives are used to delay mold formation.

Fresh-keeping agents contain the following:
— *substances increasing water absorption during dough preparation (pre-gelatinized starch, guar gum flour);*
— *substances increasing the content of soluble matter in the flour (agents containing enzymes); and*
— *substances forming complex compounds with the starch and thereby delaying retrogradation of the starch (fats and emulsifying agents).*

Commercial fresh-keeping agents usually contain two or three of the above substances. Pure enzymatic compounds, which contain a large amount of soluble substances, achieve a moister product crumb, but at the same time, the risk of an inelastic crumb is present when flour is weakened by additives.

A combination of agents to increase water absorption during dough preparation, through vegetable thickeners (hydrocolloids), fats or emulsifying agents, has a favorable effect. This improves the swelling in the dough through increased water absorption (about 3%). This increased amount of water can be stabilized during baking, when the emulsifying agents form complex compounds with the amylose of the starch, thus allowing the starch to maintain its solubility in water.

Although fresh-keeping agents can delay the retrogradation processes in the starch, they cannot prevent the loss of substances which generate product smell and flavor.

Fig. 393 **Packages containing partially-baked products**

The addition of "day-old" bread to the dough can also increase the bread's fresh-keeping properties. However, it is important to note that only a clean, mold-free, day-old bread (soaked and reduced to pieces) of the same kind, produced in the same bakery, can be added. The quantity added cannot exceed 3% of the total quantity of flour used.

In the case of whole meal bread and Pumpernickel, the maximum amount of leftover bread that can be added to a dough is 10% of the grain products. Leftover bread containing preservatives can only be added to bread varieties which can themselves be preserved.

Measures Used During the Baking of Bread

The conditions under which bread is proofed and baked also have an influence on its fresh-keeping properties.

→ Cool and soft doughs containing a small amount of yeast yield a moister bread crumb = they keep fresh for a longer period of time.
→ Optimum fermentation maturity yields a tender, voluminous product with a good crust and crumb, enhancing fresh-keeping characteristics of the bread.
→ High initial baking temperatures, decreasing after a certain time, have a favorable effect on the formation of crust and crumb.
→ When the baking temperature and the baking time are adjusted correctly, an optimum crust and the desired moist-elastic crumb can be achieved. When the baking time is exceeded, the product dries out and the crust turns thick.

Measures that can be taken during the baking of bread in order to delay the aging process of bread
1. Do not speed up dough development through high amounts of yeast
2. Prebake or bake at initially high, then decreasing, temperatures
3. Respect the correct baking time
4. Possibly interrupt the baking process for products that are to be stored

Table 61

Partially-Baked Products

While the interrupted baking method can be used for large bread loaves, small products, like baguettes, can be sold in a partially baked condition. These "brown-and-serve" products are prebaked for about two-thirds of the normal baking time. After they have cooled, they are packaged in sealed water/steamproof or carbon dioxide-proof foils. Such products can be stored as follows:

— at normal room temperature in waterproof bags = 2 to 3 days;
— in a deep freeze in waterproof bags = 2 to 3 weeks;
— in a deep freeze in waterproof bags containing a carbon dioxide protective gas = 2 to 3 months.

Interrupted Baking Method

The interrupted baking method can also be considered as a measure to prolong fresh-keeping properties of the bread. In this method, breads are discharged from the oven after about four-fifths of the normal baking time has elapsed. The bread loaves are stored in this condition. After storage, they are baked again, this time for two-fifths of the normal baking time. However, the starch retrogradation process has already started after the end of the first baking period. Therefore, the bread's normal minimum freshness period is reduced after the second baking phase.

Measures Used During Storage of Bread

In a bakery, bread is sold fresh from the oven. It is important to create hygienic conditions for short-term storage. For longer-term storage of whole bread loaves or sliced bread, the storage temperature and the air humidity are of even greater importance.

The process of starch retrogradation causes a change in the freshness characteristics that can be detected by a sensorial examination. The aging process can be slowed down by delaying the process of starch retrogradation.

> *Starch does not undergo retrogradation at temperatures:*
> *— below -7°C (due to ice crystal formation); and*
> *— above 55°C (in the temperature range where the starch remains pasty).*

Therefore, two methods for keeping bread fresh can be used:
➤ deep-freezing
➤ storage in a warm environment

Keeping Bread Fresh Through Deep-freezing

It is technically possible to store whole bread loaves, as well as small and fine bakery products, in a deep freezer.
However, the baker needs a high-performance shock freezer that can cause the temperature to rapidly drop from 35°C to -7°C. A prolonged stay in this critical temperature range promotes the aging of bread. Prolonged exposure to this critical temperature range also leads to premature aging and to a separation of crust and crumb.

> *Prerequisites for correct deep-freezing of bread:*
> → *Freeze bread when it comes out of the oven, with a core temperature of 70°C.*
> → *Use shock-freezing in a highly agitated environment until the core temperature has decreased to -7°C.*
> → *Store in a non-agitated environment at temperatures ranging between -15°C and -18°C for up to a week.*
> → *Avoid defrosting the product or introducing new products during storage.*
> → *Defrost at temperatures ranging between 220 and 240°C under heavy steam application (if possible), whereby the defrosting time depends on the product weight.*

Reference: *The interrupted baking method is described in more detail in the chapter entitled **Baking Processes**.*

Fig. 394 **Storage of bread**

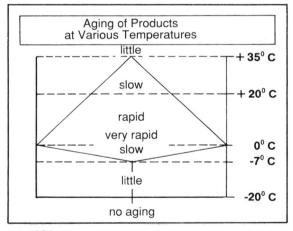

Fig. 395

Food for Thought: *Why should bread not be stored in a refrigerater?*

Measures that can be taken during the storage of bread in order to delay the aging process
1. High storage temperature of about 50°C with relatively good humidity
2. Deep-freezing
3. Packaging with waterproof materials

Table 62

177

Keeping Bread Fresh Through Warm Storage

Bread can be stored for up to two days without losing its freshness at an air humidity of about 80% and temperatures over 50°C.

In this warm environment the starch remains pasty, and starch retrogradation does not occur.

When bread with a high wheat-flour content is stored at temperatures of more than 50°C, the crumb turns brown. The reason for this is the browning albumen-sugar-compounds (Maillard Reaction), the effects of which are especially apparent in the brown crumb of Pumpernickel.

The following method should not be mistaken for having the same effect as warm storage: Bread loaves are packaged, after having cooled to about 50°C, in sealed, waterproof bags made of synthetic material. This method is used to keep the crust and the crumb soft; it prevents evaporation of the water, but not the process of starch retrogradation.

For appropriate storage of bread loaves, it is important to avoid factors that may cause premature aging, softening of the crust, attacks by mold spores, dirt and the absorption of foreign odors.

More details regarding packaging methods and materials are given in the chapter entitled **Sliced Bread Production**.

Additional Information
Special compartments are available for warm storage of bread. These chambers are equipped with fully-automated temperature and air humidity controls.
However, warm storage temperatures and inappropriate air humidity could provide the bread mold with ideal living conditions. Therefore, the air in the storage chambers is circulated and "washed" in a liquid that destroys mold germs. But even under these conditions, bread can only be stored for a short time. The crust turns so soft that rye and mixed rye bread must be baked for a short period of time prior to selling. For mixed wheat bread, a combination of the interrupted baking method and warm storage should be used for best results.

Summary:
Important information about the aging process of bread and how it can be delayed

Bread loses its freshness due to retrogradation of the pasty starch, water migration from the crumb to the crust, water evaporation, and the loss of substances generating smell and flavor.
The minimum freshness period is the period of time during which bakery products maintain their freshness characteristics when stored under appropriate conditions. The minimum freshness period is to be indicated on products sold in a prepackaged format to the consumer.
The minimum freshness period of bread can be prolonged by delaying the retrogradation process of the starch. Such measures can be taken during dough makeup, during baking, or during storage of the bread loaves.

Mold as a Bread Disease

Fig. 396 **Bread mold**

The mold filaments of blue cheese indicate that the cheese is mature. The mold has formed the desired aroma substances.

However, this does not apply to bread mold. When we see white, yellow, green or blue mold patches, the bread is no longer fit for consumption.

Desirable and undesirable molds are both generated by mold fungi. Although they are closely related to each other, they have very different effects.

Mold Fungi

The mold patches appearing on bread are each composed of a whole colony of mold fungi. Although we cannot recognize the individual plants with the eye, they can be identified under a microscope. There are many species of mold fungi. *Figs. 397 to 400* show microscopic pictures of the most common bread fungi:

— watering-can mold
— brush mold
— head mold
— chalk mold

The multi-cellular composition of mold fungi can be clearly recognized with the exception of the chalk fungus, which is actually a form of yeast. "Chalk mold" is generated by many different unicellular yeasts on the bread, and is so named because it appears as a chalky film on the bread surface.

Fig. 397
Watering-can mold
Mop-shaped
(Aspergillus glaucus)

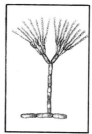

Fig. 398
Brush mold
(Pennicillium glaucum)

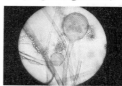

Fig. 399
Head mold
(Mucor mucedo)

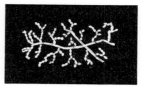

Fig. 400
Chalk mold
(Trichosporon variabile)

Living Conditions of Mold Fungi

Not every bread turns moldy. The following test investigates the conditions for mold growth.

Test 27:

Put two slices each of bread from the same loaf into four plastic bags. Store each package for five days:
A) closed at room temperature
B) open at room temperature
C) closed in the refrigerator
D) closed in the freezer

Observations:

A) The bread has turned moldy.
B) The bread has not turned moldy, but it is very dry.
C) The bread has not turned moldy, but it is somewhat dry.
D) The bread has not turned moldy, and its crumb is moist.

Conclusions:
— Mold requires nutrients to live. Bread is a good nutrient medium.
— Mold requires moisture to live. Dry bread does not turn moldy.
— Mold requires a certain temperature to live. Bread stored in a cool environment or in a freezer does not turn moldy.

Additional Information
After the mold fungi have germinated on the surface of the bread, tube-like fungus filaments grow into the bread. There, they branch out and form a root-like structure called mycelium that is invisible to the eye. The mycelium absorbs the nutrients from the bread. These are decomposed, then used to build the cells of the mold fungi and noxious matter that penetrates the bread crumb. In some places, spore carriers grow from the mycelium. Mold fungi can be recognized by the differing forms and colors of the spore carriers. The spores themselves cannot be recognized by the naked eye. They are dispersed and, under favorable conditions, they can germinate into new mold fungi.

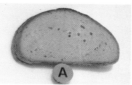

Fig. 401   **Fig. 402**

Slices of bread stored at room temperature in a moist (A) and in a dry (B) environment

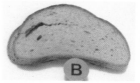

Fig. 403   **Fig. 404**

Slices of bread stored in the refrigerator (C) and in the freezer (D)

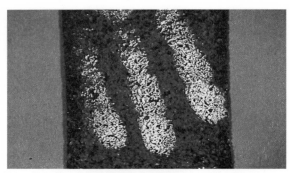

Fig. 405 Chalk mold has been transmitted by hand to the bread. Prevent mold infections by establishing sanitary conditions.

Fig. 406

Example:
A bakery owner takes strict measures to control bread mold in his/her bakery. The economic damage caused by mold makes hygienic measures a must. Bread quickly turns moldy during the summer months. For that season, technological measures for mold control are also recommended.
What kind of measures can be used for mold control?

Hygienic measures for mold control

1) *Avoid moist-warm room temperatures (to avoid growth of mold on the walls, etc.).*
2) *Remove moldy raw materials and products and destroy them.*
3) *Wash wooden storage shelves with water containing vinegar.*
4) *Reduce flour dust development.*
5) *Remove residues and waste material from equipment and tools.*
6) *Wash "molded areas" with a 1% formalin* solution (*a very weak aqueous solution of formaldehyde).*
7) *If necessary, use air filters and air circulation in storage rooms.*
8) *Store packaging materials in a cool, dry environment and protect them against dust.*
9) *Pay strict attention to personal hygiene.*

Bread mold needs moisture and warmth to grow. In bread, it is the free water that promotes mold growth. Except for Knackebrot (Swedish rye crackers), all bread varieties contain so much free water that they can easily turn moldy.

Mold fungi grow best in the temperature range between 4°C and 40°C.

With the exception of chalk mold, all mold fungi need oxygen to live.

Freezing temperatures do not destroy the mold fungi. After food products have been defrosted, the fungi continue to live. Mold fungi and spores are only destroyed during baking.

Some mold fungi form dangerous poisonous substances (mycotoxins) during nutrient transformation. These can be carcinogenic (e.g., aflatoxin, patulin) or have a directly poisonous effect (e.g., penicillin acid).

These poisonous substances continue to exist in the food product. They are not destroyed during baking.

Therefore, the baker must ensure that moldy (spoiled), and thus unhealthy, products are not stored. Raw materials must also be free from mold.

Mold Control

Hygienic Measures in the Bakery
The air in the room, the walls, the floor, the raw materials, the equipment, the tools, and also the staff (food-handlers) can at all times transmit mold spores.

The most important measures for mold control must therefore be taken in the bakery itself.

The cooling area (cooling rooms) for bread and bread storage in large bakeries is equipped with:
— filters for dust separation;
— "magnetic" ceilings attracting dust; and
— ultraviolet lights.

Ceilings and walls can be coated with a special mold-resistant paint.

Exposed areas, rough surfaces and areas difficult to access should be given special attention during cleaning and should be washed, if necessary, with a 1% formalin solution or vinegar water.

The staff must also pay attention to personal hygiene and keep work clothing impeccably clean.

Technological Measures

Bread mold control starts as soon as the dough is prepared.

Test 28

Prepare six rye breads, each with 100 g of rye flour. Use the following sour contents: 0%, 10%, 20%, 30%, 40% and 50%.
Store two slices of each of these bread loaves in plastic bags, at room temperature, for up to 10 days.
Evaluate the growth of the mold.

Observations:
— Bread loaves without sourdough and with a small sour content turn moldy first.
— Bread loaves with a sour content of 40% and 50% do not turn moldy for about seven days.

Conclusion:
— Mold growth can be delayed through changes in the dough formula.
— Sourdough forms acids (especially acetic acid) which control mold.

Fig. 407
Bread with a sour content of 40% and 50% is protected against mold attacks for up to 7 days

For a longer-lasting protection against mold attacks, for example, when the bread is to be stored, mold inhibitors can be added to the dough.

When using baking agents containing mold inhibitors, the manufacturer's instructions must be carefully followed because:

— the finished product must be labelled accordingly (e.g., the use of sorbic acid as a preservative must be identified);
— certain maximum quantities of added preservatives per kg of finished product must not be exceeded;
— the use of certain substances is only allowed for bread with a reduced calorific value and for sliced bread;
— the fermentation process could be delayed and an increase of the amount of yeast added (by about 1/4 of the normal quantity) could be required.

Additional Information

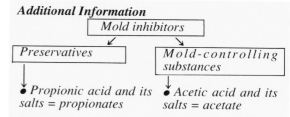

• *Propionic acid and its salts = propionates*

Two forms used — Sodium Propionate and Calcium Propionate.

Recommended usage is 0.3% to 0.5% of flour in white bread and buns; 0.2 to 0.4 % of flour in rye, whole wheat and dark breads.

• *Sorbic acid and its salts = sorbates*

Inhibits yeast fermentation. Consequently, its use is restricted to spraying on finished product.

• *Acetic acid and its salts = acetate*

In the past, it was used extensively in the form of vinegar. However, it is not as cost-effective as the propionates. Some manufacturers can justify a higher cost by its natural vs. chemical connotations in the ingredient list.

• *Acetic acid salt = sodium diacetate is an effective mold protector; proofing, smell and flavor of the bread are, however, affected by its age.*

Three helpful hints:
1. The preservatives and the mold-controlling substances should not be dissolved in water added to the dough, as this would reinforce the retarding effect on the fermentation process.
2. It is important to avoid simultaneous use of the preservative, calcium propionate, and of other fresh-keeping agents because this would greatly reduce the elasticity of the crumb.
3. Leftover dough containing preservatives can only be used to make bread that also contains preservatives (e.g., sliced bread or bread with a reduced calorific value).

During the **baking process** in the oven, other measures for mold control can be taken.
— A closed, firm bread crust is important because mold spores cannot germinate due to the low water content.
— Increase the spacing between bread loaves baked in a pan for a short period of time towards the end of the baking phase so that the sides of the loaves can dry.
— Although a well-baked bread is desirable, a longer baking time (= decrease of the amount of free water in the product) does not significantly contribute to mold control. Only the loss of a large amount of water (e.g., in the case of Swedish rye crackers) is an effective means of mold control.

During **storage and packaging** of bakery products, mold control can be achieved:
— through cool storage = heat abstraction; the disadvantage being, however, premature aging of the bread;
— through evaporation or by not storing bread loaves too close together;
— through heat sterilization of sliced bread; and
— through storage of sliced bread in carbon dioxide protective gas.

Packaging materials and techniques are discussed in detail in a special chapter.

Production of Whole-grain and Specialty Breads

Whole-grain Products

Fig. 408
Whole-meal bread varieties

Whole-grain bread was traditionally produced in the northern part of Germany. As consumers all over the world became increasingly health conscious, these bread varieties became more popular. This is a positive development from the nutritional point of view as whole grain contains desirable fibre substances (cellulose, hemicellulose and lygnin).

Whole-grain Bread Varieties
➤ Their main ingredient is meal.
➤ They contain all components of the grain
➤ They are baked in enclosed (sandwich bread-type) pans or in cellophane bags.
➤ They do not have a strong crust.
➤ The color of the crumb is dark.

Coarsely-ground Whole-meal Breads

This bread type can be produced with coarsely-ground rye and/or wheat meal and must contain the wooden outer shell of the grain, and all other components of the grain, including the germ.
For coarse-meal products, yeast, salt, water, dairy products and sourdough made with whole-grain products are used. The percentage of other wheat or rye flours and/or other additives should not exceed 10%.

Whole-meal Breads

This bread type is made from medium-to-coarse-milled flour (meal) containing all the components of the grain, and can be made with wheat or rye. The percentage of the other rye and/or wheat products should not exceed 10%. In Europe, meals do not contain the germ of the kernel. It is removed in a special milling process.

Bread with a Whole-meal Content

Bread with a whole-meal content of more than 10% and less than 90% cannot be sold as "whole-meal bread." The bread type and the phrase "containing whole meal" should appear on product packaging, e.g., mixed rye bread containing whole meal.

Bread made with Stone-ground Flour

When wheat is ground between stones, the heat generated produces flour with a nutty flavor, but with a short shelf life. Stone-ground flour differs from whole-wheat flour in that whole-wheat flour does not contain any germ components. Because stone-ground flour is produced in one milling stage, it cannot be blended or modified.

Quality Characteristics of Whole-meal Bread

The production of high-quality whole-meal bread requires extensive technical knowledge. The shell material contained in whole-grain or whole-meal products:
— has a negative impact on the cohesiveness of the dough;
— causes the dough to absorb a high amount of water; and
— does not have a strong aroma.

The consumer wants a whole-meal bread:
— with a moist crumb;
— with a sliceable crumb;
— with good fresh-keeping characteristics;
— with an aromatic flavor; and
— with visible, swelled grain particles.

Selection of Whole-meal Products

Coarse particles are visible in some whole-meal bread varieties.

When selecting the meal, the baker must know the correct type of flour and he or she must also be able to distinguish between the various degrees of fineness, e.g., very coarse, coarse, medium and fine meal.

The adjectives "hard" and "soft" are also frequently used to provide additional information about the meal, from which the baker can establish the type of milling process used.

While soft meal is obtained by means of grinding, hard meal is obtained through hammering the grains. While soft meal easily absorbs water, hard meal swells better.

At one time, the meal had to be processed "fresh from the mill," but modern processing and storage techniques have lengthened the fresh-keeping qualities of whole-grain products. Because they contain the germ, whole-grain products are particularly rich in fats and enzymes. They are fit for processing for up to four weeks, provided they are stored in an appropriate, cool environment.

Swelling of Meal Products

In order to obtain a good quality whole-meal bread, measures must be taken to ensure adequate swelling of the meal.

It is recommended that a mixture of about 50% coarse meal and 50% fine meal be used. The coarse meal should be allowed to swell prior to incorporation into the dough.

Fig. 409 **Whole-grain pumpernickel (left) and whole-meal bread (right)**

Fig. 410 **Bread containing whole meal**

Fig. 411
Whole meals with various degrees of fineness

Additional Information

Whole meals must be thoroughly soaked in water. Establish the swelling conditions of whole-meal products:
— *Scale 100 g each of rye meal with the following degrees of fineness: coarse, medium and fine.*
— *Put each meal sample into a beaker and soak in 100 g of water with a temperature of 20°C.*
— *Evaluate the swelling after four hours.*
— *Perform, for comparison purposes, a test with the same sample types, but add boiling water.*
— *Evaluate the swelling after four hours.*

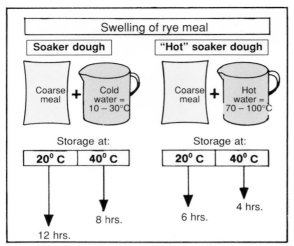

Fig. 412

Food Regulatory Guidelines

Reference:
*For further information about preservatives that can be added to whole-meal breads, refer to the chapter entitled **Sliced Bread Production**.*

Fig. 413 **Whole-meal bread deficiency due to insufficient swelling of the coarse meal**

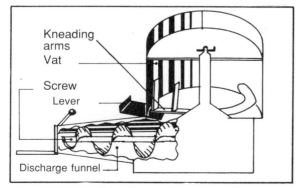

Fig. 414 **Vat kneader for meal doughs, with discharge device**

Between 30 and 40% of the meal quantity is to be used for a sourdough made from whole meal. As meal doughs significantly stiffen, a very soft dough should be prepared with a dough yield (DY) of 200.

The soaker dough and the "hot" soaker dough are prepared with identical amounts of water and meal (DY = 200). The swelling process aims at optimum swelling of the coarse meal. In addition, the baking properties of the meal are changed through the enzymes.

The baking properties are changed even more when the "hot" method is used. Here, hot water with a temperature ranging between 70 and 100°C is added to the meal, turning the starch partly into a paste. Depending on the use of cold or warm storage during these preliminary stages, the enzymatic maturing process can be controlled.

In addition to the sourdough method used and the use of the swelling or "hot" process, adding soaked, leftover bread significantly contributes to increasing the quality of whole-meal bread. While, in principle, only 3% of leftover bread (related to the total flour quantity) can be used for whole-meal bread, up to 10% of the same bread type can be added as leftover bread. This leftover bread must be produced in the same bakery and cannot be spoiled or dirty. Leftover bread containing preservatives can only be added to bread which also contains preservatives.

The soaked leftover bread must be prepared in such a way that it can be easily distributed in the dough; e.g.,
— reduced to pieces and soaked in water to form a paste,
— in the form of bread crumbs, up to a maximum of 6.5% of the total flour content (corresponds to 10%, minus water content, of the moist bread)
  a) mixed with the meal,
  b) soaked in cold water for about 3 hours,
  c) soaked in hot water for about 1 hour.

The leftover bread has the same effect as the addition of high-gluten flour (pasty starch).

The quantity of "hot" soaker dough and leftover bread added must be adjusted to the properties of the rye meal:
— for meal containing a low amount of enzymes = increase of their quantity;
— for meal rich in enzymes = decrease of their quantity.

> **Remember:**
>
> *Whole-meal bread should have the following characteristics:*
>
> — *The bread should be easy to slice.*
> — *The crumb should be aromatic.*
> — *The bread flavor should be well-rounded to sweet.*
> — *The bread should have good fresh-keeping characteristics.*

Model for the Production of Whole-meal Bread

Table 63 shows a model for the production of rye-meal bread. This model incorporates all the measures that can be taken to enhance the swelling.

A whole-meal dough is not mixed very intensively (as in the case of a wheat flour dough). Instead, it should be mixed for 20 to 30 minutes on a very low speed in order to achieve an intensive swelling of all meal particles. The mixing process can often be interrupted for about 10 minutes halfway through the mixing time before continuing.

In bakeries with large-scale, whole-meal bread production, a special mixer equipped with a rotating vat and discharge device is used (see *Fig. 414* on page 184).

Shaping and Baking of Whole-meal Bread

The strand of rye-meal dough (prepared manually or by mechanical equipment) is usually cut and shaped to be baked in special pans. In this case, the end product does not have much of a crust and does not dry out as easily, even with a long baking time.

In special steam baking chambers (at 100°C and pressurized), the baking time varies between 12 and 24 hours. When bread is baked for a long time in hot steam (similar to steam bread), it has a moist crumb and no crust. The products of starch decomposition formed during the baking process produce a sweet flavor and longer-lasting freshness.

It is best to consume this type of bread at least 12 hours after baking.

Small Bakery Products Containing Meal

Meal is not used solely for large bread loaves and sliced bread. With the increasing popularity of country-style bakery products, small bakery products made of rye meal or wheat meal have become more and more popular.

The table below is a model for the production of wheat/rye whole-meal rolls with the following components:

— Wheat meal (fine)	= 6.000 kg
— Rye meal (fine)	= 3.500 kg
— High-gluten flour	= 0.300 kg
— Mixed baking agent with lecithin	= 0.200 kg
Total quantity	= 10.000 kg

Because the whole-meal dough is moist, the dough for buns/rolls is prepared with a theoretical dough yield of 170.

The recipe yields 10 batches, each comprising 30 pieces of whole-meal rolls with a dough weight of 60 g. The dough pieces are placed onto plates, without having been rounded, and baked at full proof under strong steam application, where applicable (baking temperature = 260/230°C) for about 25 minutes.

These rolls do not have the same crisp crust as light-colored wheat rolls, but their enjoyment value remains unchanged for up to 24 hours.

Model for the production of whole-meal rye bread using 100 kg of meal
Sour content = 35% one-phase sour

Starter = 3.500 kg (do not include quantity in the calculation)

Sour:

Coarse rye meal	= 35.000 kg	Temp.	= 28°C
+ Water	= 35.000 kg	DY	= 200
= Sourdough	= 70.000 kg	Resting time	= 12 hrs.

Soaker dough:

Coarse rye meal	= 20.000 kg	Temp.	= 20°C
+ Water	= 20.000 kg	DY	= 200
= Soaker dough	= 40.000 kg	Resting time	= 12 hrs.

Leftover bread:

Dried leftover bread	= 6.500 kg	70°C broth	
+ Water	= 6.500 kg	temperature,	
= Leftover bread	= 13.000 kg	Resting time	= 1 hr.

Dough

Sourdough	= 70.000 kg		
+ Soaker dough	= 40.000 kg	Dough	
+ Leftover bread	= 13.000 kg	temperature	= 28°C
+ Fine meal	= 38.500 kg	DY	= 178
+ Water *)	= 16.500 kg	Resting time	= 10 min.
= Dough **)	= 178.000 kg		

*)   If necessary, adjust firmness of the dough after the first mixing stage by adding more water.

**)   Salt = 1.800 kg, yeast = 1.000 kg, added to the dough

Table 63

Reference:
*More examples for small bakery specialties are shown in the chapter entitled **Specialty Bread**.*

Model for the production of wheat/rye whole-meal rolls

Starter = 0.10 kg (do not include quantity in the calculation)

1. Sour:

Rye meal	= 2.000 kg	Temp.	= 27°C
+ Water	= 2.000 kg	DY	= 200
= Sourdough	= 4.000 kg	Resting time	= 15 hrs.

2. Soaker dough:

+ Rye meal	= 1.500 kg	Temp.	= 20°C
+ Wheat meal	= 2.000 kg	DY	= 200
+ Water	= 3.500 kg	Resting time	= 15 hrs.
= Soaker dough	= 7.000 kg		

3. Dough:

Sourdough	= 4.000 kg		
+ Soaker dough	= 7.000 kg		
+ Wheat meal	= 4.000 kg	Temp.	= 27°C
+ High-gluten flour	= 0.300 kg	DY	= 170
+ Baking agent	= 0.200 kg	Dough	
+ Yeast	= 0.400 kg	temperature	= 29°C
+ Salt	= 0.200kg	Resting time	= 10 min.
+ Lard	= 0.400 kg		
+ Water	= 1.500 kg		
= Dough	= 18.000 kg		

Table 64

Summary of important information about whole-grain products			
➤ Grain product	➤ Rye-meal (coarse type)	➤ Wheat-meal	➤ Whole-grain rye or wheat products
➤ Special methods of dough processing	➤ Swelling of grain products rich in shell material *through*	— Prolonged sourdough preparation — "Hot" soaker dough — Addition of leftover bread — Additives promoting the swelling process — Long mixing time	
➤ Special methods of baking	➤ Baked in a sandwich bread-type pan ➤ Small amount of crust or no crust	➤ Long baking time	➤ Special baking procedures to obtain a moist crumb and a sweet-sour flavor
➤ Bread category	➤ Whole-meal bread — contains all the components of the grain — up to 10% of additives and/or other grain products can be added	➤ Bread with a whole-meal content — contains more than 10% but less than 90% of the grain products in the form of meal	➤ Bread made from stone-ground flour — has a nutty flavor, but poor fresh-keeping characteristics — contains all components of grain kernel

Specialty Bread

Fig. 415 **Specialty bread**

Fig. 416 **"Stonemason" bread**

Specialty breads differ from standard varieties through their components or methods of production.

The same food regulations apply to specialty breads as to traditional bread varieties.

The German Agricultural Society (DLG) has established a systematic classification of specialty bread varieties. Based on this classification, the following well-known specialty breads are introduced.

Specialty Bread Made With Specially-Treated Milled Products

Stonemason Bread

This is a coarse-grained whole-meal bread. The grain is treated with moisture to separate it from its wooden shell. The full grain, with its valuable shell layers and the germ, is crushed or cut and must be carefully handled to avoid cell structure collapse. The bread can be baked in an ordinary bread pan, giving it its characteristic shape.

186

Steamed Bread

This is a coarse-grained, whole-meal rye bread baked without a pan, to which 15 to 20% of "steamed" flour is added. This type of flour contains shell particles plus the germ of the grain and is treated with steam and heat. During this process, the shell particles are partly decomposed into soluble sugars and become nutritionally valuable. The bread has a somewhat sweet flavor. Through caramelization, the crumb takes on a brown color.

Specialty Bread Using Special Dough Processing Methods

Graham-Rye Bread

This is a coarse-grained, whole-meal rye bread which is not acidified. A slow swelling process is typical for this bread. This type of bread is comparable, as far as the processing methods are concerned, to graham bread made with wheat-meal.

Simons Bread

This is a coarse-grained, whole-meal rye bread which is particularly wholesome and nutritious. These qualities are obtained through the means of an intensive swelling process of the pre-cleaned grain. The swollen grain is crushed in moist condition and further processed with "hot" soaked grain and sourdough. The baking process in the special steam baking chambers takes about 12 hours. This bread takes on a characteristic similar to that of the original Pumpernickel bread.

Specialty Bread Using Special Baking Methods

Bread Baked in a Wood-burning Oven

This bread variety can only be baked in directly-heated masonry ovens. During the heating-up phase, one hour prior to the commencement of the baking process, and during subsequent heating phases, only untreated wood can be used. The high initial heat during baking gives the bread a strong crust.

Bread Baked in a Stone Oven

During the entire baking time, the bread must be baked at a preset temperature level on supports made of fireproof, stone materials.

Bread Baked in Steam "Chambers"

This is a bread without a crust baked in closed pans at temperatures ranging between 100 and 130°C under continuous hot steam application. Bread varieties baked in this environment include rye-meal and Pumpernickel breads.

Pumpernickel must be made with very coarse-grained meal products and baked for at least 16 hours. In the process, the starch of the flour is partly decomposed into soluble sugar. This gives Pumpernickel its sweet flavor and its typical moist, dark-colored crumb (Maillard Reaction = sugar-albumen-compounds). Sweeteners or browning agents are not used for genuine pumpernickel (in some cases, molasses is added). The long baking process has the disadvantage of largely destroying the vitamin thiamin.

Fig. 417 **Pumpernickel**

	Fat	Bran particles	Albu-men	Mois-ture	Carbo-hydrates	kJ in 100 kg
Whole-grain rye bread	1.2	5.7	6.8	40.8	45.5	935
Swedish rye (Knackebrot)	1.7	7.9	11.4	5.4	73.6	1,554

Table 65 **Compare the nutritional value of Swedish rye and coarse-grained, whole-meal rye bread (related to 100 g)**

Reference: *Compare the nutritional value of Pumpernickel and other rye-meal breads based on Table 73 in the chapter entitled **Nutritional Value of Bread**.*

"Gerster" Bread

In the past, Gerster bread was baked in heated ovens through flame application to the dough pieces. The dough skin formed in the process locks in the aroma substances. The flame application process gives a special aroma to the dough skin and the outer layers.

Today, the use of special chambers equipped with gas flames is preferred for producing this type of bread.

The skin of the dough pieces is cut along the sides to ensure that the increase in volume during baking can take place without irregular cracking.

Fig. 418 **"Gerster" Bread**

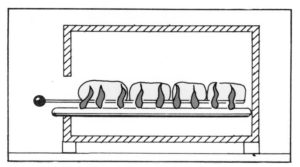

Fig. 419 **Schematic function of the special flame chamber for "Gerster" Bread**

Swedish rye crackers/flat dry bread (Knackebrot)

This type of bread is baked in flat sheets. It is aerated through the use of yeast, sourdough, incorporated air, and also by chemical leavening agents.

While all other bread varieties have a moisture content between 30 and 45%, Knackebrot contains less than 10% water. This is why it is crisp and brittle in texture and has a long, durable life.

The calorific value (per 100 g baked bread) is correspondingly high, but it is actually lower per slice than other bread varieties.

The low water content makes it difficult to make any meaningful comparisons with the nutritional values of other bread types.

"Crisp" bread differs from Knackebrot in that it is not baked, but aerated and heated just like potato chips. This process is explained in more detail under the heading *Additional Information*.

Additional Information
Extruded Products

The correct name of crisp bread is "Extrudat." It is not a specialty bread because it does not fulfil the requirements of bread production and is similar to chips and other snack foods. It is produced in an extruder. The extruder resembles a mincer. It blends, mixes, presses and heats the ingredients in a single process. At the end of the process, the extruder evacuates the substance through a narrow die which causes the substance to solidify.

Specialty Bread Made by Adding Grain Products not Derived from Rye or Wheat

Three-Grain Bread

This type of bread can be made with various specialty grains, e.g., oats, barley, rice, millet or corn, whereby the percentage added must amount to at least 5% per grain product.

Multi-grain bread varieties must contain rye or wheat. An example for three-grain bread is given in Table 66.

When either barley or corn is added, the volume of the bread is smaller than usual and the crumb is darker. When corn is added, the crumb takes on a yellowish color.

Model for the production of three-grain bread made with 10 kg of grain products		
Starter = 0.4 kg (do not include this quantity in the calculation)		
Sour:		
Rye Flour	= 2.000 kg	Temp. = 23°C
+ Water	= 1.600 kg	DY = 180
= Sourdough	= 3.600 kg	Resting time = 12 hrs.
Soaker dough		
Coarse rye-meal	= 2.000 kg	Temp. = 23°C
+ Rice flour	= 1.000 kg	DY = 180
+ Oats	= 0.500 kg	Resting time = 12 hrs.
+ Water	= 3.500 kg	
= Soaker dough	= 7.000 kg	
Dough:		
Soaker dough	= 7.000 kg	
+ Sourdough	= 3.600 kg	Temp. = 26°C
+ Rye flour	= 2.500 kg	DY = 176
+ Wheat flour	= 2.000 kg	Resting time = 10 mins.
+ Water *)	= 2.500 kg	
= Dough	= 17.600 kg	
*) Yeast = 0.4 kg salt = 0.2 kg added to the dough		

Table 66

Fig. 429   **Three-grain bread**

Fig. 421   **Milk-Albumen Bread**

Specialty Bread made by adding Dairy Products

Butter Bread

This type of bread should contain at least 5 kg butter or 4.1 kg pure butter fat per 100 kg flour/grain products.

It cannot contain any other fat matter, with the exception of 0.5% monoglycerides and diglycerides in the dough and the usual baking agents for shaping.

Milk Bread

It should contain at least 50 litres whole milk per 100 kg grain products.

Other types of liquid cannot be added. However, the whole milk content can be achieved by using other diluted milk products.

Sourmilk Bread, Buttermilk Bread, Yogurt Bread and Whey Bread

These bread varieties should each contain 15 parts of the dairy product used per 100 parts grain products. Concentrated dairy products can be used in the corresponding diluted quantity.

> **Reference:**
> *Refer to the chapter entitled Milk and its Importance to the Baking Process to find out more about guidelines applying to bakery products made with dairy products.*

Milk-Albumen Bread

It should contain at least 2 kg milk albumen powder per 100 kg grain products. This quantity is achieved by adding 6 kg commercial, dried skim milk.

Quark Bread

It should contain at least 10 kg quark or a corresponding quantity of dry product per 100 kg grain product. The following *Table 67* shows a model for production of quark rolls made with 20% quark.

Model for the production of quark rolls made with 10 kg of wheat flour

Bread flour (baker's patent)	= 10.000 kg	
+ Quark	= 2.000 kg	
+ Milk powder	= 0.300 kg	
+ Lecithin baking agent mix	= 0.300 kg	Temp. = 26°C
+ Baking margarine	= 0.200 kg	Dough resting
+ Yeast	= 0.500 kg	time = 15 Min.
+ Salt	= 0.200 kg	
+ Water	= 4.800 kg	
= Dough	= 18.300 kg	

Dough input per roll = 55 g
Proofing = 30 minutes
Dough is cut crosswise before baking

Baking temperature = 240°C
Baking time = 20 mins.

Table 67

Specialty Bread made by adding Vegetable Matter

Spice Bread

The amount of spice added to breads such as caraway seed bread, pepper bread and paprika bread should be enough to allow the spice to be detectable by taste.
In caraway seed bread, this is achieved by adding about 8 g caraway seed or 6 g ground caraway seed per kg flour.

Linseed or Sesame Bread

These bread varieties have a higher nutritional value due to the fat content of the oily seeds added. However, this fat content has no effect on the bread baking technique. The required amount is 8 kg of "oily seeds" (the fat of which has not been removed) per 100 kg flour. When a smaller amount is added, the term "bread with linseed" or "bread with sesame" can be used.

Sesame is roasted prior to its incorporation in the dough but it is not roasted when spread over the surface.

To enhance the linseed flavor, use 1/4 of linseed in the form of meal. It is important that the linseeds are fresh and clean. Due to the enormous swelling capacity of the whole linseed bodies, they must soak for four hours in about twice their weight in hot water (100°C).

Fig. 422   **Linseed Bread**

Fig. 423   **Sesame Bread**

Wheat germ Bread

It contains at least 10% wheat germ (with a minimum fat content of 8%) in ratio to bread flour.
Only sugar, yeast and fat are to be added because wheat germ already contains salt from its "cooking" treatment.
A higher than normal dough temperature, short intermediate proof and careful final proof are strongly recommended.

Granary Bread (Malt bread)
This bread contains at least 8 kg **malted** rye or wheat per 100 kg grain products.

Bran Bread
This bread variety meets current consumer needs for high fibre content by adding at least 10 kg clean bran per 100 kg grain products. Although bran still contains 15% dry starch, the nutritional value of bran bread is clearly less than that of other bread.
The bran in the crumb is unsettling to some consumers due to the presence of occasional black specks or spelts (wheat husks). The volume of the bread is also smaller.

Composition of offal and bran as % of dry substance		
Substance	Offal	Bran
Glucose polymers	4.8	10.0
Proteins	10.7	15.7
Fat	7.0	3.6
Ash	4.7	7.4
Fibre material	72.8	47.3
Total	100.0	84.0

Fatty acid composition of fats in offal and bran		
Fatty acid	% of total fatty acids	
	Offal	Bran
Palmitic acid	20.4	17.5
Stearic acid	1.1	1.1
Oleic acid	12.4	16.3
Linoleic acid	57.7	58.7
Linolenic acid	7.1	5.6

Table 68

Compare the proportion of fibre material in offal and bran.
Note the proportion of unsaturated fatty acids in the fat of offal and bran. Draw conclusions with regard to the nutritional value of offal and bran.

Bread enriched with fibre matterial contains additional bran. But the addition of specially-treated offal (residue of beer production) is also possible. The addition of offal is nutritionally desirable. It is also preferable in flavor to the spelty bran (bran with a large percentage of husk content).

Soya Bread

It must contain at least 10 kg soya products per 100 kg grain products. The baker uses soya flakes (= soya grits) with a fat content ranging between 20 and 25%, causing the dough to be short and the volume of the bread to be small. To avoid a crumb that is too moist, a dough acidifying agent must be added even when a strong baker's flour is used. The recipe shown in *Table 69* for soya rolls takes this into account.

Model for the production of soya rolls with 10 kg of wheat flour		
Straight Baker's flour	= 10.000 kg	
+ Soya grits	= 2.500 kg	
+ Dough acidifying agent	= 0.125 kg	Temp. = 26°C
+ Mixed baking agent	= 0.300 kg	Dough resting
+ Baking margarine	= 0.250 kg	time = 10 mins.
+ Yeast	= 0.600 kg	
+ Salt	= 0.250 kg	
+ Water	= 8.750 kg	
= Dough	= 22.770 kg	
Dough input	= 45 g per roll	
	Place dough pieces with the seam (oiled) side up on the baking sheet	
Proofing		
(Final proof)	= 30 minutes	
Baking temperature	= 240°C	
Baking time	= 20 minutes	

Table 69

Specialty Bread with Modified Nutritional Value

— ***Bread enriched with albumen***
 The dry matter of the bread must contain at least 22% albumen;
— ***Bread with a reduced amount of carbohydrates***
 The bread must contain at least 30% less carbohydrates than comparable bread;
— ***Bread with reduced calorific value***
 The bread cannot contain more than 840 kilojoules (kJ) or 200 kilocalories (kcal) per 100 g of bread.

Dietary Bread

Dietary bread must conform to the applicable food regulations. It must be identified as dietary bread and a list of ingredients should appear on the packaging.

Bread with a Low Amount of Sodium (Common Salt)

It cannot contain more than 120 mg sodium (or 40 mg when it is a bread with a very low amount of sodium) per 100 g bread.
Although salt substitutes are added for spicing, they do not have the technological effect of cooking salt on the dough.

Gluten-free Bread (Bread without gliadin)

This bread cannot contain any wheat gluten or products made of bread grains, oats or barley. However, soya, egg or dairy products are allowed.
It is consumed by individuals who cannot digest albumen substances. The baker uses starch, hydrocolloids, rice and potato flour because cohesiveness of the dough cannot be achieved by adding gluten substances.

Fig. 424 **Graham bread**

Graham Bread (Wheat-meal Bread)

In order to be classified as a dietary bread (without salt and yeast), this bread must be produced in accordance with the instructions of the American physician, Dr. Sylvester Graham.
Bakers now produce products similar to Graham bread with wheat-meal, yeast and salt to enhance the flavor.

Diabetic Bread

This bread is produced for diabetics. It cannot have a calorific value of more than 840 kilojoules or 200 kilocalories per 100 g. The recipe in *Table 70* shows how the nutritional value of the bread is reduced through the addition of meal, vital gluten and soya grits. Meal and vital gluten are made to swell prior to dough preparation.

It is difficult for the baker to ensure that dietary bread has the required composition. Therefore, it is recommended to adopt proven recipes. Such recipes can only be changed under expert advice, whereby the nutritional value must be re-evaluated.

Sample recipe for diabetic bread	
Wheat flour, (first clear)	= 4.000 kg
+ Rye flour, (light)	= 2.000 kg
+ Wheat-meal, (medium)	= 4.000 kg
+ Vital gluten	= 4.500 kg
+ Soya grits	= 3.500 kg
+ Yeast	= 0.800 kg
+ Salt	= 0.800 kg
+ Water	= 13.500 kg
= Dough	= 32.700 kg

Table 70

Specialty Bread with Added Vitamins

This bread is enriched with vitamins, especially vitamin B. For this purpose, special nutrient yeast and flour containing grain germ are used. This bread must be baked very carefully to prevent destruction of the vitamins added.

Fig. 425 **Gluten-free bread**

Fig. 426 **Diabetic bread**

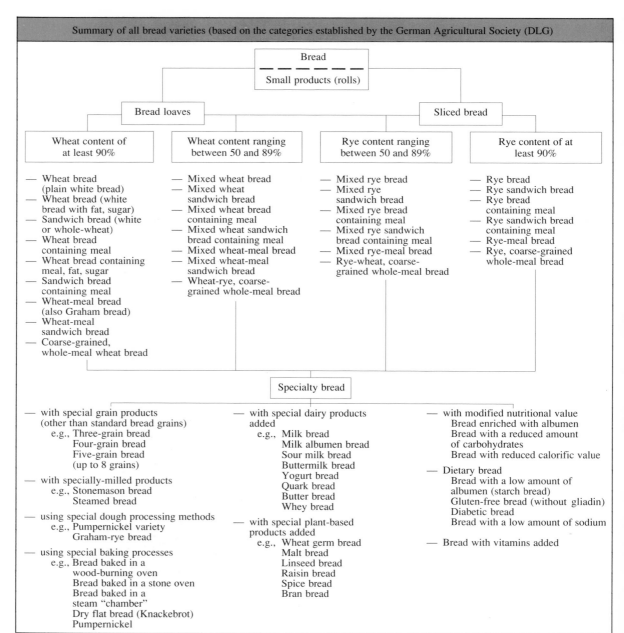

Summary of all bread varieties (based on the categories established by the German Agricultural Society (DLG)

Bread
— — — — —
Small products (rolls)

Bread loaves | Sliced bread

Wheat content of at least 90%	Wheat content ranging between 50 and 89%	Rye content ranging between 50 and 89%	Rye content of at least 90%
— Wheat bread (plain white bread) — Wheat bread (white bread with fat, sugar) — Sandwich bread (white or whole-wheat) — Wheat bread containing meal — Wheat bread containing meal, fat, sugar — Sandwich bread containing meal — Wheat-meal bread (also Graham bread) — Wheat-meal sandwich bread — Coarse-grained, whole-meal wheat bread	— Mixed wheat bread — Mixed wheat sandwich bread — Mixed wheat bread containing meal — Mixed wheat sandwich bread containing meal — Mixed wheat-meal bread — Mixed wheat-meal sandwich bread — Wheat-rye, coarse-grained whole-meal bread	— Mixed rye bread — Mixed rye sandwich bread — Mixed rye bread containing meal — Mixed rye sandwich bread containing meal — Mixed rye-meal bread — Rye-wheat, coarse-grained whole-meal bread	— Rye bread — Rye sandwich bread — Rye bread containing meal — Rye sandwich bread containing meal — Rye-meal bread — Rye, coarse-grained whole-meal bread

Specialty bread

— with special grain products (other than standard bread grains)
  e.g., Three-grain bread
      Four-grain bread
      Five-grain bread
      (up to 8 grains)

— with specially-milled products
  e.g., Stonemason bread
      Steamed bread

— using special dough processing methods
  e.g., Pumpernickel variety
      Graham-rye bread

— using special baking processes
  e.g., Bread baked in a
      wood-burning oven
      Bread baked in a stone oven
      Bread baked in a
      steam "chamber"
      Dry flat bread (Knackebrot)
      Pumpernickel

— with special dairy products added
  e.g., Milk bread
      Milk albumen bread
      Sour milk bread
      Buttermilk bread
      Yogurt bread
      Quark bread
      Butter bread
      Whey bread

— with special plant-based products added
  e.g., Wheat germ bread
      Malt bread
      Linseed bread
      Raisin bread
      Spice bread
      Bran bread

— with modified nutritional value
    Bread enriched with albumen
    Bread with a reduced amount
    of carbohydrates
    Bread with reduced calorific value

— Dietary bread
    Bread with a low amount of
    albumen (starch bread)
    Gluten-free bread (without gliadin)
    Diabetic bread
    Bread with a low amount of sodium

— Bread with vitamins added

Production of Sliced Bread

In most small bakeries, sliced bread is simply an option offered to the customer as a convenience. In this case, no special considerations are made in regard to fresh-keeping properties, durability, packaging and labelling of the bread.

The following information must be indicated on the package when sliced bread is produced and offered in the bakery:

— net weight
— price
— ingredients
— best-before date

Food Regulatory Guidelines

Large-scale production of sliced bread is advantageous to the baker in various ways.

➤ The baker can attract new customers (Example: consumers of specialty bread varieties).

➤ The baker can supply large-scale consumers or retailers (Example: delivery to an area where the baker does not have a branch outlet).

➤ The baker can produce large quantities of bread in advance (Example: bread with a long shelf-life through the addition of preservatives).

Sliced Bread Varieties

When sliced bread is produced on a large scale, it is worthwhile to choose suitable bread varieties.
The baker can select bread varieties that are particularly suited to selling and storing in a sliced condition.

Fig. 427

Processing Methods for Sliced Bread Varieties

It is appropriate to take measures to improve fresh-keeping properties of the bread, e.g.,
— increasing the sour content,
— adding high-gluten flour, fresh-keeping agents and "hot" soaker dough.

In order to increase the durable life of this bread, it is possible to add mold-preventing agents. These must be specified on the label.

In order to reduce sliced bread waste and to obtain more uniform slices, the individual bread loaves are produced in large weight units. Large-scale sliced bread producers make "strands" of bread which are up to 1.50 meters long. This requires special shaping machines, baking molds, foils and slicing machines.

The consumer prefers untreated, natural foodstuffs. Therefore, the following hygienic measures are especially important when producing and packaging sliced bread:
— cooling the bread loaves in a dust-free environment until the crumb is sliceable and the crust no longer breaks into fragments
— removal of bread crumbs from areas where the bread loaves are cut into slices and from the storage area
— storage of packaging materials in a clean, dust-free environment
— cleaning slicers immediately after the slicing process
— washing the storage room and the slicers with mold-preventing additives

Reference:
*Read the chapters **Fresh-keeping of Bread** and **Mold as a Bread Disease** if you require more information on how the durable life of bread can be prolonged.*

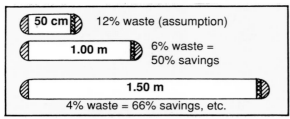

Fig. 428 **End waste in the case of normal and extra-long bread loaves**

Fig. 429 **Special bread slicer**

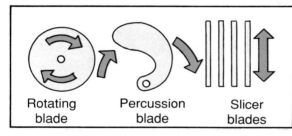

Fig. 430 **Blades for various bread slicers**

Bread slicer operation and maintenance

When cleaning bread slicers of any type, the following guidelines should be observed:
— *disconnect power source*
— *use only approved, specialized tools*
— *check maintenance procedures in the slicer manual*
— *handle blades with caution*
— *do not leave blades and knives unattended while cleaning*
— *wear protective handgear if possible*

When slicer is in operation:

— *do not push bread toward the blades with your hands (use an unsliced loaf or a specially-designed wooden block)*
— *do not attempt to free dislodged bread slices or crumbs*
— *do not clean, brush or adjust guides and trays*
— *do not remove protective devices*

If, for some reason, your fingers or hand sustain injury, stop the operation of the slicer and attend to your injury. Before re-starting the slicer, discard the bread nearest to the blades and completely clean and disinfect slicer blades.

Even when no sharp knives are involved, please respect the accident prevention guidelines.

Slicers

Knives and blades used:

Bread slicers use various kinds of blades and knives:
— Rotating knives which rotate at high speed around their own axis. They slice the crust. The knife is cleaned by a moving waste stripper.
— Percussion knives which cut the bread through circulating movements (like a sickle) into slices. They are primarily suited for bread with a firm crust and crumb.
— Slicer blades which are a whole series of knives moving in alternate directions, cutting a whole loaf of bread at one time into slices (usually 32 blades, 16 moving up, 16 down, at high speed). They are especially suited for soft bread varieties (white and whole-wheat breads, French bread, etc.).

Accident Prevention

The bread slicer is one of the most dangerous machines in a bakery. The machines, which contain knives driven by electric motors, are equipped with special protective devices:

➤ The part of the knife that is not used for cutting must be protected by a shield. If this shield can be removed, the driving mechanism must be disconnected or prevented from operating when the blade is unprotected.
➤ In the area where bread slices are ejected, the knife must be totally protected by a shield (on conventional slicers, the dull side is facing down where the bread is ejected).
➤ The guides feeding the bread must be equipped with an access protection shield. It should only be opened when the knife is automatically stopped at the same time.
➤ The back side of the feeding device must be equipped with a finger protection shield extending over the entire cutting height.
➤ The knives should only be connectable when all safety devices are firmly locked.

Important:
Cleaning and operating slicers should only be performed by trained personnel.
Most accidents are caused by people who are unfamiliar with the total operation and its dangers:
— Do not let children or untrained workers operate slicers.
— Always disconnect the power source to the slicer while cleaning.
— Keep slicer, trays, guides and shutes clean.

Packaging of Sliced Bread

Bakeries specializing in the production of sliced bread adapt slicing and packaging systems to the special requirements of the bread varieties to be produced, and to the packaging format.

In addition to the actual packaging process, modern packaging machines can do the following:
— They can create a vacuum in the package, whereby mold spores are prevented from germinating (lack of oxygen).
— They can fill bags or tube sections with protective gas (CO_2), whereby mold spores in the package are prevented from germinating (protective gas).
— They can heat-seal shrinkable and sealable packaging foils, whereby the package is tightly sealed (protection against dirt).
— They can sterilize the contents of the package through microwaves, whereby the mold spores between the bread slices are destroyed.

Packaging Materials

Apart from special preservation formats (e.g., bread in cans), the usual packaging materials used for sliced bread are paper, transparent foil (weather-tight) and synthetic.
The packaging materials should have the following features:

— They should be able to receive *imprints* for advertising and labelling purposes.
— They should be as *waterproof* as possible to protect the sliced bread from drying out during storage.
— They should be *aroma-tight* so the aroma is maintained and foreign odors are kept away from the contents.
— They should be *highly-resistant to tearing*. If the package is torn, mold germs could invade the bread slices. A vacuum or protective gas packaging would then lose its effectiveness.
— They should be *sealable under heat*. Through sealing, the package is kept as tightly closed as possible.
— They should be *heat resistant*, thereby allowing heat sterilization of the package.
— They should be *gas-impermeable.* Thus, the sliced bread can be stored in a carbon dioxide protective gas.
— They should be *cold resistant*. This prolongs the durable life of sliced bread through storage in deep-freezers.

The operational requirements in a bakery and the corresponding properties of the packaging materials should match.

It is absolutely necessary to obtain advice from the manufacturer of packaging materials to determine the packaging equipment best suited for each bakery product.

Examples of characteristics of various packaging materials					Tightness		
Material	allow imprints	tear-proof	sealable under heat	heat resistant	Steam	Gas	Light
Transparent foil (simple)	–	(+)	–	(+)	–	–	–
Wax paper	+	(+)	(+)	–	–	–	+
Poly-ethylene	+	+	(+)	(+)	–	–	–
Poly-propylene	+	+	+	+	+	+	–
Aluminum foil coated with synthetics	+	+	+	+	+	+	+

+ = Characteristic is present
(+) = Characteristic is conditionally present
– = Characteristic is not present

Table 71

Measures to prolong the fresh-keeping properties of sliced bread		
Prolonged sourdough method	Microwaves	Vacuum package
Preservative	Heat sterilization	Protective gas

Additional Information

Sliced bread packages can be sterilized after-hours in the oven, once the baker has finished baking products.
Good results are achieved:
— *at oven temperatures ranging between 120 and 140°C; and*
— *at temperatures in the core of the bread packages ranging between 70 and 75°C for about 15 minutes.*

Food for Thought:
Evaluate the various measures that can be used for sliced bread preservation
a) *from the point of view of sanitation and health,*
b) *from the cost factor involved.*

Additional Information

If the percentage of composite ingredients used exceeds 25% of the final product, the individual ingredients of the composed ingredient must be listed (example: sourdough — rye flour, water).

Substances in additives must be shown as components of the recipe (also as components of the ingredients) when they have a technological effect on the product. A technological effect can be defined as having a major influence on the characteristics of the foodstuff (e.g., smell, color, flavor and durable life). If a substance could be omitted without altering the end product, then it does not have a technological effect. In this context, the following example is of interest:

A part of the agent used to separate the bread from the baking pan can remain attached to the bread. This separating agent does not have to be included in the list of ingredients because it does not have a technological effect on the product.

When the relative quantity of an ingredient is specifically pointed out (e.g., "low salt" or "high fibre"), then the percentage of the additive must be indicated, e.g., "bread with a low salt content, containing a maximum of 1.2% cooking salt," or "bread containing at least 5% linseed."

Labelling Sliced Bread Packages

Labelling regulations for prepackaged foods impose special conditions on the production of sliced bread. The following information must be provided on the prepackaged product:
— the trade name,
— the name and location of the manufacturer,
— the list of ingredients,
— the best-before date,
— the net weight of the package contents,
— the appropriate languages (eg., French and English in Canada).

The price can be indicated on the package or on a shelf label beside the package.

An example for labelling a dark bread package containing 500 g of bread is shown in *Table 72*.

City Bakery Any town, Phone 234-5678	
500 g **Dark bread** – Rye-meal Bread –	**Ingredients** Sourdough (rye-meal, water) Rye-meal Water Wheat flour Yeast
Best before ... (see package tie)	Salt Sodium propionate

Table 72

Here the preservative is included in the list of ingredients. It is not necessary to identify it separately as a preservative.

The package size in our example is the most frequently used unit of 500 g.

The average loaf of bread in North America weighs 20 oz. or 567 g net weight (after baking). Other common sizes are 16 oz. (454 g) and 24 oz. (680 g). However, there are no restrictions regarding bread weight as long as the weight is clearly defined on the package. Bakers should always be aware of local food regulations.

The average bread weight of several samples cannot deviate from the weight indicated on the package (nominal weight).

Example:

When 10 packages of sliced bread (each with a nominal weight of 500 g) are weighed, they must total at least 5,000 g.

Weight Regulations

Reference:

*For further details on lists of ingredients, please read the chapter entitled **Working Recipes for Bread Doughs.** If you require information on the establishment of the minimum freshness date, refer to the chapter entitled **Keeping Bread Fresh.***

Specially-suited bread varieties
Measures to improve bread freshness
Sanitary production conditions

↓

Braided bread
Regular bread loaves

↓

Bread Slicers
- *Cutting systems to suit the bakery variety*
- *Accident prevention*

↓

Packaging
- *Closing and protecting the contents*
- *Labelling and advertising*

↓

Sliced bread

↙   ↘

produced and offered for sale in the same bakery for immediate consumption

for sale in prepackaged format in the producing bakery, self-serve environments, branch outlets or through retailers

↓

Labelling:
– trade name
– manufacturer
– list of ingredients
– best-before date
– weight
– bilingual (where applicable)

↓

The price and weight indication on the package or on a shelf label beside the merchandise

Price on the package or on a label beside the merchandise

↘   ↙

Weight units:
— average loaf of bread weighs 567 g net weight (after baking),
— there are no restrictions regarding bread weight as long as it is indicated on the package.

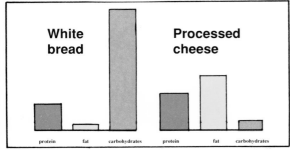

Fig. 432

Nutritional Value of Bread

Fig. 431

Those wishing to lose weight often feel they should reduce their consumption of bakery products. This practice is recommended by many dietitians and in printed information on weight control.

However, this notion is no more than a popular misconception. In fact, bread is a very important part of a balanced diet.
Bakers must educate their customers in the nutritional benefits of baked products.

Calculation of the Nutritional Value of Bread

First, we have to explain what we understand by nutritional value and how it is determined.

Let us use a nutritional value table and compare the values of 100 g processed cheese and of 100 g white bread. We then obtain the following comparable orders of magnitude:
— 1,100 kilojoules for the cheese,
— 1,104 kilojoules for the bread.

These values indicate how much energy the body gains when burning (metabolizing) 100 g of food products.

Generally, the energy value is expressed in kilojoules (kJ), but also in kilocalories (kcal). Energy value is determined by adding the fat, protein and carbohydrate contents of a food product using the following ratios:

➤ *38 kJ (9 kcal) per gram of fat*
➤ *17 kJ (4 kcal) per gram of protein*
➤ *17 kJ (4 kcal) per gram of carbohydrate*

Nutritional Value

197

However, in our examples of white bread and processed cheese, these three energy-supplying nutrients have a rather different composition. At identical calorific values, the cheese supplies, above all, fat and protein. However, the bread supplies carbohydrates. Therefore, the nutritional value is only informative when both the calorific value (in kJ, also in kcal) and the composition of the nutrients is shown.

> *Note:*
> *An identical calorific value does not mean identical composition in terms of nutrients!*

Nutritional Values of Various Bread Varieties

Table 73 summarizes the nutritional value of various bread varieties. If we compare whole-wheat bread and white bread, we find they contain approximately the same nutrients, but different calorific values, e.g., 931 and 1,104 kilojoules, respectively.

This difference is partly due to a somewhat lower fat content, but mainly due to the different composition of the carbohydrates.

	Grams per 100 g of fresh matter					Calorific Value	
	Fat	Fibre	Protein	Moisture	Carbohydrates	kJ	kcal
Wheat rolls	1.0	1.0	8.0	34.0	56.0	1,126	265
Wheat (flour) bread	1.8	1.0	8.0	37.2	52.2	1,104	258
Whole-wheat bread	3.9	1.0	8.5	35.7	49.9	1,141	269
Mixed wheat bread	1.2	5.4	7.2	42.3	43.9	931	219
Mixed rye bread	1.5	2.0	7.5	40.0	49.0	1,018	240
Mixed rye bread containing coarse meal	1.4	3.1	7.0	40.5	49.0	1,005	237
Rye (flour) bread	1.3	3.3	6.9	41.3	47.2	969	228
Rye-meal bread	0.9	3.3	6.8	41.2	47.8	935	220
Swedish rye crackers	1.2	5.7	6.8	42.8	43.5	935	220
(Knackebrot)	1.7	7.9	11.4	5.4	73.6	1,554	366

Table 73
Nutritional value and calorific value of various bread varieties

Based on the nutritional value table for various bread varieties, dark rye, whole-meal and whole-grain breads have a considerably higher proportion of fibre (ballast matter) and, therefore, lower calorific values. However, it should be noted that the vitamin B content is destroyed in whole-grain bread with a high proportion of crust or a long baking time (Pumpernickel).

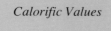
Calorific Values

➤ Identical quantities of carbohydrates in bakery products do not mean that the carbohydrates all have the same nutritional value!
➤ Fibrous material has a very positive nutritional effect; it can be added to bakery products along with vitamins and mineral matter!

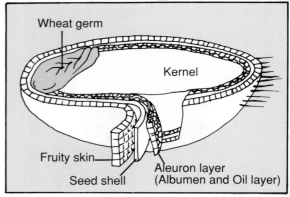

Fig. 433
The shell components of the grain and the outer layers of the grain are rich in fibrous matter

Bread with a High Fibre Content

Whole-wheat bread contains, in addition to starch and soluble sugar, shell components of the grain. These are cellulose, hemicellulose and lygnin (an indigestible carbohydrate), which are known as fibrous matter.

Fibre does not supply energy, but it has the following positive nutritional effects:
— increases the chewing intensity (salivation helps break down the food),
— prolongs the sense of satiation,
— has a soothing effect on excessive gastric acid,
— increased activity of the intestines,
— strengthening of the digestive organs,
— absorption of toxic matter in the intestines,
— shortening of the period of time it takes the food to pass through the system.

Flour containing a higher proportion of fibre also contains a higher proportion of the valuable components of the outer layers of the grain:
— grain protein of a higher value (with vital amino acids),
— a higher proportion of vitamins (especially vitamin B-complex),
— a higher proportion of mineral matter.

Bread with Modified Nutritional Value

Compared with the nutritional habits of 50 years ago, the following can be generally stated:

— average daily fat intake has tripled,
— average daily intake of sweet sugar substances has increased 10 times,
— fibrous matter has been neglected.

The cause for all this is a change in eating habits. People in the western hemisphere eat:

— more than they need,
— too much fat, and
— too many sweet sugar substances.

Alcohol consumption and sweet beverages rich in nutrients are contributing factors.

Diseases caused by the lack of a nutritional diet are on the rise, including obesity, heart diseases, high blood pressure, diabetes and malfunction of the digestive system.

But, of course, a bakery cannot change clients' eating habits by enlightening them with nutritional information.

However, as people become more health-conscious, the demand increases for whole-grain and whole-wheat breads and products enriched with fibre.

If the amount of a certain nutrient contained in a bakery product is reduced or increased, this change must be identified by indicating the nutrient and the percentage found in the product.

A reduction in the calorific value should only be referenced, if:

— the calorific value is reduced by at least 40%, compared with comparable food products, or if
— the calorific value per 100 g bread and fruitcake does not exceed 840 kJ, and per 100 g fine bakery products (with the exception of fruitcake) does not exceed 1,260 kJ, and
— at the same time, the component with reduced calorific value and its quantity are indicated.

With the exception of certain dietary products, baked goods with lower calorific values cannot be commercially advertised as "weight-reducing."

To make people more aware of the interrelationship between food and health, it is sensible to highlight the nutritional value of bread. This is the only way to inform the public at large about the important nutritional characteristics of bread.

Although bread is a food product with a low fat and sugar content, it is rich in carbohydrates and fibres.

Reference:
For more details on bread with modified nutritional value and additives containing fibrous matter, please read the chapter entitled **Specialty Bread**.

Nutritional Value Table

| Average content in 100 g of food | Basic Nutrients | | | Energy |
	Fat g	Pro-tein g	Carbohy-drates g	in kJ
Bakery product made with yeast	7.0	5.0	33.0	903
Whole milk chocolate	30.0	8.0	56.0	2,209
Whipped cream	31.5	2.4	3.4	1,298
Butter fat	99.5	0.3	–	3,767
Oats	7.0	14.0	66.0	1,680
Wheat flour, (top patent)	1.0	10.6	74.0	1,457
Whole-grain rye bread	1.2	7.3	46.4	949
Rolls	1.0	7.0	58.0	1,130
Apples (raw)	0.6	0.2	13.5	251
Red currants (raw)	0.2	1.1	9.7	188
Apple juice	–	0.1	11.7	197
Strawberry jam	–	0.4	65.4	1,100
Lemonade	–	–	12.0	206
Vanilla ice cream	16.5	12.5	60.5	1,848

Table 74

Food Regulatory Guidelines

Specialty bread with modified nutritional value

1. Bread enriched with protein	→ The dry matter must contain at least 22% protein.
2. Bread with reduced carbohydrate content	→ This bread must contain at least 30% less carbohydrates than comparable bread varieties.
3. Bread enriched with fibrous matter	→ This bread must contain at least 10% bran (related to the flour content).

Table 75

Food for Thought:
In bread with modified nutritional value, a portion of the carbohydrate is replaced with protein. What influence does this have on the calorific value of the bread?

Production of Sweet Yeast-Raised Goods

Classification and Composition of Yeast-Raised Pastries

When a customer goes into a bakery to buy sweet bakery products, he or she will ask for cakes, tarts, cream products, or simply for pastry.

It will not occur to him/her to ask for "fine bakery products." But this is the correct trade name for cakes, tarts and other desserts.

"Fine bakery products" is the generic term used for all bakery products other than bread and rolls (including all other small bakery products made with unsweetened yeast dough).

> *   *Fine bakery products differ from bread in that their content of added fats and sugars amounts, in total, to at least 10 parts per 90 parts of flour products or starch.*

Therefore, fine bakery products contain at least 11.1% of fat and/or sugar (related to amount of flour used).

Fine bakery products made with yeast doughs are generally designated as yeast cake or fine yeast pastry.

All fine yeast pastries are normally produced using the following six ingredients:
- Wheat flour,
- Milk/Water,
- Fat,
- Sugar,
- Salt,
- Yeast.

In addition, the following ingredients are used to produce fine yeast pastry:
- Eggs,
- Dairy products,
- Dried fruit, fruit products,
- Raw paste, such as almond paste, kernel paste, nougat,
- Seed kernels, such as almonds or nuts,
- Sugar substitutes, sweeteners,
- Spices, aromatic substances.

Dough made with pre-mixed flour or convenience products contains substances such as emulsifiers, sugar products of the starch and invert sugar.

Look at the window displays in various bakeries. You will probably discover unfamiliar yeast pastries that are produced only in specific regions of a country. But you will also see certain yeast pastries that can be found worldwide.

Maybe your bakery produces and sells special yeast pastries that are only available in a few other bakeries.

The following chapters describe the best known fine yeast pastries and their production processes.

Fine yeast pastries are normally grouped according to their composition, in categories such as "light," "medium," and "heavy" yeast doughs.

When the level of sugar content exceeds 5% in a dough, fermentation activity begins to slow. At levels between 10 and 20% sugar content, yeast must be increased to compensate for the retarding effect of the sugar.

* *Whether a yeast dough is classified as light or heavy depends exclusively on the fat/sugar content in the dough.*

A dough with a low sugar/fat content ferments easily (= fast) and yields "light" bakery products with a large volume, and which are easy to digest.

Fig. 434
Fine pastries made with a light yeast dough

Fig. 435
Fine pastries made with a medium yeast dough

Reference: *For more information on convenience products, please refer to the chapter entitled* **Convenience Products Made From Fine Yeast Doughs**.

Fig. 436 **Fine bakery products made with a heavy yeast dough**

Doughs with a high sugar/fat content ferment with difficulty (= slowly) and yield "heavy" bakery products with a small volume, and which are difficult to digest.

Fig. 437 "Mixed" yeast dough

Fig. 438 "Beaten" yeast dough

Fig. 439 "Pulled" yeast dough

Fig. 440 "Batter-type" yeast dough

Fig. 441 **Deep-fried bakery products made with fine yeast dough containing egg**

The method of production is so typical for certain fine yeast bakery products that it is used to name the final products.

Classification based on the production method	
Production method:	Bakery product:
Mixed fine yeast dough	➤ for almost all fine yeast bakery products
Master sweet dough	➤ for yeast doughnuts
Laminated yeast dough	➤ for Danish - style pastries
Batter-yeast dough	➤ for yeasted cakes

Fine yeast bakery products can also be classified based on typical group characteristics.

Group characteristic:	Bakery product:
Special ingredients in the dough	➤ product containing egg ➤ product containing butter ➤ product containing milk ➤ product containing fruit
Filling, topping	➤ Poppy seed cake ➤ Pastry ➤ Apple cake ➤ Cheese cake ➤ Sugar cake ➤ Almond paste cake ➤ Bee hive cake
Shape of product	➤ Braids ➤ Pretzels ➤ Pockets ➤ Yeasted cake
Size of product	➤ Large bakery product ➤ Small bakery product
Baking process	➤ Oven-baked products ➤ Fried bakery products
Storability	➤ One-day products ➤ Weekend products ➤ Durable products

Standard data for the sugar/fat content in fine yeast doughs per 1,000 g of flour			
	Type of bakery product	Sugar content	Fat content
Light fine yeast dough ● without egg	Small yeast products, basic dough for Danishes	75 to 150 g	75 to 150 g
● containing egg	Doughnut dough	100 to 125 g	100 to 125 g
Medium fine yeast dough	Sugar cake, Butter cake, Bee hive cake, Coffee cakes	150 to 200 g	150 to 200 g
Heavy fine yeast dough	Stollen	75 to 150 g	300 to 500 g

Table 76

Preparation of Fine Yeast Doughs

The following methods are used for making fine yeast doughs:
— sponge method,
— straight dough method using the usual ingredients,
— modified straight/creaming method, creaming sugar, fat, milk powder and salt, then adding eggs gradually, flour, water and yeast last.
— direct method with pre-mixed flour or convenience products.

Indirect Method Using Sponge Dough
The sponge dough used in the indirect method is also often called the "short preliminary dough."
The sponge dough is normally used for making heavy yeast doughs (e.g. Stollen). But a sponge dough is often prepared for lighter doughs, like doughnuts (using the normal ingredients).

Food for Thought:
Joe thinks: "Dough preparation using a sponge dough is outdated and time consuming! A few grams more or less of yeast doesn't make a difference!"
Is this correct?

---

* *Characteristics of a sponge dough:*

➤ *The dough is started with 1/3 to 2/3 of the flour quantity required by the recipe and the total amount of yeast and milk or water (Fig. 442). Sometimes up to 2% of sugar (= 20 g per kg of flour) is added.*
➤ *The dough is made soft and warm (28 to 30°C).*
➤ *The maturing time ranges between 30 and 60 minutes.*

---

* *Reasons for the use of the sponge dough:*

➤ *The yeast is able to ferment completely before ingredients are incorporated into the dough.*

➤ *A sponge dough is supposed to be strongly leavened. During preparation of the main dough, the cells of the sponge dough are finely compressed.*

These very fine cells guarantee a minimum degree of aeration, even if the main dough rises only slightly.

The sponge dough is mature when it has almost doubled in volume.
Now the main dough is prepared with the sponge dough and all other ingredients are added at the same time.

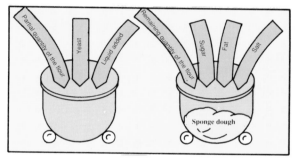

1. Sponge dough   **2. Main dough**

Fig. 442
Indirect dough method (with sponge dough)

Straight Dough Method using Common Ingredients

The direct method does not use a sponge dough.
When the dough is prepared with high-speed and high-intensity mixers, it is not necessary to dilute the yeast in water, to dissolve the sugar, or to cream the fat and the sugar.

All ingredients are put into the mixing bowl and blended at the same time ("all-in" method).

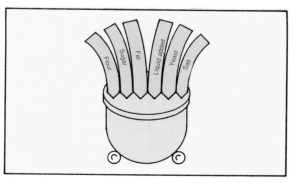

Fig. 443
Preparation of a fine yeast dough using the direct method ("all-in" method)

A client asks Joe: "Can you give me a good recipe for doughnut dough?" Joe's face turns red and he replies: "I'm sorry! I don't know any doughnut dough recipes. In our bakery, the doughnut dough is prepared with pre-mixed flour!"
This is embarrassing!
Could something like that happen to you?

Direct Method with Pre-mixed Flour or Convenience Products

The expert baker who uses pre-mixed flour or convenience products should also be able to produce the bakery product with the usual ingredients. Otherwise, he or she is not able to compare and evaluate the production methods of bakery products made with pre-mixed flour and products made from scratch.
What are pre-mixed flours?

> * *Pre-mixed flours contain mixed ingredients for specific product groups. They consist of durable ingredients in certain proportions.*

Pre-mixed flours for fine yeast doughs contain
— Wheat flour,
— Fat,
— Sugar,
— Salt,
— Milk powder;
In addition, they contain other optional ingredients, such as
— Invert sugar,
— Emulsifiers

➤ Invert sugar improves freshness properties.

➤ Emulsifiers improve fat distribution in dough, dough characteristics and product quality.

> The following must be added to the dough:
> — Liquid,
> — Yeast,
> — Eggs (if required for the type of bakery products to be produced).

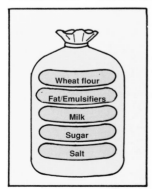

Fig. 444 Composition of pre-mixed flour for fine yeast doughs

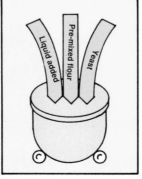

Fig. 445 Direct method using pre-mixed flour

This is how fine yeast doughs using pre-mixed flour are prepared:
→ Scale the pre-mixed flour,
→ Scale the yeast,
→ Measure the liquid to be added,
→ Blend all ingredients simultaneously without further preparations (Fig. *445*).

> *The use of pre-mixed flour for yeast doughs has certain advantages over the traditional method:*
> ➤ *Dough preparation is easier, takes less time and the risk of making errors is reduced.*
> ➤ *The fermentation stability and the fermentation tolerance are higher.*
> ➤ *The product has a larger volume and a tender, aerated crumb.*
> ➤ *The product has better fresh-keeping characteristics.*

Definitions

What is the difference between convenience products and pre-mixed flour?

> * *Convenience products are well-proportioned, pre-treated food preparations used for the production of bakery products, fillings and toppings.*

Convenience products contain mixed ingredients which have already undergone a process, e.g. through roasting, cooking or emulsifying. Therefore, pre-mixed flours are not counted among the convenience products.

Convenience products play an important role in the production of yeast products, especially in fillings.

Baking "creams" are important to the production of fine yeast doughs.

> * *Baking "creams" are preparations made of fat, emulsifiers, beet or cane sugar (or other types of sugar) and sometimes thickeners.*

Thickeners increase the dough yield and improve the fresh-keeping characteristics of the products.

> *The use of baking creams has advantages:*
> ➤ *The fermentation stability of the dough is higher.*
> ➤ *The product volume is bigger.*
> ➤ *The crumb is tender and light.*
> ➤ *The products have better fresh-keeping characteristics.*

When bakery products are being produced, the sugar-fat-ratio of the baking cream may not be sufficient and fat (e.g. for Stollen) or sugar must be added to the dough in addition to the baking cream.

Procedures for the Preparation of Fine Yeast Doughs

For the production of fine yeast doughs, there are:
— general rules applying to all product groups; and
— special rules applying only to certain product groups.

In this chapter, we present the generally applicable methods of the production of fine yeast doughs.

Special preparation methods are discussed in the following chapters together with the corresponding fine bakery product group.

General rules for the preparation of fine yeast doughs	
Rules:	**Comments:**
— The ingredients should be prepared prior to dough preparation, so that they can warm up to room temperature.	➤ Cold ingredients make it more difficult to obtain the desired dough temperature. Cool fats, especially butter, are solid. They are difficult to distribute during dough preparation.
— When very solid fat is being used, the fat and the sugar should be creamed.	➤ Creaming fat and sugar makes it easier to distribute the fat in the dough.
— The amount of sugar used should not exceed 40% of the liquid added. Or: The sugar content of light fine yeast doughs should not exceed 20% of the flour quantity; that of fine yeast doughs rich in fat, should not exceed 15% of the flour quantity.	➤ The fermentation of the yeast is significantly determined by the sugar concentration of the dough liquid. High concentrations of sugar stop the activity of the yeast.
— The dough temperature should range between 24 and 30°C; for doughs rich in fat, it should not exceed 26°C; for doughs rich in butter, it should not exceed 24°C.	➤ Very cool doughs reach their optimum level of dough maturity only after a dough resting time of several hours. Very warm doughs have a tendency to dry out and cause the fat in the dough to melt. During dough makeup, the melted fat leaves the dough structures. Consequently, fermentation stability is reduced. The product volume remains small, and the crumb shows large cells.
— The dough should be mixed intensively.	➤ An intensively-mixed dough matures faster. It also has a higher fermentation stability. The product will have a large volume and a tender crumb.
— These types of yeast doughs require a longer dough resting time than bread dough to mature.	➤ The higher the sugar content, the longer it takes for the dough to develop the desired dough properties and the desired degree of yeast fermentation required for dough makeup. For better aeration of the product, it is recommended to let the dough resting time proceed in two phases. First, the dough should be well-developed. After punching, the dough is allowed to rise again.
— After the dough pieces have been scaled and rounded they should be allowed an intermediate proofing period.	➤ The dough needs some time to relax the gluten. After a resting period of 10 to 20 minutes, it can be easily made up without tearing.

The fermentation gases that have formed during intermediate proofing, yield, during dough makeup, additional very firm cells due to the pressing and punching of the dough.

- *Final proof should happen in a humid proofer at temperatures ranging between 30 and 40°C. Extra rich yeast doughs should be baked when 1/3 of the fermentation maturity has been attained; light fine yeast doughs at 2/3 of the fermentation maturity.*

➤ *Doughs containing a large amount of butter and Danish doughs with a roll-in fat content should not be exposed to temperatures of more than 35°C in the proofer. Otherwise, the fat melts. Extra rich yeast doughs have a lower fermentation stability. Gluten formation occurs to a lesser degree. Therefore, cohesion of doughs containing a large amount of fat results partly from the other dough components sticking together with the fat. When the dough rises in the oven, the fat melts. Doughs with an excessive degree of fermentation maturity flatten out or collapse.*

In order to prepare fine yeast doughs, the baker must know the effects of the ingredients on the dough.
The ingredients influence the:

— dough firmness;
— dough characteristics;
— dough maturing process;
— dough behavior during fermentation;
— processing characteristics;
— fermentation stability;
— fermentation tolerance; and
— product quality.

Milk and its Significance for the Baking Process

Food for Thought: *Joe maintains: "The consumer has no means of knowing whether milk or water was used for fine yeast doughs!" What do you think?*

Many bakery products are produced with milk or dairy products:

— milk rolls
— some roll varieties with milk and water
— sandwich bread
— fine yeast pastry
— yeasted cakes
— choux paste (pâté-à-choux)
— poppy seed and quark-cheese preparations
— vanilla pastry creams
— ice cream and other products

Milk as an Ingredient of Baking Products

The use of milk for the production of fine yeast bakery products is not mandatory, but it is recommended because it increases the quality of the product.

The difference in quality between fine bakery products containing milk and those containing water is detectable from the lighter texture of the dough.

Find out which products in your bakery are made with milk or powdered milk.

The Effect of Milk on Dough Characteristics

Doughs made with milk are dryer and lighter than doughs made with water. Doughs containing milk also retain a better shape. They can be made up more easily because they are less sticky and easier to form (see *Fig. 446*).

Their fermentation stability (capacity to retain gas) and their fermentation tolerance (insensitivity towards under or over-development) are higher.

The positive effect of milk on the dough characteristics is due to the improved properties of the gluten. The finely distributed milk fat makes the gluten smooth and slows down the aging processes in the dough. The emulsifying effect of milk is due to the special composition of the milk fat (lecithin content) and the albumen of the milk.

with water   with whole milk   with skim milk

Fig. 446
Yeast doughs with water (left), with whole milk (center), and with skim milk (right)

Compare the "shape" of each dough piece.

206

The Effect of Milk on Fermentation

Doughs containing milk ferment somewhat slower than doughs made with water. However, this slowing down of the fermentation process is insignificant. It is often stated that this phenomenon is due to the milk fat. But this explanation does not hold up because the fermentation process is slowed down to about the same extent when skim milk is used (see *Fig. 447*).

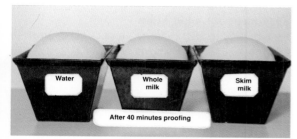

Fig. 447 **Yeast doughs after a final proofing time of 40 minutes: with water (left), with whole milk (center), and with skim milk (right)**

Compare the volume of the doughs.

* *The milk sugar (lactose) cannot ferment, therefore, it cannot further the fermentation process. It remains totally intact in the dough and in the product.*

Due to the higher fermentation stability of doughs containing milk, the final proofing time can be extended. Therefore, doughs containing milk reach a larger dough volume during the final proof.

The Effect of Milk on the Quality of the Product

Bakery products containing milk have a larger volume (see *Figs. 448* and *449*).

The crust is deep brown due to the milk sugar. During baking, the milk sugar reacts with amino acid browning agents to form ***melanoidines***.

The crumb is cottony-tender and has fine cells. The palatability is distinctly improved. Bakery products containing milk keep fresh for a longer period of time.

The Influence of Milk on the Production Method

Doughs made with milk have a higher dough yield because of the lower water content (12.5% of the milk is made up of dry components).

Doughs containing milk can be mixed more intensely, which has a positive effect on the maturing process.

Doughs containing milk do not age as fast as doughs prepared with water.

Due to the higher fermentation tolerance, the optimum fermentation maturity level can be slightly exceeded without product deficiencies occurring.

Fig. 448 **White bread made with partly-skim milk (left) and with water (right)**

Compare the volume and the color of the crust of the loaves.

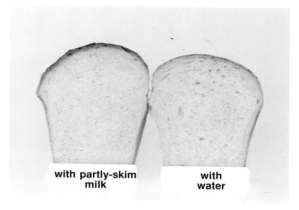

Fig. 449 **Cross-sections of white bread made with partly-skim milk (left) and with water (right)**

Compare the cells of the crumb.

The Composition of Milk

Fig. 450 on page 208 shows the components of the milk in per cent. Milk is primarily composed of water. But it has, nevertheless, a very high nutritional value because milk contains all the essential nutrients.

→ *The milk albumen contains all the essential amino acids.*
→ *The milk fat supplies energy. In addition, it carries fat-soluble vitamins. The proportion of essential fatty acids is insignificant.*
→ *The milk sugar supplies energy.*
→ *The minerals in milk include calcium, magnesium and phosphorus.*
→ *The vitamin content of milk is very high. Milk contains vitamins A, B1, and B2.*

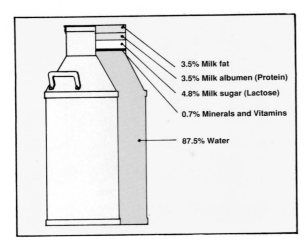

Fig. 450
Percentage of milk components

- 3.5% Milk fat
- 3.5% Milk albumen (Protein)
- 4.8% Milk sugar (Lactose)
- 0.7% Minerals and Vitamins
- 87.5% Water

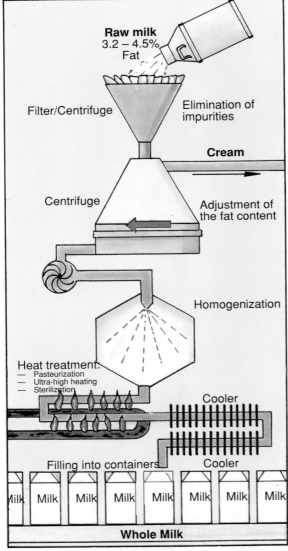

Fig. 451
Treatment of raw milk to obtain whole milk

Production of Liquid Milk

When we talk about milk, we always refer to cow's milk.

When milk is derived from other animals, the name of the corresponding animal must be included in the trade name, e.g. goat's milk.

Treatment of Liquid Milk

Raw milk is treated in dairy product plants prior to distribution to the consumer:

> ➤ *Elimination of impurities*
> ➤ *Adjustment of the fat content*
> ➤ *Heat treatment*
>   • *Pasteurization*
>   • *Sterilization*
>   • *Ultra-high heating*
> ➤ *Homogenization*

Any impurities in the milk are immediately separated in centrifuges.
The fat content of whole milk must be at least 3.5%. Because raw milk has, on average, a higher fat content, it is adjusted in the centrifuges to the desired percentage.

Heat Treatment

Milk is treated with heat in order to reduce or destroy bacteria. Heat treatment has the following purposes:
— to avoid contamination/infection,
— to improve the fresh-keeping qualities of the milk.

Pasteurized Milk is milk with a low number of germs. If it is kept in a cool environment, it keeps fresh for about two to three days.
Sterilized Milk is germ-free, durable milk. It can be stored for an almost unlimited period of time in sterile packages. The milk is heated for 20 to 30 minutes to temperatures ranging between 110 and 115°C. The disadvantage is that cooking causes a change in the taste of the milk.
Ultra-high heated Milk (UHT-milk) is an almost germ-free milk. The milk is heated for 2 seconds to temperatures ranging between 135 and 150°C. The UHT-milk also has a slightly changed taste caused by boiling (due to caramelization of the milk sugar).
UHT-milk can be stored for at least six weeks in sterile packages, even when it is not stored in a cool environment. Because it is easy to store and is reasonable in price, UHT-milk is suitable for baking purposes in remote areas.
Heat-treated milk is offered as whole, partly-skim and as skim milk.

Pasteurization methods for milk	
• High temperature heating	= 5 seconds at 85°C
• Short time heating	= 40 seconds at 71°C
• Prolonged heating	= 30 minutes at 65°C

Table.77

Homogenization

Fat is distributed in raw milk in the form of tiny droplets. Because of the milk proteins, the fat droplets are temporarily held in suspension in the milk. After a few hours the droplets are released and rise as cream to the milk's surface.

During homogenization (= uniform distribution), the milk is forced under high pressure through fine nozzles. In the process, the fat droplets are decomposed into tiny fat particles. In this fine mixture, the fat remains uniformly distributed in the milk for days. Through homogenization, neither the composition nor the durable life of the milk is changed.

Milk Varieties

Raw milk is untreated cow milk. Immediate delivery to the consumer is not permitted under any circumstances.

Preferred milk is high-quality raw milk with a natural fat content of at least 3.5%. The milk is poured into containers by the producer and directly supplied to distribution channels. The supply of preferred milk to consumers is subject to very rigorous conditions with regard to the:
— health condition of the animals;
— composition and characteristics of the milk;
— hygienic conditions in the barn; and
— hygienic conditions of the dairy for storage and filling of the milk into containers.

Preferred milk has no advantages over whole milk with regard to the baking process.

Whole milk is treated raw milk.
It is:
— heat-treated (pasteurized, ultra high-heated or sterilized);
— adjusted to a fat content of 3.5%; and
— normally homogenized.

Partly-skim milk (= milk with a low fat content) is also heat-treated. The fat content ranges between 1.5 and 2.0% and is adjusted through the removal of the cream in centrifuges.

Skim milk cannot contain more than 0.3% of milk fat. Skim milk has a less positive effect on the dough characteristics and on the quality of the bakery product than whole milk.

Whole milk and skim milk slightly delay the fermentation process in fine yeast doughs. Both milk varieties equally improve the processing characteristics of the doughs. But the fermentation stability of whole milk doughs is considerably higher than that of doughs made with skim milk. Therefore, the volume of the product is larger and the crumb structure is improved (*Figs. 453 and 454*).

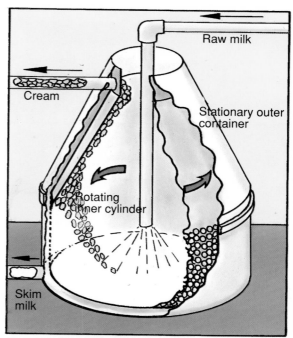

Fig. 452 **Working principle of a centrifuge**

Explain why, in a rotating cylindric container, the watery part of the milk is transported to the bottom, and the fatty part of the milk to the top of the cone.

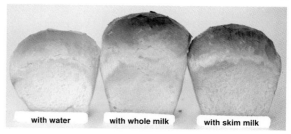

Fig. 453 **Bread loaves baked in pans made with water (left), with whole milk (center), and with skim milk (right)**

Compare the volume and the color of the crust of the bread loaves.

Fig. 454 **Cross-sections of bread loaves baked in pans, made with water (left), with whole milk (center), and with skim milk (right)**

Compare the cells of the crumb.

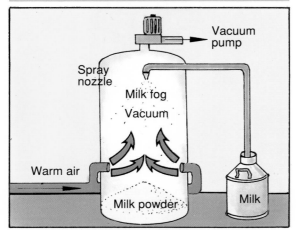

Fig. 455 **Production of milk powder using the spray method**

The following dry milk products are available to the baker:
— powdered cream with a fat content of at least 42% (where available)
— whole milk powder with a fat content of at least 26%
— partly-skim milk powder with a fat content of at least 1.5%, but less than 26%
— skim milk powder with a fat content of no more than 1.5%
— buttermilk powder with a fat content of no more than 15%

Table 78

Reference: *For more information about whipping cream, please read the chapter entitled* **Production of Tarts and Desserts.** *Preparations made with quark cheese are discussed in the chapter entitled* **Fillings and Toppings for Fine Yeast Doughs.**

Fat content of cream	
Minimum fat content of coffee cream	10%
Minimum fat content of sour cream	10%
Minimum fat content of cream yogurt	10%
Minimum fat content of whipping cream	30%

Table 79

Bakery products made with whole milk have better fresh-keeping qualities than bakery products made with skim milk.

Dairy Products as Baking Ingredients
Powdered milk, cream, sour milk, quark cheese and yogurt are significant to the production of bakery products.

Powdered Milk
Many bakeries use powdered milk instead of liquid milk.
The process is very simple. The powdered milk is distributed in the liquid added or simply mixed with the flour.

Powdered milk has hardly any disadvantages for the baking process compared with the corresponding milk varieties.

Powdered milk must be stored in a cool, dry environment and protected against foreign odors.

Powdered milk is normally produced by means of the spray-dried method. The milk is diffused in a spray tower and is dried through the rising warm air (see *Fig. 455*).

Cream

Whipping cream, coffee cream and sour cream have a variety of applications in the production of fine yeast products:
— as a dough ingredient,
— as toppings for sugar cake, butter cake and Streusel cake,
— as components of fillings and toppings, e.g. in custard and quark-cheese preparations.

Cream does not only increase the nutritional value of fine yeast products, but also the palatability.
Cream has a considerably higher milk fat content than milk. The part of the milk containing a large amount of fat is separated from the rest of the milk (skim milk) by means of separators (= centrifuges).

Quark Cheese
Quark cheese is the cheese variety most frequently used in bakeries today as an alternative to cream cheese. Quark cheese is used:
— as a filling in bakery products;
— as a topping for shortcake bottoms, flat yeast cake;
— as a cream-cheese substitute for cheesecake.
— as an ingredient for Stollen and coffee cakes.

Quark cheese is normally made from skim milk. The milk is thickened by adding lactic acid bacteria. The whey is separated. The desired fat content is achieved by adding cream.

Using Dairy Products in Baked Goods

Bakery products designated as containing dairy products must comply with certain regulations with regard to the proportion of milk used and the fat content of the milk. Specific percentages are taken from German federal regulations and reflect good manufacturing practices in many countries.

> *   *Per 100 kg of grain products (flour, meal, starch), the following quantities must be used:*
>
> — *for bread and rolls: at least 50 litres of whole milk,*
> — *for fine yeast baking products: at least 40 litres of whole milk, and*
> — *for baking products without yeast: at least 20 litres of whole milk.*

Instead of whole milk, corresponding quantities of
— whole milk powder, or of
— skim milk or skim milk powder supplemented with the corresponding quantity of milk fat (cream or butter) can be used.

Refer to *Table 81* and *Fig. 456*.

Fig. 456

Proportion of powdered milk used for the preparation of whole milk
For 1 litre of whole milk = 139 g of whole milk powder + water to yield 1 litre.   For 1,156 g of whole milk = 156 g of whole milk powder + 1 litre of water.

Table 81

Additional Information

Condensed milk plays a minor role in the production of bakery products because it is expensive. Condensed milk has been concentrated through the elimination of water and has been made germ-free through heat treatment.
Condensed milk contains all dry milk matter in concentrated form and a minimum of 40% sugar.

Fat content of condensed milk varieties	
➤ Condensed milk: at least	7.5%
➤ Condensed milk with a high fat content: at least	15.0%
➤ Partly-skim condensed milk: more than	1.0%
less than	7.5%
➤ skim condensed milk no more than	1.0%

Table 80

Food Regulatory Guidelines

Summary of the most important information about milk and its significance for the baking process

* Composition of milk:
  3.5% Milk fat
  3.5% Protein
  4.8% Milk sugar (lactose)
  0.7% Minerals
  87.5% Water

* Milk treatment:
  ➤ Adjustment of the fat content
  ➤ Heat treatment
  ● Pasteurization
  ● Ultra-high heating
  ● Sterilization
  ➤ Homogenization

* Milk varieties:
  ➤ Raw milk
  ➤ Preferred milk
  ➤ Whole milk
  ➤ Partly-skim milk (2% milk)
  ➤ Skim milk
  ➤ Evaporated milk
  ➤ Condensed milk
  ➤ UHT milk

* Baked products containing milk:
  ● 6% milk solids must be used

* Effect on the baking process:
  ➤ Dough characteristics
  ● light and dry
  ● firm
  ● easy to shape
  ● high fermentation stability and high fermentation tolerance

  ➤ Fermentation process:
  ● insignificant slowing down of the fermentation process
  ● longer proofing time

  ➤ Quality of the bakery product:
  ● large volume
  ● deep-brown crust
  ● light-tender crumb
  ● fine cells with thin walls
  ● high enjoyment value
  ● longer fresh-keeping properties

Sugar and its Significance on the Baking Process

Fig. 457 **Types of sugar**

Fig. 457 shows icing sugar, granulated sugar (coarse and fine), hagel sugar (a decorative sugar), cone sugar and white and brown rock sugar.

The baker uses sugar in the production of bakery products for various purposes:
— to sweeten and tenderize the product;
— to increase fresh-keeping qualities;
— to brown the crust;
— to provide food for the yeast (in small amounts); and
— for decorating purposes.

The baker uses various types of sugar:
→ Granulated Sugar - white sugar with a crystal size from coarse to medium to fine (Berry Sugar).
→ Liquid Sugar is a solution of highly-refined sucrose or invert sugar. Recently a series of liquid sweetener blends have been developed combining refined sucrose and/or invert sugar with dextrose and/or various corn syrups.
→ Glucose syrup made from corn starch.
→ Sugar substitutes, such as sorbitol and xylose and dietary baking products.

The baker uses sugar
— as an ingredient for doughs and pastes;
— as an ingredient for desserts and ice cream;
— as an ingredient for fillings and creams; and
— as a means of decorating bakery products.

Food for Thought: *Is it possible to distinguish between a dough containing sugar and one containing no sugar?*
Joe thinks: *"It is impossible to see or feel whether or not there is sugar in a dough or in a bakery product. You can only taste it!"*
Is this correct?

More precise information about the effect of sugar on dough, fermentation and product quality can best be obtained by performing a baking test while increasing the sugar content.

Sugar as an Ingredient for Baking Products

Perform a small test.
Test 29:
Incorporate 30 g powdered sugar (powdered sugar dissolves better in dough than crystal sugar) into 250 g bread dough.
— Compare the firmness of this dough and the processing characteristics with those of the original dough.
— Make up the dough containing sugar and a piece of bread dough without added sugar of identical weight into a pan-baked loaf. Compare the fermentation behavior.
— Bake both samples.
Compare the product volume, the color of the crust, the structure of the crumb and the consistency of the crumb.

The Effect of Sugar on Dough Characteristics

The higher the sugar content
— the softer the dough; the amount of liquid added must be reduced accordingly.
— the "shorter" the dough. It loses elasticity. Therefore, it is easier to shape (easier to mold).
— the slower the dough maturing process. The dough resting time must be prolonged accordingly.

The Effect of Sugar on the Fermentation Process

The fermentation process of fine yeast doughs is almost exclusively determined by the proportion of sugar contained in the dough (*Fig. 458*).

➤ *Doughs with a low sugar content ferment better than doughs without any added sugar. The best fermentation is obtained at 2% (referred to as baker's per cent, related to the amount of flour used). However, this low proportion of sugar is not sufficient to sweeten fine yeast doughs.*

➤ *Doughs with a sugar content of more than 10% ferment slower due to the inhibiting effect of the sugar on the yeast.*

➤ *Doughs with a sugar content of more than 20% require a long fermentation time. Volume is small and the crust color is dark. Because of the long process, fine yeast doughs rarely exceed 20% sugar content.*

Fig. 458
Yeast doughs with different sugar contents but identical fermentation times

Compare the volume of the doughs.
Explain the differences.

The Effect of Sugar on the Quality of the Bakery Product

Bakery products containing sugar have a very brown crust (*Fig. 459*).

Sugar turns from light to dark brown at temperatures ranging between 160°C and 190 °C. As melanoidines (browning substances made of sugar and albumen components) form, the crust turns brown at lower temperatures.

Bakery products containing sugar have a very crisp crust immediately after baking. However, bakery products containing sugar lose their crispness much earlier than bakery products without sugar.

Bakery products with a sugar content of up to 10% (but without fat or with a small fat content) have a larger volume than sugar-free products. The biggest volume is achieved with a sugar content ranging between 2 and 5% (*Fig. 459*). Such products have an adequately-aerated crumb. However, the characteristics of the crumb and those of the cells are not improved through the addition of sugar to the dough (*Fig. 460*).

Bakery products with a sugar content of more than 12% have a smaller volume compared to products without sugar.

Bakery products with a very high sugar content (more than 20% of the amount of flour used) are characterized by a slowing down of the fermentation process of the yeast and therefore have
— a smaller volume; and
— an insufficiently-aerated crumb with thick cell walls.

Fig. 459
Bread with varying sugar contents (0%, 2%, 5%, 10%, 20% and 30% sugar, related to the quantity of flour used)

Compare the volume and color of the crust of the bread loaves.

The palatability of fine yeast products is enhanced through
— the sweet taste;
— the aromatic substances forming during the fermentation process;
— caramelization of the crust; and
— the formation of melanoidines.

Excessive sugar contents reduce the enjoyment value, especially due to the unappetizing texture of an insufficiently-aerated crumb.

Fig. 460 **Crumb structure of yeast bakery products without sugar, with a sugar content of 10% and with a sugar content of 20% (related to the quantity of flour used)**

Compare the cells of the crumb.

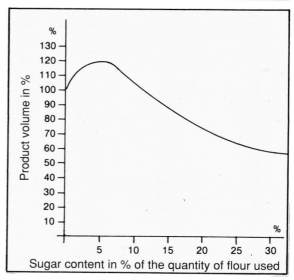

Fig. 461
Interrelationship between the size of the product volume and the sugar content

Additional Information

The crust of bakery products reaches, during baking, a temperature of 190°C or more. The sugar melts in the process. During the cooling phase, the sugar in the crust turns brittle-firm. As a result, the crust becomes crisper. Bakery products containing sugar have less of a crust than bakery products without sugar. The reason for this is the shorter baking time in the oven to avoid excessive browning of the crust.

213

Bakery products containing sugar lose their crispness rapidly,
— *because water absorption from the crumb proceeds faster due to the thin crust,*
— *because the sugar in the crust attracts absorption of humidity from the crumb and from the air (hygroscopic).*

Type of Sugar Used in Fine Yeast Doughs

Refined Sugar (in Crystals)

The baker usually purchases refined sugar or white sugar.

These two types of sugar constitute the most popular varieties used in a bakery.

Refined sugar differs from white sugar through its higher degree of purity which is, however, insignificant for the preparation of dough and batters.

Refined sugar and white sugar are offered in various forms of crystallization: coarse, medium, fine, very fine, and in the form of powder (= icing sugar, various degrees of fineness). Sugar varieties with fine crystals are most suitable for the production of doughs because they dissolve better in the dough.

Sugar with coarse crystals is ideal as a decoration on braids and smaller breads, because it is less liable to melt under normal or steam conditions in the oven.

Reference: *Special sugar varieties are described in the chapter entitled* **Gingerbread Products**. *Sugar substitutes are discussed in the chapter about dietary baking products.*

Liquid Sugar

Liquid sugar is a solution of highly-refined sucrose or invert sugar. Recently a series of liquid sweetener blends have been developed combining refined sucrose and/or invert sugar with dextrose and/or various corn syrups.

Liquid sugar can be easily scaled and proportioned. Moreover, liquid sugar has advantages for the baking process of fine yeast doughs. Dissolved sugar can be distributed more easily and rapidly in the dough than sugar in crystals and, therefore, has a positive effect on the dough characteristics.

Liquid sugar is delivered in tanker trucks, and is available in refillable tanks or disposable containers for medium-sized and small bakeries.

When using refined liquid sugar for fine yeast doughs, the water content of the liquid sugar must be considered when measuring the quantity of the liquid to be added to the dough.

Refined liquid sugar (produced in the bakery = simple syrup) has always been used for sweetening whipping cream or for the production of cakes (brushing sponge cakes with flavored syrup).

Sugar used for Decorating Purposes

Children, in particular, have a tendency to go for those bakery products which are coated with sugar. However, adults are also influenced to a large extent by the appearance of bakery products.

Therefore, sugar varieties play a significant role in decorating bakery products.

The sugar varieties used for decorating purposes are evaluated based on
— the purpose they are used for;
— their processing characteristics; and
— the durability of decorating properties on the bakery products.

Hagel sugar is made by breaking pressed sugar plates.

The hagel grains are composed of many small sugar crystals sticking together. Contrary to candy-sugar of identical grain size, hagel (hail or nib sugar) breaks into brittle pieces when chewed.

Hagel sugar is usually sprinkled onto the made-up dough pieces prior to baking (usually on braids). Such pieces should not be baked under excessive steam conditions.

Fig. 462 **Fine yeast products with hagel sugar**

Food for Thought:
Joe maintains: *"Hagel sugar is composed of large sugar crystals."* Is this true?

Powdered sugar is finely-ground refined sugar. It is used
— for decoration (dusting baked products),
— for icings,
— as an ingredient for tart dough.

Refined powdered sugar easily attracts humidity from the air and thus has a tendency to form lumps. Therefore, powdered sugar must be stored in a dry, air-tight environment.

Icing sugar, like powdered sugar, is finely-ground refined sugar. Icing sugar contains plant-based products such as cornstarch, which reduce the sugar's ability to absorb humidity. Therefore, icing sugar is more suitable for powdering bakery products than refined powdered sugar, especially
— for bakery products with moist surfaces (e.g. fruit pie),
— for bakery products that are offered for sale for a longer period of time (e.g. Stollen).

Refer to *Fig. 463*.

Fig. 463 **Danish-style pastry with refined powdered sugar (left) and with icing sugar, decorating powder, (right) after six hours of storage at high air humidity**

Fondant is a boiled icing made of refined sugar, water, glucose and/or cream of tartar.

During boiling, the sugar is dissolved and the water partially evaporates. The boiling process is interrupted when the water content is down to about 10%. This occurs when the boiling temperature has reached 116°C.

Through intensive cooling and stirring, microscopically small sugar crystals are formed that transform the thickened colorless syrup into a white fudge-like base.

The corn syrup (= glucose syrup) prevents this base from turning into candy.

Due to its tender consistency, its insensitivity to moisture, and its long-lasting shine, fondant is the most suitable icing for yeast products, and also for other fine bakery products.

Bakers can make fondant and other products with boiled sugar.

5 kg of sugar are dissolved in 2 litres of water while heated slowly.
The foam is skimmed off the surface until the solution is clear. Sugar crystals deposited on the walls of the pot are incorporated into the solution by means of a brush and some water. Through evaporation of the water, the sugar concentration in the solution increases. As the concentration of the solution increases, its boiling point increases as well. The cooking process is interrupted when the desired sugar concentration is reached. The cooking phases can be determined in various ways:
— through measuring the density by means of a spindle. The depth of immersion indicates the degree of concentration of the solution. Spindles used to determine the sugar concentration are also called "sugar scales." The spindles are usually graduated into Beaumé units.
— through measuring with a sugar thermometer – determination of the temperature of the solution. Some bakeries still use the sugar thermometer graduated into Reaumur units.
— by means of the hand test = evaluation of the condition of the sugar.

Products made in the bakery with boiled sugar			
Product	Cooking temperature	Density	Test
Simple syrup	105°C	32° Bé	light, threadlike strands
Fondant	116°C	43° Bé	brittle, hairlike strands
Caramel	between 142 and 150°C	– – –	spun sugar
Color = browned sugar	over 150°C	– – –	brown color

Table 82

Reference: *For more details on icings, please refer to the chapter entitled* **Production of Small Yeast Products**.

Production of Beet Sugar

Sugar is present in almost all plants and fruits. It can only be extracted economically from cane and sugar beets, where the sugar content is especially high.
Although the extraction of solid sugar crystals from sugar cane was performed as early as 600 A.D. in India, the extraction of sugar from sugar beets started in Europe in the 18th century.

Cane sugar and beet sugar are chemically identical substances. The sugar content of beet varieties today is around 16%.

The sugar extraction process

➡ The beets are reduced to chips; the chips are soaked in hot water.

➤ The separated turbid-gray sugar water is the **raw juice**.

➡ The raw juice is purified by means of lime solution and carbon dioxide.

➤ The filtered, light-yellow sugar solution is the **thin juice**.

➡ The thin juice is thickened in evaporators.

➤ The thickened, filtered product is the **thick juice**.

➡ The thick juice is thickened in vacuum boilers until crystals form.

➤ The thick juice containing sugar crystals is the sugar syrup or **filler**.

➡ In centrifuges, the liquid syrup is separated from the sugar crystals. The rest of the syrup is thickened again until crystals form, and then separated.

➤ The yellowish-brown crystals are the **raw sugar**.
The syrup obtained last is the **molasses**. It is sold to yeast factories as yeast food containing sugar and for other types of baking, like cookies, bread and muffins.

➡ The raw sugar is separated in centrifuges from any syrup residue through steam or water-jet treatment.

➤ The purified crystal sugar is the white sugar (EG Quality II). The purest sugar is the **refined sugar** (EG Quality I). It is purified by means of a special method.

Reference: *Fig. 464 on page 217 is a schematic representation of the production of beet sugar.*

Summary of the most important information about sugar

1. Sugar as an ingredient for yeast doughs:

— quantity to be added to the dough	➤ 75 – 200 g per kg of wheat flour
— effect on the dough characteristics	➤ Decreasing elasticity Increasing plasticity
— effect on the fermentation behavior	➤ Fermentation enhanced through the addition of a small amount of sugar; fermentation slowed down when a high amount of sugar is added
— effect on the quality of the bakery product	➤ Better browning of the crust; large volume when a small amount of sugar is added; smaller volume when a large amount of sugar is added; slight improvement of the fresh-keeping characteristics

2. Sugar varieties and their suitability for the baking process

Sugar type	Product description	Suitability
— Refined sugar	➤ purest crystal sugar	➤ ingredient for doughs and pastes; fine berry sugar; for boiling sugar
— White sugar	➤ white crystal sugar	➤ ingredient for doughs and pastes
— Hagel ("Hail") sugar	➤ refined sugar crystals the size of hailstones or small peas, sticking together	➤ decoration
— Refined powdered sugar	➤ finely-ground refined sugar	➤ for powdering purposes; for icings
— Icing powder	➤ refined powdered sugar with additives to prevent crystallization	➤ for powdering purposes
— Glazing sugar	➤ refined powdered sugar with stabilizers	➤ for icings
— Fondant	➤ refined sugar boiled with starch syrup	➤ for icings
— Refined liquid sugar/simple syrup	➤ concentrated solution made with refined sugar	➤ to soak cake bottoms, sweeten cream, to dilute icings and as a dough ingredient

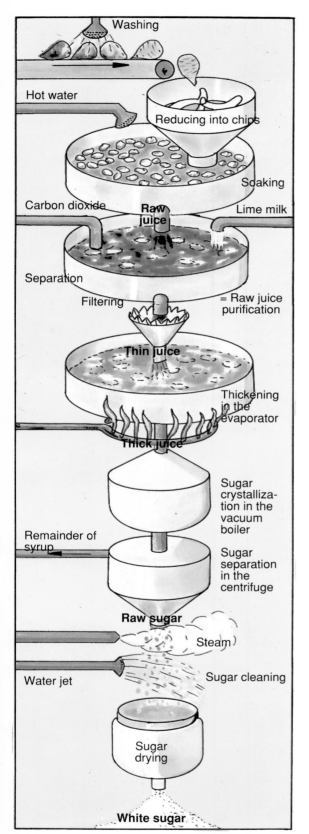

Fig.464 **Schematic representation of the production of beet sugar**

Fats and their Effect on the Baking Process

Food for Thought:
An essential characteristic of fine bakery products is their sweet taste.
Is it necessary to add fat to the dough of fine bakery products to enhance their nutritional value?
What do you think?

All fine bakery products made with a yeast dough contain fat. Besides sugar, fat is an ingredient for fine yeast doughs that determines the quality of the end product.

Bakery products receive through fat
— *a higher enjoyment value*
  ● *through the flavor typical for fat,*
  ● *through the crumb structure typical for fat,*
— *better fresh-keeping characteristics,*
— *a higher nutritional value.*

Fat is added to the dough in various ways:

→ as a dough ingredient
→ as roll-in fat (e.g. for Danish-style pastry)
→ as coating fat (e.g. for Stollen)
→ as an ingredient of fillings (e.g. in creams)
→ as a topping (e.g. streusel)
→ as a deep-frying fat (e.g. for doughnuts)

The purposes of using fats in baking are:
— to increase flavor
— to improve fresh-keeping qualities
— tenderization and softening of the texture
— to aid leavening in puff dough

The fats used in bakeries include margarines, butter, lard, shortenings and oils.

Margarine and deep-frying fats are composed primarily of the following fats:
— Vegetable oils: coconut, palm kernel, peanut, palm, soya, cornseed, sunflower, canola.
— Animal fats: lard, tallow, fish and whale oil (whale oil is becoming less popular).

 **Reference**: *Deep-frying fats and their suitability are discussed in principle in the chapter entitled* **Doughnuts**.

The Effect of Fat on the Dough, on Fermentation and on the Baked Product

 Joe maintains: *"Fat slows down the fermentation activity of the yeast. This is obvious, because fat coats the yeast cell membrane."*

217

Test 30:

Determine how fat blended with yeast influences the fermentation behavior of the dough.

Prepare three equally firm doughs, each with 250 g Straight Baker's flour, 15 g yeast, and 4 g salt.

Dough A with 150 g water, with no fat added;

Dough B with 130 g water and 50 g shortening (= 20% of the flour content). Add the smooth shortening to the dough only after dough formation has started.

Dough C with 130 g water and 50 g shortening. Mix the shortening and the yeast intensely prior to dough preparation.

Observation:

All three doughs show the same fermentation behavior. Doughs containing fat ferment just as well as doughs without fat. The mixing of yeast and fat (Dough C) has no effect.

Conclusion:

Fat in doughs without sugar does not slow down the fermentation process.

Joe's statement that fat coats the yeast cell membrane could not be proven.

When comparing fine yeast doughs and wheat flour doughs and their products, noticeable differences can be found in the dough characteristics, in the fermentation behavior and in the quality of the product. Since fine yeast doughs contain sugar as an ingredient, besides fat, it is not obvious whether the difference is due to the fat or to the sugar.

In order to show the effect of fat on the baking process, the characteristics of yeast doughs without sugar are listed.

The effect of fat

* *Effect on the dough properties:*

➤ *The higher the fat content, the softer the dough. In order to achieve the desired dough consistency, the proportion of the liquid added must be reduced by 20% of the quantity of fat added, when margarine is used.*

➤ *When a normal quantity of fat is added (up to 20% of the quantity of flour added), the dough is easier to shape and more extensible. The fermentation stability is somewhat higher, most distinctly when a small quantity of fat is added (up to 10%). The favorable effect of a small quantity of fat added on the dough properties can be explained by the improvement of the extensibility of the gluten.*

➤ *When a higher quantity of fat is added (more than 20%), the dough is "short." It tears easily when extended.*

Fig. 465 Doughs without sugar and varying fat proportions

Compare the volume of the doughs.

* *Effect on the fermentation behavior:*

➤ *Fat has no influence on the fermentation behavior in doughs without sugar. Doughs with a fat proportion of 50% ferment just as well as doughs without fat (Fig. 465).*

* *Effect on the quality of the product:*

➤ *Fat has no influence on the browning of the crust.*

➤ *Bakery products with a fat content of up to 20% of the total flour content have a larger volume than bakery products without fat. The largest volume is achieved at a fat proportion ranging between 5 and 10%.*

➤ *Bakery products with a fat content of more than 30% of the quantity of flour used, show, with increasing fat content, an increasingly smaller volume (Fig. 466).*

➤ *Bakery products with a low fat content have a better crumb structure. The cells are somewhat finer, and the crumb appears to be "velvety." The higher the proportion of fat used, the more tender and "short" the crumb. It loses its fine, velvety consistency.*
Well-aerated, large bakery products with a fat content of more than 20% have a crumb prone to tear when cut. The cause is the insufficient gluten swelling and gluten netting
— due to the smaller amount of liquid added to the dough,
— due to the isolating effect of the fat (Fig. 467).

➤ *Bakery products with a high fat content differ distinctly in terms of enjoyment value from bakery products without fat:*
— The taste and the odor are characteristic for bakery products with fat.
— The chewing characteristics are determined by the tender-short crumb.

➤ *With an increasing proportion of fat, the product keeps fresh for a longer period of time. This is because the fat largely determines the properties of the crumb. The crumb remains soft. The aging process through starch retrogradation is delayed through the fat. The drying-out process plays a minor role due to the small proportion of liquid. Therefore, many bakery product varieties with a high proportion of fat are classified as durable baking products.*

Food for Thought: *Doughs without sugar and a fat content of more than 30% reach, at identical proofing time, the same volume as doughs with a low proportion of fat. The volume of the end product is, however, smaller than that of bakery products with a low fat content. This means that the fermentation stability is significantly weakened only at the time when the product is baked in the oven.*

What is the reason? Think about the gluten formation in doughs with a low amount of liquid and about the fat characteristics during heating.

Fat content of the yeast doughs and in the corresponding end products		
	Fat content of the dough in % of the quantity of flour used	Fat content of the end product in % of the product quantity
Doughnut doughs	10 – 15	16 – 22 including deep-frying fat
German Stollen with fruit	40 – 50	20 – 25 including fat coating
German Danish	10 – 15	25 – 30 including roll-in compound
Danish	10 – 15	45 – 55 including roll-in compound

Table 83

Food for Thought:

A light, fine yeast dough contains 100 g sugar and 100 g fat per kg flour. Such a dough ferments well. A heavy yeast dough (e.g. for Stollen) contains per kg flour only 100 g sugar, but about 400 g fat. This dough ferments very slowly.

The answer seems to be simple: Fat slows down the activity of the yeast. But is this true?

Also Consider: Light yeast doughs contain per 1 kg flour about 0.5 l added fluid; heavy fine yeast doughs only about 0.3 l added liquid. The activity of the yeast is primarily determined by the sugar concentration of the dough liquid. The sugar concentration in the dough increases with a decreasing proportion of liquid added.

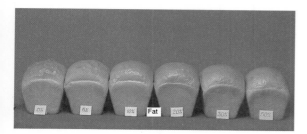

Fig. 466 Bakery products without sugar and with varying proportions of fat

Compare the volume and the color of the crust of the loaves.

Fig. 467
Cross-section of bakery products without sugar and with varying proportions of fat

Compare the structure of the crumb of the loaves.

Margarine and its Suitability as a Baking Ingredient

Fig. 468
The composition of the fat determines the consistency of the margarine

The baker can choose between various types of fats varying in composition:
— pure fats (such as coconut fat, peanut fat, olive oil, lard, pure butter fat, etc.). They are 100% composed of pure fat matter.
— Fat emulsions (such as butter and margarine). They are only composed of 80 to 82% of fat matter; the rest is water and other substances.
For yeast cake doughs, fat emulsions (i.e. butter and margarine) are more suitable than pure fats.

Advantages of fat emulsions as a baking ingredient
— They are more plastic!
Therefore, it is easier to achieve the desired dough characteristics such as dough stability, workability, and fermentation stability.

> — They have a positive effect on the water balance because the water emulsified in the fat has little effect on the dough consistency. Therefore, the dough receives water in addition to the normal liquid added to the dough.
> — They can be distributed more easily in the dough. This has a positive effect on the dough characteristics and, hence, on the volume and the crumb structure of the finished product.

For the preparation of creams, tart-pastes and roll-in doughs, margarine is also more suitable than pure fats because the producer can adjust its consistency specifically to its end use.

Margarine producers offer the baker special types of margarine depending on the use:
— baking margarine,
— roll-in margarine,
— colored and uncolored margarines.

For fine yeast doughs, only a specifically suited type of margarine or shortening should be used.

Baking margarine is adjusted to the consistency of the dough and to dough fermentation temperatures.

Special requirements with regard to baking margarine	
→ *The upper melting range must be higher than the fermentation temperature.*	▶ *Thus, the fat remains plastic even during the fermentation process and does not affect the fermentation stability.*
→ *The upper melting range should be lower than the mouth temperature.*	▶ *The fat can melt in the mouth during consumption, and the enjoyment value is maintained (palatability).*
→ *Its consistency should be smooth, but not soft or greasy.*	▶ *Yeast doughs with a high fat content can be produced without losing their required consistency. They still absorb enough liquid to guarantee yeast activity.*
→ *It should keep its smooth-stable consistency even when it is stored in a cool environment.*	▶ *The baking margarine does not need to be conditioned hours before it is to be incorporated into the dough.*

Baking margarine is equally well suited for the production of shortbread dough and tart-pastes. Contrary to household margarines, the risk of stored shortbread

dough turning soapy is very low when using baking margarine, due to the special composition of the fat.

Reference: *Roll-in margarine and its processing are discussed in principle in the chapters entitled* **Production of Danish-style Pastry** *and* **Production of Puff Pastry Dough**.
For more information about margarine for the purpose of creaming refer to the chapter entitled **Cream Cakes and Cream Desserts**.

Production of Margarine

Margarine is a spreadable *water-in-oil-emulsion*.

The fat content should be at least 80%.

The oils and fats used for the production of margarine are 90% derived from vegetable sources. These include, in particular, soya oil, sunflower oil, peanut oil, canola oil, cotton seed oil, palm oil/palm kernel fat (from the same fruit) and coconut oil.

Animal fats, i.e. lard, tallow, fish oil and whale oil, are only used in small quantities. The vegetable oils are produced through pressing and extraction (= separation by means of a fat dissolvent). Through refining, the foreign matter is eliminated and the durable life of the oil is improved.

For the production of margarine, more solid fats (= fats that are solid at room temperature) than oils (= fats that are liquid at room temperature) are required.

The supply of solid fats on the world market is, however, lower than that of oils. For the production of margarine, oils are transformed into solid fats by means of special methods. This process is called fat solidification. Fat is usually solidified by causing hydrogen to attach to the unsaturated fatty acids (hydrogenation – see *Fig. 469*).

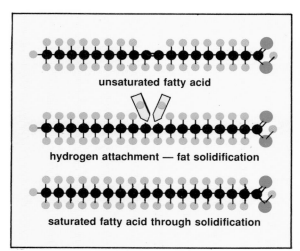

Fig. 469 **Principle of fat solidification**

Through blending naturally solid fats, solidified fats and oils with varying melting ranges, the manufacturer of fats, oils and shortenings can produce an edible fat specifically suited for almost any purpose.

In addition to the various oils and fats (minimum of 80%), margarine contains the following ingredients:
—*Water or skim milk (16%),*
—*Vitamins (A and D),*
—*Carotene (= provitamin A) as color,*
—*Salt (3%),*
—*Lecithin as an emulsifier (0.2%),*
—*Whey powder (1.4%),*
—*Vegetable mono- and diglycerides (0.5%),*
—*Sodium benzoate,*
—*Artificial flavor.*

Production process of margarine

➤ *Blending of the fatty phase: Oils, fats, fat-soluble (liposoluble) vitamins, carotene, and lecithin are blended while they are slightly heated.*

➤ *Blending of the aqueous phase: Salt, starch and other non-liposoluble ingredients are dissolved or blended in water/skim milk.*

➤ *Emulsification: The fatty phase and the aqueous phase are emulsified initially through stirring in the "rapid cooler."*

➤ *Cooling and kneading: During the emulsifying process, the emulsion is cooled at the same time. The emulsion solidified on the walls of the rapid cooler is continuously scraped off and kneaded. The finished margarine is ejected from the rapid cooler (Fig. 473).*

Fig. 470 Soya seed oil is a component of many margarine varieties

Fig. 471 Cross-section of a sunflower
Sunflower oil is a component of many margarine varieties

Fig. 472 **Cotton flour with cottonseed**
Cottonseed oil is a component of many margarine varieties

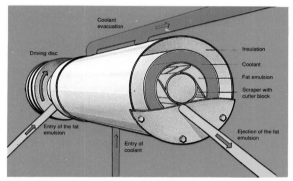

Fig. 473 **Margarine production: Emulsification, cooling and kneading in the rapid cooler**

Margarine maintains its full quality for up to 10 weeks when it is stored at a temperature below 16°C.

Butter and its Suitability as a Dough Ingredient

Butter as a Dough Ingredient

Butter is just as suitable as baking margarine as a dough ingredient for doughs with a low or normal fat content. In the production of heavy fine yeast doughs with a high fat content, butter is more difficult to work with than baking margarine or shortening because butter has a lower melting range.

Joe thinks: *"Butter is much too expensive to be used as a dough ingredient. The customer can not taste the difference between a product made with butter or margarine anyway."*
What do you think? Remember that the temperature of fat in the crust rises to about 180°C during baking. Is there a difference in flavor between butter that has been heated and margarine that has been heated?

→ Butter is hard at refrigeration temperatures.	➤ Therefore, the butter must be adjusted to room temperature prior to its incorporation into the dough.
→ Butter has, at yeast dough temperatures, a softer consistency than baking margarine.	➤ Therefore, the quantity of liquid added to a yeast dough with a high butter content must be slightly reduced.
→ Butter has a lower upper melting range than baking margarine (butter melts earlier).	➤ Yeast doughs with a high butter content must be made cooler. The same applies to the temperature in the proofer. Excessively warm doughs containing a lot of butter have a tendency to "flow" and they have a lower fermentation tolerance.
→ Butter spoils faster than baking margarine.	➤ Therefore, only very fresh butter of the highest quality should be used for bakery products with a long shelf life.

When using pure butter fat, the higher fat content in the pure butter fat should be taken into account.

Consult the conversion formula in Table 84.

Food Regulatory Guidelines

Conversion formula for pure butter fat

1 kg butter contains on average
= 0.8 kg pure butter fat
Pure butter fat quantity = quantity of butter x 0.8

Table 84

Average composition of butter

80 – 85%	Fat (minimum content)
16 – 16.5%	Water (maximum content)
2 – 2.3%	Salt
0.7%	Casein (protein, lactose and minerals) Vitamins: A, D, E, K and Provitamin A = Carotene

Table 85

Regulations Regarding Bakery Products Made with Butter

Joe thinks: *"The term, butter pastry, applies to all bakery products made with butter. It does not matter how much butter has been used and if other fats have been added to the dough in addition to butter."*

Is this true?

Butter is produced from milk or cream, or both, and contains no less than 80% milk fat and may also contain milk solids, bacterial culture, salt and approved coloring matter.

Guidelines	Explanations
➤ The proportion of fat added should be only butter.	➤ This applies to doughs, toppings (butter streusel), fillings, deep-frying fat, and to the fat used for coating. It also applies to thin shortcake bottoms used for the bottom of a buttercream tart. The fat used for greasing of baking tins and molds does not have to be butter. If only a part of the bakery product contains butter (butter streusel), this can be pointed out in the name "streusel with butter."
➤ The products should contain a minimum amount of butter.	➤ The following minimum quantities per 100 kg ground grain products or starch should be used for European pastries: — Butter pastry in general: 10 kg butter — Streusel cake, butter cake: 30 kg butter including topping — Butter Stollen: 40 kg butter — Almond Stollen: 30 kg butter For almond Stollen, the best fat to use is butter. This applies even if the term "butter" is not part of the trade name.

Food for Thought: *Does butter pastry always have to be identified in the commercial name or through a clear reference?*

Fig. 474 **Butter cake**
Unlike margarine toppings, butter toppings on a cake have a brown-speckled appearance caused by browning of the milk sugar component of the butter

Production of Butter

Butter is a **water-in-milk/fat-emulsion**. In addition to the milk fat, it contains other ingredients such as water, milk sugar, and milk albumen.

Butter can be made with sour or sweet cream.

Joe is supposed to prepare whipped cream. He whips the cream with the mixer at high speed. When he checks the consistency of the whipped cream, he is surprised to see little fat balls swimming in a water-milky liquid. Joe has just produced butter!

The process of butter production

➡ *The cream is separated from the milk in a centrifuge.*

➡ *The cream is whipped in the butter maker.*

➡ *The buttermilk (water remains) is separated. The butter globules are washed while they are kneaded.*

➡ *The butter is shaped and packaged.*

➤ *The products obtained are cream and skim milk.*

➤ *In the process, the milk fat conglomerates into butter globules and separates from the rest of the milk (= buttermilk).*

➤ *In the process, the milk residues attached to the butter globules are eliminated. The durability and the plasticity of the butter are thus increased.*

Types of Butter

The following are quality characteristics of three kinds of butter used in the North American baking industry:

1. *Salted butter* = most widely used in bakery products; salt acts as a preservative and enhances flavor

2. *Unsalted butter* = poor fresh-keeping characteristics, but used for glazing Stollen and in butter icing because of its pure taste

3. *Cooking butter* = better known as "drawn" butter; its lack of moisture limits its value in baking

For bakery products which are normally stored for some time prior to consumption, only salted butter should be used. The lower quality of unsalted butter and of cooking butter is frequently due to a long storage time prior to shaping. It spoils quickly, reducing the quality of the bakery product.

Sweet cream butter is made with sweet or slightly sour cream.

Cultured butter is made with sour cream, to which milk acid bacteria can be added. It has a stronger flavor. Cultured butter is widely used in Europe.

Pure butter fat is made by melting the butter and subsequently separating the water and other non-fatty matter. The fat content amounts to 99.5%.

➤ Advantages over butter:
Pure butter fat can be stored for a longer period of time. However, it is of limited use as a deep-frying fat (for butter pastry).

➤ Disadvantages over butter:
Pure butter fat does not have the full aroma of butter.

Pure butter fat is frequently made with butter that has been stored for a long time and has lost most of its quality characteristics. This butter fat spoils faster in bakery products than regular butter. Therefore, caution must be taken when using butter fat (that has been stored) for the production of bakery products.

Spoiling of Fats

When food with a lower water content spoils, it is often because of the fats. This applies to durable baking goods, to flour, to milk powder and to chocolate.

All fats spoil eventually. Spoiled fats taste rancid and soapy.

Here are the main reasons why fat spoils:
— Enzymes in the fat matter;
— Enzymes of micro-organisms, especially mold fungi;
— Oxygen.

How fat spoils	
— Enzymes separate fatty acids from the fat molecule.	➤ Depending on the type of fatty acids separated, the fat tastes rancid or soapy.
— Enzymes split up the fatty acid chains.	➤ In the process, methyl-ketones are produced.
— Oxygen combines with the unsaturated fatty acids.	➤ Stale and odorless products with a rancid taste are also formed. Some products of oxidation are resiny and can be detrimental to one's health.

In a simplified manner, the following rules can be set for the storability of fats:	
➡ Fats without water are more durable than fat emulsions.	➤ Example: Pure butter fat is more durable than butter.
➡ Refined fats (purified by means of the hot method) are more durable than unrefined fats.	➤ Example: Margarine is more durable than butter.
➡ Fats containing primarily unsaturated fatty acids are more durable than fats with a high content of unsaturated or multiple unsaturated fatty acids.	➤ Example: Solidified peanut fat is more durable than peanut oil.

The spoiling process of fat is accelerated through
— **Heat,**
— **Moisture,**
— **Metal traces,**
— **Light.**

The following apply to the storage of fat:	
➡ Store fats in a cool environment!	➤ Store butter below 12°C, margarine below 16°C in the: — storage room, — refrigerator, — freezer!
➡ Store fats in a dry environment!	
➡ Store fats in an airtight environment!	➤ In airtight packages.

➡ Store fats in a dark environment!	➤ Store in tightly-sealed packages; darken the storage chambers!
➡ Protect fats from foreign odors!	➤ Do not store fats along with odor-producing substances!

In principle, the same storage conditions apply to bakery products containing fat. However, the storage conditions must also be adjusted according to the preservation of quality characteristics typical to the baking product, e.g. maintenance of the moisture of the crumb.

Summary of the most important information about fats and their significance for the baking process
* Effect of fats when used as a dough ingredient:
➤ Low to normal additions of fat improve the dough yield, the product volume, the condition of the crumb and the fresh-keeping characteristics of the end product.
➤ High amounts of added fat have a negative effect on the dough characteristics, reduce the volume of the end product, and have a negative effect on the condition of the crumb.
➤ Fat in sugar-free doughs has no influence on the fermentation activity of the yeast and on the browning of the baking product.
➤ The addition of fat makes the dough soft. By reducing the amount of liquid added, the sugar concentration in doughs is increased. This results in a slowing down of the fermentation process.
* Margarine is an emulsion consisting mainly of vegetable fats.
➤ Margarine contains at least 80% fat.
➤ Special types of margarine are adjusted to special purposes:
• baking margarine as a dough ingredient
• roll-in margarine used for Danish and puff pastry dough
• special creaming margarine used for icings and pastes.
* Butter is an emulsion produced from milk.
➤ Butter contains at least 82% fat.
➤ "Butter pastry" contains butter as the only added fat product.

Eggs and their Significance for the Baking Process

Fig. 475

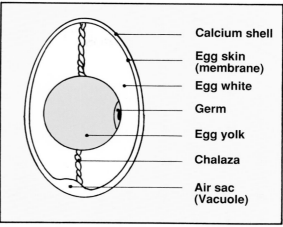

Fig. 476 **Composition of an egg**

No other baking ingredient has such a manifold effect on the finished product:

➤ Eggs are used as an ingredient for baked goods and sweets, for icings and ice-cream.
➤ Eggs improve the condition of doughs, pastes, cakes, cookies, icings and ice-cream.
➤ Eggs improve the enjoyment value.
➤ Eggs aerate and emulsify. They have a smoothing effect. They bind water and have a solidifying effect. They give color and have a browning effect.

Composition and Properties of Eggs

The special suitability of eggs as baking ingredients is partly due to their composition.

The egg is not a uniform substance. *Fig. 476* shows the composition of an egg in a simplified fashion.

The egg content is composed as follows:

— 36% egg yolk, and
— 64% egg white.

The egg yolk significantly differs in composition from the egg white (*Table 86*).

The egg yolk has
— a higher fat content,
— contains lecithin, and has
— a higher albumen content. The water content is correspondingly lower.

The differences in the composition of egg yolk and egg white account for different effects on the baking process.

Characteristics of the Egg Yolk

Due to its special characteristics, the egg yolk has various applications in the bakery.

Contrary to the egg white, the egg yolk cannot be stiffly beaten. It can, however, be whipped to a foam and blended with water or milk in spite of its high fat content (e.g. for coatings).

Compositions of eggs			
Components	Whole egg	Egg yolk	Egg white
Albumen	13.0%	16.0%	11.5%
Fat	11.5%	32.0%	Traces
Carbohydrates	0.5%	0.5%	0.5%
Water	74.0%	50.0%	87.5%
Minerals	1.0%	1.5%	0.5%
Vitamins	A, B_1, B_2	A, B_1, B_2	B_2

Table 86

Properties of egg yolks:	Applications of egg yolks:
— Egg yolk has an emulsifying effect and thus increases the stability of fat-water-mixtures.	➤ For voluminous yeast bakery products, e.g. for yeast doughnuts, for smooth, pliable short-bread, for homogeneous, voluminous pastes and creams, for smooth ice-cream
— Egg yolk can swell and makes batters smooth.	➤ For pâtés made with cooking starch (as a substitute for flour gluten)
— Egg yolk binds water when heated.	➤ For crumb formation in choux paste products
— Egg yolk browns when exposed to high heat.	➤ For all baked goods with a deep brown crust
— Egg yolk enhances flavor.	➤ For all baked goods, creams and ice-cream
— Egg yolk enhances color due to its carotene content.	➤ For a yellow crumb

Properties of Egg White

Due to its composition, egg white has different properties and thus different effects on the baking process than egg yolk.

Properties of egg white:	Applications of egg white:
— Egg white can be stiffly beaten.	➤ For foam batters (angel food cake) and meringues, for aeration of biscuits, cheese cake or light vanilla cream
— Egg white makes pastes smooth.	➤ For macaroon cookies, for egg white sprayed glazes and royal icings
— Egg white locks in water when it coagulates.	➤ For macaroon pastes

When incorporated into the dough, egg white is always used in conjunction with egg yolk. Egg white alone makes the crumb dry and accelerates the aging process of the product.

Reference: *For the ability of egg white to be stiffly beaten, refer to the chapter entitled* **Bakery Products Made with Meringue**.

without egg content   with egg white

Fig. 477 **Cross-sections of coffee cake made from fine yeast dough, without egg content (left) and containing 200 g egg white per kg flour (right)**

Evaluate the volume and the cell structure of the crumb.

Caution! *The use of duck eggs is prohibited in bakeries! Duck eggs can be infected with salmonellae (= typhoid bacillus and paratyphoid bacillus).*

Eggs as Baking Ingredients

Baker Smith says: *"Fine yeast bakery products containing eggs have a nicer appearance and the cells of the crumb are more tender; they taste better and keep fresh for a longer period of time."*

Are eggs a mandatory dough ingredient for fine yeast products?

For certain fine yeast baking products, the use of eggs as dough ingredients is required in order to obtain their characteristic properties.

For other fine yeast doughs, the use of eggs as dough ingredients is not necessary from the point of view of the baking process. But the addition of egg generally yields a better product quality.

The following count among the fine yeast products for which egg is used:

— Yeast doughnuts,
— Brioche (a French breakfast baking product, containing a low amount of sugar, but a high amount of butter and egg),
— Stirred yeast cake (specialty product),
— Savarin (small yeast ring) soaked in a syrup-rum-solution, glazed with apricot glaze, and topped with fruits and whipped cream,
— Croissants,
— Danish dough.

The effect of whole egg on the production of fine yeast products:

➤ *Through the addition of egg, dough development is improved. During the mixing process, the dough is developed to the point where it can absorb the air incorporated during kneading into the dough structure.*

➤ *Through the addition of egg, dough characteristics are improved. The dough is more extensible and plastic. It has a high dough maturing tolerance. It ages less rapidly and thus tolerates a long dough resting time. Through this, the dough has better processing characteristics.*

➤ *Through the addition of egg, fermentation stability and fermentation tolerance are increased. Even older doughs that have been punched back several times maintain their fermentation stability for a very long time. Shaped dough pieces can be exposed to a longer proofing time than those without egg content.*

➤ *Through the addition of egg, the product volume is increased.*

➤ *Through the addition of egg, the crumb structure is improved. The crumb has fine pores with thick walls. It is aerated, but nevertheless, very moist.*

➤ *Through the addition of egg, the browning of the crust is improved.*

➤ *Through the addition of egg, fresh-keeping characteristics of the end product are improved.*

The favorable effect of the whole egg on the production of fine yeast products is primarily due to the egg yolk; the egg white plays a lesser role.

Through its high lecithin content, but also due to the composition of its albumen substances, the egg yolk has an emulsifying effect. Thus, the egg yolk makes, in particular, the gluten more extensible and plastic. In addition, the albumen substances of the egg white improve the water retention in the dough and increase the gas retention capacity.

The special browning capacity of the egg yolk is due to its composition. When heated, the egg yolk favors the formation of melanoidines (browning substances composed of amino acids and sugar).

The better fresh-keeping characteristics of the end product are due to the fat content of the egg yolk. The fatty matter not only increases the fat content of the end product, but it also delays the retrogradation process of the starch and, thus, increases the fresh-keeping characteristics of the bakery products.

Fig. 479 **Coffee cakes made with light yeast dough, without egg content (left), and containing 200 g whole egg per kg flour (right)**

Evaluate the volume and the brown color of the crust of the loaves.

Fig. 478 **Brioche**

Requirements Regarding the Quality of Eggs

Eggs must be fresh!

How can the baker determine if eggs are fresh?

Fig. 480 **Cross-sections of coffee cakes made with light yeast dough, without egg content (left) and containing 200 g whole egg per kg flour (right)**

Evaluate the appearance of the crumb.

Evaluation of the freshness of eggs			
Evaluation method	fresh eggs	old eggs	spoiled eggs
Evaluation of the shell	faint luster	lusterless, dull	lusterless, gray or discolored with speckles
Illumination test	small air sac, transparent, egg yolk only visible as a shadow	medium-size air sac, transparent just like fresh eggs	large air sac, turbid spots in the egg white, color changes in the egg yolk, the yolk "sticks" to the egg shell
Shake test: shake the egg close to the ear	no wobbling	faint wobbling	watery wobbling
Pour test: pour the egg onto a plate	high curvature of the egg yolk; the egg white surrounds the egg yolk in a ring which is a thick liquid on the inside and a thin liquid on the outside	the egg yolk and the inner egg white ring are clearly flattened out	the egg yolk is flat and has changed color; the egg white is turbid, has coagulated and has a watery consistency
Smell test	fresh smell	old smell	foul smell

Fig. 481 **Pour test: fresh egg**

Fig. 482 **Pour test: old egg**

Old eggs are less suitable for the baking process because of a:
— loss in emulsifying capacity,
— loss in swelling capacity,
— loss in capacity to be stiffly beaten.
Moreover, they lose some of their flavor-improving effect.

Only fresh eggs can be separated into egg yolk and egg white without causing deficiencies.

Thomas is at a loss: *The yeast doughnuts he is baking have a foul smell. Yet the eggs he has used showed no deficiencies.*
Baker Smith knows this smell!
"Thomas! You have used a hay egg!"
Thomas is puzzled: "What is that?"

Even fresh eggs can be spoiled due to an infection in the hen's ovaries. Such eggs look like fresh eggs. The expert recognizes the *"hay egg"* by its somewhat strange smell. The foul smell occurs only during baking.

Eggs are traded by quality and weight classes. The quality classes are based on the freshness of the egg.

Class A: Fresh eggs, untreated, unrefrigerated, without deficiencies

Class B: Older eggs and/or eggs with a dirty shell and/or refrigerated eggs and/or eggs which have been treated for better fresh-keeping properties

Class C: Broken eggs and/or sorted out eggs with large air sacs (= old eggs). Class C eggs can only be supplied to industrial plants for the production of egg products.

Labelling of eggs

Every container of eggs should be marked with:
1) the word "eggs" or "oeufs;"
2) the number of eggs;
3) the name and full address of:
   — the producer,
   — the registered egg station that graded or packaged the eggs, or
   — the wholesaler or retailer;
4) the "best-before" date;
5) the grade and size;
6) the country of origin, if the eggs are imported.

Table 87

Weight classes for eggs	
Jumbo:	71 g or more
Extra large:	64 g or more
Large:	56 g or more
Medium:	49 g – 56 g
Small:	42 g – 49 g
Peewee:	under 42 g

Table 88

Storage of Eggs

Eggs age during storage!

Through the enzymatic decomposition of the egg substances, the egg white turns liquid. Through the products of decomposition, the eggs taste "old." During storage, the egg content shrinks due to the evaporation of the water (the air sac increases in volume).

At room temperature, eggs keep their essential freshness characteristics for 2 weeks, and in the refrigerator, for about 3 to 4 weeks.

Eggs easily adopt a foreign odor. Therefore, they should not be stored together with food products having a strong smell.

Eggs can be stored in cold storage houses for a longer period of time at temperatures of around +/- 0°C and simultaneous application of carbon dioxide. In that case, the eggs must be identified as having been "treated for better fresh-keeping properties."

Egg Products

The baker can obtain a supply of fresh eggs all year long.
But egg products, such as frozen egg and egg powder, can be stored at a lower cost and without any deterioration problems.

Frozen Eggs

Frozen eggs are offered as
— frozen whole eggs,
— frozen egg yolk, and
— frozen egg white.

They are stored in deep freezers at -10°C.
When using frozen eggs, the following rules should be observed:
— Defrost in refrigerator overnight and use as soon as possible.
— Do not place frozen eggs in hot water.
— Stir defrosted eggs thoroughly prior to taking them out of the container!
— When a small quantity is used, the remainder should be portioned into smaller batches, then re-frigerated or refrozen. Avoid repeated defrosting of the entire contents of the container.

Quantity conversion table for frozen eggs	
1 whole egg	= 50 g frozen whole egg
1 egg yolk	= 17 g frozen egg yolk
1 egg white	= 32 g frozen egg white

Table 89

Dried Egg

Dried egg is offered as
— dried whole egg,
— dried egg yolk, and
— dried egg white in the form of a powder — also in the form of crystals.

Due to the fat content, the whole egg and egg yolk powder can only be stored for a limited period of time. Egg powder is mixed with the corresponding quantity of water (*Table 90*) and can be used after a short swelling (hydration) time. Egg white in the form of crystals must be mixed with water several hours prior to its use. Egg white powder should be hydrated with 50% water and whisked vigorously before adding the remaining 50%.

Quantity conversion table for dried egg
1 litre whole egg = 275 g whole egg powder + 725 g water
1 litre egg yolk = 525 g egg yolk powder + 475 g water
1 litre egg white = 150 g egg white powder + 850 g water

Table 90

Caution! Follow the manufacturer's instructions when using dried egg white.
The water/dried egg white ratio does not necessarily correspond to the composition of fresh egg white.

Suitability of eggs for the baking process			
Properties	egg yolk	egg white	whole egg
can be stiffly beaten	–	+	(+)
makes glazes suitable for spraying	–	+	–
has an emulsifying effect	+	(+)	+
makes smooth pastes	+	+	+
improves the fermentation stability	+	(+)	+
has a browning effect	+	–	+
increases the volume of the end product	+	+	+
improves cell structure (fine crumb)	+	–	+
improves the fresh-keeping characteristics of the baking product	+	–	+

+	=	property is present
(+)	=	property is conditionally present
–	=	property is not present

Table 91

Summary of the most important information about eggs as baking ingredients

➤ *Eggs improve*
   — *the condition of doughs, batters, creams and ice-cream;*
   — *the fermentation stability of yeast doughs;*
   — *the quality of baked goods.*

➤ *Egg yolk*
   — *has an emulsifying effect;*
   — *makes doughs, batters, creams and ice-cream smoother;*
   — *locks in water when coagulating;*
   — *browns the crust of the bakery product;*
   — *improves the enjoyment value of baking goods, creams and ice-cream;*
   — *produces a yellow color.*

➤ *Egg white*
   — *can be stiffly beaten;*
   — *makes batters smooth;*
   — *absorbs water when coagulating;*
   — *makes glazes suitable for spraying.*

➤ *Egg products are*
   — *frozen eggs, and*
   — *dried eggs.*

➤ *Bakery yeast products containing eggs are:*
   — *doughnuts and sweet dough products,*
   — *stirred yeast cake,*
   — *brioches,*
   — *savarins,*
   — *croissants,*
   — *Danish doughs.*

Fillings and Toppings

Fig. 483

Yeast product fillings or toppings are of major importance to the consumer. Specific fruit toppings for custard, marzipan and preserve fillings, poppy fillings and streusel toppings are very much in demand.
The shape and appearance of the product are also significant to the customer.

The baker should use special care in selecting and preparing fillings and toppings for his products.

> *The following fillings are normally used for fine yeast bakery products:*
> — *fillings made with fruits and fruit products;*
> — *fillings made with preparations containing starch (starch custards);*
> — *fillings made with quark-cheese preparations;*
> — *fillings made with pastes;*
> — *fillings made with poppy seed preparations.*

Fillings and Toppings Made with Fresh Fruits

Although the baker offers fine yeast bakery products with fruity fillings and toppings made of durable fruit products all year long, the customer prefers products made with fresh fruits.
No durable fruit product has the same aroma as fresh fruits.

Fig. 484 **Fillings and toppings made with fresh fruits**

Classification of fruits		
Stone fruits	➤	cherries, peaches, apricots, plums, etc.
Kernel fruits	➤	apples, pears, etc.
Berry fruits	➤	strawberries, red currants, gooseberries, raspberries, blackberries, blueberries, etc.
Tropical fruits	➤	oranges, lemons, pineapple, bananas, etc.
Dried fruits	➤	raisins, etc.
Shell fruits	➤	almonds, walnuts, hazelnuts, peanuts, etc.

Table 92

Fresh fruits primarily used for yeast baking products include apples, blueberries and cherries.

In order to prevent the depletion of the fruit's juices, fruits with a high water content, e.g. cherries, are steamed prior to their use and mixed with starch or another thickener.

Other fresh fruit varieties, such as strawberries and raspberries, are seldom used for yeast products. These fruits have their special enjoyment value when they are used as fresh toppings on tarts and desserts.

Fillings and Toppings made with Fruit Products
Jams and Marmalades

Jams and marmalades are spreads made with fruits and sugar. The solid consistency is achieved through the gelling pectin of the fruits or through the addition of pectin.

The name "jam" is given to a product made by boiling fruit, fruit pulp or canned fruit to a suitable consistency with water and a sweetening ingredient. Marmalades are made exclusively from citrus fruits.

Jam should contain no less than 45% of the named fruit and 66% water-soluble solids. It may contain added pectin, an antifoaming agent and a preservative. Jam should not contain apple, rhubarb or fruit pulp preserved in sulphur dioxide.

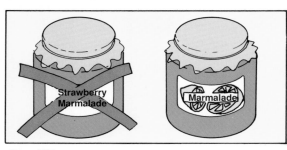

Fig. 485
Cannot be used for preparation made with non-citrus fruits   **Can only be used for preparations made with citrus fruits**

230

Preserves

Preserves are spreads made with sugar and fruits (with some exceptions, such as citrus fruits, apples, pears) in small pieces or in the form of a paste. They can be made with one or several fruit types. The terms "simple preserves" and "extra preserves" indicate a low and high fruit content, respectively.

Jams and preserves used for fillings are spread smoothly.

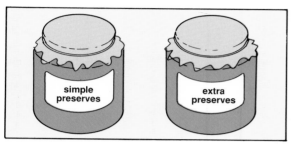

Fig. 486
— made with one or several fruit types
— in pieces or in paste form
simple = low fruit content
extra = high fruit content

Jellies

Jellies are spreads made with sugar and the juice of one or several fruit types. Simple jellies have a low fruit juice content; extra jellies have a high fruit juice content.

When baked, jellies have a tendency to flow out of the baked product. Therefore, they are primarily used for fillings of baked products, e.g. for double-layer tea-cakes.

Jellies made with apples or pears are called "apple-jelly" and "pear-jelly" respectively.

Fig. 487
simple = low fruit content
extra = high fruit content

Plum Jam

Plum jam is thickened primarily through the evaporation of water from the plum paste, but rarely by means of gelling agents. The fruit content is correspondingly higher than that of preserves.

Fruit Pulp and Fruit Paste

Fruit pulp and fruit paste are made with fruits reduced to small pieces and from which the non-edible parts have been eliminated. Pulp and fruit paste do not contain any sugar or other ingredients.

The baker primarily uses apple pulp and apple paste, e.g. for filling of doughnuts or turnovers or for covered apple cake.

Fig. 499   without sugar
in pieces   paste

Fillings and Toppings made with Durable Fruit Products

The baker tries to offer tasty bakery products made with fruits all year long — even after the fresh fruit season. Fruit varieties from overseas and hothouse fruit from southern and tropical countries are available all year long, but these fruits are
— very expensive, and
— often poor in aroma.

Bakers can use durable fruit products of excellent quality which are offered in a large variety:
— steamed fruits,
— frozen fruits, and
— dried fruits.

Steamed Fruits

Fig. 489 **Steamed fruits**

231

Steamed fruits are sterilized fruits in cans or glass jars. They are either whole fruits or cut fruits in a watery-sugar solution. The following steamed fruits are used for toppings or fillings of fine yeast products:

— apples in slices or in pieces,
— cherries,
— strawberries, red currants, cranberries,
— apricots,
— sliced mandarins,
— pineapple in pieces or in rings,
— blueberries, wild and cultivated.

Fig. 490 **Copenhagen fruit pockets with steamed fruit toppings**

Frozen Fruits

The use of frozen fruits increases every year. Frozen apples are often used for yeast products. Frozen apples can be processed in the same way as fresh fruits after defrosting.

For desserts and tarts, bakeries primarily use frozen raspberries, strawberries and blueberries (cultivated and wild).

Fig. 491 **Frozen red currants**

Dried Fruits

Dried fruits can be stored, are always available and are low in price. However, they are less aromatic than fresh fruit.

232

Dried fruits are:
— evaporated fruits, such as apples, plums and apricots. These fruits are soaked in water prior to their use for bakery products.
— dried fruits, such as raisins, figs and dates.

Dried Apples

Among the evaporated fruits, bakeries primarily use dried apples for the production of baked goods.
Fully-ripe, large apple varieties with a small core and a sour flavor are used.
Dried apples are cut into pieces or rings (= ring apples).
Prior to use, dried apples must be soaked in water for an extended period of time (*Fig. 492*). It is recommended that apples be steamed after they have been soaked and that a small amount of thickening agent be used. Apple fillings are readily available in the form of apple pie and apple turnover fillings.
Dried apple pieces with a cold starch mixture are also available.
During soaking, the starch binds the excess water without heat application.

Fig. 492 **Dried apples must soak prior to use**

Fig. 493 **Products made with yeast dough and dried apples**

Dried apples can be used for fillings or toppings of small yeast bakery products, for Danish and for apple cake (*Fig. 493*).

Raisins

Raisins are used as ingredients of many types of fillings and toppings:

➤ in yeast products (Danish, raisin bread and rolls, coffee cakes, Stollen, fruit cake),
➤ in pies and cinnamon rolls,
➤ in puff pastry products.

> * *Raisins are very sweet, aromatic dried grapes. They are primarily dried on the vine.*

Not all raisins are suited for the production of bakery products. They must meet the following requirements:

— They must be free from earth residues and other impurities.
— They must be free from squashed, sticky berries and berries with stems.
— They must be seedless.
— They must be firm and dry.
— They must be durable.
— They must be sweet and aromatic.

Sultana raisins are best suited for bakery products. They are, in principle, seedless, very sweet and aromatic. Depending on their country of origin and on the variety, they have a purple-brown (from California) or an amber to waxy color.

The major producers of sultana raisins are in California, Australia, and also in Iran, Turkey and Greece.

Currants are small, black, slightly sour-aromatic, dried grapes. They grow mainly in Greece (Korinth = town in Greece). The use of currants for bakery products is limited.

> *Tips for the processing of sultana raisins:*
> → *Sort out any impurities!*
> → *Wash the raisins in cold water and let them drip off thoroughly, immediately after washing!*
> → *When sultana raisins are to be used for dry cakes, soak the raisins overnight in a small amount of rum.*
> → *When they are to be used for pound cakes or fruit cakes, coat the raisins with flour prior to incorporating. (This will prevent the raisins from sinking to the bottom during baking.)*

Additional Information

If conditioned raisins are incorporated into a dough too early in the mixing process or at too high a speed, the raisins will break open and leach the solids. The dough will discolor and the acid released from the raisins will accelerate oxidation. The leached raisin solids are high in fructose and dextrose which interferes with yeast activity, gives low volume, increases final proof time and results in a poor-quality product.

> Caution! *Make sure raisins have been properly conditioned before incorporating into a dough.*

Nuts

Fig. 494 **Hazelnut**

Nuts or shell fruits — unpeeled fruits — include almonds, hazelnuts, walnuts, peanuts, Brazil-nuts, cashew nuts, pistachios and pecans.

Almonds, peanuts, hazelnuts, pecans and walnuts are the most widely-used nuts as baking ingredients.

The green pistachio kernels are used simply for decorating purposes and as flavor carriers for tarts, desserts and ice-cream.

Almonds

Almonds are an ingredient of many fine bakery products;

➤ as a dough ingredient for Stollen, stirred yeast cake, shortcakes and cookies;
➤ as an ingredient of cake batters;
➤ as an ingredient of fillings;
➤ as an ingredient for croque-en-bouche (crunch in the mouth), florentines, etc.;
➤ as a main raw material for marzipan and macaroons;
➤ as a decoration on gingerbread, tarts and pralines.

Almond fruits are similar in appearance to peaches. Their fruit pulp is not edible. The almond is the kernel inside the fruit shell.

Unlike sweet almonds, bitter almonds
● are very small,
● have an aromatic-bitter smell,
● have an intensively bitter flavor,
● have a high amygdalin content.

233

Commercial almond brands

— Whole almonds with skin
— Blanched almonds, without skin
   • whole
   • sliced
   • flaked
   • slivered
   • ground

Table 93

Caution: *Store bitter almonds away from the access of children!*
An infant can die after eating only 5 to 6 bitter almonds!

Practical tips:

— *Removing the almond skin:*
 • *Pour hot water over the almonds.*
 • *Let them soak for 10 minutes.*
 • *Pinch the almond skin off.*
— *Processing of chopped almonds (ready-made)*
 • *Pour some hot water over the chopped almonds. This will prevent the almonds from absorbing moisture from the crumb of the bakery product. The almonds are more "juicy."*

Caution!

It is risky to produce candied orange peel in the bakery. Almost all orange peels have been treated, often with pre-servatives.

Only untreated lemons or oranges should be used in the bakery to produce candied peels.

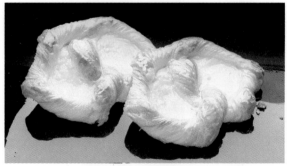

Fig. 495 **Danish dough pretzels filled with vanilla pastry cream**

Reference: *For more information about the preparation of vanilla pastry cream, refer to the chapter entitled* **Cream Tarts and Cream Desserts**.

After the consumption of bitter almonds, poisonous hydrocyanic acid is formed in the body by the amygdalin.

Bitter almonds are the wild variety of sweet almonds, and are used exclusively in the production of almond flavorings.

Almonds are cultivated mainly in the Mediterranean countries and in California.

Candied Fruits

Candied fruits are fruits candied in sugar. For bakery products, the following are primarily used:

➤ Candied lemon peel
➤ Candied orange peel
➤ Decorative fruits (e.g. candied cherries), and
➤ Rutabaga or turnip is colored and candied and is used extensively in North America for mixing with fruits or it is sold on its own.

Candied Lemon Peel and Candied Orange Peel

Candied lemon peel is made from the thick peels of the large cedrat lemons.

The blanched (= steamed) fruit shells are candied, in phases, in sugar solutions of increasing concentration.

Candied lemon peel is available in the form of shell halves and in cubes. The candied shells have a faint green color and they are somewhat translucent.

Candied orange peel is made from the shells of bitter oranges (pomerances), using the same process as for candied lemon peel.

Thecandied peels have the color and flavor is like oranges.

Fillings and Toppings Made with Vanilla Pastry Cream

The bakery prepares vanilla cream every day:
— as a filling for fine yeast baking products, Danish and dessert items;
— as a basic cream for European-style butter cream.

The cream can be produced
— in a cooking process using cream (custard) powder, or
— in a cold process with cold cream powder (pre-gelatinized starch).

Product:	Composition:
— Custard powder ➤	*raw rice starch, wheat starch, or corn starch;* *added color;* *added flavor*
— Instant powder ➤	*pre-gelatinized, dry starch;* *plant-based thickeners and gelling agents;* *added color;* *added flavor*

Can you produce a vanilla pastry cream from scratch? The following table describes the production process.

How to make a cream with vanilla flavor:
— *Use the recipe from Table 94.*
— *Take some milk off the quantity indicated in the recipe; blend the cream powder and the whole egg with the milk until you obtain a smooth batter.*
— *Heat the remainder of the milk and sugar until they boil.*
— *Pour the prepared cream powder into the boiling milk, while stirring continuously.*
— *After the cream has become smooth, cook for another three minutes, while stirring continuously.*

Basic recipe for a cream with vanilla flavor	
1,000 g	of milk
200 g	of sugar
90 g	of custard powder
0 – 200 g	of whole egg

Table 94

Cooked vanilla cream for fillings can best be prepared when it is still somewhat warm, shortly before it turns firm.

For yeast-cake fillings, egg foam is incorporated into the cream while it is still hot.

Caution! *Custard powder usually contains the artificial flavoring agent, vanillin. The use of vanillin does not have to be identified on bakery products sold in unpackaged format. The filling cannot, however, be designated as "vanilla cream," and is often referred to as "Bavarian cream." The label on packaged products with added vanillin must have a reference to added artificial flavor.*

Fillings and Toppings made with Quark-cheese Preparations

The usual ingredients for quark-cheese fillings and toppings are quark cheese, sugar, eggs, salt, cream/milk and lemon as flavor.

For cheese cake, the filling must be stiff. Stiffness is achieved by adding starch or other thickeners. Aeration is achieved through egg white foam.

For quark-cheese fillings, a moist, creamy consistency is required. Therefore, the baker should dispense with the addition of thickeners.

Fillings Made with Raw Pastes

Starting products are raw marzipan, persipan (apricot kernel paste) and nut pastes.

Marzipan Fillings

Almond paste is blended with milk or egg yolk and sugar until it is smooth.

For *fruity marzipan fillings*, preserves are blended into the almond paste until the paste is smooth.

Marzipan fillings can be extended by adding clean, white-cake crumbs.

Frangipane is a filling paste made with almond paste, butter/margarine, eggs and some flour.

Persipan Fillings

Persipan fillings are prepared in the same way as marzipan fillings.

The use of persipan should be identified as apricot kernels on the end product offered for sale.

Fig. 496 **Fillings and toppings made with quark-cheese preparations**

Fig. 497 **Danish filled with a nut paste**

Poppy seed Fillings and Toppings

Fig. 498

Boiling milk is poured over ground poppy seed and sweetened with sugar.

To obtain a better consistency of the paste, cooked vanilla custard is mixed into the poppy seed paste.

To enhance the poppy seed paste, the following can be used: sultana raisins, candied lemon peel, candied orange peel, chopped almonds, almond paste, rum and spices.

Fillings and Toppings Made with Convenience Products

The making of apple, quark-cheese and poppy seed fillings takes a long time. The baker can buy ready-made fillings to which individual products can be added to improve the flavor. Cake crumbs can be added to extend the product.

Declaration of Fillings and Toppings

In principle, there is no requirement to give bakery products fillings a special name. But the name of the bakery product must correspond to the general trade concept and describe the bakery product sufficiently.

Example 1:

Poppy seed coffee cakes offered unpackaged. Labelling is not required.

Example 2:

Poppy seed coffee cakes prepared and offered for sale in the bakery, sealed in transparent packaging. Labelling is required: name, address of manufacturer, name of product, count or weight, price, best-before date.

Example 3:

Poppy seed coffee cake sealed in transparent foil is offered for sale in a self-serve environment or in a food store.

In this case, poppy seed coffee cake is considered a prepackaged item; the bakery product must be labelled. The trade name should read: "poppy seed coffee cake" or "with poppy seed filling."

Regulations regarding packaging and labelling can be obtained from the appropriate regulatory body.

If the proportion of poppy seed used for the filling is less than 20%, the trade name should read simply "filled" or "coffee cakes filled with poppy seed."

Beware!

The following applies to second two examples:

If the filling contains added substances (such as artificial color, preservatives, artificial flavors) or food substitutes, such as kernel paste, their use must be identified on the product in the ingredient listing.

Reference:
In connection with the labelling of bakery products, please also refer to the chapters entitled **Spices and Flavors**, **Preservatives and Artificial Color**.

Additional Information

Minimum quantities of ingredients determining the value of fillings		
Item	Minimum content	
Quark-cheese filling	20%	Quark-cheese
Poppy seed filling	20%	Poppy seed
Nut/almond filling	20%	Nuts/almonds
Marzipan filling	20%	Almond paste
Fruit filling or fruit products	30%	Fresh fruit
Preserves filling	100%	Preserves

Table 95

Food Regulatory Guidelines

Food for Thought:
A baker offers filled yeast products for sale, with the special indication "filled with almond paste." The filling is composed of the following ingredients:

1.0 kg   Sugar
1.0 kg   Apricot preserve
1.0 kg   Cake crumbs
0.5 litres Milk
1.5 kg   Almond paste

The filling is thus primarily composed of non-almond products.
Is the label "filling made of almond paste" permitted in this case?

236

Products Made with Light Fine Yeast Dough

Fig. 499 **Pastry made with light fine yeast dough**

The following pastries are made with light fine yeast dough:

- ➤ cinnamon rolls
- ➤ sweet rolls
- ➤ tea buns
- ➤ hot dog and hamburger buns
- ➤ Danish (basic dough)

The consumer has specific expectations with regard to the quality of light yeast pastries purchased in retail and franchise bakeries.

- *— They must be fresh.*
- *— They must have a good flavor.*
- *— They must have a well-leavened, cottony crumb with fine cells.*
- *— They must be easy to digest.*

Even on the day of production, light fine yeast bakery products have a reduced enjoyment value:

- — The crust loses its luster and shrinks.
- — The crumb is somewhat firm and dry.
- — The pastry has little flavor.

The short shelf-life period is due to the low fat/sugar ratio of the dough.

Production of Small Yeast Pastry

Makeups, Fermentation and Baking
Small yeast pastry is produced with or without fillings, or with a topping.

Fig. 500
Small yeast pastry made with poppy seed paste

Fig. 501 **Makeup of yeast dough for filled small pastry, using a makeup machine**

Basic recipe for light fine yeast dough	
1,000 g	Bread flour
500 g	Milk
100 g	Sugar
100 g	Margarine
60 g	Yeast
12 g	Salt
	Flavor

Table 96

Breakfast crescent rolls, made of light yeast dough, are an example of the production of unfilled small yeast pastry.

237

Fig. 502

"Silicone parchment paper has a special coating that prevents dough from sticking to the baking pan. It helps keep pans clean and prevents the burned residue from previous products from sticking to the bottom of the baked goods."

Fig. 503

Fig. 504

Joe says: "If everybody working in a bakery is concerned about safety and sanitation first, the bakery soon would go into bankruptcy." What do you think? Discuss his statement.

Makeup of Crescent Rolls	
Working steps:	*Explanations:*
— *Prepare the baking pans!*	➤ *Make sure the baking pans are clean! Coat the baking pans with some fat or place silicone parchment paper on the pans. The fat on the baking pans prevents the dough pieces from sticking.*
— *Make sure the work place is clean!*	➤ *Remove flour dust and dough scraps! Use only impeccably clean equipment! Clean your hands!*
— *Make sure the work place is safe!*	➤ *Do not place any containers or equipment on the floor! Follow safety instructions when working with dough cutting devices, mixers, sheeters, etc.!*
— *Make sure the work process runs smoothly!*	➤ *Arrange your work place in such a manner so that — the number and length of work steps is as small as possible, — the physical work is reduced to a minimum, — the tools and equipment are handy in the sequence of the work process!*
— *Prepare the egg wash.*	➤ *Liquids normally used are milk, eggs or egg yolk and water, a pinch of salt/sugar can be added.*

Fig. 505 **Shaping of crescent rolls**

Working process for production of crescent rolls	
Working steps:	**Explanation:**
— Scaling and rounding of heads (units)	➤ Rounding ensures finer and more uniform cells in the crumb and is a prerequisite for obtaining pieces of identical size when using the bun rounder
— Intermediate proofing	➤ The round pieces must be allowed to relax. Immediate further processing would cause the dough surface to tear.
— Pressing and rounding using the bun rounder	
— Short intermediate proofing	➤ The round pieces must be allowed to relax.
— Rolling out	➤ Rolling-out and rolling-up by means of the crescent-rolling machine is performed in two successive work steps. When the crescents are rolled up by hand, they can be rolled up easier when the flat dough pieces can rest for a moment.
— Shaping and placing of the rolled up dough pieces onto the baking pans	➤ The rolled-up dough pieces are placed onto the baking pans in the shape of a horseshoe. Proper spacing will allow products to bake and look better as they do not stick together. When placing the dough pieces onto the pans, it is important to ensure that the tapering of the last rolling on the crescent runs from the outside to the inside (see Fig. 507).
— Fermentation of the dough pieces	➤ The final proofing should be between 35 and 40°C and at a corresponding humidity. If the humidity is too low, the dough skin dries out and turns tough. This leads to a rough lackluster crust of the baked product. When the air in the proofer is too dry, the dough pieces should be coated with egg wash before and after makeup.
— Baking of the shaped pieces	➤ Crescents are baked at 2/3 proof. At full fermentation maturity, the contours of the rolled pieces would disappear. The dough pieces are baked in the oven at temperatures ranging between 220 and 240°C. When the baking temperature is too low, the crust of the crescents turns too hard and the crumb too dry. Crescents with egg wash coating should not be baked in steam. The wash runs off to form black lines at the base.
— Preparation after baking in the oven	➤ The crescents can be coated with some water or a thin liquid starch paste right after they come out of the oven. This gives them an additional luster (sheen). This does not, however, apply to crescents which have previously been coated with egg.

Food for Thought: *Why does water applied to bakery products coming right out of the oven give them a better luster? For more information, please refer to the section on Bread Production in the chapter entitled **The Baking Process**.*

Fig. 506 **Makeup of crescents by means of special equipment**

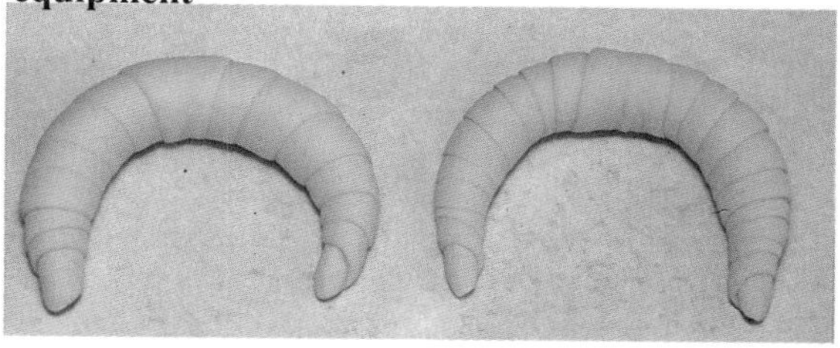

Fig. 507 **Shaping of the rolled pieces: correct (left), wrong (right)**

Production of Apple Turnovers using Yeast Dough

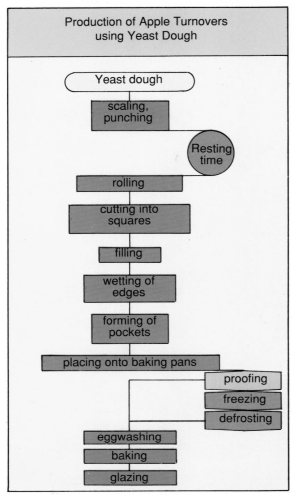

Yeast dough
→ scaling, punching
→ Resting time
→ rolling
→ cutting into squares
→ filling
→ wetting of edges
→ forming of pockets
→ placing onto baking pans
→ proofing
→ freezing
→ defrosting
→ eggwashing
→ baking
→ glazing

Table 97

Joe thinks: *"Coating with hot apricot glaze is too expensive and time consuming! The customer won't notice the difference anyway!"* What do you think?

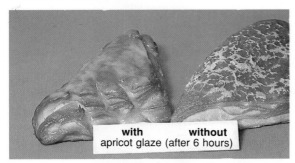

with apricot glaze | without apricot glaze (after 6 hours)

Fig. 508 **Glazed pastry with apricot coating (left) and without apricot coating (right) after 6 hours of storage**

Evaluate the glazing of the pastries.

Preparation of an Apricot Glaze

All yeast pastries that are to be coated with a sugar icing or fondant should receive an application of hot apricot glaze prior to icing.

> * *Apricot glaze = applying hot apricot preserve to the baking product*

Why apply an apricot glaze?

→ It delays the "dying" of the water icing/fondant glaze.
➤ The apricot preserve gelling on the crust of the baking product prevents rapid absorption of the moisture from the glazing by the crust.

➤ When the glazing dries out, large sugar crystals form. The glazing loses its luster; it "dies."

→ It delays the cracking of the sugar glazing.
➤ Icings tear easily off the crust when they dry out. On baked products that have received an apricot glaze, the glazing and the apricot coating form a strong compound.

→ It improves the fresh-keeping characteristics of the baked product.
➤ Baked products with an apricot coating do not dry out as fast as others.

→ It increases the enjoyment value of the baking products.
➤ The enjoyment value is increased
  • through the flavor of the preserve, and
  • through the improved appearance of the glazing.

And this is how an apricot coating is prepared:
— Pass the apricot preserve through a strainer.
— Cook the apricot preserve until it forms a fine liquid.
— Apricot preserve reaches its optimum consistency at 105°C.

And this is how the apricot coating is applied:
— Use only brushes resistant to boiling.
— Apply a coat of apricot preserve to the baked product right after it comes out of the oven.

Glazing

Sugar glazings for fine yeast pastry are composed primarily of icing sugar and glucose, with a low proportion of water.

The sugar industry offers the baker the following types of sugar for glazings:
— powdered sugar,
— glazing powder,
— fondant.

Powdered sugar is blended with water at a ratio of 5 to 1 (0.2 litres water per 1 kg powdered sugar). Glazings made of powdered sugar are very sensitive to moisture. The fine sugar crystals dissolve quickly. Thus, the coating deteriorates. Powdered sugar glazings have the same reaction when the baked goods are stored in a very dry environment.
The drying out of the glazing leads to the formation of large sugar crystals (*Fig. 510*). The glazing "dies." Water glazings made with powdered sugar are, therefore, only suited for baked goods that are consumed on the day of production.

Glazing powder is a mixture of powdered sugar and glazing stabilizers derived from plant products and hard fat flakes. The stabilizers delay the crystallizing process of the dissolved sugar. Glazing powder can be stored easily. It does not have a tendency to turn lumpy as quickly as powdered sugar.

The selection and use of the different types of glazing powders will depend on:
— temperature of product during application,
— length of storage, and
— climate during storage and at sales point.

Fondant is a special icing made by boiling sugar, water, and cream of tartar or glucose, and cooling slowly while agitating the mixture. It is very solid when stored in a cool environment. Prior to being taken out of the container, the fondant should be kept at room temperature for an extended period of time. When prepared for use, 1 kg fondant is blended with 50 ml water and heated to a maximum temperature of 40°C. If the fondant is heated up to a higher temperature, the minuscule sugar crystals dissolve and form large, transparent sugar crystals during the cooling process. The glazing turns translucent and cloudy.

Additional Information

The preparation of a glazing is based on the solubility of the sugar in water. Through over-saturation of the solution, a part of the sugar remains in the form of undissolved crystals. The smaller the undissolved crystals, and the finer these remain distributed in the solution, the smoother the glazing.
The larger the crystals, the duller and more unappealing the appearance of the glazing.

Fig. 509 Glazed jelly doughnuts

Note the smooth and silky glaze.

 **Reference:** *The production of powdered sugar and of fondant is described in the chapter entitled* **Sugar for Decorating Purposes**.

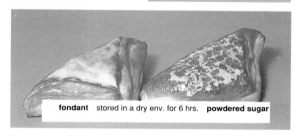

fondant   stored in a dry env. for 6 hrs.   powdered sugar

Fig. 510 Danish coated with fondant (left) and with a glazing made with powdered sugar (right) after having been stored for 6 hours in a dry environment

Describe the glazings in the pictures.

fondant   stored in a humid env. for 6 hrs.   powdered sugar

Fig. 511 Danish coated with fondant (left) and with a glazing made with powdered sugar after having been stored for 6 hours in a humid environment

Describe the glazings in the pictures.

 Joe says: *"I always have trouble with fondant! When I knead it, it is too firm! When I heat it, it turns glassy!"* What is he doing wrong?

241

Suitability of fondant and powdered sugar glazings for fine yeast baking products — a comparison		
	Fondant	Powdered sugar glazing
Production of the glazing:	The production is complicated. Therefore, the fondant is purchased as a ready-made product.	Simple production: Blend powdered sugar and water.
Processing of the glazing:	The fondant must be heated up carefully, while water is being added. Although the fondant should be applied onto the pastry while it is still somewhat warm, it dries even on cool pastry. When applied on hot pastry, the glazing turns glassy.	Powdered sugar glazings only dry sufficiently on warm pastry. On hot pastry, the glazing turns glassy!
Durability of the glazing:	Fondant is not very sensitive to air humidity and moisture from the pastry (e.g. moist fillings). Fondant "does not die fast." The glazing keeps its luster for a few days.	Powdered sugar glazing deteriorates very fast at high air humidity on covered Danishes (Fig. 511). It also "dies very fast" (Fig. 510).

Production of Danish-style Pastry (Plunder)

Fig. 512 **Assorted coffee pastries**

Quality and Composition

Compare Danish-style pastry with a simple small pastry made with a fine yeast dough.

Observations:

— The crust of the Danish pastry is flaky.
— The crust of the Danish pastry is crisper.
— The crumb of the Danish pastry shows distinct layers.
— The Danish pastry keeps fresh for a longer period of time.

The reason for these quality characteristics is the roll-in shortening fat incorporated in layers into the dough.

> * A Plunder or Danish-style pastry is a fine baking product rich in fat, made with rolled-in (laminated) yeast dough.

When a customer asks for a Danish pastry, he or she gets a product made of unsweetened fine yeast dough in various shapes.

These pastry items have sweet fillings or toppings.

In recent years, a new variety of baking product has been developed in the bakeries: Danish-style specialty products made with yeast doughs with a low sugar content, such as croissants (filled and unfilled), Danish rolls and Danish snacks with cheese, ham, hamburger and pizza toppings.

The roll-in fat content depends on how heavy the product is intended to be (see *Table 98*).

The roll-in fat proportion per 100 parts flour must amount to at least 25.6 parts pure fat. When converted into the dough quantity of a light fine yeast dough, the minimum requirement is as follows:

> * Per 1,000 g of light fine yeast dough, at least 170 g of roll-in margarine must be used.

German Danish (Plunder) has a relatively low roll-in fat content. Therefore, this variety is easier to digest. But don't be misled! The fat content of German Danish is comparable to that of Christmas Stollen.

Danish has a high content of roll-in fat.

Kopenhagener Danish is Danish with a particularly high roll-in fat content.

242

Butter Danish must exclusively contain butter as a fat (in the dough as well as for roll-in purposes).

Roll-in fat content in Danish per 1,000 g yeast dough			
German Danish	170	–	300 g
Danish	400	–	600 g
Kopenhagener Danish	700	–	1,000 g

Table 98

Production Processes
Basic Yeast Dough

Danish-style pastry is made with yeast dough (= basic dough) and roll-in fat.
The composition of the yeast dough depends on the pastry type to be made:

→ for coffee pastry ➤ a light fine yeast dough

→ for croissants ➤ a fine yeast dough with a low amount of sugar

→ for rolls ➤ a simple yeast dough

The basic yeast dough for coffee pastry must be light: Too high a fat content in the dough reduces the isolating effect of the roll-in fat.
Too high a sugar content in the dough reduces the elasticity of the dough.
The dough can be folded more easily when egg is added.

> * *Caution! For Danish-style pastry with a high roll-in fat content, the basic dough must be made cool.*

Due to the large amount of fat layers, the yeast dough must have especially good roll-in properties. Cool, slightly rested doughs can be rolled-in (laminated) more easily.

Basic recipe for a yeast dough for Danish-style pastries	
1,000 g	Bread flour, or a blend of bread/pastry flours
100 g	Baking margarine or shortening
100 g	Sugar
450 g	Milk
50 g	Egg (= 1 egg)
60 g	Yeast
12 g	Salt
	Lemon flavor or spice

Table 99

Dough temp./dough resting time for basic yeast dough, based on proportion of roll-in fat (for 1,000 g dough)		
Roll-in fat	Dough temp.	Dough resting time
170 – 300 g	26 – 28°C	30 min. at room temp.
400 – 600 g	22 – 24°C	30 – 60 min. at cooler temp.
700 – 1,000 g	20 – 22°C	60 min. in the refrigerator

Table 100

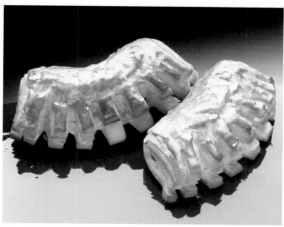

Fig. 513 **The bears claws show the structure typical for Danish-style pastry**

Roll-In Shortening

The baker has special requirements with regard to the fat rolled into the dough (= roll-in fat):

> — *Roll-in fat must be smooth and extensible so that it does not break when folded into the dough.*
>
> — *Roll-in fat must be as firm and formable as is required to obtain the proper dough characteristics. When the roll-in fat is too soft, it is pushed outside the dough when rolled into it. When the fat is too solid, it cannot be distributed uniformly enough and penetrates the dough layers.*
>
> — *Roll-in fat must maintain its firmness whether the oven temperature is high or low.*
>
> — *Roll-in fat must melt at mouth temperature (37°C). Fats with a higher melting range give a tallowy flavor to the pastry.*

The producers of margarine offer special types of roll-in margarine which fulfil these requirements to a large extent. The desired properties are achieved by selecting the proper fat raw materials and production processes and through the high fat content (85 – 90%). The proportion of fat not melted at room temperature is higher in roll-in margarine than in other special types of margarine.

Butter is not as well suited to Danish production as roll-in margarine. If you want to make Butter Danish pastry, you will obtain a good quality product when you follow these principles:

— The butter should not be warmer than 18°C.
— The butter must be mixed with some flour to obtain a plastic paste.
— The basic yeast dough must be stored in a very cool environment prior to the fat being folded in.
— The dough must be folded and kept in a cool room.

243

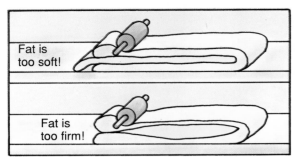

Fig. 514

Fig. 515
Laminating by means of the reversible sheeter: Folding in the roll-in margarine

Fig. 516
Laminating with the aid of a sheeter: Placing of a single fold

Joe says: *"Those who haven't got enough work make Danish-style pastry! Why go out of your way and fold the fat into the dough? Just use more fat in the dough — a better fat distribution is achieved and time is saved!"*

What do you think about this?

Laminating (folding the dough)

The number of fat layers in Danish-style dough depends on how "rich" the Danish is to be (*Table 101*).

Beware! The higher the roll-in shortening or butter content, the more layers the Danish must have!

➤ *When the fat layers are too thick, they melt out of the dough layers during proofing or baking.*
➤ *When the fat layers are too thin, they tear during folding — the dough layers stick together and prevent the formation of layers.*

Working process for Danish-style pastry	
— Blend some flour into the roll-in shortening to make it more workable	➤ Dough is ready for make-up purposes and is better adjusted to the dough properties. It does not tear easily during folding.
— Shape the roll-in margarine into an oblong block	
— Roll out the pastry dough into a rectangular shape	➤ The dough is rolled out twice as long as the roll-in fat. After folding, the dough is pressed together at the edges in order to prevent the fat from squeezing out during rolling.
— Place the block of shortening onto the dough	
— Give the dough the first turn, known as the Roll-in Turn	➤ Roll the dough into a rectangle the thickness of a finger. Brush the flour off the dough. Fold the dough into a three-fold layer.
— Give the dough the second single fold, repeat	➤ Proceed in the same way as for the first fold.
— Let the dough relax, preferably in a refrigerator for a few hours or overnight	➤ The Danish dough must be stored in a cool environment.

Number of folds for Danish depending on the proportion of roll-in fat used		
Roll-in fat per 1,000 g dough	Folds	Fat layers
200 g	2 single	= 9 layers
300 g	1 single 1 double	= 12 layers
500 g	3 single	= 27 layers
700 g	2 single 1 double	= 36 layers
900 g	3 single 1 double	= 108 layers

Table 101

Reference: *Guidelines and hints on roll-in shortening, the types and uses, are given in the chapter entitled* **Puff Pastry**.

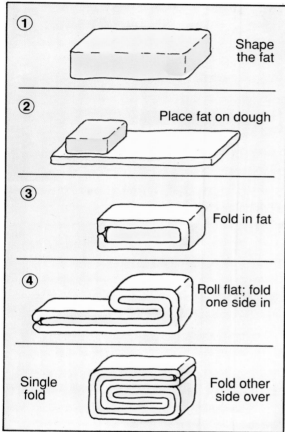

① Shape the fat

② Place fat on dough

③ Fold in fat

④ Roll flat; fold one side in

Single fold

Fold other side over

Fig. 517

Laminating Danish Dough — single fold

Reference: *For a detailed description of lamination, including "book folds," please refer to the chapter entitled* **Puff Dough**.

Makeup, baking and preparation of Danish-style pastry is done in the same way as small yeast pastry, with the exception of the following:

— The temperature in the proofer (80°F/85% humidity) should not exceed 35°C. At higher temperatures, the roll-in fat melts out.

— The optimum development time for light Danish is reached at 3/4 proof, that for Kopenhagen Danish is reached at 1/3 proof.

The baking temperature ranges between 190 and 210°C. The heavier the Danish and the heavier its filling, the lower the baking temperature must be.

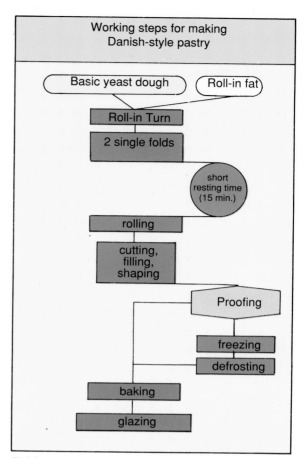

Working steps for making Danish-style pastry

Basic yeast dough — Roll-in fat

Roll-in Turn

2 single folds

short resting time (15 min.)

rolling

cutting, filling, shaping

Proofing

freezing

defrosting

baking

glazing

Table 102

Croissants

Fig. 518 **Croissant**

Table 103 shows a basic recipe for fine yeast dough with a low sugar content. It is especially suited for croissants with meat, cheese or vegetable fillings.

245

Rules for the production of croissants:

→ *Make a cool dough, with the temperature ranging between 22 and 24°C.*

→ *Let the dough rest in the refrigerator for 30 minutes (cover it up).*

→ *Fold the roll-in fat or butter into the dough, using the single-fold method.*

→ *Let the dough relax for a few minutes between folding and makeup (15 – 20 minutes).*

→ *Roll the dough flat (about 3 mm thick); Cut it into triangles: Long side = 10 cm; height = 20 cm.*

→ *Cut the triangle in the center of the long side. This small cut allows you to achieve a better shape when rolling the dough piece up. Contrary to crescent rolls, croissants are rolled up loosely.*

→ *Let the croissants proof at 35°C at a moderate air humidity (65% of relative air humidity).*

→ *Give the croissants an egg wash at 2/3 proof.*

→ *Let the croissants dry slightly until they reach 3/4 proof.*

→ *Bake the croissants in the oven at temperatures ranging between 210 and 220°C, without steam. The baking time ranges between 15 and 17 minutes.*

Basic recipe for fine yeast doughs with a low sugar content (e.g. croissants)	
1,000 g	Bread flour
100 g	Butter
25 g	Sugar
450 g	Milk (water + milk powder)
100 g	Egg (2 eggs)
60 g	Yeast
15 g	Salt
= 1,750 g	basic dough
+ 450 g	roll-in margarine or butter
= 2,200 g	croissant dough

Table 103

Baker Smith and Joe discuss how the loose layers of the Danish are achieved.
Joe says: "It's obvious that the fat aerates the Plunder!"
Baker Smith says: "The fat has no aerating effect, but it prevents the steam from leaving the dough!"
Who is right? Joe, Baker Smith, or neither?

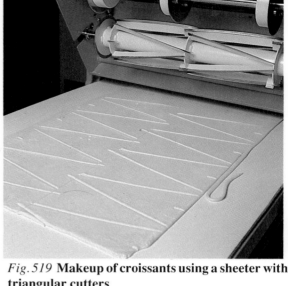

Fig. 519 **Makeup of croissants using a sheeter with triangular cutters**

Aeration

The Danish is aerated in two ways:

➤ *The dough is aerated through the fermentation gases of the yeast (= biological aeration).*

➤ *The spaces between the dough layers are aerated through steam (= physical aeration).*

The quality of the aerated layers depends on:

— the composition, condition and temperature of the basic dough,

— the quality of the fat/butter,

— the ratio between fat content and the number of layers,

— how uniform and intact the layers are.

Therefore, it is up to you to obtain a well-aerated Danish by using the proper technique.

Reference: *The aeration of laminated doughs is described in detail in the chapter entitled **Puff Pastry**.*

Pastry Deficiencies

In order to properly evaluate baked goods, one must know both the general and specific quality characteristics of a group of baked goods.

In the case of Danish-style pastry, the following four quality characteristics determine the value of the final product:

— The individual layers must be thoroughly aerated with fine cells.

— The crumb layers must be distinct, but should not detach from each other.

— The crust must be flaky, but it should not detach when an icing/fondant is applied.

— The crust must be brown, smooth and silky in appearance.

The following table lists the most frequent deficiencies of Danish-style pastry and its causes, and makes recommendations on how they can be avoided.

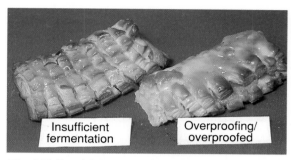

Insufficient fermentation

Overproofing/ overproofed

Fig. 520 **Danish baked at insufficient proof and at excessive proof**

Deficiency (Faults)	Causes	Corrections
— The pastry is flat and heavy. The fat has melted out during baking.	➤ Overproofing at high proofer temperature. *Or:* ➤ The dough was not folded correctly, therefore, the fat layers were too thick.	➤ Keep the temperature in the proofer below 35°C. ➤ Adapt the number of folds to the proportion of fat used.
— The crust detaches from the pastry during glazing.	➤ The dough does not have enough layers; the fat layers are too thick.	➤ Increase the number of layers by extra folds.
— The pastry shows no layers, or only indistinct layers.	➤ The roll-in proportion is too low, or the number of folds is too high. *Or:* ➤ The dough was not folded properly — rolled too thin, — rolled out irregularly, — torn during folding (insufficient rest period), — dough temperature too warm.	➤ Adjust the number of folds to the proportion of fat used. ➤ Use better care while laminating.
— The pastry is flat and heavy.	➤ The basic dough is too rich. *Or:* ➤ The dough did not sit long enough before it was made up.	➤ Check the fat and sugar content of the dough. ➤ Let the dough rest for a sufficient period of time.
— The crust is porous and shows an uneven brown color.	➤ The dough was proofed at a high humidity. *Or:* ➤ Steam application during baking in the oven.	➤ Let the proofed pieces dry off prior to placing them into the oven. ➤ Do not use steam.
— The crust is gray and bark-like.	➤ The dough pieces dried out during proofing.	➤ Make sure that sufficient air humidity is available during proofing.
— The pastry is small. The shape has been affected, e.g. the pockets have opened.	➤ The dough pieces were baked at insufficient proof.	➤ Bake the Danish at 3/4 proof.
— The pastry is flat and has an indistinct shape.	➤ Overproofed!	➤ Bake at 3/4 proof.

How to Make Rusks (Melba toast)

Have you ever tasted freshly-roasted butter rusks?

Discover rusks as oven-fresh coffee pastry.

Baker Smith says: *"It does not pay to make rusks in a small-sized bakery!"* Is this generally true?

Baker Smith should consider offering this light, aromatic and easy-to-digest pastry to his customers! Rusks are generally recommended as part of a diet for babies, infants, sick and elderly people. The reasons are

— it is easy to digest,
— it can be stored for several months,
— it is ready for consumption, and
— it can easily be made into a bread pudding.

* *Rusks are crisp, durable baked products made with a light, fine yeast dough.*

The dough is first baked like sandwich bread in the oven, then sliced and roasted.

During the roasting and drying processes, the water content in the rusk is reduced to less than 10%. Therefore, rusks can be stored for up to a year.

It is easy to make rusks for immediate consumption.

The baker requires extensive knowledge with regard to the selection of ingredients, the production process and the storage conditions in order to preserve the freshness characteristics of rusks for several months.

Product quality requirements :	Measures:
— Rusks must break "short" and the crumb must be brittle. An essential prerequisite is a crumb with fine cells.	➤ A crumb with fine cells is achieved through: — a sponge dough, — the addition of egg yolk, — the addition of lecithin or emulsifiers, — intensive mixing of the dough,
	— a sufficient dough resting time and vigorous working of the dough during dough make-up, — low proof prior to baking in the oven.

The brittleness of dough is improved through the addition of sodium bicarbonate. Through the addition of syrup and of malt extract, a better brown color can be achieved during roasting.

— Rusk slices should keep their shape during roasting. Concave sidewalls are undesirable.	➤ Concave sidewalls during the roasting process are due to a contraction of the drying crumb. This can be reduced — with a fine texture, — through special methods of dough makeup, — by keeping the crust thin during baking in the oven.
— Rusks should have an oven-fresh crispness that lasts for months.	➤ The baked product is cut into slices and roasted golden-brown on both sides at a temperature of around 220°C. Then, the rusk is dried in the oven (below 160°C). During storage, the water content is maintained below 10% by wrapping the product in vapor-proof packages.
— Rusks should not taste rancid, even after they have been stored for several months.	➤ The risk of the rusk turning rancid is reduced — by using a special baking margarine or a vegetable fat with mainly saturated fatty acids, — by adding ascorbic acid, — by using air-tight packages.

Light fine yeast dough for rusk	
1,000 g	Bread flour or cake flour
100 g	Sugar
60 g	Fat
50 g	Whole egg (= 1 egg)
450 g	Milk
60 g	Yeast
15 g	Salt
20 – 30 g	Baking agent (with lecithin or emulsifier)

Table 104

Fig. 521 **Rusks with concave sidewalls**

Do you know the causes of concave sidewalls?

Steps for the production of rusk

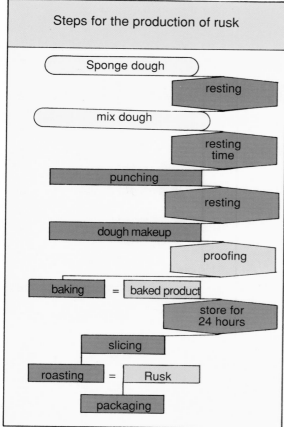

Sponge dough

resting

mix dough

resting time

punching

resting

dough makeup

proofing

baking = baked product

store for 24 hours

slicing

roasting = Rusk

packaging

Table 105

Rusk varieties

— *Conventional Rusk* ➤ *It contains about 6% fat and 10% sugar (related to bakery percentage of flour).*

— *French Rusk* ➤ *It has a low fat and sugar content. The dough liquid is mainly composed of water.*

— *Nutritional Rusk* ➤ *It contains at least 10% butter, at least 10% whole egg or 3% egg yolk. The dough liquid must be whole milk or the equivalent of whole milk. Due to its butter and whole milk content, the nutritional rusk can be stored for a shorter period of time than normal rusk (rancidity).*

— *Butter Rusk* ➤ *It must contain at least 10% butter to flour.*

— *Egg Rusk* ➤ *It must contain at least 4 whole eggs or 4 egg yolks per 1 kg of flour.*

— *Coated Rusk (coated with macaroon or coconut paste, sugar or chocolate glazing)* ➤ *Due to the fat content of the almond paste, the coconut chips and the chocolate, rusk cannot be stored for more than 6 to 9 months.*

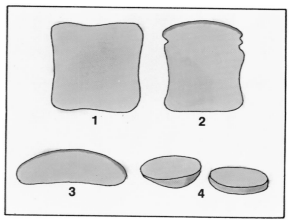

Fig. 522 **Rusk slices in various shapes:**

1. Baked in a closed box (sandwich pan)
2. Baked in an open box (bread pan)
3. Baked on a tin or in loaf shape
4. Baked as round rusk (crimped pan)

249

Products Made with Medium Fine Yeast Doughs

The following are among fine pastries made with medium fine yeast doughs:
➤ Cakes baked in cake pans of various shapes and sizes, such as streusel cake, butter cake, bee sting cake, cheese cake and poppy seed cake
➤ Large pastries, e.g. braids and filled coffee cakes
➤ Pastry in special shapes, such as baskets, animals, etc.

Fine yeast pastry, which is supposed to keep its quality characteristics for several days, should be made with medium fine yeast doughs.

The production processes used for baked goods made with medium fine yeast dough are comparable to those used for light fine yeast doughs, with the following exceptions:

Joe says: "We make one dough for all fine yeast products. I don't see why the dough for some products should be different from the dough for doughnuts, for example." What do you think?

Basic recipe for medium fine yeast dough	
1,000 g	Bread flour
150 g	Sugar
200 g	Margarine/butter
450 g	Milk
80 g	Yeast
12 g	Salt
	Lemon, vanilla

Table 106

Production of Yeast Pastries Baked on Pans (Kuchen)

Fig. 523

The scaled dough pieces are shaped into rectangles. The weight of the dough is
— for pan size, 40 x 60 cm (16" x 24") = about 1.2 kg dough

After a short intermediate proofing period, the dough is rolled out, maintaining a uniform thickness throughout. Then the dough is placed onto greased pans or pans lined with silicone paper.

A rolling pin or a mechanical sheeter is used for rolling out the dough.

Rolling-out Dough Using a Dough Sheeter

Most small bakeries use a dough sheeter, either a single or a multi-purpose type. With interchangeable pressure plates and guides, sheeters can be used to mold a variety of bread shapes and weights. Their main use is to laminate and sheet a variety of puff and Danish pastries.

Working with the sheeter must be
— safe, and
— hygienic.

Work Safety

To ensure safety in the work place, you must operate the machine carefully while respecting the rules for accident prevention.

> *The dangerous points of sheeters are*
> — *the feeder areas around the rollers,*
> — *the area where the conveyor belt runs onto the deflection roller,*
> — *any cutting devices.*

The feeder area around the rollers is secured by means of a protective grating equipped with lateral screens. Movable protective gratings activate a switch when they are lifted. The machine is then switched off or put into reverse gear.

Cleaning

The machine must be in perfect hygienic condition when used.
The machine should be cleaned after each use, or at least at the end of the day.

Standard baking pan sizes
16 x 24 inches (40 x 60 cm)
18 x 26 inches (45 x 65 cm)

Table 107

> *Suggestion: Take a look at the pan sizes used in your bakery.*

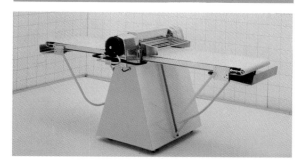

Fig. 524 **Sheeter model**

Joe is smart. *He says: "When the dough piles up in front of the rollers, the protective grating is in the way. I know a technical trick to lift the grating without switching the machine off!"*

How smart is Joe?

Fig. 525

→ The flour container is emptied and cleaned.

→ The roller scrapers are taken out and cleaned with warm water.

→ The conveyor belts are brushed dry.

→ Metal and synthetic parts are wiped off.

→ For maintenance work, such as oil changes and lubricating, follow the manufacturer's instructions.

Fig. 526 **Rolling out the dough using reversible sheeter**

Caution!
Operation and cleaning of the reversible sheeter should only be performed by persons who are familiar with such tasks.

Food Regulatory Guidelines

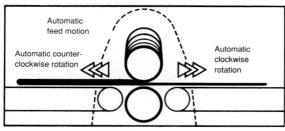

Automatic feed motion

Automatic counter-clockwise rotation

Automatic clockwise rotation

Fig. 527
Representation of the working principle of a sheeter model with automatic feed motion

Fig. 528 **Streusel cake**

Function

The dough is rolled out in phases. The desired dough thickness must be adjusted prior to each rolling process. When a fully-automated machine is used, only the desired final thickness must be adjusted.

And this is how the reversible sheeter works:
— The conveyor belt feeds the dough through the rollers, where the dough is rolled flat to the selected thickness.
— The conveyor belt on the other side of the rollers picks up the dough. In order to prevent the rolled dough from folding on the conveyor belt, a synchronized gear ensures that the pick-up belt moves twice as fast as the feeder belt.
— The dough piece is now rotated by 90° and fed in the opposite direction through the rollers.
— The desired dough thickness is achieved after 3 to 4 passages through the machine. Most automatic sheeters have a setting device to avoid rolling the dough too thin.

Streusel Cake

After intermediate proofing, the dough placed onto the pan is coated with milk. The moist dough surface improves adhesion of the streusel to the dough. Streusel is made by hand-blending flour, sugar and fat to a crumbly consistency. The amount of streusel to be used for a pan size of 40 x 60 cm is about 1 kg.

The cake is baked at 2/3 proof for about 18 to 20 minutes at a temperature ranging between 210 and 220°C.

For butter streusel cake, the dough and the streusel must contain 51% butter as shortening. The percentage of butter used must amount to at least 30% of the quantity of flour. Butter streusel and heavy streusel (650 g margarine and 650 g sugar per kg flour) must be made cool. Otherwise, the crumbs have a shortbread-like consistency.

Typical deficiencies of Streusel	
Deficiency:	*Cause:*
— *The crumb crumbles when cut and during consumption.*	➤ *The dough surface was too dry when the streusel was applied.* ➤ *The streusel mixture is too fine.* ➤ *The proportion of flour used for the streusel is too high.*
— *The streusel melts during baking.*	➤ *The proportion of fat used in the streusel is too high.*
— *The streusel is brittle and hard.*	➤ *The proportion of sugar used in the streusel is too high.*
— *The cake forms bubbles during baking.*	➤ *The dough was too young or too soft. The bubble effect is reinforced when the initial baking temperature is too high.*

Basic recipe for Streusel	
1,000 g	Bread flour
500 g	Margarine/butter
500 g	Sugar
	Vanilla, lemon or cinnamon

Table 108

Bee Sting Cake (Bienenstich)

Bee sting cake is a flat yeast cake baked with a topping of almond/honey paste. The paste is prepared with sugar, honey, fat, cream, almonds and other nuts (see *Table 109*). Bee sting cake is usually filled with a light vanilla pastry cream.

The bee sting paste is spread on the flatly rolled yeast dough. The paste should still be warm:
— When the paste is cool, it is solid and tears up the dough surface during application.
— When the paste is hot it "burns" the yeast in the dough surface.

The industry offers the bakery basic bee sting paste as a convenience product:
— The basic paste is offered as a ready-made product. It is heated prior to use and mixed with chopped almonds or almond chips (or nuts).
— The basic paste is also offered in powdered form. First, the almonds are spread onto the dough, then onto the ready-made product. During baking, the powdered basic paste melts.

Bee sting paste made with convenience products is easy to prepare and has no disadvantages.

For bee sting cake, at least 200 g bee sting paste should be used per 1 kg dough. The proportion of almonds or other nuts in the paste should be at least 30%.

Fig. 530 **Bee Sting Cake**

Basic recipe for Bee Sting paste
200 g Sugar
100 g Honey
200 g Fat
100 g Whipping cream
300 g flaked Almonds or Peanuts

Table 109

Reference: *For more details on the preparation of the basic paste for Bee Sting Cake, please refer to the chapter entitled* **Pastry Made with Roasted Products**.

Food Regulatory Guidelines

Butter Cake, Sugar Cake

Butter cake is a yeast cake containing mostly butter as a fat in the dough and in the topping. It also usually contains chopped almonds.

Fig. 531 **Sugar cake**

The dough is placed onto the baking sheet. At half proof, butter flakes are spread onto the dough, then granulated sugar. The higher the proof of the dough at the time the butter flakes are placed onto it, the deeper the butter holes that will be formed during baking.

Fig. 529 **Cheese cake**

To improve the flavor and to achieve a better adhesion of the sugar, the dough can be coated with sour cream prior to applying butter flakes.

After the butter flakes have been applied, the temperature and the humidity level should be kept low in order to avoid premature melting of the butter flakes and dissolving of the granulated sugar.

The total butter content of the butter cake should be at least 30% of the flour used. When margarine is used, the cake is called "sugar cake."

Fruit Desserts

Fig. 532 **Fruit Desserts**

Fruit desserts made from yeast dough are baked on flat pans and are made with fillings from apples, plums, sour cherries, apricots, blueberries, and also rhubarb stems.

The fruit most frequently used for yeast cakes is apples. They are available in various forms.

Apples are available as:	They are prepared as follows:
— Fresh apples	➤ Peel the apples, remove the core, cut the apples into cubes or slices and use them raw or steamed.
— Steamed apples	➤ Let them drip off or use a thickener.
— Apple pulp/paste	➤ Add only sugar. Use a thickener for liquid pulp.
— Frozen apples	➤ Defrost; add sugar. Use a thickener for watery products.
— Dried apples	➤ Soak in water. Convenience products already contain sugar and a thickener that will work in cold water.

Caution! Raw, peeled apples turn brown so they should be baked or steamed immediately!

The following toppings are normally used for fruit desserts:
— Lattices or tops made with yeast dough, puff dough, tart paste or pie dough;
— Streusel;
— Custards;
— Meringues;
— Cake batters.

Cake batters and meringues are only applied onto the fruit after 2/3 of the baking time has elapsed. Depending on the fruit type and the quantity of fruit used, fruit desserts are baked in the oven for 25 to 45 minutes at a baking temperature ranging between 200 and 210°C.

Food for Thought: *Why do raw, peeled apples turn brown?*

Fig. 533 **Diced apple filling made from dried apples**

Fig. 534
Lattice and Streusel used as fruit dessert toppings

254

Production of Braids

Braided pastries are sold in many bakeries. Braiding is fun.

For durable show pieces and ornamental braids, bakers use a salt dough or doughs made from rye flour without sugar and shortening.

For small braids to be consumed on the day of production, the baker uses a light fine yeast dough or a bun dough.

For large braids, a medium fine yeast dough is best suited. This type of dough differs from the ordinary bun dough because:
— It is made firmer.
— It is made with eggs — about 2 eggs per kg flour.

Joe says: *"Braided pastry? We don't have any time for that! Coffee cakes taste just as good as braided pastry!" Comment on this statement!*

> *Makeup procedure of the dough:*
> → *Round the dough pieces after scaling.*
> → *After a short resting period, roll the dough pieces approximately 30 cm long using both hands and working the strands from the inside to the outside.*
> → *Braid loosely.*
> → *Use light rye flour for dusting to avoid sticking.*
> → *Egg wash prior to final proofing and at 1/2 proof. Do not allow the egg wash to run into the points of contact between the strands. Allow the egg wash to dry slightly before baking.*
> → *Do not overproof.*
> → *Bake at a temperature decreasing from 200 to 180°C.*

Figs. 539 to 542 **Braiding technique for the production of two-stranded braids**

Figs. 543 to 544 **Braiding technique for the production of three-stranded braids**

Figs. 535 to 538 **Braiding technique for the production of one-stranded braids**

Fig. 545 **Braided pastry made with two- and three-stranded braids**

255

Figs. 546 to 550
Technique for the production of four-stranded braids

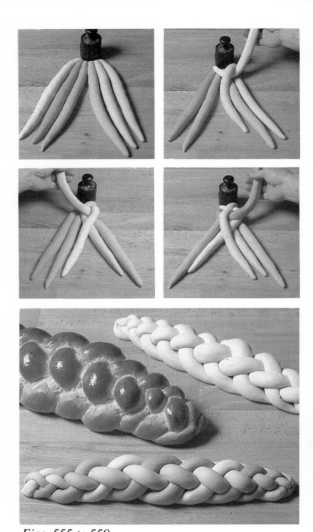

Figs. 555 to 559
Technique for the production of six-stranded braids

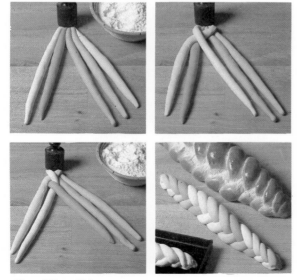

Figs. 551 to 554
Technique for the production of five-stranded braids

Summary of important information about pastry made with medium fine yeast doughs

➤ *Yeast pastry baked on baking pans, such as:*
— *Streusel cake, butter cake, filled coffee cakes, braids, bee sting cakes*

➤ *Composition:*
15 – 20% sugar
15 – 20% shortening/butter

➤ *Quantity of dough used for a 40 x 60 cm (16" x 24") baking sheet is approximately 1.2 kg.*

➤ *Butter cake and butter Streusel cake should contain at least 300 g of butter per kg of flour. Almonds are best suited for bee sting cake.*

Doughnuts and Other Deep-fried Pastries

Fig. 560 **Doughnut types**

Deep-fried pastry is the result of a long-standing tradition. In accordance with a very old farmers' custom, a large feast was prepared prior to a period of fasting. The final and high point of this meal was the fried fritter.

Today the doughnut is an integral part of our diet, whether as a snack food between meals or as a dessert item after a main meal.

In the past, doughnuts were only available at certain times of the year. Now they are offered at all times, and at all hours — the 24-hour doughnut shop has become a part of North American life.

The lard once used to fry doughnuts has been replaced with vegetable oils, and this change, combined with modern baking techniques, allows bakers to offer customers pastries with a lower fat content.

> * *Deep-fried pastries are baked goods baked in frying fat.*

The hot fat transfers the heat immediately to the baking product, giving fried products an extremely short baking time. These products are made of various doughs and batters.
➤ Yeast Doughnuts:
— glazed, sugar, cinnamon, raisin, apple and jam filled,
— various flavored glazes include chocolate, vanilla, caramel, maple,
— toppings include sugar sprinkles, nuts and nut mixtures and chocolate vermicelli.
➤ Cake Doughnuts:
A very viscous batter, normally deposited by machine, comes in a variety of flavors and types:
— plain, whole-wheat, chocolate, blueberry, cherry, and orange.

The quality of such deep-fried pastries depends
— on the formulation of the dough and batter,
— on the dough makeup (method used),
— on the baking method, and
— on the quality of the deep-frying fat.

Fig. 561 **Sugar Twist Doughnut**

Production of Yeast-Raised Doughnuts

Take a look at doughnuts in the display windows of specialty bakery shops. You may notice significant differences in quality.

In addition to the general requirements with regard to fine baked goods, the following specific quality characteristics apply to yeast-raised doughnuts:

> ➤ *Doughnuts should have a large volume. The exterior feature is the large ring (collar) which is not browned.*
>
> ➤ *Yeast-raised doughnuts should have a low fat content. They should absorb only a small amount of fat during frying.*
>
> ➤ *The crust should show a uniform brown color.*
>
> ➤ *The doughnut should keep its shape for several hours, without shrinking.*
>
> ➤ *The crumb should be aerated with fine cells. It should be moist.*

Basic recipe for yeast doughnuts	
1,000 g	Bread flour
100 g	Shortening
100 g	Sugar
150 g	Whole egg (= 3 eggs)
35 g	Egg yolk (= 2 eggs)
430 g	Milk
100 g	Yeast
12 g	Salt
	Flavors (i.e. vanilla, lemon)

Table 110

Reference: *For more information about French Crullers, please refer to the chapter entitled* **Pastry Made with Pâte-à-Choux**.

257

Composition and Preparation of the Dough

Doughnuts are made from light fine yeast dough containing egg. The production process should be geared, in principle, toward three quality characteristics:

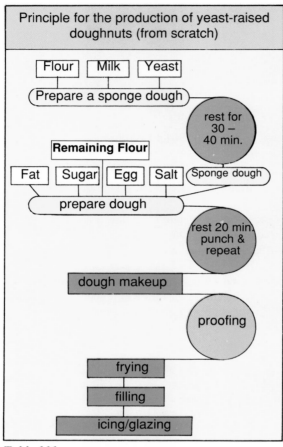

Principle for the production of yeast-raised doughnuts (from scratch)

Flour | Milk | Yeast
Prepare a sponge dough
rest for 30 – 40 min.
Remaining Flour
Fat | Sugar | Egg | Salt | Sponge dough
prepare dough
rest 20 min. punch & repeat
dough makeup
proofing
frying
filling
icing/glazing

Table 111

Super-raised yeast doughnuts contain baking powder and other additives to enhance volume and dough stability.

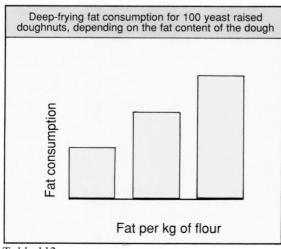

Deep-frying fat consumption for 100 yeast raised doughnuts, depending on the fat content of the dough

Fat consumption

Fat per kg of flour

Table 112

— to obtain formed units with a large volume,
— to achieve a low absorption of fat by the units during frying, and
— to obtain a tender, moist crumb.

In order to be able to make voluminous pastries with a large, light-colored ring, the dough must have a particularly high fermentation stability.

The fermentation stability is increased
— through the preparation of a sponge dough,
— with the addition of whole egg and of egg yolk,
— with reduced fat and sugar content in the dough,
— by making a soft dough,
— through intensive mixing, and
— through repeated punching of the dough.

The consumption of fat during frying is influenced primarily by the fat content in the dough and by the proportion of egg used.

> * *The lower the fat content in the dough, the lower the fat absorption during frying.*

To achieve the desired tenderness and fresh-keeping properties, the dough must contain a minimum of 100 g per kg flour (see basic recipe in *Table 110*).

> * *The higher the egg content in the dough, the lower the absorption of fat during frying.*

The lowest deep-frying fat consumption is achieved when 250 g (= 5 eggs) are added per kg flour (*Table 113*).
For a sufficiently moist texture, an egg content of 150 g (= 3 eggs) is required. The best doughnut quality is achieved with 150 g whole egg (= 3 eggs) and 35 g egg yolk (= 2 egg yolks).

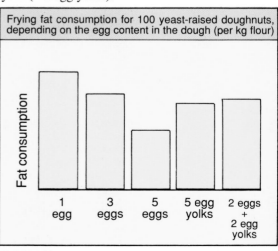

Frying fat consumption for 100 yeast-raised doughnuts, depending on the egg content in the dough (per kg flour)

Fat consumption

| 1 egg | 3 eggs | 5 eggs | 5 egg yolks | 2 eggs + 2 egg yolks |

Table 113

Because the dough preparation process is time-con-suming, the traditional method is gradually being replaced by bases and mixes.

> * *Baking creams are blends of fat, emulsifiers, forms of sugar and sometimes thickeners.*

When a dough is made with the aid of baking cream, all ingredients, with the exception of fat and sugar, are added as usual.

> * *Mixes for yeast and cake doughnuts are special blends of flour, sugar varieties, fat, emulsifiers, salt, flavors and chemical leavening agents.*

For dough preparation, water and yeast, or water only (for cake doughnuts) must be added.

The use of baking creams and ready-mix flour have the following advantages:
— The dough rises and matures faster.
— The fermentation stability and the fermentation tolerance are increased.

This will eliminate the necessity of a sponge dough and reduce the resting periods, allowing doughnuts to be fried at almost full proof.

Frying of Doughnuts
For the appearance and fat absorption of yeast-raised doughnuts, proper development and proofing is es-sential.

> * *Fat absorption is reduced with increased proofing times (see Table 114).*

However, remember that overproofed doughnuts lose their shape rapidly after frying. They shrink and form a fold in the light color ring.

The frying temperature should range between 170 and 180°C. Lower, but also higher, frying temperatures lead to higher fat absorption (*Table 115*).

In addition, a very high frying fat temperature will have the following effects:
— The volume of the final product is smaller (through rapid crust formation).
— The crust is too dark and softens rapidly after frying.
— The core of the texture is raw (inelastic).
— The frying fat breaks down faster.

Fig. 562 **Yeast-raised doughnuts with 1 egg yolk (left) and with 5 egg yolks (right) per kg flour**

Fig. 563

Joe says: *"It doesn't matter what the dough-nuts look like! The most important thing is that they taste good!"* What do you think?

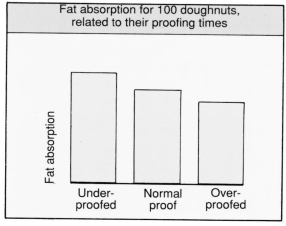

Table 114

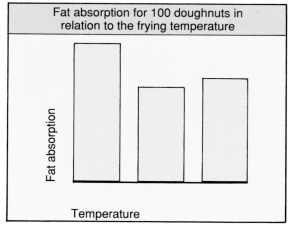

Table 115

Food for Thought: *Doughnuts are fried in hot fat. Why can't they be fried in hot water?*

259

Fig. 564
Yeast doughnuts with normal proof (left) and overproofed (right) dough

Fig. 565
Doughnuts fried in fat temperature of 180°C (left) and at 210°C (right)

Helpful hints for frying doughnuts:

→ *Begin frying doughnuts at 3/4 proof.*

→ *After 1 minute of frying, turn doughnut gently to the other side; after doughnuts have reached a nice brown color, turn them once more with the smooth part on top.*

→ *Let doughnuts drip off on drip-tray for at least 30 seconds before processing further.*

→ *Some yeast-raised doughnuts are filled with smooth preserves, jams, jellies and vanilla custards.*

Only granulated sugar may be applied while doughnuts are still warm. Powdered sugar should not be applied until the doughnut has cooled off (to prevent premature melting of the sugar).

Other doughnuts are glazed or dipped into chocolate, coated with nuts or colored sprinkles, decorated with icings and also left plain for the production of cream-filled doughnuts.

Food for Thought: *Is there a difference in appearance between the first and second side of a fried doughnut?*

Doughnut Faults

Joe fries yeast-raised doughnuts. Baker Smith is not satisfied with the quality of the finished product. The yeast-raised doughnuts have only a narrow ring, they are small, and they shrink shortly after they have been fried.

The cause of these faults may include the following:
— the fat content in the dough is too high,
— the egg content in the dough is too low,
— the dough has been undermixed,
— the dough was made up too soon (too young),
— the doughnuts were underproofed.

Baker Smith will closely monitor the production process the following day in order to determine the faults.

The following deficiencies also occur frequently:

— *Fold formation in the "collar" (ring)*	➤ *excessive proofing*
— *Rough crust*	➤ *excessive dry proofing*
— *Formation of bubbles on crust*	➤ *humidity in proofer too high*
— *Too much fat absorption*	➤ *too much fat content in dough* ➤ *or underproofing* ➤ *or frying temperature too low* ➤ *or egg content too low*

Food for Thought: *Joe is in the process of frying doughnuts when he realizes the fat level is too low. Joe is too lazy to go to the storage room for more frying fat.*
He gets one of his bright ideas!
The box of baking margarine is much closer. "Nobody will notice the difference between vegetable oil fat or margarine."
Well, Joe is the first one to find out what the difference is.
Can you explain what happened?

Frying Fats

Some consumers believe that fried bakery products tasted better years ago. They remember when lard was used exclusively for frying purposes.
In today's world of "you are what you eat," fried pastries dripping with lard are hardly sought after.
Such pastries are hard to digest and are not acceptable. Moreover, the lard decomposes especially fast when heated and forms substances which are detrimental to our health.

Fig. 566
Fruit of the oil palm-tree

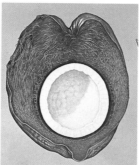

Fig. 567 **Cross-section of a coconut with the fruit pulp (= copra) containing fat**

Unhardened fats made from palm oil are suitable as frying fats because they are heat-resistant.

Coconut oil fat is not suited as a deep-frying fat
— because it foams during frying,
— because it spoils very fast when heated, due to the separation of fatty acids.

Characteristics of Frying Fat

The quality of fried products depends largely on the quality of the frying fat used.

The following points should be considered when selecting frying fats:

➤ *The fat should melt without splashing.*
➤ *The fat should not foam during frying.*
➤ *The fat must be neutral in flavor and free of odor.*
➤ *The fat should melt in your mouth, otherwise the product will have a tallowy taste.*
➤ *The fat should have a high smoke point; it should not release smoke at frying temperature.*
➤ *The fat should be heat resistant for a long period of time.*

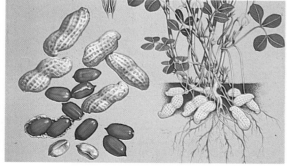

Fig. 568 **Peanuts with plant**

Hardened peanut fat is particularly well-suited as a frying fat, because it is highly heat-resistant.

The following are suitable deep-frying fats:

— hardened peanut fat, and
— unhardened fat made with palm oil.

These fats have a high smoke point; they are especially heat-resistant, they do not foam and they have a neutral taste.

The Effect of Spoiled Fats on Your Health

The composition of fats change over a period of time. This change accelerates when they are heated to high temperatures. Frying fats have an unpleasant flavor after exposure to normal frying temperatures for 20 to 60 hours.

Fig. 569 **Resination of various fats and oils after being heated to 180°C for 24 hours (not used for frying yet)**

The heated fats spoil due to the chemical reactions taking place, i.e.:
— separation of fatty acids from the fat molecules, and
— deposit of oxygen on unsaturated fatty acids.

In the process, substances detrimental to the health are formed.
The higher the baking temperature, the faster fat spoils.
The color or taste of the fat does not necessarily reveal the degree to which the frying fat has been decomposed through heat.

Warning signals indicative of spoiled frying fat:

— Strong smoke formation at normal frying temperatures.
— Strong odor of burnt fat.
— Rancid after-taste.
— Continuous foaming of the fat and formation of small bubbles.
— Deposit of sticky dark residue.
— Dark color of the fat.

When using fats that are sensitive to heat, such as coconut fat or oils with a high proportion of unsaturated fatty acids, the fat is spoiled after only a few hours of use.

261

A reliable test can be performed by the baker using a special formula. Such a test set can be obtained from some manufacturers of shortenings.

Rapid test for frying fat

— *Mix some frying fat with the reagent solution. Depending on the degree of spoiling, the frying fat turns more or less dark.*
— *Compare the test sample with color samples.*
— *Evaluate conclusions with regard to the use or non-use of the fat.*

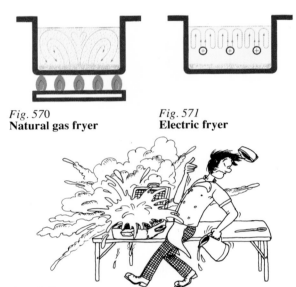

Fig. 570
Natural gas fryer

Fig. 571
Electric fryer

Fig. 572

Caution! You can be burned!
Never pour water into hot fat!

Summary for the use of frying fat

→ *Use only heat-resistant fats.*

→ *Melt the fat prior to pouring into the kettle. This will prevent initial overheating.*

→ *Avoid frying at temperatures over 180°C.*

→ *If you add to the existing fat in the fryer, take the proper precautions to avoid splashing.*

→ *Check the quality of the fat at regular intervals and check for possible spoilage.*

→ *Clean the fryer on a regular basis. Drain, filter or discard and rinse. Always use a small amount of vinegar for your final rinse.*

Frying Equipment

The industry offers a large variety of doughnut frying equipment. Regardless of the performance and the methods of operation, there are general technical requirements applying to all types of equipment.

Requirements of baker:	*Industry offers:*
➤ *Frying equipment must maintain the selected frying temperatures. Overheated fats spoil faster. "Cold" fat is absorbed by doughnuts.*	➤ *Electric and natural gas-fired equipment which operates with a thermostat. The temperature of the fat is measured in the frying zone and kept constant.*
➤ *The residues should not burn and should sink to the bottom without being stirred up again and again.*	➤ *A buffer at the bottom of the fryer keeps the force of heat away from the fat, hence creating a "cold" zone and preventing turbulence in the oil.*
➤ *Frying equipment must be made of material that does not favor fat oxidation. Copper and iron especially decompose the fat.*	➤ *All components of the frying equipment which come into contact with the fat must be made of stainless steel. Local fire codes will explain all requirements and regulations.*
➤ *Frying equipment must be easy to operate and clean without presenting the risk of an accident.*	➤ *The heating coils, etc. can be removed for easy cleaning. All frying equipment has some fire-extinguishing device installed or is directly connected to one.*
	➤ *For the purpose of changing fat or the cleaning of accumulated residue, the fat can be drained through a spout.*
	➤ *The draining spout is secured by a valve to prevent unintentional opening.*
	➤ *Lifting devices are designed in such a way that the risk of splashing is reduced to a minimum.*
	➤ *The cover of the deep-frying pan is a safety feature in case of a fat fire.*

Frying equipment differs
— in the size of the kettle,
— in the method of frying,
  • frying in individual kettles,
  • conveyor method,
— in the method of loading,
  • in lowering and lifting devices,
  • in turning devices,
— in the style,
  • table-top fryers,
  • free-standing models,
  • single, double and continuous systems
  • complete doughnut streets.

Fig. 574 **Electric continuous system**

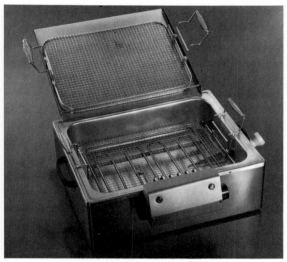

Fig. 573 **Electric fryer, table-top model**

Summary of the most important information about yeast-raised doughnuts
* *Frying fats must be suited for their intended use: they must be heat-resistant, have a high smoke point, low foam formation, neutral taste, and a melting range below 37°C.*
* *Frying equipment must conform to approved standards, must be clean and safe to operate, must be of stainless steel material, and must provide for fat drainage.*
* *Quality characteristics of yeast-raised doughnuts:* — *large volume,* — *wide "collar,"* — *moist, tender texture with fine cells.*
* *Important tips for the production of yeast-raised doughnuts:* — *low fat and sugar content,* — *high egg content,* — *intensive mixing of the dough,* — *proper floor time,* — *frying temperature between 170 and 180°C,* — *avoid excessive humidity and overproofing.*

Products Made From Heavy Fine Yeast Dough

The following are products made from heavy fine yeast dough:
— Stollen
— Yeasted "Pound Cake"

Stollen has become more popular than yeasted pound cake in North America and is available all year long in many bakeries.

How to Make Stollen

Joe makes Stollen for the first time in his career. He thinks of himself as a "progressive" baker. He does not believe in the traditional production methods. To him they are outdated.

Against the explicit instructions of his bakery manager, he dispenses with the sponge dough.

Fig. 575 **Christmas Stollen**

Joe mixes all of the ingredients including the fruits. He watches the dough during mixing and becomes nervous: the Stollen dough turns gray-brown. And, in spite of plenty of dough resting time, the dough hardly rises (poor fermentation).

263

Joe says: *"Stollen is not difficult to make. It's made the same way as raisin bread. Adding fruits only after the dough has rested is an outdated method!"*
What do you think?

Fig. 576 **Filled Stollen**

Basic recipe for Stollen	
1,000 g	Bread flour
500 g	Butter
125 g	Sugar
50 g	Almond paste
280 g	Milk
80 g	Yeast
12 g	Salt
	Lemon/vanilla flavor
800 g	Sultana raisins
250 g	Candied lemon peel
100 g	Candied orange peel
250 g	Chopped almonds
80 g	Rum

Table 116

Fig. 577 **Preparation of the fruit for the Stollen**

264

But Joe knows what to do! He increases the temperature in the proofer. And, in fact, the dough does ferment better now.

Joe runs into problems during dough makeup: The warm dough is shiny. Fat melts out. The dough falls apart like shortbread.

The finished Stollen is not any better: The texture is gray. It is poorly leavened. The texture is very dense immediately above the bottom of the Stollen.

A sample taste confirms his worst fears. The Stollen tastes terrible.

The next day, Baker Smith takes a lot of time to produce the Stollen. He explains every step in detail.

Production Method

The production of Stollen requires extensive knowledge. The production method cannot necessarily be compared with that of other yeast products.

The difficulties encountered during Stollen production are due to the following:
— the high fat content,
— the high sugar content (due to certain fruits),
— the low amount of liquid in the dough.

Due to the high fat content and the low water content, the flour albumen swells insufficiently. The dough is "short" and barely extensible. The cohesiveness of the dough is affected partly through the binding of dough components and dough fat. The fermentation stability is correspondingly low.

The sugar concentration in the free dough liquid is extremely high due to the low amount of liquid added. This significantly reduces the activity of the yeast (*Table 117*). Therefore, the baker must make adjustments:
— to improve the condition of the dough, and
— to improve leavening.

The condition of the dough and the absorption of liquid can be improved by the use of special baking agents.

Sugar content in the Stollen dough — a comparison with a light fine yeast dough		
	per 1,000 g flour	per 1,000 g milk
light fine yeast dough ⟶	100 g	200 g
Stollen dough ⟶	125 g*	450 g*
* The sugar content in the Stollen dough is also increased through the sugar content of the fruits.		

Table 117

Tips for the production of Stollen

Tips:	Reason:
→ Let the dried fruits soak in rum overnight.	➤ This will ensure that the fruit in the Stollen is correctly conditioned, preventing moisture loss from the dough.
→ Make sure that all ingredients, including the fruits, have the right temperature. The dough temperature should be 25 to 26°C, that of all-butter Stollen at 24°C.	➤ The desired dough temperature will be achieved. Cool doughs ferment too slowly. Excessively warm doughs melt the fat.
→ Prepare a soft sponge dough. Let it rest for 30 to 40 minutes.	➤ The yeast can develop its full fermentation power before the ingredients slow down the fermentation. The addition of sponge dough helps create the needed fine cell structure in the Stollen and increases the amount of aromatic substances.
→ Mix the dough first — without the addition of fruit.	➤ This will prevent the fruits from crushing during mixing the dough. Squashed fruits change the color of the dough. The fruit's sugar would have a negative effect on the activity of the yeast.
→ Let the dough rest for 30 minutes, then add the fruits.	➤ This way, the fruits can be distributed easily in the leavened dough.
→ Let rest for a maximum of 10 minutes — not in the proofer.	➤ This will prevent the Stollen "spreads" (flattening) during baking.
→ Bake the Stollen at a temperature decreasing from 220/210 to 190°C.	➤ High initial temperature ensures quick coagulation of the proteins, preventing the Stollen from spreading. Dropping the temperature prevents — the Stollen from darkening too quickly and ensures an evenly baked product; — the Stollen from drying out.

Fig. 578 **Mixing of Stollen dough**

Fig. 579 **Stollen makeup method**

Fig. 580 **Shaping by means of Stollen forms**

Finishing

The Stollen is processed further after baking
— to improve the storability,
— to increase the enjoyment value.

First, any burnt fruits on the Stollen surface must be eliminated (when baking forms are used, the fruits do not burn).

While the Stollen is still warm, it is coated with melted butter or margarine. This will seal in the moisture, and prevent the Stollen from drying out.

Immediately after this process, fine-grained sugar is sprinkled over the Stollen. The sugar prevents mold formation on the surface. After the Stollen has cooled, it receives a coating of powdered or icing sugar.

The outer fat layer of the Stollen is particularly sensitive to spoiling.
— Oxygen,
— Light and
— Humidity have a tendency to make fat turn rancid.

Therefore, the fat for the outer treatment of the Stollen must be selected with special care.

The most durable fat is hardened peanut fat. Baking margarine is less durable, but still perfectly suitable.

Butter has the highest tendency to spoil. For butter Stollen, butter must be used for the outer treatment. When selecting butter type, durability must be a deciding factor.

The use of high-quality butter is recommended because freshness can be guaranteed. Care must be taken when using pure butter fat. Pure butter fat could have been made with butter that has been stored for an excessive period of time.

Good manufacturing practices for Stollen production	
Stollen type	Quantity of ingredients per 100 kg flour:
simple Stollen (no filling)	➤ at least 30.0 kg Butter, *or* 30.8 kg Margarine, at least 60.0 kg Dried fruits
Dresdner Stollen	➤ at least 20.0 kg Butter *and* 20.0 kg Margarine, at least 70.0 kg Dried fruits, at least 10.0 kg Almonds
Butter Stollen	➤ at least 40.0 kg Butter, no other fat, at least 70.0 kg Dried fruits
Almond Stollen	➤ at least 30.0 kg Butter, no other fat, at least 20.0 kg Almonds

Table 118

Food for Thought: *Stollen keeps fresh for a long period of time.*
If this is so, is storage of Stollen in deep freezers unnecessary and, moreover, uneconomical? What do you think?

Stollen is best stored in a very cool, dark room.

Stollen can be stored in a deep freezer without losing its quality characteristics.

Heavy Stollen attains its full enjoyment value only two days after production. It will keep their quality characteristics for at least four weeks.

Yeasted "Pound Cake" (Guglhupf)

Fig. 581 **Yeasted "Pound cake"**

Yeasted pound cakes are made from heavy fine yeast dough. They differ from Stollen

— in terms of their composition	➤ through their higher milk content, ➤ through their higher sugar content, ➤ through their high egg content (30 to 50% of the quantity of flour used).
— in terms of the production method used	➤ through the technique used for dough preparation. The dough is mixed with a paddle, giving it a soft appearance.
— in terms of the shape	➤ through baking in special baking molds ("bundt pans").
— in terms of the taste	➤ through the high egg content.

The creaming method is applied in the production process of this product. Butter or shortening is creamed with sugar. Eggs are added gradually until the batter is smooth. At this stage the sponge dough and the flour are added. Mixing continues until the dough has a smooth consistency.

Quality Control For Yeast Products

Most fine yeast products made with yeast dough taste best when they are fresh.

Unfortunately, some products lose their freshness characteristics when they are stored:
— They dry out.
— They lose some aroma.
— They change in terms of taste and condition.
— They absorb moisture from the air and they adopt foreign odors.
— They can mold.
— They can turn rancid.

Reference: *For more information about the aging of baking products, refer to the chapter entitled* **How to Prolong the Freshness of Bread.**

The baker can preserve the freshness characteristics for a prolonged period of time and delay spoiling and mold formation
➤ through the composition of the baked products,
➤ through proper dough preparation methods,
➤ through cool doughs,
➤ through special packaging procedures.

Composition and Quality Preservation

Stollen will keep fresh longer than lighter yeast products because of its higher fat content.

However, it is impossible to simply increase the fat content of all products in order to improve their fresh-keeping properties. A higher fat content has a distinctive influence on the character of the baked products.

By adding suitable ingredients or additives, it is possible
— to increase the water content in the dough,
— to achieve a better distribution of the fat in the dough,
— to delay starch retrogradation.

All three measures improve the fresh-keeping properties of baking products.

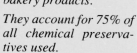

Attention! Calcium and sodium propionate are the most important antimicrobial agents used in bakery products.

They account for 75% of all chemical preservatives used.

They are the least expensive and have little effect on yeast activity.

The addition of preservatives like sodium and calcium propionate delays molding in baked products.

Their use should only be applied to products with high moisture content, i.e. for filled poppy seed cake.

Joe says: *"I can understand that bakers use preservatives for baked goods. But I don't think that this is in the best interest of the consumer!"*

What do you think?

Ingredients or additives prolonging freshness

• Egg yolk	➤	*It has an emulsifying effect due to certain fat substances, but especially because of its lecithin content.*
• Shortenings	➤	*Their effect is based on the composition of their fat and the additional emulsifier content.*
• Emulsifiers	➤	*They improve fat distribution in the dough and retard the starch.*
• Thickeners	➤	*They bind additional liquids during dough preparation. This will retain moisture in the crumb for a longer period of time.*

Dough Preparation Methods and Quality Preservation

Yeast products of identical composition can keep their freshness characteristics for varying periods of time, in spite of identical storage conditions.

The reason is the use of different dough preparation methods.

The following methods have a favorable effect on the shelf life of yeast products:
— doughs made with a sponge dough,
— cool temperatures,
— intensive mixing of the dough,
— sufficient dough resting time until an optimum maturity of the dough is achieved,
— avoidance of excessive proofing.

Cool Handling and Quality Preservation
The same principles apply to cool handling of yeast products as those already described in the chapter en-

titled **Wheat-flour Products**. In any event, fine yeast doughs are more suitable for cool handling than wheat-flour doughs because of the high sugar and fat content.

Retardation and Interruption of the Fermentation Process

Do you remember from the early chapters?

— Retarding the fermentation process involves reducing the temperature without freezing the dough.
— Interrupting the fermentation process involves stopping fermentation through freezing the dough.

Yeast doughs can be retarded for up to 18 hours without undergoing a distinct loss of quality.

* *For both methods, the following rules must be observed:*

➤ *Dispense with the preparation of a sponge dough.*
➤ *Use shortening or baking agents containing emulsifiers.*
➤ *Make sure you give the doughs their final shape prior to retardation or interruption of the fermentation process.*
➤ *Make sure the humidity in the cooler (retarder) is sufficient.*

* *In addition, the following applies when the fermentation process is retarded:*

➤ *Make cool doughs (22 to 24°C).*
➤ *Reduce the dough resting time.*
➤ *Do not let the finished products rise. Refrigerate products immediately after makeup.*
➤ *The temperature during retardation of the fermentation process must range between +8 and -5°C, depending on the time period stored.*

* *In addition, the following applies when the fermentation process is interrupted:*

➤ *Make the dough warm (25 to 27°C).*
➤ *Let the dough rest (for about 15 minutes).*
➤ *Make sure the temperature is reduced rapidly to -18°C, immediately after dough makeup.*
➤ *Defrost the dough pieces first at cooling room temperature (to 4°C). Otherwise, the surface of the dough pieces becomes too moist through condensation of the air moisture.*

Deep-freezing of Baking Products

Fine yeast products must be frozen unglazed. Sugar coatings lose their gloss/shine during freezing. Moreover, they dissolve during defrosting due to the condensating air moisture. When an glazed pastry is defrosted in the oven, the glaze will melt.

Fine yeast doughs lose quality during storage in a deep freezer.

➤ They dry out over a period of time.
➤ They lose flavor.
➤ The crumb contracts and detaches from the crust.
➤ Starch retrogradation occurs gradually.

Light fine yeast doughs maintain their quality characteristics for about six days when they are deep-frozen. Heavy fine yeast doughs can be stored for a longer period of time, depending on their fat and water content.

The same methods apply to freezing fine yeast products as to any other wheat-flour products.

Some baked goods are not suited for freezing.

— Baked goods with watery fruit toppings or watery fillings, like apple or vanilla cream fillings,
— baked and iced products.

During freezing, some of the juice leaves the cells of the fruits. The destroyed cells are not able to reabsorb the juice during defrosting. This causes a significant loss in aroma.

In the case of pastry creams, the water is frozen out of the starch. Thus, the cream loses its binding capacity and tastes old.

Packaging and Preservation of Quality

At one time, traditional packaging methods had the following functions:

— to prepare the goods for transportation,
— to protect the goods from being contaminated by dust and insects,
— to give the products an attractive appearance.

In recent years, packaging has also assumed the following tasks:

➤ protection against drying out or against absorption of moisture from the air,
➤ protection of the aroma,
➤ protection against contact with the air,
➤ protection against bacteria,
➤ merchandising effects.

The exposure to mold is reduced

● *through sterilization* ➤ *The packaged goods are heated to a core temperature of 70 to 80°C. The mold germs are destroyed. Packaging prevents new infection.*

● *through the exchange of atmosphere* ➤ *Air is withdrawn from the package and carbon dioxide is added. Thus, no oxygen is available for mold formation or for the baking goods to turn rancid.*

Products made with Special Doughs and with Batters

Production of Puff Pastry, Short Pastry and Gingerbreads

Puff Pastry

The pastries in *Figs. 582 – 584* are examples of the wide range of puff pastries available today.

Products made from puff doughs are:
— Coffee rings such as turnovers, palm leaves, apple strudel, vol-au-vents, Napoleon/vanilla slices, pin wheels
— Spicy products and snacks such as sausage rolls, cheese sticks
— Semi-finished products such as creamhorns, patty shells

Fig. 582 **Puff pastries**

Fig. 583 **Savory puff pastry snacks**

Fig. 584 **Palm leaves, fans and bow ties**

Tips for subsequent working steps:

There are several types of puff dough methods used.
Make up a list of puff pastries produced in your bakery, including their usual names. Categorize the pastries into coffee pastries, spicy/snack pastries, and semi-finished products.

Basic recipe for Puff dough		
Basic dough		**Roll-in fat**
1,000 g	Bread flour	1,000 g roll-in fat
600 g	Water	
20 g	Salt	
20 g	Sugar	
60 g	Fat	
= 1,700 g	Basic dough	
+ (if required) addition of:		
Egg		
Acetic and citric acid		
Flavor		
Alcohol		

Table 119

Although puff pastries seem to be, at first glance, quite different from one another, they do have quality characteristics common to all puff pastry products:
— They are strongly leavened.
— They have a layered, flaky structure.
— They show a uniform, but not intensive, browning.
— They are generally less sweet than other bakery products.

These common characteristics of puff pastry products are due to the composition and production methods.

Composition of Puff Doughs

Puff dough is composed of a basic dough and roll-in fat.

Unlike Danish-style pastry dough, the basic dough for puff pastry does not contain any yeast. It is prepared using only flour, water, some salt, sugar and fat. To improve its characteristics or flavor, egg, and vinegar can be added.

Basic dough and the roll-in fat are made into many thin dough-fat layers through folding, repeated rolling-out of the dough and laminating. These layers are required for leavening of the dough and give the puff dough its special characteristics.

Each individual fat or dough layer is thinner than a sheet of silk paper or a razor blade. But, nevertheless, the layers must remain undestroyed during rolling-out, cutting, forming and baking of the dough. Therefore, it is important that the dough and the roll-in fat are suitable and of the same plasticity.

Basic Dough

Cohesiveness and extensibility are the desirable characteristics of the basic dough.

The baker can achieve these characteristics
— by selecting a suitable type of wheat flour,
— by adjusting to the correct consistency of the dough,
— by intensively mixing the dough and allowing the dough to relax.

Top Patent or baker's bread-making flours are best suited for making the basic dough. Their gluten content ensures good elasticity and strength.

The baker can modify the gluten properties in the basic dough.

➤ Baking margarine and egg yolk reduce the toughness of the dough and make it more extensible.

➤ Acetic or citric acid and egg white improve the cohesiveness of the dough. The gluten is relaxed.

➤ Salt slows down the swelling process of the gluten and makes the dough tougher.

In general, the basic dough is improved when these principles are followed:

> → Adapt the basic dough to the firmness of the roll-in fat in order to avoid the dough layers from breaking or sticking together during the rolling process.
> → Make the basic dough cool to prevent the roll-in fat from flowing out.
> → Mix the basic dough intensively, as a smooth dough makes the rolling process easier.
> → Let the basic dough relax to prevent it from contracting during the rolling and dough makeup processes.
> → Wrap the basic dough in a plastic sheet during storage to prevent formation of a hard dough skin.

Roll-In Shortening

Next to wheat flour, the roll-in shortening is the main ingredient of puff dough in terms of quantity. Therefore, it has a significant influence on the quality of the final product. Liquid or hard fats are not suitable because they cannot be rolled.

In order to evaluate the suitability of various solid fats as roll-in, a simple test can be performed.

Test 31:

Prepare a basic dough based on the basic recipe in Table 119. Separate this basic dough into four parts of equal size. Fold in each quarter with 250 g fat under identical conditions. Use the following fats for the laminating process:

A = Creamed margarine, B = Baking margarine, C = Butter, D = Roll-in margarine.

Make up the laminated doughs into unfilled pieces of 10 x 10 cm, 3 mm high. Form the pieces into triangles. Bake these, after a resting time of 60 minutes, on a baking sheet for 25 minutes at an oven temperature of 210°C.
Evaluate the laminating characteristics of the fats.
Evaluate the quality of the products.

Observations:

— Creamed margarine is not a suitable roll-in fat. Laminating is almost impossible. The finished product is hard, irregular and has large cells.

— Baking margarine and butter are somewhat suitable as roll-in fats. The product shows a satisfactory degree of leavening. The crust of the puff pastry made with butter is browner than that of pastries made with margarine. The baking margarine or butter is easier to work with if it is mixed with some flour when it is cool.

— Roll-in margarine is the most suitable as a roll-in fat. The end product is uniform and well leavened.

Tips for subsequent working steps:

Low-gluten flours or extremely high-gluten flours must sometimes be used to prepare basic doughs. However, a suitable basic dough can be obtained from each type of flour to produce puff pastry.
In what way would you change the basic recipe in Table 119 when you use extremely high-gluten or extremely low-gluten flour?

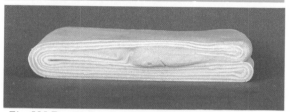

Fig. 585 Poorly-laminated puff dough: Basic dough and fat have not been conditioned to each other and their respective firmness has not been considered

Reference:
In the chapter on the production of Danish pastries, you will find the requirements of roll-in margarines. Please refer to that chapter for more information.

Additional Information
How do you distinguish roll-in margarine from other types of margarine?
— Roll-in margarine is almost exclusively composed of vegetable fats. The vegetable fats are combined in such a manner that a longer melting range is achieved.
Example:
Coconut fat turns immediately to liquid in its melting range when heated up by 1°C. Therefore, it has a low melting range. Hardened palm oil softens more gradually when heated in its melting range of approximately 24°C. Therefore, it has a large melting range and is suitable as a component of a roll-in margarine.
— During margarine production, the fat mixtures used for roll-in margarine are processed in a similar way as ice-cream during the cooling phase. There, many small fat crystals form. Moreover, the roll-in margarine is allowed to rest prior to shaping, ensuring crystallization.
— The fat content of roll-in margarine used for puff pastries, ranging between 85 and 99%, is somewhat higher than that of other margarine types.

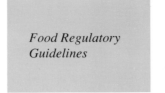

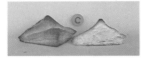

Fig. 586
Pastries made with doughs containing different roll-in fats
A = Creamed margarine, B = Baking margarine, C = Butter, D = Roll-in margarine

What happens when an unsuitable roll-in fat is used?

During rolling with unsuitable roll-in margarine, fat-dough layers cannot form. When the fat is too hard, the dough is damaged. When the fat is too soft, it flows in the dough. *Fig. 587* shows a microscopic picture of a well-layered puff dough and that of a puff dough laminated with running fat.

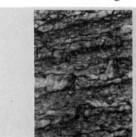

Fig. 587 **Puff dough (frozen cross-section 40 μ, 1/125). Unsuitable roll-in fat (left) and suitable roll-in fat (right) used for laminating**

Tips for the use of roll-in fat:
➤ *Roll-in fat should be selected based on its suitability. Creamed margarine or baking margarine, deep-frying fats, tallow or pure butter fat are unsuitable because of their characteristics.*
➤ *Roll-in fat should never be melted or dissolved. This would destroy its structure; it would no longer be suitable for laminating.*
➤ *Roll-in fat should be stored at cool temperatures at all times.*
➤ *If butter is used, it should be sprinkled with flour to improve its workability.*

Roll-in fat Content

The basic recipe in *Table 119* indicates that 1,000 g roll-in fat should be used for 1,000 g flour. This is the generally used ratio of 1/1 for flour and roll-in fat in puff doughs.

A puff dough of good quality can also be prepared with a lower fat content.

According to good manufacturing practices, the minimum fat content should be 70% (related to the total quantity of flour used).

In order for a puff dough to be qualified as "made with butter" the minimum butter content should be 68.3% (related to the total quantity of flour used).

Methods of Puff Dough Preparation

Several methods can be used for the preparation of puff doughs:

→ **English puff Dough**
— prepare a basic dough,
— prepare the roll-in fat,
— work the roll-in fat into the basic dough.

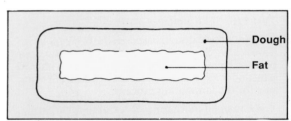

Fig. 588
English puff dough (dough outside, fat inside)

* *English puff dough = basic dough on the outside*

→ **Dutch puff dough**
— prepare a basic dough,
— prepare the roll-in fat,
— wrap roll-in fat around the basic dough

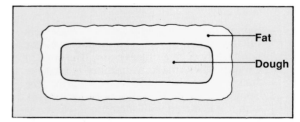

Fig. 589
Dutch puff dough (fat outside, dough inside)

* *Dutch puff dough = fat on the outside*

When making a Dutch puff dough, the roll-in fat is combined with a substantial quantity of flour (up to a third of the flour to be used for the basic dough). Thus, it can be easily used as the outer layer. The dough should not be too tough/elastic. Cool handling and folding is recommended in order to prevent the fat from running.

This method has the following advantages:
— Rapid folding process because long resting times are not required.
— No skin develops on the dough surface.
— The product is more tender due to the outer fat layer.

→ *Scotch Puff Dough*
— The dough ingredients and the refrigerated roll-in fat cubes are incorporated in one step into the dough (all-in method).

In this method, the roll-in fat cubes should not form a connected fat layer.

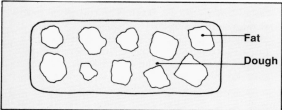

Fig. 590
Scotch puff dough (fat pieces in the dough)

> * *Scotch puff dough = roll-in fat cubes in the dough*

This method is also called "quick method" or "blitz puff dough," because dough preparation is simpler and fewer turns are required.
Scotch puff doughs are, however, not as suitable for some products as other methods that rise more uniformly.

Folding Puff Dough
The working steps used for folding are described using the example of the English method.

1. Incorporation of the roll-in fat
The dough should be of uniform thickness and wrapped around the fat. Excess dusting flour is brushed off the dough surface.
2. Laminating using a single fold
The folded dough is rolled out into a rectangular shape under a uniform pressure from the roller, or by gradually reducing the distance between the rollers of the reversible sheeter or rolling pin. The dough should be the thickness of a finger (no less).

The dusting flour is brushed off the dough. The dough is placed in three layers, one on top of the other, in exact rectangular shape (single turn).

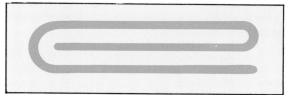

Fig. 591 **Dough layers of the single fold method (single turn)**

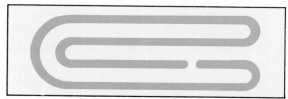

Fig. 592 **Dough layers with a "book" or "double" fold**

3. Application of a double fold
After single folding, the dough is rolled out again into a rectangle one finger thick. It is important to note that, in the subsequent fold, the dough must always be rolled out in the opposite direction to the previous turn.

The flour is brushed off the dough, which is placed with each end flipped over towards the center, then folded over one more time in an exact rectangle (double turn). Care should be taken to prevent the dough from overlapping at the centre (see *Figs. 592* and *593*).
Next, the rolled dough is wrapped in a plastic sheet. Then the dough is kept cool during a resting period of at least 10 minutes.

Fig. 593 **This is what a well-laminated dough with a double fold looks like**

4. Folding with a single turn
After the resting time (which can last until the next working day) the rolled-in dough is rolled out again. The dough is freed from dust flour and placed in three layers, one on top of the other, as described in the second working step (= single fold).
5. Folding with a double turn
The dough is rolled out again, in the opposite direction to the previous fold. As in the third working step, the dough is placed in four layers (= double turn).

The expert calls this standard folding process of puff dough two single and two double turns. Other variations are also used, depending on the fat ratio.

The folding process demonstrated using the example of the English puff dough is almost the same for other production methods.

The folding of Dutch puff dough is performed in a similar fashion but the resting time is shorter. For pastry shells made from Dutch puff dough, five single turns are often used.

For the Scotch puff dough, two single and one double turns are sufficient, or even two double turns.

When folding with two single and two double turns, 144 dough-fat layers are created.

Calculation of the fat or dough layers:

1. *Single turn*   *= 3 layers*
2. *Double turn*
    = 3 layers x 4   *=12 layers*
3. *Single turn*
    = 12 layers x 3   *= 36 layers*
4. *Double turn*
    = 36 layers x 4   *= 144 layers*
    of fat or dough

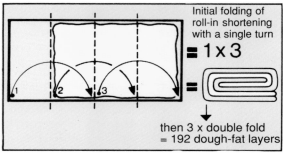

Fig. 594 Incorporation of the roll-in fat using one single turn

A somewhat modified folding method is shown in *Fig. 594*. Here, a single turn is used during incorporation of the roll-in shortening. Dough and roll-in fat must be rolled out for this purpose and folded in for the first turn. Then, only three double turns follow. Using this method, 192 dough-fat layers are achieved. Quality roll-in shortenings are stable enough for this type of fine layering.
What happens if the correct number of turns is not applied?

Fig. 595 Test products made with puff dough, using insufficient (left), correct (center) and excessive (right) folding

Test 32:
Prepare a basic dough following the recipe given in *Table 119*. Then fold it, using the method for English puff dough.
After the first two folds, cut off a third of the dough for makeup.
Fold the remainder again using a single and a double fold.
Now, take off about half of the dough for makeup. The remaining third of the dough is folded again with a single and a double fold.
Make up the three doughs with a different number of folds, varying frequencies, as is described in *Test 31*.
Evaluate the quality of the puff pastries.

Observations:
The test pastries (*Fig. 595*) show that a good quality puff pastry can only be achieved with optimum folding.
This test included the pastries made with dough which was folded in two single and two double turns.
When the layers are insufficient in numbers, the pastry turns out to have uneven flakes. The fat-dough layers are too large. The roll-in fat partly flows out of the dough.
When the dough is folded too much, the fat-dough layers are destroyed. Sufficient flakiness cannot be obtained. The end product is small in volume.

---

*   *Remember*

➤ *insufficient folding*   ➤ *uneven flakes*
                              ➤ *the fat flows out*

➤ *optimum folding*   ➤ *good leavening, good flakiness*

➤ *excessive folding*   ➤ *insufficient flakiness, large cells*

Fig. 596 **Puff pastries are given an apricot preserve coating after baking, while they are still hot. Then the fruit topping is applied and glazed with fondant.**

Makeup and Shaping of Puff Pastry

Makeup

From the folded and relaxed puff dough, portions, as needed, are cut off with a sharp knife for dough makeup.

To achieve rising of the puff dough pieces, the following fundamental rules must be followed:

→ Gently press the cutting points of the dough together.
  Try not to damage the fat-dough layers.

→ Do not work or stretch the puff dough.

→ Be sure to roll the dough out uniformly.
  Adjust the rolling machine in phases to a lower dough thickness.

→ Cut off the border pieces of the rolled-out puff dough and use them for other items (e.g. for bottoms, Eccles cakes, palm leaves).

→ Do not apply any egg wash to cut edges of puff dough pieces, otherwise they stick together.

→ Place dough pieces for high-rising puff dough pastries on pans coated with water.

Fig. 597
Makeup of puff dough pieces

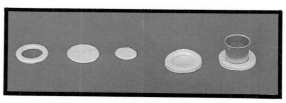

Fig. 598 **Shaping of shells, making vol-au-vents (patty shells)**

Shaping

For pastries made with puff dough, various types of sweet fillings, i.e. pastes, creams, fruits or fruit products, are used. Other puff pastries are unsweetened, spicy and salty items, such as sausage rolls, shells and cheese pretzels. Semi-finished products include patty shells, cream horns, etc.

For puff pastries that are not meant to rise, leftover puff dough is used. It can be quickly worked through and single-folded again.

For palm leaves and fans, the puff dough is rolled out in sugar instead of flour. The sugar is incorporated into the dough structure. After they have been folded together, the dough pieces are cut crosswise into layers and then placed onto pans to which a coating of fat has been applied. Thus, the puff dough expands laterally (*Fig. 599*).

Freezing

Puff dough does not age to the same extent as yeast dough or Danish dough. Therefore, it can be easily stored in coolers or deep freezers.

The production of puff dough is very time-consuming. Therefore, it is not economical to make small quantities of dough every day. It is preferable to make larger quantities of puff dough and to store the rolled dough of the shaped dough pieces at –20°C. When the dough is stored for a prolonged period of time in deep freezers, the dough pieces must be protected against drying out.

Puff dough should not be frozen after baking. Pastries with a high fat content turn brittle during freezing. Therefore, the already brittle structure of the puff pastries would be destroyed and the product would be far too brittle and dry.

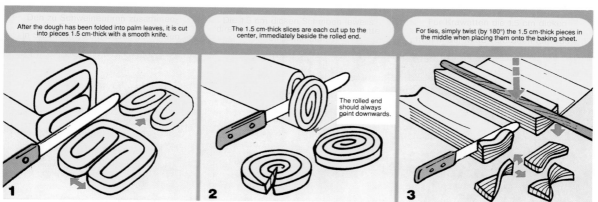

After the dough has been folded into palm leaves, it is cut into pieces 1.5 cm-thick with a smooth knife.

The 1.5 cm-thick slices are each cut up to the center, immediately beside the rolled end.

For ties, simply twist (by 180°) the 1.5 cm-thick pieces in the middle when placing them onto the baking sheet.

The rolled end should always point downwards.

1   2   3

Fig. 599 **Shaping of palm leaves, fans and bow ties**

Baking and Leavening of Puff Dough

Puff dough leavens and expands at the same time during the baking process. Baking temperatures and baking times depend upon the type of pastry made, the size of the pastry and the filling used.

Examples: Palm leaves, cream horns, layers for Napoleon slices, etc., are baked at temperatures ranging between 210 and 230°C. Products with meat or fruit fillings are baked at temperatures ranging between 190 and 210°C.

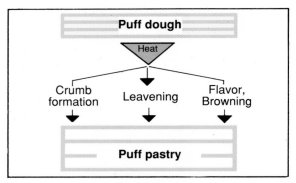

Fig. 600 Baking of puff pastry

How does leavening of the puff dough occur during baking?

→ The fat layers insulate the dough layers from each other, even when the roll-in fat turns liquid.

→ At temperatures above 60°C in the dough piece, the starch turns pasty. At the same time, the gluten coagulates.

→ At a temperature around 100°C, the water evaporates from the dough layers.

→ The steam exercises an inner pressure, which makes the dough layers rise. The freshly-formed crumb solidifies during leavening and thus obtains its typical structure.

→ After the steam has evaporated, the temperature in the outer layers of the pastry can increase to more than 100°C. Roasted substances, made of dough and fat components, form. Sugar that has been added can caramelize.

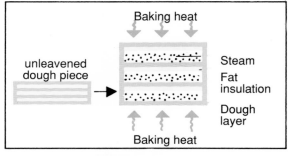

Fig. 601 Leavening of puff pastry

> ***Remember:***
> *Puff dough leavens through the pressure exercised by the steam = physical leavening*

Quality Characteristics and Deficiencies of Puff Pastries

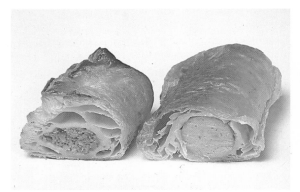

Fig. 602
Sausage rolls made with puff dough

Faults in Puff Pastry

Faults	Possible Causes
The pastries contract during baking	➤ the basic dough is too tough; ➤ the puff dough is too fresh; the resting time is too short; ➤ the dough pieces are not allowed to rest for a sufficient period of time (on the pans); ➤ the pans are coated with an excessive layer of fat
The roll-in fat flows out of the puff dough	➤ the puff dough has not been sufficiently laminated; ➤ the dough layers are too thick; the oven is too cold
The crumb is doughy	➤ the baking time is too short (the oven too hot); ➤ the filling is moist, heavy
The pastries do not rise uniformly	➤ the dough is not folded properly (some areas of the dough are not sufficiently coated with fat); ➤ the layers are partly destroyed; ➤ dull cutting tools are used; ➤ the cutting points are coated with egg
The pastries are "gray" and dull	➤ the flour is not brushed off; ➤ the dough has formed a skin; ➤ lack of sugar

Quality Characteristics

The puff pastries should leaven, have a brittle-crisp crust, a tender crumb and a good aroma. Puff pastries fresh from the oven best meet these requirements.

Some puff pastries (filled with sausage or cheese) should be consumed while still warm. Other pastries, e.g., those filled with cream or those coated, are best consumed cold.

Although puff pastries have a high fat content, their shelf life is not improved by the addition of more fat.

Why not?

— The pasty starch in the dough layers is not incorporated into a fat layer. Therefore, it rapidly retrogrades and the pastry flakes in the crumb quickly firm up.

— The roll-in fat is still liquid in the first hours after the pastries have been baked in the oven. The longer the pastries are stored, the more the roll-in fat returns to a crystallized state. This becomes obvious through the fatty-sticky feeling of the palate when consuming older pastries.

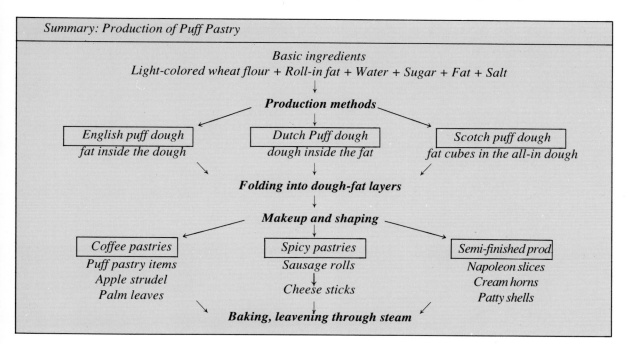

Summary: Production of Puff Pastry

Basic ingredients
Light-colored wheat flour + Roll-in fat + Water + Sugar + Fat + Salt
↓
Production methods
↓

| English puff dough | Dutch Puff dough | Scotch puff dough |
| fat inside the dough | dough inside the fat | fat cubes in the all-in dough |

Folding into dough-fat layers
↓
Makeup and shaping
↓

Coffee pastries	Spicy pastries	Semi-finished prod.
Puff pastry items	Sausage rolls	Napoleon slices
Apple strudel	Cheese sticks	Cream horns
Palm leaves		Patty shells

Baking, leavening through steam

Short Pastries

Fig. 603 **Pastries made with short paste**

The Use of Short Paste

Many recipes indicate a short paste as the basis for fine baked goods, desserts, tarts, and fruit flans. Next to yeast dough and puff dough, short paste is an important dough type for fine baking goods. A good short paste must guarantee the following:

— during processing	— in the final product
• good dough properties, even when the paste is stored for several days in a cool environment	• short consistency, e.g. as bottoms for fruit flans
	• pleasant flavor, e.g. as a part of nut wedges
• it must be easy to roll out without breaking or contracting	• long fresh-keeping properties, e.g. as a part of durable goods
• long durability without turning rancid	• stability, e.g. as a bottom for tarts
	• low tendency to wet through, e.g. as a bottom for fruit flans

Basic recipe for rich short paste, suitable for rolling	
1,000 g	Pastry flour
650 g	Butter/margarine
350 g	Sugar
	+ Salt/flavor

Table 120

Basic recipe for light short paste, suitable for rolling	
1,000 g	Pastry flour
500 g	Baking margarine
500 g	Sugar
125 g	Milk
15 g	Baking powder
	+ Salt/flavor

Table 121

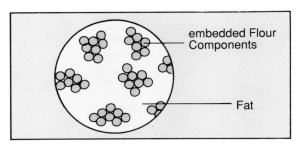

Fig. 604 Easily worked short paste
The flour components are embedded in a fat structure

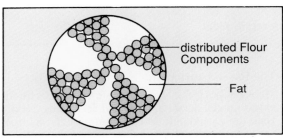

Fig. 605 Short paste that easily breaks apart; impossible to work with
The flour components have interrupted the cohesive structure of the fat. The dough breaks

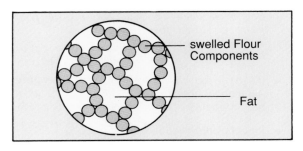

Fig. 606 **"Tough" short paste; impossible to work with.** The flour components have absorbed liquid. The fat is embedded in a dough structure

278

The processing characteristics of the paste and the quality of short pastries depend on the composition of the short paste and on the production methods used.

Composition of Short Pastes

Short paste contains the basic ingredients: pastry flour, fat and sugar. To improve the quality of the paste and the flavor, the following can be added: salt, flavor, eggs.

Short pastes suitable for rolling out are prepared based on the following basic recipes:

1 part sugar, 2 parts fat, 3 parts flour (1/2/3 – heavy short paste)

or

1 part sugar, 1 part fat, 2 parts flour (1/1/2 – light short paste)

> *Remember:*
> *For rich short paste, use sugar, fat and flour at a ratio of 1/2/3.*

Preparation of Short Pastes

Unlike the basic yeast dough or the basic puff dough, a short paste should not be made elastic by developing the gluten content.

Therefore, pastry flour or a pastry flour/patent flour blend rich in starch, but low in gluten content should be used. The fat should distribute easily, but should not become embedded in the dough structure. The sugar should be as fine grained as possible, so that it can dissolve rapidly.

> *The following rules apply to the preparation and processing of short pastes:*
>
> → *Use cool ingredients; never dissolve the fat.*
> → *Cream sugar and fat until smooth.*
> → *Add eggs gradually, in stages, to avoid curdling.*
> → *Incorporate the flour.*
> → *Avoid overmixing.*
> → *Store the short paste in a cool environment.*
> → *Make short paste cool.*

Reasons for Specific Properties of Short Pastes

The short, fat condition of the short paste is due to the high fat and sugar content. The gluten and the starch grains of the flour are wrapped in fat. Thus, they stick together (*Fig. 604*), but the dough does not swell.

The starch cannot completely turn pasty during baking. It is wrapped in fat. Moreover, it does not have a sufficient amount of dough water at its disposal. Therefore, the cells of the crumb form a short rather than cohesive structure.

Faults of Short Pastes

When warm ingredients are used to make the short paste, or it becomes so warm during processing that the fat melts, the short paste breaks (see *Fig. 605*). It cannot be rolled out or shaped.

Such short paste yields firm, hard pastries.

When a short paste containing milk is overmixed, the gluten swells. The paste turns tough and shrinks. Tough short paste cannot be rolled out. It shrinks back to its original size. Tough short paste yields light-colored, shrunken and misshaped pastries with bubbles.

When the sugar is too coarse and undissolved, it can cause the baked product to spread excessively.

When the short paste is made too soft, or if the sugar and the fat have been creamed too much, the pastries lose their shape.

Baking and Leavening of Short Doughs

Short pastes are baked at temperatures ranging between 180 and 210°C without steam. As the pastries are often very flat, they bake dry within a short period of time.

Rich short pastes do not require any leavening agents. They are short/brittle. Light short pastes (to which liquid has been added) require the addition of baking soda or powder as leaveners.

The effect of these chemical leaveners will be examined in connection with the leavening agents used for gingerbread pastries.

Pastries made with Special Short Doughs

The 1/2/3 short paste is modified through the addition of spices, cocoa, nuts, almonds, or through the use of special processing techniques. Such special short pastes are used for the production of coffee pastries and durable pastries.

Examples:

— *cutout coffee pastries*
A 1/2/3 short paste is rolled out, cut out and decorated. Sometimes, parts are put together with a filling in between, after baking.
Fig. 607 is an example of cutout cheese shortbread pastries.

— *ice box shortbread cookies*
Instead of coarse sugar, the short paste contains icing sugar. All the ingredients are blended together at slow speed to form a smooth paste. Cocoa powder is added to half the paste. Both colored pastes are refrigerated in frames or forms. The pastes are then cut up and arranged to form patterns. After slicing 5 mm thick, the pastries are baked.

Fig. 607 **Cutout cheese shortbread pastries**

Fig. 608 **Fancy ice box shortbread cookies (black-and-white pastries)**

Fig. 609 **Piped shortbread cookies**

Fig. 610

| cutout short paste | piped short paste | patterned short paste |

Categorize the short pastries in your bakery according to the makeup techniques used for the short paste.

279

— *piped shortbread cookies (pastries)*

Egg or milk is added to a 1/2/2 short paste with a high fat content, in order to allow the paste to be piped (squeezed through a tube). For softer, more tender pastries, replace up to 10% of the flour with corn starch or rice flour. After baking, the dough pieces receive a topping, or they are filled or coated after they have been baked in the oven (see *Fig. 609*).

Linzer Short Paste

The Linzer short paste contains ground nuts or almonds. Sugar, butter and flour are mixed with almonds/nuts at a ratio of 1/1/1. Typical is a coating of tangy preserves (raspberry jam) topped with a short paste grid (lattice topping).

Fig. 611 **Linzer torte**

Amandines

The basic dough is a 1/2/2 short paste to which egg and almonds are added. The soft paste is cooled, cut into pieces shaped in the form of hearts and fried in frying fat. After they come out of the fryer, the Amandines are rolled in cinnamon sugar.

Cheese Short Dough

The paste used for cheese pastries does not contain any sugar. Flour, fat and grated cheese are mixed together, using a ratio of 1/1. Salt, paprika and egg are added. The cutout dough pieces receive a spicy topping and are then baked in the oven.

Fig. 612 **Speculos**

Speculos (Spicy short dough)

Simple spicy speculos is made with a large amount of sugar (2 parts sugar, 1 part fat, 3 parts flour). Special spices used include cinnamon, cloves, coriander and cardamom. This type of speculos is crisp, hard/brittle, dark and very aromatic.

Almond speculos is made with a 1/2/3 short paste to which roughly grated almonds are added as a base.

Butter speculos should only contain butter fat or pure butter.

At one time, only wooden molds were used for baking speculos. Today, machines can be used to make the production process more economical.

Fig. 613
Wooden mold and shaping rollers of a machine

Summary of the most important information about short pastries					
Short Pastries					
short doughs		*light short pastes*	*spiced short pastes*		*short pastes with many ingredients*
			sweet	*salty*	
rich	**light**	*1/2/2 – short paste*	Spices	Salt	*pastes with high fat*
1/2/3	*1/1/2*	*addition of egg-milk*	Sugar	Cheese	*content (1/1/1)*
dough	*dough*	*and wheat starch*			*grated nuts, almonds*
Bottoms		*Piped short paste*	*Speculos*	*Cheese*	*Linzer short paste*
Tortlets				*short paste*	*Amandines*

Gingerbread

Among the Christmas pastries in a bakery count a multitude of gingerbread pastries. The following are the typical characteristics of these pastry types:

— they are very sweet,

— they are not very moist,

— they are flavorful,

— their crumb is short,

— they are very durable.

These characteristics are, in particular, due to the high amount of sweeteners contained in gingerbread.

Composition and Production of Gingerbread

Because gingerbread pastries are durable, they should contain:

→ per 100 parts flour, at least 50 parts sugar (and/or powdered honey, invert sugar cream, invert sugar, sugar syrup, maltose syrup, dextrose, fruit sugar or sugar produced by starch).

→ for honey cakes/honey gingerbread, at least half of their sweeteners in the form of honey.

Composition of Gingerbread Doughs

Due to their high sweetener content and an almost complete lack of water, the flour components of the honey or gingerbread doughs do not swell.

The viscosity of the doughs is achieved by means of the viscous-sticky properties of the sweeteners.

The baker can achieve the desired quality of gingerbread or honey cake doughs by selecting the proper ingredients.

Fig. 614 Christmas pastries made with gingerbread dough

Food Regulatory Guidelines

Basic recipe for honey cakes	
1,000 g	Flour (700 g Baker's Patent and 300 g rye)
800 g	Honey
100 g	Egg
30 g	Gingerbread spices (cloves, cinnamon, mace, nutmeg, allspice, fennel, coriander, anise, cardamom)
10 g	Soda
10 g	Potassium (where available)

Additional Information

Gingerbread was first produced during the middle ages in monasteries and, later, on a commercial basis, by "gingerbread bakers." These bakers differed from sugar pastry bakers and belonged to their own guild.

The famous "Nuernberger Gingerbread War" between gingerbread bakers and sugar pastry bakers was a dispute over who was allowed to produce the popular delicacy.

However, the conflict was solved in 1808 when the Bavarian King decided that both trades could produce gingerbread.

Measure	*Reasons*
→ *Use bread flour (baker's patent)*	➤ *short dough due to the weak gluten flour; higher water absorption of baker's patent flour*
→ *Add rye flour (light and medium rye) up to one-third of the total quantity of flour used*	➤ *improved spreading characteristics of the dough; less sweetness; better flavor*
→ *Use syrup or liquid sugar instead of crystallized sugar*	➤ *better dough characteristics due to the higher content of dissolved sugar; longer fresh-keeping of the products*

Fig. 615 **Gingerbread bakers produced ginger-bread in the Middle Ages**

Sample recipes for gingerbread	
Gingerbread	
1,000 g	Flour (wheat/rye)
800 g	Honey (part invert sugar optional)
100 g	Candied lemon peel
100 g	Candied orange peel
100 g	Nuts (or almonds, grated)
100 g	Egg
30 g	Gingerbread spice
15 g	Ammonia bicarbonate
15 g	Sodium bicarbonate
Nut gingerbread	
1,000 g	Flour (700 g wheat, 300 g rye)
900 g	Invert sugar syrup
300 g	Candied orange peel
500 g	Hazelnuts (roasted, grated)
50 g	Gingerbread spices
20 g	Ammonium bicarbonate
20 g	Sodium bicarbonate

Table 123

Fig. 616 **Pastries made with gingerbread dough**

Preparation of Gingerbread Doughs

Gingerbread doughs are traditionally made to be *stored doughs*. This means that all the ingredients (with the exception of spices and leavening agents) are combined into a dough which is then stored for several months. During this period of time, the products of the fermentation process form aromatic substances. The carbonic acids separating from the sugar create a chemical reaction that leavens the dough.

As *fresh doughs*, gingerbread doughs are prepared with all ingredients. However, they must also be stored for about one to three days in order to guarantee good processing characteristics and baked goods of high quality.

The following basic rules must be observed when preparing and processing doughs:

→ Warm the sweeteners to ensure better processing.

→ Do not warm honey to more than 80°C; otherwise the flavor substances of the honey are destroyed.

→ Let heated sweeteners cool down to 40°C before they are added to the flour; otherwise the albumen coagulates and the flour starch turns pasty.

→ Store the basic dough in a covered plastic or wooden container for long periods of time; otherwise it dries out too much (cool storage).

→ Allow basic dough to warm up to room temperature; otherwise it cannot be worked very easily.

→ Add different leavening agents separately; otherwise they could react to each other.

Modifications of Gingerbread Doughs

As you can see from the recipes given in *Table 123*, different pastries can be made by varying the ingredients, e.g.:

➤ Brown gingerbreads (simple)
— are the only ones that should contain fat;

➤ Honey cakes
— should contain at least 50% sweeteners in the form of honey;

➤ Brown almond gingerbreads,
Brown nut gingerbreads
— when they are labelled as "the finest," they should contain at least 20% grated almonds and/or hazelnuts or walnuts.

The following are some baked goods made with gingerbread dough:

— Domino stones = filled goods shaped as cubes and composed of layers of gingerbread and fruit jelly; marzipan cover with couverture or chocolate coating.

— Pfeffernuesse = a spicy gingerbread dough containing egg, cut out in round pieces and coated, after baking, with a boiled sugar glaze.

— Cookies	=	Cookies with candied sugar in the dough; soft cookies, containing nuts, almonds, marzipan or chocolate; rectangular-shaped, baked dry, coated with glaze or couverture.
— Gingerbread men and Gingerbread houses	=	dough rolled out to about 1/4" thickness, cut out with a variety of cutters, baked and decorated accordingly.
— Swiss gingerbread	=	honey cake pieces, trapezoid-shaped, filled with marzipan, couverture cover.
— Swiss Leckerli	=	very fine honey cake dough, to which candied lemon or orange peel is added; after baking, almonds receive a boiled sugar glazing; cut into squares or triangular shapes.

Baking and Leavening of Gingerbread Doughs

Prior to the makeup of gingerbread doughs, a small sample quantity is baked in the oven. Thus, the leavening of the product can be evaluated. Through the addition of leavening agents or modification of the doughs, major errors can be avoided.

The following rules apply to the baking process:
— no steam in oven,
— bake at uniform heat (at temperatures ranging between 160 and 180°C),
— bake with vent or oven doors slightly open.

Leavening of the dough is achieved during baking through the gases produced by the chemical leaveners.

Wafer Gingerbread

Fig. 617 **Wafer Gingerbread**

These types of gingerbread are made with a paste similar to a macaroon paste. They are usually spread onto wafers because the paste is very soft.

They are of the highest quality and very durable. *Fig. 617* shows a number of different shapes and types. The following glazings are commonly used: boiled sugar glaze, fondant, royal icing and couverture. Chocolate coatings are also used, but are not as durable for wafer gingerbread.

Bee honey is essentially composed of 70 to 80% invert sugar and 15 to 25% water. Among other components, a high proportion of aromatic substances is important to the production of baked goods. Invert sugar is a mixture composed of equal parts of dextrose and fruit sugar. In honey, it is formed through the enzyme invertase.

Beet and cane sugar can be inverted through the addition of acid or through the effect of the enzymes. Because of its fruit sugar content, invert sugar is much sweeter than beet sugar, but it does not crystallize as easily.

Invert sugar cream (artificial honey) is made of invert cane or beet sugar and sugar produced by the starch (up to 38.5%), with the possible addition of honey.

Liquid invert sugar and invert sugar syrup contain at least 50% invert sugar in the dry substance. They also contain water. Therefore, the quantity added to the dough must be quantitatively converted into dry sugar. Example: Syrup with a water content of 20% = required sugar quantity divided by 80 x 100 = quantity of syrup to be used.

Caramel sugar, with various degrees of browning, is obtained through heating cane or beet sugar. It is available in the form of crystals or in liquid state. Caramel sugar has an influence on the flavor and color of gingerbread.

Glucose (also called corn syrup) is produced through the chemical or enzymatic decomposition of starch. It contains 40% dextrose, 40% dextrine and 20% water. Therefore, it has a low sweetening power, but it increases the fresh-keeping characteristics of products.

The essential effects of sweeteners are as follows:

— Honey has a high content of natural invert sugar and of aromatic substances.

— Invert sugar improves the characteristics of gingerbread doughs and has a high sweetening power due to its fruit sugar content. It does not crystallize to the same extent as cane-beet sugar, but it retains the moisture of baked goods.

— Caramel sugar lends a caramel flavor to the product and provides additional color to gingerbread products.

— Corn syrup has similar effects as invert sugar, but has less sweetening power.

Gingerbread batters are spread onto special molds (see *Fig. 618*).

Examples:

— White gingerbread
  = made with 15% whole egg or egg products and no more than 40% flour products;

— Almond gingerbread
  = no less than 25% almonds and/or hazelnuts or walnuts, and no more than 10% flour products or 7.5% starch in the batter;

— Nut gingerbread
  = a nut content of at least 20%, mainly consisting in the type of nut included in the name of the pastry.

Fig. 618 **Gingerbread molds**

Summary of all gingerbread types		
← **Brown Gingerbread** →		**Wafer Gingerbread**
Brown almond or nut gingerbread honey cakes	Domino stones, Pfeffernuesse, Swiss gingerbread, Swiss Leckerli, Gingerbread men, etc.	Almond/macaroon gingerbread Nut gingerbread White gingerbread
↓	↓	↓
Gingerbread dough	Gingerbread with special ingredients, fillings, glazings	Batters with a high content of egg white, sugar, nut products

Fig. 619
Wafer gingerbread with a variety of spices

Fig. 620
Important spices used in bakeries: A = vanilla beans, B = cloves, C = ginger, D = anise, E = cardamom, F = saffron, G = cinnamon stick and finely-ground cinnamon, H = Star anise

284

Spices and Aromatic Compounds Used in Baking

Spices and Aromas
The fragrance and aroma of baked goods are predominantly determined by the ingredients used. Products with a low amount of added spices or aromatic compounds are flavored mainly by means of salt and sugar, but also through the aromatic substances formed during baking. Products containing a large amount of spices or aromatic compounds receive their smell and taste from the multitude of aromatic ingredients. The ingredients of wafer gingerbread summarized in *Fig. 619* are a good example. Gingerbread also contains special spices, including cinnamon, anise, nutmeg and allspice.

Spices used for Fine Baked Goods
Spices are unprocessed parts of plants which are simply dried.
What causes these plant parts to have a spicing effect?
Spices contain, as flavoring components:
— etheric oils = very volatile substances resembling fat, with an aromatic smell and flavor;
— tannins = mildly volatile substances, soluble in water, with a bitter or acidulous flavor;
— resins = non-volatile substances, liposoluble, with a sharp flavor.

From old documents and recipes, we know about the value attributed to spices in former times. Spices were precious. Their mixtures and the quantities used were often a secret of the producer.

Today, bakeries have access to a large variety of spices:

Important spices used are:	
Root spices	Ginger
Bark spices	Cinnamon
Flower spices	Cloves, Saffron
Fruit spices	Vanilla, Nutmeg, Lemon peel
Seed spices	Anise, Star anise, Fennel, Cardamom, Coriander, Caraway, Poppy seed, Pepper, Allspice, Sesame

In what form are spices used as ingredients for fine baked goods?

Spices are added as ground substances to doughs or pastes. Thus, they easily release their aromatic substances and they can be distributed more finely.

Spices are often used as mixtures. Thus, they compliment their respective flavoring effects, e.g., spice mixtures for gingerbread or Speculos.

The aromatic substances of spices lose some of their effect when the ground spices are stored for too long or in an inappropriate way. The smell and flavor of substances are very volatile. They are easily decomposed under the effects of oxygen, heat, moisture and light.

The following rules apply to the storage of spices:

— *Store in an airtight container (protection against oxygen)*

— *Store in non-absorbent materials (protection against spices turning rancid)*

— *Store in light-tight materials (protection against sunlight)*

— *Store in cool, dry rooms (protection against heat and moisture)*

Aromatic Compounds used for Fine Baked Goods

The spicy components of spices are more durable and easier to proportion in the form of aromatic compounds.

* **Aromatic compounds** *are preparations of smell and/or flavor substances which are exclusively meant to give aroma to foodstuffs.*

Additional Information

The oldest known gingerbread recipe dates back to the 16th century; the following ingredients are listed:
1 lb. sugar
1/2 mug honey
4 lot cinnamon
1-1/2 trump nutmeg
2 lot ginger
1 lot cardamom
1/2 trifle pepper
1 heap flour

These old-fashioned units of measurement do not mean anything to us. But does the spice mixture sound familiar?

This is how you can put together spice mixtures:

Spice mixture for Gingerbread
100 g	ground Cinnamon
50 g	ground Cloves
50 g	ground Allspice
50 g	ground Cardamom
10 g	ground Anise

Spice mixture of Speculos
100 g	ground Cinnamon
20 g	ground Allspice
20 g	ground Cloves
20 g	ground Cardamom
10 g	ground Mace flour

Food for Thought:
The use of ready-made spice mixtures offered in the marketplace has advantages:
— *They guarantee a uniform composition of flavor.*
— *They save time.*

But: Does their use ultimately lead to a uniform flavor of the baking goods?
What do you think?

Tips for the use of spices

➤ *Store spices appropriately in order to preserve the aromatic substances.*
➤ *Adjust the quantity of spices used to the type of baked good produced. Heavy baked goods containing a high amount of fat lose less smell and aroma substances during baking than "light" baked goods.*
➤ *Always weigh spices with precision. An insufficient quantity of spices used does not yield the desired aroma. An excessive quantity can destroy the taste of bakery products.*
➤ *Do not incorporate spices into sponge doughs or doughs that are to be stored for a long period of time. They may lose a large amount of their aroma.*

Preparations of aromatic substances are also called **essences** (= the essential, concentrated form), or **extracts**. In addition to the aromatic substances, they contain carriers, solvents and emulsifiers.

Categories of Aromatic Compounds

What does the baker have to know when purchasing aromatic substances?

➤ Besides the trade name (often a fantasy name, e.g., "orchid-vanilla essence"), the following should be identified on the label of the package:

— The trade name, e.g., lemon essence,
— The purpose, e.g., to give flavor to creams, etc.,
— The quantity to be used, e.g., 3 to 5 g per 1,000 g paste.

➤ In addition to the trade name, the type of aromatic substance should be identified.

* **Natural aromatic substances** are exclusively derived from natural raw substances (e.g., through pressing, extraction, fermentation, distillation). Therefore, they are usually a mixture of several natural aromatic substances (substances conveying aroma).

* **Nature-identical aromatic substances** are not of natural origin. They are individual aromatic substances produced in pure form. They correspond in their composition and effect to natural aromatic substances and should be identified as artificial flavors.

* **Artificial aromatic substances** are chemically produced. They correspond to the natural aromatic substances in terms of flavor, but not in terms of their composition and effect.

The Use of Aromatic Substances

The baker must know the following when using aromatic substances:

Aromatic substances differ in terms of their applications and some can be resistant to baking. Aromatic substances that are resistant to baking are mildly volatile and those that are not resistant to baking often contain a large proportion of highly volatile alcohols. In order to select the appropriate types of aromatic substances for a given purpose, follow the manufacturer's instructions.

The composition of an aromatic substance must be adapted to the specific type of baking product. For some doughs and pastes, a wide variety of aromatic substances can be used, e.g., for yeast doughs, yeasted cakes and Stollen doughs. For other doughs and pastes, however, only certain aromatic substances can be used. For example, vanilla and rum extract should be used in nut cakes, but not lemon essence.

Aromatic substances have their optimum effect when they are used in certain proportions. These are indicated by the manufacturer. Generally, 3 to 5 g of essence or aroma per 1,000 g paste are used. For pasty aromatic substances or fruit concentrates (also called compounds), between 30 and 200 g per 1,000 g paste can be added.

The optimum quantity to be added, based on common recipes in a bakery, can be established by means of baking tests using two or three different quantity ranges.

Under certain conditions, artificial or nature-identical aromatic substances should not be used.

When a product is supposed to be designated, for example, as "almond cake," the almond flavor has, for this type of product, a significance in terms of value. Therefore, only natural aromatic almond substances should be used. Even if their use is identified, nature-identical aromatic almond substances should not be used in this case.

When using nature-identical or artificial aromatic substances, the product should be called "pastry with almond flavor."

When a baked product is offered for sale in prepackaged format, the list of ingredients should always indicate the type of aromatic substances used (e.g., cherry, vanilla). It is sufficient to label as follows:

— Natural flavor
    or
— Artificial flavor

Food Regulatory Guidelines

Summary of important information about the use of aromatic substances

➤ *Take note of the applications specified for aromatic substances and essences.*
➤ *Respect the recommended quantity proportions. The optimum quantity to be used for a bakery's specific recipes can be established by means of flavor tests.*
➤ *Use the aroma suited to the type of baked good to be produced.*
➤ *Respect the food regulations applying to the use and labelling of natural and artificial aromatic substances.*

Vanilla beans are the fruits of a tropical orchid. Vanilla grows in Central America (Mexico). Right after they have been harvested, vanilla beans have no aroma. Only through a fermentation process does the bean receive its aromatic substances and its typical black and brown color.

Vanilla contains about 150 different aromatic substances, the main one being vanillin. By means of appropriate solvents and by using pressure and specific temperatures, the natural vanilla aroma is extracted from the beans.

Through a precise analysis of the natural vanillin, it has become possible to artificially produce this main aromatic substance of the vanilla bean. The vanillin thus produced is a white powder. It has the same composition, the same flavor and the same effect (in terms of the quantity to be added) as the natural vanillin. Therefore, this vanillin is nature-identical. Nature-identical vanillin yields a pure vanilla flavor. Baked goods spiced with vanilla require labelling. But if the flavors of the product are supposed to be included in the trade name, this should be done as follows, when vanillin is used: "contains artificial flavor."

An artificial vanilla flavor is a substance called ethyl vanillin. This substance is similar in terms of smell and flavor to that of vanillin. However, its effect is much stronger. Baked goods containing the artificial aromatic substance ethyl vanillin must be labelled as follows: "with artificial flavors."

Chemical Leavening

Short pastes contain a high amount of fat and sugar. A 1/2/3 short paste has a fat content of about 67% and a sugar content of about 33%, related to the quantity of flour used. It does not contain any additional quantities of water or milk. Under these conditions, the yeast can no longer ferment.

Gingerbread doughs are rich in sugar. Their content of sweeteners amounts to about 50% of the flour products used. When used in such a quantity, sugar has a preserving effect. Therefore, yeast cannot serve as a leavener.

However, leavening agents which release leavening gases through chemical reactions can leaven these doughs.

Potassium Carbonate

The producers of gingerbread discovered several hundred years ago that potash is a leavener. In former times, it was obtained through leaching plant ash. This is where its name comes from.

In chemical terms, it is the potassium of the carbonic acid (potassium carbonate).

Test 33:
Dissolve 5 g potassium carbonate in 50 g water in a beaker glass.
a) Watch to see if changes are occurring in the solution.
b) Now heat the solution (carefully) and watch if changes are occurring.
c) Add a few drops of lactic acid to the solution. Hold a burning wood shaving over the foaming solution. Watch what happens.

Observations:
Potassium carbonate is soluble in water. No change occurs in the potassium carbonate solution when it is heated. When acid is added, gas bubbles up and suffocates the flame.

* **Conclusion:**
  Potassium carbonate decomposes when acid is added, and releases carbon dioxide.

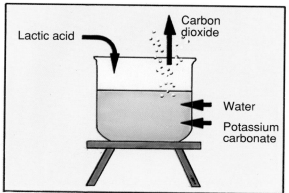

Fig. 621 Potassium carbonate releases the leavening gas carbon dioxide under the effect of acid and heat

When potassium carbonate is added to a gingerbread dough that is to be stored, the acids formed from the added honey and sugar have an decomposing effect on the potassium carbonate. Carbon dioxide is released as a leavening gas, water is also released and a potassium salt forms. The potassium salt makes the dough soft due to its alkaline state and makes it expand laterally.

Additional information about the chemical reaction occurring during leavening with potassium carbonate

Potassium carbonate + Lactic acid

$$K_2CO_3 + 2\ CH_3 - \underset{\underset{OH}{|}}{CH} - COOH$$

$$2\ CH_3 - \underset{\underset{OH}{|}}{CH} - COOK + H_2O + CO_2$$

Potassium lactate
(a salt of the lactic acid)
+ Water + Carbon dioxide

Remember:
* *Potassium carbonate has a leavening effect on gingerbread and causes it to expand laterally.*

Sal Volatile

Sal volatile is a mixture composed of three ammonium salts. The main component is ammonium hydrogen carbonate (salt of the carbonic acid).

In pure form this salt is also used as an ABC rising agent (derived from the name = ammonium bicarbonate). Let us test the leavening effect of ABC rising agents using the following three tests:

Test 34:

Dissolve 5 g ABC rising agent in 50 g water in a beaker glass.
Now heat the solution (carefully) and watch what happens.

Observations:
ABC rising agents are soluble in water. When heated to over 60°C, leavening gases are released (*Fig. 622*).

Conclusion:
* *ABC rising agents decompose when heated and release a leavening gas.*

You can easily smell the pungent odor escaping from an open bottle containing ABC rising agents.
Let us conduct the following test:

Test 35:

Put 2 g dry ABC rising agent into a test glass and heat it in dry state over a Bunsen burner.

Watch the changes occurring in the ABC rising agents; smell the vapors released.

Observations:
ABC rising agents decompose completely without any residue when they are heated in dry state. Carbon dioxide, steam and ammonia gas are released (*Fig. 623*).

Test 36:

Taste a little bit of the water from *Test 34*.

Observations:
The water has an alkaline flavor.
Add a little bit of phenolphthalein or a strip of red litmus paper to the water from *Test 34*.

Observations:
When phenolphthalein is used, the water takes on a pink color; when litmus paper is used, it turns blue.

Conclusion:
* *When ABC rising agents are heated in water, the residue forms an alkaline solution.*

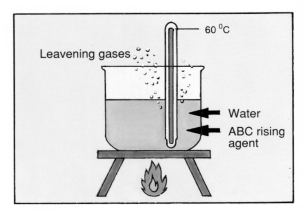

Fig. 622
ABC rising agents, dissolved in water, release the leavening gas carbon dioxide when heated

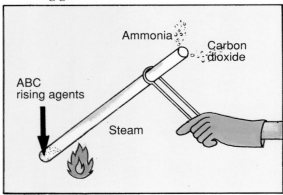

Fig. 623
Dry ABC rising agents release the leavening gas carbon dioxide when heated

---

Additional Information
Chemical reaction taking place during the leavening process, using ABC rising agents

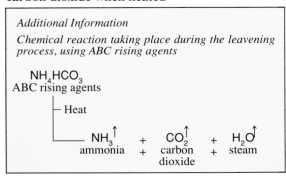

NH_4HCO_3
ABC rising agents

— Heat

$NH_3\uparrow$ + $CO_2\uparrow$ + $H_2O\uparrow$
ammonia + carbon dioxide + steam

The ammonia gas has a pungent odor and is very aquaphilous. It combines with water to form ammonium hydroxide. Ammonium hydroxide is a component of detergents known for its pungent odor and its bleaching effect. Products using ABC as a leavener must be baked thoroughly.
In the moist crumb of the baked good, ammonium hydroxide is formed when the ABC rising agents cannot completely evaporate. The crumb then takes on a greenish color and produces an alkaline taste.

* **Remember:**
  ABC rising agents must only be used for leavening of dry, flat baking products.

Sodium Bicarbonate

The sodium salt of the carbonic acid is often used instead of potassium carbonate for the production of gingerbread.

Test 37:
Dissolve 5 g sodium bicarbonate in 50 g water in a beaker glass.
a) Watch the solution to detect if any changes are occurring.
b) Now heat the solution and watch what happens.
c) After the first bubbles have settled, carefully add a few drops of lactic acid. Hold a burning wood shaving over the foaming solution.

Observations:
Sodium bicarbonate is soluble in water.
When it is heated, gas bubbles appear.
When acid is added, the solution again produces a strong foam (*Fig. 624*). The released gas suffocates the flame.

Conclusion:
* *Sodium bicarbonate decomposes when heated in water and releases carbon dioxide. When acid is added, it releases more carbon dioxide.*

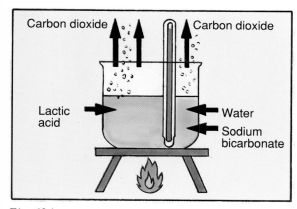

Fig. 624
When sodium bicarbonate is exposed to heat and acid, the leavening gas carbon dioxide is released

Sodium bicarbonate can be used for leavening gingerbread dough that is supposed to be stored, because the acids formed in the dough cause the sodium bicarbonate to completely decompose.

However, in fresh gingerbread doughs, the only effect is produced by heat. Therefore, only a part of the carbon dioxide is released and soda remains as the residual salt of the sodium bicarbonate.

Baking Powder
Baking powder contains sodium bicarbonate as the carrier of carbon dioxide.
In addition, it contains acid or acid salts as carbon dioxide developing agents.
It contains salt as a separating agent between sodium bicarbonate and acid salt. Therefore, baking powder can be stored.
When baking powder is added, it must be sifted with the last portion of flour to be incorporated into the dough. It has an effect on the dough prior to its being baked in the oven (preliminary rising power).
However, the main part of the carbon dioxide is released only during baking.

---

* **Remember:**
  Baking powder leavens the baked goods through the carbon dioxide released from the sodium bicarbonate under the effects of heat and acid.

Additional Information
The German chemist Justus von Liebig (1803 – 1873) is often cited as the inventor of baking powder. This is partly true. Justus von Liebig wrote many articles and lectured about the production of bread during his years at the University of Giessen. His efforts were mainly geared toward producing a nutritional food. Because bread was the main staple for a large part of the population, Liebig wanted to improve the nutritional value of finely-ground flour through the addition of nutrient salts.
For that purpose, he introduced, in an article, a baking powder that had been developed by Professor Horsford from Cambridge in North America. This baking powder was composed of an acid powder and an alkali powder. From these powders, Liebig derived the desired nutritional salts to be added to flour. At the same time, he considered baking powder to be a good leavening agent for bread.
However, the advent of baking powder has not contributed to a major breakthrough in the production of bread because its use results in bread that tastes flat and dry. But baking powder has undergone further modifications, and today it is an indispensable leavening agent for cookies, cakes and pastries.

Additional Information
Baking powder can contain various agents that develop carbon dioxide, e.g., cream of tartar, citric acid and salts of phosphoric acid. Sodium pyrophosphate, a salt of the phosphoric acid, is used most frequently. Using the example of this acid salt, the following is its chemical reaction with sodium bicarbonate:

$$2\ NaHCO_3 \quad + \quad Na_2H_2P_2O_7 \quad \xrightarrow{\text{Heat}} \quad Na_4P_2O_7 \quad + \quad 2\ H_2O \quad + \quad 2\ CO_2\uparrow$$

Sodium bicarbonate + Sodium pyrophosphate   *Sodium phosphate + Water + Carbon dioxide*

Products Made with Batters

To determine the difference between doughs and batters, make a list of products in your bakery. Categorize the individual items depending on whether a dough or a batter is used as the basis.

Fig. 626   Fig. 627
Batters can be spread or poured

Fig. 628 **Batters can be piped**

Fig. 625

Distinction between Doughs and Batters

Yeast doughs, puff doughs, short pastes and gingerbread doughs differ very strongly in terms of their composition, the production methods used and the processing methods, and in terms of their use for baked products. However, they all have one thing in common — they are called ***doughs***.

Doughs have common characteristics:
➤ The ingredients in the recipe are based on the flour.
➤ The production techniques/processes used consist primarily of blending and kneading.
➤ The doughs are extensible and elastic through the formation of gluten, or have a pliable consistency like short pastes. In the case of most dough types, the dough properties are determined by their absorption, by the liquid added and by the flour components.
➤ Leavening is caused through yeast fermentation, steam (in the case of puff dough), and through chemical leaveners (in the case of short pastes and gingerbread doughs). The gas absorption capacity of the swelled albumen in the gluten allows the products to leaven.

For ***batters*** used in bakeries, sugar or eggs are the basis for the recipe.

Batters have common characteristics:
➤ The recipe is, if based on eggs, high in sugar and fat content. To make the batter cohesive, wheat/cornstarch or mixtures of flour, wheat and cornstarch are used.
➤ The production techniques/processes used consist of beating, whipping and creating roux.
➤ Batters are primarily foamy, and soft to flowing.
➤ Leavening is, in principle, achieved by physical and chemical means.

The expert categorizes various batters, according to their quantities of ingredients used, into light or heavy batters. Depending on the production methods used, he/she distinguishes between cold or warm batters, and whipped or beaten batters.

Machines used for the Production of Batters

For the production of bread and rolls, even small bakeries normally use large machines and equipment. Mixing, shaping, manipulation, fermentation and feeding of bread and small wheat-flour products is almost never done manually.

But what about the production of baked goods with batters in the bakery?

Large bread-mixing machines and plants cannot always be used due to the large variety of products made. Moreover, the tools required are different, e.g., whipping attachments, bowls, piping bags, palette knives, decorating combs, turntables, cake pans, forms and other decorating tools.

The most important machine used is the cake mixer with its various mixing attachments. This machine replaces the bothersome, continuous physical work required to make batters. It mixes, homogenizes (uniform distribution), and aerates the batter.

What kind of requirements does the baker have with regard to a mixing system used for the production of batters? The baker expects

— high efficiency,
— ease of manipulation,
— appropriate functioning, regardless of whether small or large quantities are handled,
— suitability for several working steps, e.g., beating, whipping, blending, kneading,
— a device for heating the bowl (on some of the equipment shown here),
— uncomplicated maintenance,
— work safety.

What types of mixers are on the market?

The following basic types are available:
➤ conventional mixers, with whipping and paddle attachments,
➤ planetary mixers with circulating function,
➤ continuous batter mixing systems.

The Functions of Mixing Systems

Besides the composition of ingredients, several factors in the mixing system influence the ideal development of a batter:

— the use of the appropriate mixing system,
— the selection of the appropriate working tools,
— the control adjustment of the correct working speed,
— the respect of the correct working time.

Continuous Processes

The operation of continuous process mixers allows for uninterrupted batter production. It is suited for large bakeries. First, the ingredients are blended in a preliminary mixer. The blended batter is fed by means of pumps via a storage tank into the actual blending head, whereby the quantity of air to be incorporated is measured and blown in. The homogenization and beating processes are more intensive and shorter than in the case of the previously mentioned machines.

Fig. 629
Cake mixer with special action

Fig. 630
Cake mixer with planetary action

Cake Mixers

The cake mixers shown in *Fig. 632* can be equipped with various bowl sizes and attachments. The agitator, installed in the center, can be used for mixing and whipping.

During the mixing of batter, the attachments — paddle or wire whip — turn around their own axes.

In the special cake mixer (*Fig. 629*), the attachment does not turn around its own axis. It is moved around in circles of adjustable widths (radiuses) through the batter. Through the centrifugal effect, the batter is moved and worked through from the center of the bowl to the outside.

Wire whip (light) Wire whip (heavy) Paddle Dough hook

Fig. 631
Attachments for planetary cake mixers

Fig. 632
Special cake mixer (left) and planetary mixer (right)

Planetary Mixers

The planetary mixer (*Fig. 632*) is a modified version of the special cake mixer. In the planetary mixer, the attachments rotate like the earth around the sun. It turns around its own axis and at the same time, reverses direction, rotating about two to four times as fast as it is moved in a circle. The batter is completely worked through by the attachment (millimeter by millimeter), from the walls to the center (see *Fig. 633* and the working diagram in *Fig. 634*).

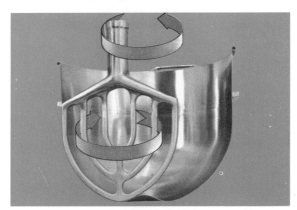

Fig. 633
Working principle of the planetary mixer

Fig. 634
Working diagram of the planetary mixer

292

Work Safety, Cleaning and Maintenance

The danger points in mixers are:
— the bowl wall with the mixing tools, and
— the driving axis.

Loose pieces of clothing or hair can be caught in the turning driving axis.

→ Carry hair protection!
→ Wear tightly-fitting clothes!

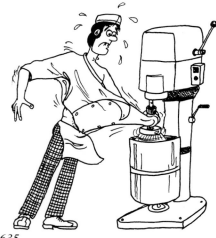

Fig. 635

Fingers can be caught between the bowl wall and the attachment.

→ Switch the mixer off when you want to scrape the bowl.

→ Use the appropriate bowl size. Between the upper rim of the bowl and the uppermost point of contact of the attachment on the bowl walls, there should be a distance of at least 12 cm.

→ Maintain the effect of protective devices. Mixers with a bowl diameter of more than 50 cm are usually equipped with safety guards.

The same principles apply to cleaning cake mixers as to bread-mixers. Moreover, it is important to note that cleanliness is imperative to achieve optimum results for the mixing process. Fatty residues must be removed using hot water and detergent. Then rinse with hot, clean water. Prior to use, the bowl must again be rinsed with clean, cold water.

Maintenance work includes checking the lubricated areas in accordance with the manufacturer's instructions and continuous maintenance of the attachments. Through whipping and beating movements, metal can be rubbed off the bowls and the tools. Metal shavings and rust leave a dirty appearance. The whipping and beating devices are damaged when they are not firmly attached. Loose wires on whips must be replaced.

Products Made From Egg Whites

Composition of Egg-white-foams

Meringues and Japonais — these popular names for light egg-white-foams are indicative of especially light and fluffy bakery products.

Meringues or foam batters consist solely of egg white and sugar. Foam batters differ, depending on their sugar content:

➤ Light foam batters contain about the same amount of sugar and egg white.

➤ Heavy foam batters contain significantly more sugar than egg white.

Basic recipe for foam batters	
light	**heavy**
1,000 g (ml) Egg white	1,000 g (ml) Egg white
1,000 g Sugar	3,000 g Sugar
5 g Cream of tartar	5 g Cream of tartar
+ Flavor	+ Flavor

Table 124

Whipping Egg-white-foams
The following rules apply to the mixing of egg white with sugar to achieve a good result:

→ Ensure clean separation of egg yolk and egg white; eliminate any traces of egg yolk from the egg white.

→ Use clean bowl and attachments; make sure no fat is attached to them; clean them with hot water and rinse them with cold water.

→ Use the correct quantity of sugar and choose the appropriate moment for adding it to the egg white; cream of tartar enhances stabilization of the foam.

In order to establish the best possible whipping conditions for foam, the following tests are performed:

Test 38:

Whip under identical conditions and for an identical period of time:
Sample A = 100 g egg white
Sample B = 100 g egg white + 50 g sugar
Sample C = 100 g egg white + 100 g sugar
Sample D = 100 g egg white + 150 g sugar

Now, evaluate the volume and the condition of the egg foam obtained.

Observations:
Sample A yields an unstable egg foam volume and a batter with large cells. The egg foam falls apart (*Fig. 639*). Sample B yields a stable egg-white-foam with good cells. The cells of the egg-white-foam of samples C and D decrease in size the higher the sugar content. But the volume is not significantly affected by changes in the egg white/sugar ratio. Egg foam has a tendency to "flow."

Fig. 636 **Products made with heavy meringue**

Fig. 637 **Light meringue foam as a pie topping**

Reference:
*In the chapter entitled **Eggs and their Effect on the Baking Process**, you will find fundamental statements on the composition and treatment of eggs and egg products.*

Fig. 638 **Volume of meringue foams (after they have been beaten stiff) for which varying amounts of sugar have been used**

Fig. 639 **Egg-white-foam without sugar added (left) falls apart; the heavy foam batter (right) is stable**

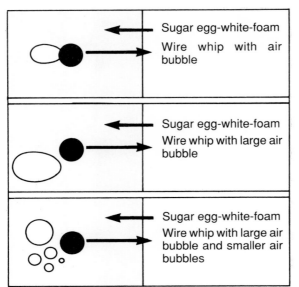

Fig. 640 **Formation of air bubbles in egg-white-foam batters**

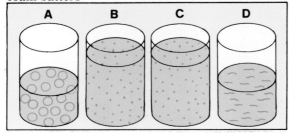

Fig. 641
Condition of foams to which sugar was added at different times

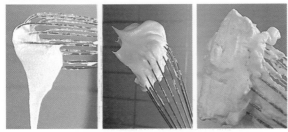

Fig. 642
Well-whipped egg-white-foam with stable surface and protruding peaks (center)
Insufficiently beaten egg-white-foam; it is "runny" (left)
Over-whipped egg-white-foam; it forms flakes (right)

Food for Thought:
Using the example of foam, we have introduced you to the process of physical leavening based on the incorporation of air.
The leavening of puff dough is also achieved by means of a physical process, e.g., through the effect of steam.
Compare the two leavening processes. What do they have in common? How do they differ?

Theory:

As shown in *Fig. 640*, the foam forms through the air bubbles incorporated into the egg whites. Each wire of the whip draws in air during the whipping process.

This air is incorporated in the form of bubbles into the sugar egg-white-batter. As the whipping continues, tiny bubbles form and already existing bubbles are divided into smaller ones. The egg white/sugar films around the air bubbles become thinner and firmer in the process.

Due to its hygroscopic properties, sugar increases the viscosity of the batter. A small amount of cream of tartar causes the tough albumen substances to dissolve and thus achieves a larger foam volume.

For the mixing process, the quantity of sugar used and the timing of its addition are both important.

Test 39:
Whip 100 g egg white with 150 g sugar under identical conditions and for an identical period of time. The timing for the addition of sugar varies as follows:
Sample A = whipping without sugar, whereby the total amount of sugar is added toward the end of the mixing stage;
Sample B = whipping with 50 g sugar, whereby 100 g sugar is incorporated toward the end;
Sample C = whipping with 50 g sugar, whereby 50 g sugar is added twice, after 1/2 and then after 3/4 of the whipping time has elapsed.
Sample D = whipping with the total amount of sugar for the total length of the whipping process.

Observations:
The egg foam from sample A has a tendency to turn flaky.
Samples B and C yield stable, creamy egg foams with fine cells. In the case of sample D, the solidification of the foam is retarded. The whipping time would have to be increased.

Tips for the preparation of foam batters

➤ *Use only equipment from which all fat has been removed. Only when the egg yolk is cleanly separated from the egg white can the batter be whipped stiff.*
➤ *A high amount of sugar makes the egg-white-foam stable, but also heavy. Granulated sugar is the most suitable for meringues.*
➤ *When batters with a high sugar content are prepared, 1/3 of the quantity of sugar to be used is incorporated immediately; the remainder is added toward the end of the mixing stage.*
➤ *Part of the sugar can also be added at the end in the form of boiled sugar (heated to 117°C for Italian or Swiss meringues).*

Makeup and Baking of Meringues

Light meringues are usually spread or piped into prebaked pie shells. They are flash-baked at temperatures ranging between 220 and 260°C.

Other products made in this fashion are fruit tarts and Baked Alaska.

The upper crust of the meringue solidifies due to the coagulation of the albumen, and the sugar turns brown. However, the inside of the meringue should remain moist.

Heavier meringues, like meringue shells and Japonais, are usually piped with star-shaped or round tubes onto baking pans. These products are more dried than baked at temperatures between 100 and 110°C.

Meringues are leavened by means of incorporated air. During baking in the oven, the expanding air fills the cells. The batter stabilizes due to the solidification of the egg white.

Tips for further processing

Meringues and Japonais are made to be used for the production of dessert items.

Establish the principles applying to appropriate storage based on the composition of these products.

Common Errors Made with Egg-White-Foams

Fault	Cause
➤ The product has a small volume	➤ Fat or egg yolk particles in the batter
➤ The product is flat and it has lost its shape	➤ Very high amount of sugar used; the batter is too soft
➤ The product is browned, but the inside is still raw	➤ Very high temperatures during baking have prevented the core from drying
➤ The product has a cracked surface	➤ Steam present in oven

Due to the high sugar content, products made with egg white-foam batters have a tendency to absorb water. They are supposed to remain dry on the surface and on the inside. Therefore, pastries made with meringues must be stored in a dry environment. If meringue products are refrigerated, they become soft and mushy.

Goods Made With Sponge and Viennese Batter

Fig. 643 **Sponge cake layers, slabs and flans**

The method of whipping egg whites separately before folding them into the yolk/sugar mixture, increases the aeration of the batter. This method known as "Biscuit de Savoie" (separated sponge method) originated in France in the 1600s.

Othellos, Desdemonas, Jagos and Rosalinds all fall under the general category of sponge cake batters. What are sponge batters?

➤ Sponge batters are whipped batters.

➤ Sponge batters contain whole egg, sugar and wheat flour/wheat starch.

Composition of Sponge Batters

We determine the differences between egg white batters (meringues) based on the quantity of sugar used, i.e., light and heavy foam batters.

The same applies to sponge batters. Depending on the composition, we distinguish between:

Light sponge batters = 1,000 g whole egg + 400 g sugar + 400 g wheat flour/wheat starch.

Heavy sponge batters = 1,000 g whole egg + 1,000 g sugar + 1,000 g wheat flour/wheat starch.

How to remember the composition of sponges:

Sponge batters

with identical amounts of Whole egg

light	**heavy**
less Sugar	more Sugar
less Flour/Starch	more Flour/Starch
less Egg yolk	more Egg yolk

It is easy to beat egg white. Therefore, it is possible to obtain foam batters with a very large volume. We will now examine to what extent an egg can be whipped.

Fig. 644
Volume of whipped egg white, egg yolk and whole egg

Basic recipe for sponges	
1,000 g	Whole egg
600 g	Sugar
600 g	Wheat flour/wheat starch
	Salt + Aroma

Table 125

Fig. 645   **Othello baking cups**

Fig. 646   **Othellos**

Sample recipe for light sponge batter			
Othello batter			
1,000 g	Egg white	400 g	Egg yolk
400 g	Sugar	200 g	Water
400 g	Wheat starch	400 g	Wheat flour
	Some Salt		

Table 126

Summary of mixing methods for sponge batters
Sponge batters
light   **heavy**
whip up cold   whip up hot/cold
separated sponge method   one-stage method

Test 40:
Whip together for five minutes (each sample separately)
Sample 1 = 100 g Egg white + 60 g Sugar
Sample 2 = 100 g Egg yolk   + 60 g Sugar
Sample 3 = 100 g Whole egg + 60 g Sugar
Then evaluate the volume and condition of the batters.
Observations: As expected, egg white yields the highest volume. Egg yolk, however, can hardly be whipped. Whole egg can be whipped, but it has a smaller volume and a softer consistency than egg white.

Reasons: Due to the high fat content of the lipophilous albumen substances resembling albumin in the egg yolk, its capacity to be whipped is reduced. The same applies to whole egg. But egg yolk contributes to the formation of an emulsion (fatty substances of the egg yolk + water content of the whole egg).

Conclusions:
→ Sponge batters can be whipped more easily when a higher amount of egg white is used. The batter is then lighter.

→ Sponge batters with a higher egg yolk content are more difficult to whip and the result is not as favorable.

→ Goods made with light sponge batters are dry. Products made with heavy sponge batters, however, have a moist crumb structure.

Mixing of Sponge Batters

Light and heavy sponge batters differ also in terms of the methods used for mixing.

> *   *Light sponge batters are mixed cold using the separated sponge method (egg white and egg yolk are whipped separately).*

Othello Batter
as an Example of a Light Sponge Batter

Egg yolk, sifted wheat flour, water and flavor are whipped together in a bowl until the batter is smooth.

Egg white, sugar and salt are beaten together in a second bowl. The egg-white-foam should be mixed to a "soft peak" or flakes will form. The sifted flour is "folded" into this mixture by hand. Be careful not to overmix.

After both batters have been blended together, the Othello batter is piped from a round tube onto paper or button tins (see *Fig. 645*), then immediately baked at a temperature around 200°C, under an open steam vent.

Similar production processes are used for

— Ladyfingers, and
— Swiss chocolate rolls.

Batters for ladyfingers and Swiss chocolate rolls contain more egg yolk. In heavy sponge batters, the egg yolk fat and water form an emulsion through slight heating of the batter or the eggs and sugar.

> *   *Heavy sponge batters are best mixed warm. Heavy sponge batters are whipped using the one-bowl method (eggs + sugar).*

Sample recipe for heavy sponge batter
Jelly rolls, etc.
1,000 g   Whole egg
500 g   Sugar
Salt + Flavor
250 g   Cake flour
250 g   Starch

Table 127

Jelly roll batter
as an Example for a Heavy Sponge Batter

Whole egg, sugar, salt and flavor are mixed together in a bowl. After a short mixing time, the batter is heated (if a heating device is installed under the bowl). While the batter is heated, it is whipped until it reaches body temperature. Then the batter is allowed to mix until it becomes cool again.

> *Why a "warm" batter?*
> — *The fat contained in the egg yolk emulsifies easier when warmed.*
> — *The sugar dissolves better when heated.*
> — *The air incorporated during beating expands when the batter is heated. When the batter cools off, the cells tighten. The batter obtains greater viscosity.*

Optimum mixing has been obtained when the volume is sufficient and a silky shine appears on the surface. The batter should be firm enough so that it does not slide off the hand when held sideways.

Cake flour and starch are sifted together several times to make sure that the batter remains aerated and fluffy. Then this mixture is incorporated into the whole egg batter by hand.

The finished batter must be processed quickly. When jelly rolls or a similar product are made, the batter is spread with a palette knife onto a pan, which is lined with silicone paper. It can be piped through a savoy bag into small decorative circles to create special dessert items. The batter is baked in the oven at a temperature of about 220°C to prevent it from drying out.

Batters can be modified through the addition of cocoa or nuts. These are incorporated into the flour/starch mixture.

Vienna Batter

Vienna batter contains whole egg, sugar, cake flour/starch and fat. The fat yields a moist product with better fresh-keeping characteristics.

Vienna batter is used, for example, for layers, flans and berry cups. Vienna batter can also be modified through the addition of cocoa powder, nuts, almonds, etc., to make cakes and pastries for flavored desserts.

Basic Recipe for Vienna Batter
1,000 g   Whole egg
600 g   Sugar
Salt + Flavor
300 g   Wheat flour
300 g   Starch
300 g   Butter (folded in last)

Table 128

Mixing Method for Vienna Batter

One-stage Method

Just like any heavy sponge cake batter, ingredients for the Vienna sponge should be at room temperature or warmer for optimum results. The blended Vienna batter must be able to emulsify an extra amount of fat.

This fat to be added should be melted, but not added hot or the albumen substances will coagulate. Nor should the fat be added prior to the addition of the flour/starch mixture because it would sink. If it is added before the flour/starch has been thoroughly worked through, fat bands or small flour/fat lumps form.

All-in Method

When emulsifiers are used, the emulsion for Vienna batter can be achieved even if the batter is mixed cold. With the all-in method, all ingredients and emulsifiers can be combined into a batter. However, leavening is not exclusively achieved by the incorporation of air, but also through the use of baking powder.

The production process for Vienna batter or sponge batter using ready-mix flour is similar. Only eggs and water should be added to the ready-mix flour to obtain a batter.

Makeup and Baking

When Vienna batter is used to make jelly rolls or sheets, it is spread onto baking pans and lined with silicone paper. When it is used to make cakes, it is poured into cake rings or cake pans.

The batter is baked at a temperature of about 200°C. The touch method is used to check whether the cake is done. Fully-baked batter rebounds easily and shows no imprints. After baking, the cakes are immediately turned over onto a flat surface covered with a sprinkling of sugar and flour.

Faults in Sponge and Genoese Products

The majority of product deficiencies that occur in egg-foam batters can best be shown using the example of a flan.

Fig. 647

Undulated and contracted surface on the flan

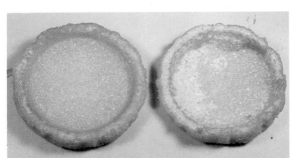

Fig. 648 **Badly-formed walls of sponge mini-flan cases**

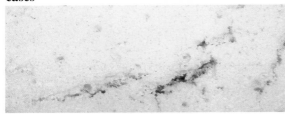

Fig. 649 **Dry cracks**

Fine Cells	Large Cells
• higher starch content	• higher flour content (instead of starch)
• lower sugar content	• higher sugar content
• smaller amount of baking powder added	• larger amount of baking powder added
• higher egg content	• shorter mixing time
• addition of egg white	• higher amount of water added
• excessive or insufficient use of emulsifiers	• higher volume after mixing
• batter overwhipped or too stiff	

Table 129
Influencing factors on cell structure of sponges

Fig. 650 **Ring formation**

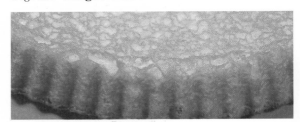

Fig. 651 **Excessively large pores**

Deficiency	Cause	Remedy
— undulated and contracted surface (Fig. 647)	➤ overwhipped batter; ➤ underwhipped batter	➤ reduce the flour content and increase the starch content; ➤ whip the batter appropriately
— improper walls with disappearing contours (Fig. 648)	➤ excessively aerated batter; ➤ excessive use of pan grease on the walls	➤ whip batter less; if necessary, reduce the amount of baking powder; ➤ let the pans cool and use less grease; use a pan grease mixture containing release agents
— dry cracks in the crumb structure (Fig. 649)	➤ batter too warm; ➤ batter too firm	➤ maintain batter temperature between 24 and 26°C; ➤ reduce flour and starch content
— ring formation in the crumb of the flan (Fig. 650)	➤ fat not emulsified	➤ add fat only after the flour has been completely blended into the batter
— cells too large or too small	➤ see Table 129	

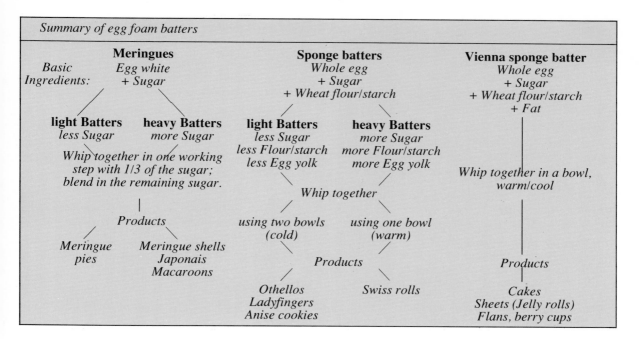

Summary of egg foam batters

	Meringues	Sponge batters	Vienna sponge batter
Basic Ingredients:	Egg white + Sugar	Whole egg + Sugar + Wheat flour/starch	Whole egg + Sugar + Wheat flour/starch + Fat

Meringues

light Batters — *less Sugar*   **heavy Batters** — *more Sugar*

Whip together in one working step with 1/3 of the sugar; blend in the remaining sugar.

Products

Meringue pies   Meringue shells / Japonais / Macaroons

Sponge batters

light Batters
less Sugar
less Flour/starch
less Egg yolk

heavy Batters
more Sugar
more Flour/starch
more Egg yolk

Whip together

using two bowls (cold)   *using one bowl (warm)*

Products

Othellos / Ladyfingers / Anise cookies   Swiss rolls

Vienna sponge batter

Whip together in a bowl, warm/cool

Products

Cakes / Sheets (Jelly rolls) / Flans, berry cups

Pound Cake Varieties

Fig. 652 **Pound Cakes**

Some durable baking goods maintain a moist crumb for a long time. Such goods are those made with pound cake batters. Their long fresh-keeping characteristics are primarily due to their high fat content. Due to their high fat content, however, pound cake batters cannot be mixed in the same fashion as foam or sponge batters. Their ingredients are creamed, rather than whipped. This is known as the creaming method.

Composition of Creamed Batters

Based on the fat content in proportion to the egg content of the batter, a distinction is made between light and heavy pound cake or creamed batters. Light batters can be mixed warm, somewhat like Vienna batter; fat and flour are blended together. However, heavy batters are mixed cold.

Heavy batters contain the basic ingredients at a ratio of 1/1/1/1. Good emulsification of the ingredients is imperative to obtain the desired volume and tender-moist crumb of the products. But volume and crumb condition are also significantly determined by the binding capacity of the flour in the batter.

Test 41:

Under identical conditions, we mix three batters composed as follows:

a) 150 g fat, 150 g sugar, 150 g whole egg, 150 g cake flour

b) 150 g fat, 150 g sugar, 150 g whole egg, 75 g cake flour/75 g wheat starch

c) 150 g fat, 150 g sugar, 150 g whole egg, 150 g wheat starch

The batters are deposited into small loaf pans lined with corrugated paper, then they are baked for 40 minutes at a baking temperature of 200°C. We evaluate crust, volume and crumb condition of the baking products.

Observations:

If only flour is added to the batter, cakes have a small volume. The crust is tough and firm. The crumb is firm and has large cells.

If only starch is added to the batter, cakes have a very large volume. The top is a little bit too flat. The crust is thin and has a tendency to be flaky. The crumb is short and has a very fine cell structure.

The mixture of cake flour and wheat starch as ingredients of the batter yields the desired characteristics of the cake.

Fig. 653 **Cross-sections of pound cakes with cake flour content (left), with a mixture composed of cake flour and wheat starch (center), and with wheat starch (right)**

Additional Information

Wheat powder is pure wheat starch. It is produced through washing the wheat dough. A by-product produced is wheat albumen (vital gluten for special bread varieties). The starch is washed, tumbled and dried several times, then sorted into various quality types.

Wheat starch binds water only in the batter phase. During baking, the wheat starch forms a paste with the liquid. Thus, the crumb structure is formed.

Next to wheat powder, bakers also use modified starch for batters. This starch type cannot bind as much moisture during baking as wheat starch. Modified starch is, therefore, only used in small quantities to improve the fresh-keeping properties of loaf cakes.

Fig. 654 **Pound Cake**

Fig. 655 **Marble cake (left) and Bundt cake (right)**

Conclusions:

For heavy batters, the use of flour and wheat starch at a ratio of 50% to 50% is recommended. For cakes with a firmer crumb, either a higher cake flour content or cake flour alone is used.

Examples:
— pound cakes with fruit
— marble cake,
— English cakes,
— Americanas

Basic recipe for pound cake batters			
light Batter		**heavy Batter**	
1,000 g	Whole egg	1,000 g	Whole egg
600 g	Fat	1,000 g	Fat
1,000 g	Sugar	1,000 g	Sugar
1,000 g	Wheat flour/ starch	1,000 g	Wheat flour/ starch
	Salt/Flavor		Salt/Flavor

Table 130

Production Methods for Pound Cake Batters

Pound Cakes

The ingredients for the basic recipe of heavy batter are mixed cold (old German method):

→ mix fat and flour until they are creamy,

→ mix the eggs and the sugar to a foam,

→ fold the egg foam batter into the fat/flour batter, then incorporate the wheat starch into this batter.

Pound cake is baked at a temperature of 200°C. After a short baking time, the surface of the cake can be cut lengthwise in order to obtain the desired expansion. The basic recipe for heavy pound cakes does not require the addition of baking powder.

Marble Cake

Marble cake is made with a light batter. Cocoa is added to a part of the batter. The following is a suitable recipe:

1000 g cake flour, 400 g fat, 400 g sugar, 200 g whole egg, 600 g milk, 30 g baking powder, 50 g cocoa, flavor.

→ Mix fat and sugar until creamed and add eggs gradually.

→ Blend in milk and half of the flour.

→ The remaining flour to which baking powder has been added is incorporated at the end.

→ Add cocoa to half of the batter.

Marble cake is baked for 40 minutes at a temperature of 200°C in a greased or flour-dusted pan.

English Lightly-Fruited Cakes

English fruit cakes contain from 25% raisins, currants and cherries based on batter weight. Aeration of the batter is restricted to prevent the fruit from sinking. The blending method is ideally suited for this type of cake. All of the ingredients, with the exception of the liquid and fruit, are blended to a smooth paste. The liquid is added in three stages and mixed at a slow speed. Finally, the fruit is blended into the batter. These cakes have a dense crumb with good fresh-keeping qualities (over 90 days). Baking temperature is 180°C and, after cooling, the cake is cut into pieces.

Fig. 656 **English lightly-fruited cake**

Americanas

Americanas are made with a lightly blended batter:

1,000 g wheat flour, 200 g fat, 500 g sugar, 700 g milk, 70 g whole egg, 20 g ammonium bicarbonate, aromas.

→ Fat, sugar, whole egg and aromatic compounds are blended until aerated.

→ Flour and milk are incorporated into the batter; thus, the desired degree of firmness is achieved.

→ Ammonium bicarbonate is mixed with some flour and incorporated at the end.

The batter is piped from a round tube onto pans which have been greased and flour-coated. Then it is baked at a temperature of 200°C under an open steam vent. The end products receive a fondant glazing on their flat surface.

Fig. 657 **Americanas**

Joe says:
"The typical flavor of Americanas can be achieved only when using ammonium bicarbonate. So why is baking powder sometimes used for leavening Americanas?"

Emulsification of Batters

Only when all the ingredients form a good emulsion can leavening and "short" texture of blended batters be achieved. Fresh-keeping qualities of baked goods also depend on the incorporation of emulsified fat into the starch grains.

The baker achieves this

— through the selection of suitable fats,

— through the use of specific production methods.

Respect food regulations

Ammonium bicarbonate can only be used for leavening flat baked goods in which the ammonia gas can escape from the crumb. When the recipe for Americanas results in an end product that is dry and flat, ammonium bicarbonate can be used for leavening purposes. When the baked product is high and has a moist crumb, baking powder is used as a leavening agent.

Use of Emulsifiers

Only emulsifying fats can be considered as suitable for these batters. Shortenings containing monoglycerides and diglycerides are particularly well-suited. These fats have a high air absorption capacity during the mixing process. Oils and pure fats, e.g., pure butter fat, are unsuitable.

Through the addition of emulsifiers, the batter properties during the mixing process and the fresh-keeping characteristics of baked goods can be improved. Emulsifiers also simplify the production process because all the ingredients can be blended and mixed in only one stage.

Use of Ready-mix Flours

Ready-mix flour mixtures and ready-mix flour is also available for batters which are traditionally prepared through beating and whipping.

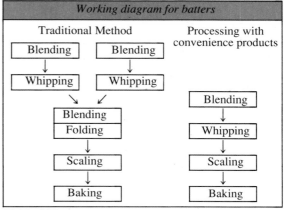

Working diagram for batters		
Traditional Method		Processing with convenience products
Blending	Blending	
↓	↓	
Whipping	Whipping	
↘	↙	Blending
Blending Folding		↓
		Whipping
↓		↓
Scaling		Scaling
↓		↓
Baking		Baking

Table 131

Cake Faults and their Causes

Fault	Cause
➤ Volume too small	➤ Batter too firm, ➤ Batter not sufficiently mixed, ➤ Possibly not enough baking powder
➤ Volume too large, brittle crust	➤ Batter too soft, ➤ Batter too strongly aerated
➤ Soggy crumb, product loses its shape	➤ Insufficient baking time, ➤ Moved too early during baking
➤ Reddish-brown color of crumb	➤ Insufficient baking temperature
➤ Tunnel formation (Fig. 658)	➤ Not enough baking powder, ➤ Batter too tough
➤ Fruits sunk to bottom	➤ Batter too soft, ➤ Fruits too moist and heavy

Additional Information

➤ *Emulsifiers reduce the tension between the fat and the water in the batter. Thus, the batter develops cells with fine walls. The volume of the end product is larger.*

➤ *Emulsifiers attach with their water-attracting component to the albumen nets, whereas the fat-attracting component attaches to the fat. Thus, the structure of the batter gains stability.*

➤ *Emulsifiers with straight-chain, saturated fatty acid esters can form compounds with the amylase of the starch. Thus, starch retrogradation is retarded.*

➤ *The following emulsifiers are used in accordance with good manufacturing practices (G.M.P.): lecithin, monoglycerides or diglycerides, polyglycerol and propylene glycol esters, ethoxylated monoglycerides and stearoyl-2 lactylates.*

➤ *Foaming agents must be used in accordance with the manufacturer's instructions. The most favorable raw material temperatures, batter temperatures, density of batters and volumes of the product must be determined through baking tests.*

It is recommended to follow these guidelines to obtain good quality products:

— batter temperature	=	24 – 26°C
— litre weight	=	600 – 900 g
— volume	=	2,500 cm³ per 1,000 g

The composition of the mixtures available on the marketplace varies, and so do the mixing methods. The following principles apply to ready-mix flour used for the preparation of whipped and beaten batters.

➤ They have a low water content (less than 10%) to improve their durability.
➤ They contain the usual ingredients of batters except
— whole egg in the case of beaten batters,
— whole egg and fat in some other mixes.
➤ They simplify the production process.
➤ They allow the elimination of errors that can be made when batters are prepared using the traditional methods.
➤ They yield products of uniform quality.

Fig. 658 **Tunnel formation on marble cake**

Summary of important information about whipped batters and beaten batters	
Leavening	
air incorporated by beating/whipping	through baking powder
in the case of batters with a high egg content	beaten batters using the all-in method
heavy batters	batters with a low fat content, using flour, not starch
Batters	
whipped batters	beaten batters
egg or egg contents and sugar whipped together	fat is creamed (with eggs and sugar) (with wheat starch)
Fresh-keeping qualities of baked goods	
shorter	longer
high egg white content	high egg yolk content
low fat content	high fat content

Products made with Choux Paste

Cream puffs are probably the best known pastry made with choux paste. The name "cream puff" also addresses the typical properties of pastries made with choux paste:
— light weight,
— large volume,
— strongly leavened, with large cells.

Although choux paste has a high egg content, this type of batter cannot be leavened through beating as, for example, meringue batter.

Choux paste must be prepared in such a way that it can be leavened through the enormously high content of liquid (steam).

Composition of Choux Paste

The basic ingredients of choux paste are: bread flour, milk/water, fat and whole eggs. The "liquid" content (milk/water, fat, eggs) is high in proportion to the flour content of the batter.

For comparison purposes: Doughs are prepared with a dough yield ranging between 150 and 200. Thus, per 100 parts flour, between 50 and 100 parts liquid are used. Choux paste contains four times as much liquid as flour!

How is this possible?

This liquid can only be bound due to the cooking (roasting/roux) process during preparation of the batter.

Production of Choux Paste

Working Steps in the Traditional Method

When bakers prepare choux paste in the traditional fashion, they prepare the batter themselves with all of the ingredients.

They can only achieve a product of high value and without any faults if they perform the following production processes very closely:

Fig. 659 **Cream puffs and eclairs**

Basic recipe for Choux Paste	
1,000 g	Bread flour
2,000 g	Milk or water
500 g	Fat
	Salt/Vanilla
1,600 g	Whole egg

Table 132

Food for Thought:
The ratio of flour or starch to water is as follows:
— *Puff pastry dough* = 1,000/500 (water)
— *Sponge batter* = 1,000/1,600 (whole egg)
— *Choux Paste* = 1,000/4,000 (water/ whole egg)

Compare the different water binding capacities and consider the respective leavening methods.

Working step	Processes	Reason
→ Heat liquid, fat and salt in a bowl until it boils	➤ The fat melts ➤ The ingredients form a mixture	➤ The fat prevents the batter from burning ➤ The fat keeps the batter short
→ Add the sifted flour to the boiling liquid; roast until a viscous batter has formed which detaches from the bowl wall	➤ The starch of the flour forms a paste or roux ➤ The albumen of the flour coagulates	➤ The batter needs to be viscous ➤ The batter needs to absorb the eggs ➤ The batter must be smooth
→ Let the batter cool to 40°C	➤ The batter solidifies as a uniform mass	➤ The albumen substances of the eggs must not coagulate when they are incorporated
→ Add the eggs one by one into the batter until it is smooth and shows the desired firmness	➤ gelatinized starch binds the egg content ➤ Lecithin emulsifies fat and water	➤ The batter must become smooth and able to retain gas due to its high egg content

Working steps for the preparation of Choux Paste		
Traditional preparation = 10 minutes		Preparation with convenience products = 3 minutes
Scaling		
↓		
Cooking		
↓		
Cooling		Scaling
↓		↓
Mixing		Mixing

Table 133

Thomas approaches his boss and says: "I don't think your cream puffs have turned out right." Thomas shows him the small, compact cream puffs.

"I think it would be easier if we used a ready-mix to make a batter. That is what they do in other bakeries," says Thomas.

"Thomas, you know that you, as a future expert, are supposed to learn how to correctly make and mix choux paste. The use of ready-made batters is certainly easier, but there are other variables to consider."

What do you think? What are the arguments in favor of the traditional preparation processes and what are the ones in favor of the use of convenience products?

Fig. 660
French crullers are deep-fried

304

Working Steps using Prepared Mixes

When making choux paste using prepared mixes, the baker must perform the following working steps according to the manufacturer's instructions:

→ Scale the desired quantity of the prepared mix products.

→ Scale the required quantity of liquid and egg, if necessary.

→ Blend and mix the batter until smooth.

Why is it, in this case, so simple to make choux paste?

The manufacturer of the prepared mix has:

— combined the ingredients required for an optimum recipe,
— carried out the cooking process,
— stirred the batter sufficiently, possibly by adding egg,
— preserved the finished batter by eliminating the moisture.

By adding liquid, the baker gives the batter the correct firmness. The composition of the batter can be modified within certain limits, e.g., by adding an additional amount of egg instead of adding water, or by adding flavors.

Prepared mixes for choux paste have the following advantages for the baker:
— less work,
— simple production,
— less room for error.

Makeup and Baking of Choux Paste

For most pastries, the finished choux paste is piped through a tube.

The pastries are either
— baked in the oven (using steam, if possible)
  or
— deep-fried (crullers).

During baking in the oven, leavening is caused by the steam pressure from the liquid in the batter.

How is this possible?

→ The starch of the flour has already formed a paste during the cooking process. Therefore, it does not form a crumb structure during baking.

→ The gluten of the flour has already coagulated during the cooking process. Therefore, it only minimally resists the steam.

→ The albumen substances of the egg content coagulate during baking. They form the crumb structure.

→ The batter solidifies at temperatures around 100°C. Therefore, crust formation must be retarded to keep the pastry extensible. Crust formation is retarded through steam application in the oven. The equivalent effect can be achieved with fried products by covering the container at the beginning of the frying process.

French Crullers

→ Pipe cruller batter onto a pan using a star tube, with two rings placed one on top of the other.

→ Place doughnut batter into the deep-frying fat using a special dye in the doughnut dropper.

→ Fry Crullers or doughnuts in deep-frying fat at 180°C.

→ Glaze Crullers, after baking, with fondant.

Cream Puffs, Eclairs

→ Pipe the batter for cream puffs onto baking sheets greased or covered with silicone paper. Use a star tube and give the puffs the shape of a rosette.

→ Bake cream puffs in steam (if possible) at 220°C, keeping the vent closed.

→ The batter for eclairs should be firmer; pipe from star tubes in the shape of ribbons and bake in the same way as cream puffs.

Bottoms for cream cakes and ornaments for decorating purposes are made with very soft choux paste.

Nut Pastries Made with and without Roux

For the uneducated eye, it is not so easy to recognize or distinguish between nut pastries made with roux and nut pastries made with raw paste. The major differences in the appearance and in the composition of such pastries are apparent using the examples of coconut macaroon pastries and almond crescents. But all nut pastries have some common characteristics:

➤ They contain ground almonds or other nut products rich in albumen, or corresponding raw pastes.

➤ They contain egg white (in parts, also egg yolk).

➤ They are made without the addition of flour or starch (exception: coconut macaroons).

➤ They are produced without the addition of leavening agents. Leavening is caused by the steam released from the egg white.

For the baker, the most important differences between nut pastries lie in the production method. Some batters are prepared starting with roux formation prior to further processing. When raw pastes are used, the roux process can be eliminated.

Food for Thought:
Cream puffs are leavened solely through the steam pressure in the pastry. Why would this kind of leavening not work for small wheat flour products?

Choux Pastry Faults

Choux pastry faults are caused primarily by incorrect cooking, incorrect firmness of the batter or through incorrect baking conditions:

Cause of deficiency	Consequence
➤ insufficient roux formation; starch insufficiently gelatinized	➤ volume of the pastries too small
➤ batter too firm, not enough eggs added	➤ volume of the pastries too small
➤ batter too soft, eggs added too quickly or too many eggs added	➤ contours of the pastries are diluted, they expand too much laterally
➤ lack of steam during baking	➤ small volume, thick crust, dense cells

Fig. 661
Cross-section of a coconut macaroon

Fig. 662 **Almond crescents**

305

Composition and Production of Nut Pastries Made with Roux

The basic ingredients are:
— nut products,
— egg white, and
— sugar.

The following nut products are customary:

Almonds, hazelnuts or walnuts, coconut. Peanuts are not normally used.

The roux process will be explained using the production of coconut macaroons as an example.

→ All ingredients are blended in a bowl. To increase the binding capacity of the roux, starch can be added (up to 3% of the total batter).

→ The coconut macaroon paste is heated until the paste reaches 70°C. Thus, the egg white/sugar basis turns viscous. The desired viscosity is achieved when the paste detaches from the wall of the bowl.

→ The finished paste is further processed while it is still as hot as possible. It is piped through a tube onto baking sheets which have received a fat and flour coating, onto baking paper, or onto wafers. It can also be spread onto prebaked bottoms made with short paste.

→ The batter is baked at a temperature of 180°C, with the steam vent open.

Composition and Production of Baked Goods Made with an Almond Paste

The basic ingredients are:
— Almond paste or kernel paste,
— Egg white, and
— Sugar.

When a paste is used, less sugar and egg white added are added because the raw paste already contains sugar and is softer than pastes prepared with the kernels themselves (compare *Tables 134* and *135*).

With raw pastes the roux process does not have to be performed in the bakery.

→ The ingredients for batters made with almond or kernel paste are mixed together in a bowl until smooth. The batter should not be overmixed or mixed until creamy. Even when convenience products are used for the production of macaroon batters, the batter is only mixed until smooth, while liquid or eggs are added.

→ Almond or kernel pastes are piped, then baked at a temperature ranging between 180 and 200°C, without steam (possibly double-panned).

Pastries made with pastes resembling those of macaroons include egg yolk macaroons, Hippen and Duchesse.

Sample recipe: macaroon batter made with almond kernels	
1,000 g	Granulated sugar
600 g	Ground almonds
600 g	Egg white

Table 134

Sample recipe for macaroon batter made with raw paste	
1,000 g	Almond paste
700 g	Granulated sugar
200 g	Egg white

Table 135

To distinguish them from almond macaroons, pastries made with coconut or nuts cannot be designated as "macaroons." Their name must indicate the nut products they contain; e.g., "coconut macaroons" or "hazelnut macaroons." When kernel paste is used, the product should be simply labelled "macaroons."

Deficiencies of Nut Pastries Made with and without Roux

Fault	Causes when roux is used	Causes when roux is not used (raw paste)
➤ The pastries expand laterally	➤ too much egg white ➤ inadequate roux formation	➤ batter too soft ➤ too much sugar added
➤ The surface of the pastries breaks easily	➤ batter is a little bit too soft ➤ steam vent not opened	➤ batter a little bit too soft ➤ steam vent not opened
➤ The surface of the pastries is dull	➤ batter too firm ➤ excessive roux formation	➤ batter too firm ➤ oven too cold

Products Made Using the Roasting (Roux) Method

Flat Florentines are composed solely of a baked roux and a chocolate coating. Moreover, bakers produce many similar pastries with a short paste bottom, e.g., nut corners, almond slices or Nutcracker. The bee hive batter spread onto yeast doughs is also prepared with a roux.

Composition and Production of Cooked Batters

The basic batter is prepared with sugar, fat and milk/cream. To prevent the sugar in the finished product from turning too hard and crystallizing, a part of the sugar is replaced with honey or corn syrup (see sample recipe: Florentines).

How is the basic batter produced?

→ Sugar, other sweeteners, fat and milk/cream are brought to a boil in a stainless steel pot.

→ In the process, a large part of the water evaporates, and the temperature exceeds 100°C. The sugar changes its characteristics.

→ At 112°C, the batter has achieved the desired degree of viscosity.

→ Nut products and fruits are added to the basic batter. It is roasted further until the appropriate degree of viscosity is achieved.

Sample recipe: Florentines	
1,000 g	Sugar products (containing 150 g honey, 150 g corn syrup)
250 g	Fat
500 g	Milk/cream
750 g	Almonds (ground)
350 g	Almonds (slivers)
150 g	Candied orange peel/Candied cherries

Table 136

Fig. 663
Products made with roux: bee hive cakes, nut corners, Florentines, nougat (croque-en-bouche) and almond barkentines

Makeup, Baking and Coating of Goods Made with Roux

Florentine batter is shaped into rings and baked on baking sheets with a good fat coating or on silicone paper at a temperature between 190 and 210°C.

After the Florentine has completely cooled, the smooth bottom is coated with couverture or chocolate coating, then combed.

The batter for nut slices, almond slices or Nutcracker is spread onto short paste bottoms. The baking temperature and the baking time depends on whether the short paste bottoms are used in raw or prebaked state. After they have cooled, the edges of the finished products receive a coating of couverture or chocolate coating.

Pastries made with roux are not leavened. A short, caramelized state is desirable. Therefore, the baked goods should be protected from moisture when stored.

	Summary of important information about batters made with roux		
Products:	Cream puff ↓	Macaroon ↓	Florentines ↓
Batter:	Pâté-à-Choux	Macaroon batter	Basic Roux
	↓	↓	↓
Basic ingredients:	Flour, Fat, Water/Milk, Whole egg	Nut products, Sugar, Egg white	Nut products, Fat, Sugar, Milk/Cream
	↓	↓	
Changes occurring during roux formation:	The egg white of the flour coagulates; the starch of the flour forms a paste (Temp.: 80–100°C)	Egg white/sugar bonding (Temp.: 70°C)	Cook the sugar until it reaches the desired degree of viscosity (Temp.: 112°C)
			↓
Leavening of the baked products:	Steam from the high content of liquid (strongly leavened)	Steam from the egg white (some leavening)	unleavened

Dietary Baking

"I don't care about dietary goods," says Joe. "I already have enough work without them!"

Thomas is critical: "Are we allowed to produce special products for sick people? How do we know what ingredients to use and how much of them are allowed?"

Following a diet is not only a method to lose weight!

A large number of people must follow a diet every day and eat special food products due to inherent or acquired diseases.

For example:
— a person who suffers from a kidney disease must eat food with a low sodium content;
— a person who is overly-sensitive to gluten must eat foodstuffs without any gluten derived from grain;
— a person who has diabetes must eat food with a low sugar content.

For such diets, special dietary baked products are required.

One of the tasks of a baker includes making dietary baked goods. And you, as an expert, should also learn how to make such products. You will acquire expertise, learn how to precisely follow a recipe and you will even perform certain consulting duties.

Because baked goods play an important role in a diabetic's diet, bakers should become more familiar with the rules relating to the production and labelling of dietary products.

Dietary Baked Goods for Diabetics

Diabetes

Diabetes (Diabetes mellitus) is a "disease of affluence" from which millions of people suffer worldwide. The disease can be in existence at the time of birth or it can be acquired through many years of overnourishment.

A diabetic cannot properly metabolize foods with sugar.

Therefore, the efficiency of bodily functions is restricted. The reason for this may be due to an excessive or to an insufficient amount of sugar in the blood. The diabetic's body protects itself against an excessive amount of sugar in the blood either by expending it through exercise or by eliminating it through the kidneys. This allows the doctor, for example, to diagnose diabetes.

Diabetes is a slow and chronic disease (it cannot be cured). If the disease is not treated, it can be fatal.

The diabetic is treated with drugs and, most importantly, the diabetic must follow a strict diet.

Dietary Prescriptions for the Diabetic

The doctor is responsible for prescribing the right combination of drugs and a proper diet for the diabetic. The diabetic must have very precise information about the food he/she is eating in order to follow the instructions of the doctor.

The following principles apply to a diet for diabetics:

→ The total energy balance of daily nutrition must be controlled because the diabetic must avoid gaining excessive weight.

→ The proportion of sugar substances contained in the daily food intake must be restricted.

How are these rules respected when producing baked goods for diabetics?

Additional Information

During the digesting process, all the sugar substances that can be used to produce energy are decomposed into simple sugar substances. These simple sugar substances are absorbed by the body through blood circulation.

The metabolic system of a healthy person regulates the blood sugar level through insulin, the hormone of the pancreas. Excess sugar absorbed is stored in the liver in the form of glycogen. This glycogen can be mobilized again in the form of simple sugars to meet the energy needs of the body.

The diabetic cannot readily produce insulin. Therefore, the storage of glycogen in the liver cannot be regulated. The sugar level in the blood is, therefore, much too high. This has a harmful effect on metabolism and many other bodily functions.

Due to the lack of glycogen formation, a lack of sugar can occur when there is a sudden need for energy. The diabetic can lose consciousness (sugar coma).

Diabetics must regulate the amount of sugar absorbed through their food intake through dieting. In serious cases, they also receive an injection of the hormone insulin.

Composition and Labelling of Baked Goods for Diabetics

Baked goods made for diabetics should contain only a small amount of carbohydrates. They should also have a low nutritive value.

What types of baked goods are especially suited for diabetics?

The following are examples of baked goods offered in prepackaged format which are especially suited for consumption by diabetics:

— Pound cake, coffee cakes, cookies with high egg content, short paste products.

The following fresh baked goods are especially suited for consumption by diabetics:

— Cream cheese cake, quark-cheese cake, apple and cherry pies, yogurt-cream dessert.

The following principles apply to the composition of baked goods for consumption by diabetics:

➤ The fat and alcohol content should not be higher than that of comparable traditional foodstuffs.

➤ The addition of dextrose, milk sugar, malt sugar, cane sugar and beet sugar, invert sugar and glucose syrup is prohibited.

➤ Only those additives expressly permitted for dietary food can be used.

Coloring substances are, for example, not allowed.

➤ For sweetening of baked goods, fruit sugar and sugar substitutes such as sorbitol, mannitol and xylose are allowed. Cyclamates are permitted only on the advice of physicians, but are generally regarded as unacceptable.

➤ The indirect addition of sugars (e.g., through raisins, dried fruit) is entirely prohibited.

In sample recipes on this page you will find sugar substitutes in place of ordinary sweeteners found in regular baked goods.

In principle, all baked goods made for consumption by diabetics must be offered for sale in prepackaged format. However, fresh products can be offered unpackaged. The same applies to baked goods which are consumed at the point of sale (e.g., in a cafe). In any event, it is necessary to label the baked goods in an obvious position on the package. The following information must be provided:

— special purpose

— special information about composition and production processes used to give the baked goods their dietary characteristics;

— the content of usable carbohydrates, fats and albumen substances per 100 g of food or in per cent;

— the calorific value in kilojoule (kj) or kilocalories (kcal) per 100 g of the foodstuff.

In the case of prepackaged products, this information must be provided along with the usual regulatory information. An example is shown in *Table 140*.

Sample recipe: Short dough for diabetics
1,000 g   Sorbitol (sugar substitute)
1,500 g   Margarine
3,000 g   Wheat flour
700 g   Whole egg
70 g   Baking powder
Salt/Aroma

Table 137

Sample recipe: Sponge cake for diabetics
1,000 g   Whole egg
350 g   Sorbitol (sugar substitute)
100 g   Water
400 g   Wheat flour
10 g   Baking powder
Salt/Aroma

Table 138

Sample recipe: Pound cake for diabetics
1,000 g   Sorbitol (sugar substitute)
800 g   Margarine
1,000 g   Whole egg
800 g   Wheat starch
1,000 g   Wheat flour
200 g   Milk
30 g   Baking powder
Salt/Aroma/Flavor

Table 139

Sample label: Pound cake for diabetics
City Bakery, Main street, Any City, Phone (403) 234-5678
Pound cake for diabetics
a special dietary product for diabetics suffering from diabetes mellitus

Contents: 250 g
Price: $ 2.89
Best before: May 12
Ingredients:
Wheat flour, egg, sorbitol, shortening, starch, milk, baking powder, salt, artificial sweetener, spices, natural flavors
Contains per 100 g:
usable Carbohydrates   = 36 g
  Fat   = 21 g
  Egg white   = 6 g
  Sugar substitute (Sorbitol)   = 24 g
  Physiological calorific value
  per 100 g   = 1,920
  Kilojoule (453 kilocalories)
Dietary foodstuff containing the sweetener cyclamate. Made without sugar, using the sugar substitute sorbitol.

Table 140

When diabetic baked goods are offered in unpackaged format, a label must be placed beside the baking product or, if in a restaurant, on a menu.

Additional Information

Instead of dextrose, milk sugar, malt sugar, cane sugar, beet sugar, invert sugar or glucose syrup, the recipes for diabetic baked goods require the use of sugar substitutes and sweeteners. The following are suitable:

1. Fruit Sugar (Fructose):

This is a simple sugar that can be stored in the liver as glycogen without needing insulin. Therefore, it is more suitable for diabetics than dextrose or complex sugars. For the production of baked goods it is important to note that fruit sugar

— *has the highest sweetening power of all sugar types (degree of sweetness 173 vs 100 = beet or cane sugar);*
— *can be directly fermented by yeast;*
— *makes the crumb of the baking product turn reddish;*
— *has a very strong browning effect on the crust of the baked product.*

2. Sugar Substitutes

a) **Sorbitol** = *a polyalcohol which occurs naturally in fruits. The high demand for sorbitol is met through technical hydrogenation of dextrose.*

Sorbitol has the same nutritive value as comparable sugar substances. It can be decomposed in the human body through fructose and can be stored in the liver without needing insulin.

For the producer of baked goods it is important to note that sorbitol
— *is easily soluble in water,*
— *has only about half of the sweetening power of beet or cane sugar,*
— *cannot be directly fermented by yeast,*
— *does not brown easily during baking.*

b) **Mannitol** = *a polyalcohol which occurs naturally in the juice of certain ash trees. Technically, it is produced through the reduction of fructose; in the process, sorbitol is also produced.*

Mannitol has similar properties to sorbitol. Unlike sorbitol, it has a browning effect when used together with albumen (Maillard Reaction).

c) **Xylose** = *a polyalcohol with only five carbon atoms. It has similar characteristics to sorbitol. However, its sweetening power is similar to that of beet/cane sugar.*

If a dietary food product contains more than 10% of the total quantity in sorbitol, mannitol and xylose, the following information should be provided: "... can have a laxative effect when used in excessive quantities."

3. Sweeteners

For diabetic food products, cyclamates are allowed. They have no nutritive value. Their sweetening power is many times stronger than that of beet sugar.

The use of a sweetener should be identified as follows: "Contains the sweetener cyclamate and should be used only on the advice of a physician."

Production of Cakes and Desserts

Cakes and Pastries

Recipes for exquisite pastries are often kept secret. Some of us will never know about the composition, processing methods and flavor mixes used for specialty products.

But you can learn other important principles about these types of specialty products, e.g.:
— the selection of ingredients, taking into account the food regulations;
— the selection of ingredients, taking into account general rules regarding the quality and composition (= standards) of cakes and dessert pastries;
— the basic principles applying to the production of cakes and pastries, taking into account the suitability of ingredients and processing methods used;
— the working steps, taking into account the principles of economical production methods.

Moreover, you can learn, based on some examples, how products made from doughs and batters are filled and finished with icings, creams and fillings.

Desserts with Light Vanilla Pastry Cream Filling

Eclairs

The eclair shells made with choux paste are cut open, filled and coated with a chocolate or caramel glaze.

The filling consists, in general, of a light vanilla pastry cream. How is this vanilla pastry cream produced?

The basis for a light vanilla pastry cream is a custard cream made with milk, sugar and custard powder. To further improve the binding power, egg yolk can be added. The pastry cream can be aerated with a light meringue.

About a third of the meringue is added to the near boiling pastry cream. The rest is incorporated shortly after. The meringue aerates the pastry cream. The albumen substances of the egg white coagulate and absorb the water.

Light vanilla pastry cream can also be used for other products, such as filled doughnuts, charlotte russe and charlotte royals, othellos and Napoleon slices (milles feuilles), etc.

Light Pastry Desserts

Dessert strips are made with puff dough strips, fruit fillings and a light creamy filling. The dessert strips are cut into slices. The light creamy filling is aerated through creamed butter and shortening.

How is this creamy filling made?
— The fat is creamed.
— A cool vanilla pastry cream is gradually added to the creamed fat, while the filling is mixed.

Fig. 664 **A colorful array of pastries**

Fig. 665 **Eclairs**

Reference:
The production of vanilla pastry cream is described in more detail in the chapter entitled **Fillings and Toppings for Yeast Products**.

Basic recipe for light vanilla pastry cream	
1,000 g	Milk
200 g	Sugar
90 g	Custard powder
100 g	Egg yolk
250 g	Egg white + 150 g Sugar

Table 141

Fig. 666 **Othellos are filled with a light vanilla pastry cream**

Fig. 667 **Pastry with a light pastry cream**

Thomas has a technical conversation with Baker Smith: "Thomas, you know that we are using cooked vanilla pastry cream to make our icings and fillings. You must make sure that the vanilla pastry cream cools properly. But it should not be too cold!"

"Yes, Baker Smith, I know. If the basic cream is too cold, the cream would gradually turn lumpy during blending."

"Right, Thomas, but do you also know how to prevent a skin from forming on the basic cream while it is cooling?"

"Well, I have noticed that a skin forms when the basic cream stands for a long time and that this skin is very bothersome when the cream is beaten. The cream doesn't become smooth!"

"Thomas, try pouring the creamy batter as usual, onto a clean, shallow pan so it can cool properly. Then sprinkle a little bit of sugar on the surface. You will see that this prevents the formation of a skin!"

Fig. 668   to   Fig. 671
Production of Yule logs and Swiss rolls

312

Because the basic cream is usually processed further after it has cooled, it is possible to use this pastry cream for butter icings. For that purpose, cold custard powder is blended with water in accordance with the manufacturer's instructions.

Cold processed custard powders contain precooked starch. The gelatinized starch has been dried. Therefore, it can absorb water in cold state.

Icings made with a vanilla pastry cream and creamed fat are called German butter icings. Light German butter icings are made with a low amount of fat; heavy German butter icings contain more fat.

The general rule for adding fat to German butter icings is 500 – 1,000 g fat for a pastry cream made with 1 litre of liquid.

German butter icing can spoil easily:

— When heated excessively, the fat melts. The cream loses some volume and the surface becomes dry.

— When stored for a longer period of time in a warm environment, the lactic acid bacteria decomposes the sugar substances of the milk. The butter icing turns sour.

The starch of the pastry cream can decompose and ferment.

Practical tips:

➤ *Pastries made with German butter icings are airy and fluffy when they are produced using a freshly prepared butter icing with a low fat content.*

➤ *Pastries made with German butter icing must be stored in a cool environment to foster a longer shelf-life.*

➤ *Pastries made with German butter icing can be preserved through the addition of chemical preservatives. The use of preservatives must be identified when the pastries are offered for sale.*

➤ *Pastries made with German butter icing should not be stored in a freezer because the pastry cream content releases water after defrosting.*

Pastries and Rolls

With sponge batter and Vienna batter, the baker makes sheets, cakes, jelly rolls and Swiss rolls, which are filled with creams or icings.

The icings are refined through the addition of flavor substances, such as fruit pulp, brandy, chocolate, nut, nougat and almond and mocha flavorings.

The consumer prefers light, easy-to-digest creamy pastries with a rounded flavor and a pleasant appearance.

Figs. 668 to 671 show how you can fill and decorate Swiss rolls and Yule logs with German butter icing.

Butter Cream Cakes and Tortes

When making high-quality cakes and tortes, the icing should not be heavy nor should it be the major component of the cake.

How does the expert achieve this? He/she prepares a fluffy icing with a large volume. Because it contains a lot of air, this icing has a low litre weight. *Fig. 672* shows a comparison between two icings of identical weight, one overwhipped and the other one whipped optimally. It is obvious that the well-aerated icing has an adequate volume, although it is lighter in weight. Therefore, the creamy pastries have a lower nutritive value and are less filling. Through the very fine distribution of the creamy components, this icing becomes fluffy and melts in the mouth. Flavor distribution is perfect. Pastries made with aerated icings have a higher enjoyment value and are more easily to digest than others.

Production of Butter creams and Icings

The fluffiness of an icing or cream with fat content depends primarily on the selection of the appropriate fat type.

Which fats are suited for icings?

Fig. 672 **Two samples of icings**
Sample A = insufficiently whipped
Sample B = well aerated

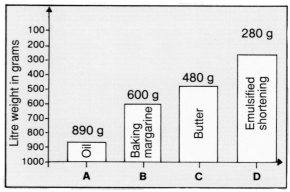

Fig. 673 **Volume of various fats after creaming**

Test 42:

We mixed, under identical conditions, but under the most favorable processing temperatures of fats, 250 g of the following fat types:
A   Vegetable oil
B   Margarine
C   Butter
D   Shortening
Compare the volume after mixing.

Observations:

Vegetable oil cannot be creamed. Margarine can be creamed minimally. Both fats are not suitable for icings.
Butter can be well-creamed. A good temperature for processing butter in icings ranges between 18 and 20°C.
Emulsified shortening yields the best volume after mixing.

The fats used to make icings have a low melting point, a high emulsification capacity and a good capacity to absorb additional moisture and air. Emulsified shortening contains emulsifiers, e.g., lecithin, monoglycerides and diglycerides.

In the case of most of the speciality fats used for icings or creams, about 2/3 of the fat content melts at room temperature. This has a positive effect on the flavor and makes it easier to aerate the fat.

In addition to the high ratio shortenings, there are also ready-mix shortenings that contain flavors suitable for butter icings and creams.

If the volume of creamed fats is compared with the litre weight, it is easy to recognize the different suitability of fats for the preparation of icings. Emulsified shortening, for example, can incorporate so much air, that a litre weighs only 280 g. The same volume of creamed margarine weighs about 600 g.

Butter is used as fat primarily for flavoring purposes. If the icing is supposed to be designated as "butter cream" or "butter icing," only butter should be used as a fat in the cream. In order to obtain a larger volume, the baker likes to use another fat that can be easily creamed. But in that case, the icing cannot be designated as "100% pure butter icing."

Joe says:
"Icings are all the same; there are no differences. You can't make any mistakes!"
Joe probably thinks only about the technological properties of butter icing! The consumer, however, judges a butter icing primarily based on its enjoyment value. Heavy, "fatty-tasting" icings are usually rejected. This type of icing is considered by the customer as a "calorie bomb."

Taste an icing sample in your bakery to see if it melts on your tongue or if a fatty flavor remains in your mouth. Check the volume of the icing using the litre weight test.

Additional Information

How is the litre weight determined?
— *Weigh an empty 100 cm³ container.*
— *Fill the container with an icing to be tested (smoothed top).*
— *Weigh the filled container. The weight of the empty container is deducted from the total weight.*
— *The net weight of the icing is multiplied by 10 = litre weight (1,000 cm³).*
What does the litre weight tell us? An icing with a large volume is created through the incorporation of air. When the weighed 1,000 cm³ of icing contains a lot of air, the weight is low. But if the 1,000 cm³ of creamy batter contains little air, the weight is high.
Are there any standard values for litre weights of icings?
— *Well-aerated German butter cream has a litre weight of 360 – 450 g.*
— *Well-aerated French butter icing has a litre weight of 420 – 500 g.*
— *Well-aerated Italian meringue icing has a litre weight of 320 – 360 g.*

Thomas says:
"Ready-mix butter icings are easy to process. The baker saves time and needs fewer ingredients. And through skillful flavoring, it is certainly possible to modify the basic icing in many ways. But does the use of identical ready-mix icing products in all bakeries not lead to too much uniformity of the products?"
What do you think?
What do your colleagues think?

Fig. 674 **Pastry made with Italian meringue icing**

Italian meringue icing has a high volume, but very little aroma of its own and is well suited for combination with fruits.

Aside from the selection of the proper fat type, what else is important to achieve a well-aerated icing?

Use:
— *optimum processing temperatures, e.g., 21 – 23°C for emulsified shortening, 18 – 20°C for butter;*
— *appropriate attachment, e.g., fine whisk in a planetary mixer;*
— *proper mixing speed, e.g., mix for 1 – 2 minutes at low speed, then for about 15 minutes at medium speed.*

Ready-Mix Icings

Icings for filling and decorating can also be made with convenience products. The following basic types are readily available:

— Basic icings in the form of powder; they are mixed with water and can be improved with various other ingredients (meringue or high ratio fat or whipping cream) and aromatic substances.
— Ready-mix icings based on fat or emulsifiers; they are mixed with water or eggs and can be flavored to taste.
— Ready-mix icings in the form of pastes; they are mixed without any further additions and can be flavored to taste.

Differentiation Between Icings
According to their Composition

Based on their composition, we can distinguish between:

➤ **German butter icing**
= Vanilla pastry cream and Fat
➤ **French butter icing**
= Whole egg batter + Fat
➤ **Italian meringue icing**
= Meringue + Fat

For French butter icing, warmed whole eggs and sugar are whipped together until a viscous foam is formed. This batter is added to the fat, which is creamed separately. For Italian meringue icing, a meringue is prepared with egg white and sugar. This meringue is mixed into the creamed fat.

French and Italian icings do not turn sour, but they have a very high fat content. Therefore their nutritive value is very high.

Basic recipe for icings		
German	French	Italian
1,000 g Fat and a Vanilla pastry cream composed of: 1,000 g Milk 200 g Sugar 90 g Custard powder	1,000 g Fat and a Whole egg batter composed of: 400 g Whole egg 400 g Sugar Salt/ Flavor	1,000 g Fat and a Meringue composed of: 400 g Egg white 600 g Sugar Salt/ Flavor

Table 142

Production of Tortes

Tortes are traditionally made with sponge cake. These cake layers can contain other ingredients depending on the flavor desired for the cake, e.g., nut meats and cocoa.

For cakes that are to be sold by the individual piece, the traditional format is a round layer with a diameter of 26 to 28 cm (10"), and divided into 12 to 18 slices per cake. For special occasion, birthday or anniversary cakes and fancily-decorated tortes, various shapes can be used. Smaller sizes are also very popular and cater to smaller groups or families.

Assembly instructions:

→ Prepare the sponge cake by brushing off any loose crumbs and cutting it with a long knife (serrated edge) into three equal layers.
→ Spread the base layer with an icing of your choice (jam can be used instead) and place the next sponge layer on top.
→ Apply a flavored simple syrup by brushing the entire layer. Do not soak.
→ Repeat this process and place the top layer with the cut side up. This will help to level the cake. Coat the top and the sides with icing.
→ Apply the decoration.

Possible Faults in Preparing Icings

Faults of desserts and cakes with icings can be attributable to mistakes made in the production of the cake layers or rolls. For more information, please refer to the appropriate chapters.

The purpose of this chapter is to reveal deficiencies in German butter icing:

Fault	Cause
➤ Icing has a small volume; it is heavy	➤ Unsuitable fat ➤ Fat insufficiently creamed
➤ Icing is granular, gritty	➤ Basic icing too soft ➤ Fat and/or pastry cream too cold
➤ Icing contains lumps	➤ Pastry cream too firm ➤ A skin was allowed to form on the pastry cream
➤ Firmness of icing decreases	➤ Pastry cream not sufficiently emulsified ➤ Water released after defrosting
➤ Icing collapses; it is sticky	➤ Fat has been processed too warm ➤ Icing is stored too warm so that the fat has melted out

Practical tips:

➤ *On cake layers, the darker top portion should be removed; otherwise it easily detaches from the filling. Its color also affects the appearance, especially if a fondant coating is used.*
➤ *The bottom layer may consist of a thin short paste bottom. It improves the stability of the torte.*
➤ *Soak thick layers more heavily with syrup. This makes the cake more moist and preserves freshness, giving the cake a rounded flavor.*
➤ *Vertical, ring or striped arrangements of cake layers and fillings makes for an interesting variety of products.*
➤ *Shape and decoration of the cakes should match the flavor.*
➤ *Cake dividers and templates help to make cake production more economical.*

Working Techniques

Diversification of the appearance of the pastries and cakes is achieved through

— Variation in the shapes, e.g., "normal torte," rounded top,
— Color differences between layers and fillings,
— Alternating techniques of layers and fillings.

Fig. 675   *Fig. 676*
Sheets are layered together with apricot jam and almond paste, then cut into strips. They can be used in many different ways for decoration purposes (see *Fig. 677*).

Fig. 677

315

Fig. 678   Fig. 679

Decorations on cakes should not be overloaded. With templates, decorations can be applied cleanly and efficiently.

Cakes with Special Finishes

Fig. 681

This ring-shaped dessert cake with a light-colored icing, jam filling and a nut crunch topping can be made from sponge cake.

Fig. 680

Fuerst-Pueckler-Torte has a typical filling with a brown/white/red color combination. The dome-shaped top on this picture suits this cake type very well.

Fig. 682

Shaped, super-imposed and layered cakes show an arrangement typical for special occasions, like Mother's Day, weddings and anniversaries.

| *Summary of important information about cakes and desserts made with icings* |

Creamy Filling

Vanilla pastry cream

Icings with Fat

| — **Basic pastry cream with custom powder**
— **Light pastry cream with the addition of meringue** | **German butter icing**
Vanilla pastry cream + creamed butter/fat | **French icing**
Whole egg/sugar foam + creamed fat | **Italian meringue icing**
Egg white/sugar (meringue) + creamed fat |

* *Fats: Suitable are butter, margarine and emulsified shortenings for icings.*
* *Durability: Vanilla pastry creams and German butter icings spoil easily. They turn sour and ferment. They are kept fresh through cooling.*
  The use of preservatives is allowed, but must be identified on the label.
  French and Italian icings do not turn sour.
* *Quality evaluation of Icings: Through flavor tests and by determining the litre weight.*
* *Flavoring of Icings: Through aromatic substances, addition of fruits, alcohol, nuts, nougat, almonds, cocoa, chocolate or mocha.*
* *Application: Light vanilla pastry cream is used for fillings in desserts, e.g., eclairs, vanilla slices, coffee cakes;*
  Fat icings are suited for filling and decorating cakes and pastries.
* *Trade name: The designation "butter cream" for icings is permitted only when the icing contains the regulated amount of butter.*
  Local regulations vary. Check with the appropriate regulatory bodies.

Cakes and Desserts made with Whipping Cream

Whipping Cream

Voluminous and stable whipped cream is a prerequisite for high-quality whipped cream cakes and desserts.

Whipping cream is a fat-in-water emulsion. It contains at least 30% fat. The emulsified fat contains the incorporated air. Thus, a foam is formed which has about three times the volume of liquid whipping cream. The whipped cream should be able to be piped through a tube and should be stable for at least one day, i.e., it should not release any water.

How is this achieved?

→ Whipping cream whips best a few days after it is produced. It should be processed only after reaching this degree of "maturity."

→ Whipping cream should be stored cool before it is whipped. Best whipping results are achieved at a temperature between 4 and 6°C. The mixing bowl should also be cool to ensure that a favorable whipping temperature is maintained.

→ Whipping cream can be whipped by hand, with a wire whip on a small mixer or with a compressed air "blower." The use of the compressed air whipping machine guarantees the best results because it is ventilated.

→ For sweetening of whipping cream and to improve the stability of the whipped cream, 60 – 100 g of sugar per litre of whipping cream are added. To improve the flavor, a part of the sugar can be replaced with vanilla sugar.

→ Whipping cream must be whipped until it has reached its highest possible volume. This occurs at litre weights between 300 and 350 g.

→ Gelatin or whipping cream stabilizers can be added to the whipping cream to prevent "settlement."

Production of Whipped Cream Cakes and Desserts

Many desserts are filled with whipped cream, e.g., cream puffs, cream horns, eclairs, cream doughnuts. In this case, the whipping cream is normally flavored with a small amount of vanilla.

When whipped cream is used for fillings in cream cakes, flavoring substances synonymous with the name are generally added to the whipped cream, such as chocolate, mocha, nut products, nougat and various fruits.

Whipped cream cakes can be made with various batters. There are no mandatory recipes for the composition and decoration of whipped cream cakes. But the characteristics summarized in *Table 143* can be considered as customary standards for the three types of cakes named.

Fig. 683
Production of whipped cream cakes using an air whip

Thomas says:
"*Making whipped cream is not an easy task. Sometimes, when the weather is warm, the whipped cream does not solidify. And at other times, the whipped cream turns into butter.*" Why?

Errors Made During the Whipping of Whipping Creams

➤ *Whipping cream is too warm*	➤ *Whipped cream does not solidify*
➤ *Whipping cream is not whipped for a sufficient period of time*	➤ *Whipped cream releases water; small volume*
➤ *Whipping cream is whipped for an excessive period of time*	➤ *Whipped cream turns into butter*

Spoiling of Whipped Cream

Whipped cream spoils fast and turns sour easily. Whipped cream must, therefore, be processed immediately under hygienic conditions. Products made with whipped cream must be stored cool. A temperature range between 0 and 3°C is favorable.

Products containing whipped cream that are stored in warm rooms or that are kept too warm after defrosting, lose some of their volume. Their surface turns yellowish and a skin forms.

317

Standards for whipped cream cakes
Example: Black Forest Cake
— Made with a chocolate sponge, thickened sour cherries (or cherry pie filling), whipped cream flavored with Kirsch and decorated with chocolate shavings
Example: Dutch Cherry Torte
— Puff pastry layers, thickened sour cherries (or cherry pie filling), whipped cream, raspberry jam and fondant glaze for the top layer as a finish
Example: Cake with Choux Paste Layers
— Layers made with choux paste, thickened fruits or preserves, whipped cream filling

Table 143

Fig. 684
Black Forest Cake (Chocolate sponge, Vienna, or Genoese cake)

Fig. 685 **Dutch Cherry Torte (layers made from puff pastry dough)**

Fig. 686 **Cake with choux paste layers**

318

Whipped Cream Fillings

What is a whipped cream filling?

The designation "cream filling" should appear on packaged cakes or desserts when fresh whipped cream has not been used.

> * *"Whipped cream cakes/whipped cream desserts" contain fillings and flavoring additives and at least 60% whipped cream. In terms of fat, they contain only milk fat or whipped cream (Exception: natural fat content of additives, such as nuts, chocolate).*

This does not apply to quark cheese, wine or yogurt-whipped cream fillings. Refer to the recipes given in *Table 145* on page 319.

> * *"Made with real whipping cream" should appear only on the label of a product containing only fresh whipping cream.*

The distinction between whipped cream fillings and synthetic cream fillings is made by the statement above. A combination of fresh and artificial creams cannot be labelled as "made with whipping cream."

Stabilizers for Whipping Cream

We know that for vanilla pastry cream, cornstarch is used as a binding agent. However, starch is not suitable for whipping cream.
— because pastry cream is too firm to be mixed together with whipping cream in cold state;
— because pastry cream cannot absorb additional liquid and would therefore release water when stored.

The most important binding agent for whipping cream is gelatine.

→ Gelatine is a natural collagen albumen substance which is obtained by cooking animal skin and animal bones.

→ Gelatine is sold in leaves, with a weight of 1.5 to 2 g per leaf, or in the form of powder.

→ Gelatine can absorb a lot of water on its surface.

→ Gelatine forms a liquid "sol" (a colloidal dispersion) when heated to more than 30°C. In this sol, the water does not firmly bind with the gelatine particles.

→ Gelatine forms a firm gel when cooled (similar to jelly). In this gel, the water firmly binds with the gelatine particles.

→ Gelatine can pass several times into the gel or sol state when heated or cooled respectively. The gelling or dissolution processes are thus reversible.

Practical tips for the use of gelatine in whipped cream:

➤ *About 6 leaves or 10 g of ground gelatine are sufficient to solidify 1 litre of whipping cream including liquid flavoring agents.*

➤ *First, let gelatine soak for about 5 minutes in cold water. In the process, gelatine can absorb about five times its own weight in water.*

➤ *Gelatine is heated in order to dissolve at a temperature of between 50 – 60°C. Gelatine should not be allowed to boil.*

➤ *Blend the dissolved gelatine with the flavoring substances into a base. Thus, even distribution is made easier.*

➤ *Do not incorporate the gelatine in cold state into the whipping cream; otherwise the gelatine forms filaments or lumps in the whipping cream.*

➤ *Do not incorporate gelatine while hot into the whipping cream; this leads to a loss of volume.*

➤ *First, blend a small part of the whipping cream with the gelatine base; then incorporate the remainder of the whipping cream gradually but quickly.*

Additional Information

Gelatine leaves and ground gelatine must be soaked in cold water prior to further use. The soaked gelatine is then dissolved while it is heated. In dissolved state, the gelatine can form a solid gel with the liquid when it cools.

There are gelatine products that can be used in a cold state, but they are not as effective as non-dissolving gelatine. Through spray crystallization, a very fine gelatine powder is obtained. This powder yields, together with milk powder, powdered sugar and swellable starches, the cold gelling agents. They absorb the liquid by means of a swelling process. Products made with these agents are, therefore, more creamy and less jelly-like.

Cold gelling agents are processed as follows:

— *when used for whipped cream: sprinkle in dry state along with the quantity of sugar indicated by the manufacturer, into the stiffly beaten whipped cream.*

— *when used for whipped cream fillings: blend together with the quantity of sugar indicated by the manufacturer until a cold base is obtained. Then incorporate the whipped cream. The blended base can also be heated to about 40°C and cooled prior to the addition of the whipped cream. In this case, the quantity of cold gelling agents should be reduced; otherwise the base loses its creamy characteristics.*

Production of Lemon-Cream Cakes

First, a fond is made with the acidic ingredients (without whipped cream). For that purpose, we mix lemon juice, white wine, egg yolk and sugar to about 85°C. After the gelatine has soaked and dissolved, it is added to this fond. Next, the fond is stirred while in a cold state. Then the whipped cream is gradually added.

Cakes and desserts with whipped cream and lemon are frequently made without a top cake cover (see the photos on this page).

Using the examples of lemon-cream cakes or cheese-cream cakes, we have learned about two different methods of production:
— preparation of a cold basic cream,
— preparation of a fond.

Fonds are primarily prepared when a large amount of liquid ingredients are combined into a whipped cream batter. When making the fond, the baker also uses the binding and emulsifying properties of the egg yolk.

Sample recipe for lemon-cream cakes	
50 g	Lemon juice
75 g	White wine
50 g	Egg yolk
150 g	Sugar
6	Gelatine leaves
700 g	Whipped cream (unsweetened)

Table 144

Fig. 678
Working steps in the production of cream desserts

Sample recipe for cream cheese tortes	
500 g	Quark cheese
150 g	Sugar
50 g	Egg yolk
	Salt/Lemon Flavoring
8	Gelatine leaves
100 g	Water
700 g	Whipped cream (unsweetened)

Table 145

Fig. 688 **Cream cheese cake with fruit**

Production of Cream Cheese Cake

The cream cheese filling is made as follows:

Strain quark cheese through a sift and blend it with sugar, egg yolk and flavor until smooth. Soak the gelatine for 5 minutes in cold water, then heat it up in 100 g water to a temperature of 60°C. The dissolved gelatine is blended with the cheese/cream. Then the whipped cream is incorporated.

The cake is made as follows: A thin, baked short paste bottom, 26 cm in diameter, is coated with preserves and covered with a thin layer of sponge cake. This layer is surrounded with a high ring. The cheese/cream filling is placed into the ring. As a cover, a second sponge cake layer, precut into 16 pieces, can be placed onto the filling. After the cake has set, it can be decorated with a dusting of icing sugar and cut into pieces.

Whipped cream fond bases are available in the form of powder as premixed products. They contain milk powder, flavor compounds, sugar and instant gelatine (dissolving in cold state).

The flavor basis for whipped cream fonds is prepared with these products under the addition of cold water. This "cold method" prevents a loss of volume when the whipped cream is added.

Summary of important information about whipping cream and fonds	
➤ Best conditions for the whipping of whipped cream	➤ a few days after production of the whipping cream ➤ at a temperature of 4 to 6°C ➤ addition of 60 to 100 g sugar per litre whipping cream ➤ use of an air blower for whipping purposes
➤ Stabilization of the whipped cream	➤ addition of gelatine or other stiffeners
➤ Shelf life of the whipped cream	➤ cool storage at 0 to 3°C to retard the souring process
➤ Storage of pastries made with whipped cream and with whipped cream fillings	➤ in a freezer at -20°C, protected against foreign odors and drying out in frosted state; slow defrosting at an appropriate air humidity
➤ Designation such as "made with real whipping cream"	➤ composed entirely of fresh whipped cream + flavoring agents; contains no artificial/synthetic products.

Fig. 689 **Strawberry tortelettes – a seasonal pastry**

Fruit Flans and Fruit Desserts

Strawberry tortelettes are a popular fresh seasonal pastry. But after the fresh fruit season, bakers can still make a variety of desserts using the broad range of canned fruits available on the market.

The expert always uses high-quality canned fruits for fruit flans and fruit desserts. A combination of fresh and canned fruits is also popular. The baker's expertise can be recognized when looking at the type of cake used and the glaze of fruit flans. What is important?

Cakes for Fruit Tortes and Fruit Desserts

Tortelettes and fruit flans are made primarily with short paste and Vienna (sponge cake) batter. The baker must ensure when preparing the cake for fruit flans,
— that the fruit can adhere to the cake used,
— that the sponge cake is protected against absorbing too much liquid.

The following three examples will demonstrate how the cakes used are treated in an expert fashion:

➤ Short paste bottoms are more stable than bottoms made with sponge batter or Vienna batter. They are also less likely to become saturated. The bottom is covered with preserves, vanilla pastry cream, or a tasty macaroon batter before the fruits are placed onto it.

➤ Short paste bottoms can be coated, prior to baking, with a mixture of short paste and macaroon batter. This layer is baked together with the short paste and is moist and tender. The bottom is coated with preserves (e.g., boiled apricot glaze) before the fruits are placed onto it (see *Fig. 691*).

➤ Short paste bottoms can be covered with a sponge batter layer. The adhesive force between the bottoms or between the sponge cake and the fruits can be achieved by applying a coating of preserves, vanilla pastry cream or macaroon base. The sponge cake bottom can absorb fruit juice and increase the moistness of the pastry (see *Fig. 692*).

Do not place moist fruits onto bottoms made with Vienna batter or sponge cake. After a short time, the bottom would become so saturated that the fruit flan could no longer be offered for sale.

Jelly Glazing for Fruit Flans and Fruit Desserts

Fruit flans normally receive a jelly glazing. This glazing should
— cover the fruits,
— be transparent,
— be easy to cut, and
— be palatable.

The use of color substances for jelly glazings is allowed. They must be identified as follows when the pastries are displayed for sale:
➤ "with artificial color" or
➤ "jelly glazing with artificial color."

The following binding agents are suited for jelly toppings:
— agar-agar,
— alginates/algenic acid
— carrageen.

Ready-mixes for flan jellies also contain some Carob gum or guar gum (guar kernel flour). The jelly is prepared by heating up the mixture of glaze, water and sugar in accordance with the manufacturer's instructions. These jellies can normally be dissolved after gelatinization through the application of heat.

Fig. 690

Joe says: *"What's the problem? I only use sponge cake bottoms to make fruit flans! At least they are soft enough and do not break when cut!"*
What do you think about Joe's statement?

Fig. 691
Short dough bottom with topping

Fig. 692
Multi-layer arrangement on a fruit flan bottom; for comparison purposes, a short paste bottom with strawberries

Reference:
For further information about the use of coloring agents for baked goods, refer to the chapter entitled **Coatings and Decorations**.

321

Additional Information

Agar-agar, algenic acid and their salts (alginates) and carrageen are complex sugar substances made of algae (water plants). Guar kernel flour and carob gum are derived from the seeds of tropical plants.

The effective components in these thickeners are high-molecular sugar substances of identical composition (homoglycanes) or of different composition (heteroglycanes).

Pectins are derived from plant cells. Therefore, they are obtained from the juice of many (especially not fully ripe) fruits. They contain galacturonic acid and complex sugar substances. In acid solutions with a sugar content of about 50%, pectins can form a gel through water absorption.

About 20 thickeners meet regulatory labelling requirements as additives to food products. The maximum quantity per kg of finished food product is set at 20 g (for pectin = 30 g).

When glaze for flans is made with juice containing pectin, sugar and fruit acids, it can be processed cold. Gelling is caused through the precipitation of pectins, (complex sugar substances in fruits) through acidification. The jellies obtained cannot be liquefied again for re-processing.

Two-crusted Pie Variations

Fruit pies are made with pie dough as bottoms and prepared with short paste, puff pastry dough or egg batters for variety. The fruits are used as a filling.

Batters (e.g., meringues) piped onto the fruit topping also serve as covers.

Food for Thought:
Why are preparations with gelatine less suitable as glazing jellies than others?

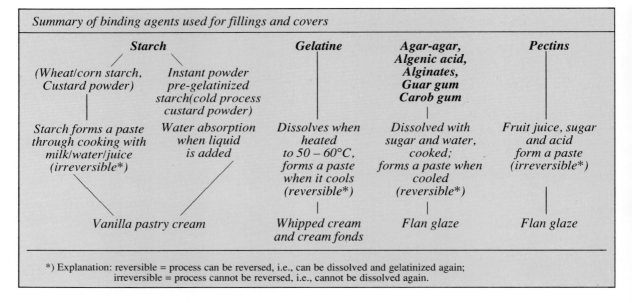

Summary of binding agents used for fillings and covers				
Starch		**Gelatine**	**Agar-agar, Algenic acid, Alginates, Guar gum Carob gum**	**Pectins**
(Wheat/corn starch, Custard powder)	*Instant powder pre-gelatinized starch (cold process custard powder)*			
Starch forms a paste through cooking with milk/water/juice (irreversible*)	*Water absorption when liquid is added*	*Dissolves when heated to 50 – 60°C, forms a paste when it cools (reversible*)*	*Dissolved with sugar and water, cooked; forms a paste when cooled (reversible*)*	*Fruit juice, sugar and acid form a paste (irreversible*)*
	Vanilla pastry cream	*Whipped cream and cream fonds*	*Flan glaze*	*Flan glaze*

*) Explanation: reversible = process can be reversed, i.e., can be dissolved and gelatinized again;
irreversible = process cannot be reversed, i.e., cannot be dissolved again.

Macaroon Tortes

Fig. 693 **Macaroon torte**

322

The production of macaroon tortes is unusual; they are baked after they have been prepared and decorated. This is how it is done:

→ Cut up Vienna sponge cake layers, fill them with preserves or macaroon batter and stack them.

→ The torte is coated with macaroon batter and fully decorated.

→ The sides can be covered with grated almonds. The torte is flash-baked at about 200°C.

→ After baking, the macaroon decoration receives a hot apricot glaze coating. The decorative pattern can be glazed with preserves or fondant.

The batter for macaroon tortes must be soft enough so that it can be easily piped through tubes. But it should also be firm enough to prevent the contours from disappearing during baking. Contrary to other macaroon pastries, the baker uses no ground nuts in batters meant for macaroon tortes. Prepared pastes are used instead.

Reference:
*For further information about macaroon batters, refer to the chapter entitled **Nut Pastries Made with and without Roux.***

Prepared and Semi-finished Products

The paste for macaroon tortes is made with almond paste, egg white and sugar. When kernel paste is used, the torte should be simply identified as a "macaroon torte."

How do marzipan and kernel paste differ?

➤ Marzipan is made with sweet almonds and sugar. Per 100 parts almonds, 50 parts sugar are used. After the peeled almonds have been soaked in hot water, they are ground and roasted with sugar. The cooled paste must contain at least 28% almond oil and not more than 17% water and 35% sugar.

➤ Kernel paste is prepared in the same way as almond paste. But instead of almonds, apricot or peach kernels that have been processed to remove their bitter taste can be used.
The finished kernel paste can contain up to 20% water and 35% sugar. About 0.5% starch must be added to the kernel paste. It is possible to distinguish it from almond paste by conducting the iodine test.

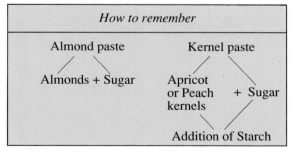

How to remember
Almond paste   Kernel paste
Almonds + Sugar   Apricot or Peach kernels   + Sugar
Addition of Starch

When marzipan covers or decorations are made, the almond paste is blended with refined powdered sugar.

For this purpose, the following maximum quantities are recommended:

— almond paste at a ratio of 1/1, 1 kg almond paste, 1 kg powdered sugar;
— kernel paste at a ratio of 2/3, 1 kg paste, 1.5 kg powdered sugar.

To ensure that the mixed pastes remain smooth, add corn syrup or sorbitol. The maximum quantities recommended are as follows:

— for almond paste = 3.5% corn syrup and/or 5% sorbitol;
— for kernel paste = 5% corn syrup and/or 5% sorbitol (always related to the total quantity of paste).

Adhere to good manufacturing practises in the processing of pastes.

Other pastes used for fillings of cakes, tortes and desserts are:
— Nut pastes and semi-finished products made with nut products,
— Nougat and nougat cream.

Prepared pastes can spoil easily
— when they are stored in too warm an environment they turn rancid through fat decomposition,
— when they are stored in a very moist environment they mold,
— when they are stored in an open, dry environment the surface turns crusty,
— when they are mixed with flour they ferment.

The baker should, therefore, ensure that such pastes are stored in a cool, dark place.

Filling pastes that have been blended and prepared for further processing are especially sensitive to spoilage through micro-organisms. They must be stored in a cool place until they are used. The baker can also add preservatives to make them more durable.

Additional Information

To prepare nut pastes, the same quality requirements applying to kernel paste must be followed. Besides the nut content, they can contain bitter almonds or apricot kernels up to a maximum of 10% of the total quantity of paste.
Besides prepared pastes, there are a multitude of semi-finished products which are available in spreadable form. They have a high sugar and liquid content. This must be taken into account when comparing the price of prepared pastes.
Nougat pastes are made with kernels (almonds or hazelnut or almond-nut), sugar and cocoa products.
Nougat pastes can contain up to 50% sugar.
Nougat pastes are not allowed to contain more than 2% water.

Additional Information

The following are permitted for use as preservatives for fine baked goods and their ingredients:

Sorbates
Sorbic acid and its salts (potassium sorbate) have a broad spectrum of activity against yeast and molds
- *normal use of 0.01 to 0.1%*
- *add after prolonged boiling (fruit jellies, etc.)*
- *inhibits yeast in yeast-raised products (primarily used to treat surface of these products)*
- *optimum effectiveness up to pH 6.5*

Benzoates
Benzoic acid and its salt (sodium benzoate); low water solubility of the free acid
- *normal use 0.05 to 0.1%*
- *more active against yeast and molds than bacteria*
- *not used in yeast-raised products*
- *optimum pH range 2.5 to 4.0 (suitable for use in acidic foods)*

Propionates
Propionic acid and its salts (calcium sodium propionate)
- *suggested upper levels 0.32 to 0.38% based on flour*
- *no activity against yeast except for rope bacteria*
- *high activity against mold (account for 75% of all anti-microbial agents used in baked goods)*
- *optimum pH range to 6.0*

Parabens
Alkyl esters of p-hydroxybenzoic acid. Parabens have a similar anti-microbial effect to benzoic acid but with a wider pH range. The methyl and propyl parabens used in sweetened fruit jellies and jam should not exceed 0.1%
- *limited solubility with a noticeable flavor*
- *inhibit yeast activity*

The following substances can be treated with sulphur dioxide or substances releasing sulphur dioxide: Dried fruits, candied fruits, candied lemon and orange peels, ground lemon or orange peels for use in bakeries, raw peeled apple pieces for use in bakeries, fruit gelatinating juices, preserves, jams, jellies, fruit pulps, fruit pastes and certain sugar products.

If the finished product contains more than 50 mg sulphur dioxide per kg/litre, this must be mentioned on the label as "sulphurized."

Preservatives

Sugar has a preserving effect on many baked goods. Other ingredients can also naturally restrict the effect of micro-organisms. However, these natural ingredients are not designated as preservatives.

> * *Preservatives, within the context of food regulations, are additives preventing spoilage through their chemical effect on micro-organisms.*

However, they have a limited use in baked goods.

Chemical preservatives can be added only up to a predetermined maximum quantity per kg of finished food product, and are not allowed at all in some products.

The use of preservatives must be identified when the food products are offered for sale. This can be done using labels such as "contains the preservative ..." or "preserved with ..." Identification is made on a label next to the baked good, on the price tag or on the list of ingredients when the food product is sold in prepackaged format.

Some examples from a pastry bakery:

➤ Macaroon batter containing almond paste can contain preservatives. In this case, the baker uses sorbic acid, among others. The baker must

— respect and precisely scale the maximum quantity allowed (1.5 g per kg batter);

— he must identify the preservative when the baked goods are displayed for sale. Example: "contains the preservative sorbic acid." When the baked product is sold in prepackaged format, the list of ingredients must include "preservative, sorbic acid." If macaroon batter is part of another product, the reference on the label should read, "macaroon batter containing the preservative, sorbic acid."

➤ An apricot cake, for example, with jelly glazing, is supposed to be preserved with preservatives. For this purpose only, propionic acid and its salts (propionates) are used in a quantity of up to 3 g per kg baked good. In this case, the baker can label the product as follows: "Jelly glazing containing the preservative, propionic acid."

➤ To press the lemon juice for lemon cream fond, the baker uses lemon peels which have been preserved with diphenyl. The lemon peels can be grated in the bakery and used as an aromatic substance without falling under labelling requirements, although diphenyl is not allowed for use as a preservative for baked goods.

➤ Apricot preserve is spread under the topping for fruit flans. The surface of the apricot is preserved with sorbic acid.

When the baker uses apricot preserve for fruit flans, he does not have to adhere to labelling requirements because the preservative has no technical effect on the finished fruit flan.

The purchaser of baked goods can tell by reading the label (declaration) whether a product has been treated with chemical preservatives. But the purchaser generally does not know anything about the use restrictions and maximum quantities allowed for these additives. Therefore, baked goods containing preservatives are often rejected.

Fig. 694

Always consider the following in your work:

→ You should give preference to untreated ingredients over ingredients with chemical preservatives.

→ You can protect untreated ingredients from spoiling through appropriate and cool storage conditions.

→ If you always make fresh products, you can dispense with chemical preservatives.

Sachertorte

Fig. 695 **Sachertorte**

In 1832, Frau Sacher, owner of a famous restaurant in Vienna, invented a recipe for a fine torte made with egg yolk, butter, sugar, chocolate and flour. Today she is remembered throughout the world for the Sachertorte, which bears her name.

The cake contains at least one part chocolate, one part whole egg and one part butter per one part flour. The batter can, therefore, be categorized as especially heavy.

After baking, the cut Sacher cake layers are soaked with red currant jelly, a wine jelly, or with hot apricot jam. Then the layers are put together and receive, on the outside, a hot coating of apricot jam. Instead of couverture, a Ganache (coating made with hot whipping cream and finely chopped chocolate) is used.

The color, appearance, flavor and quality of the Sachertorte are essentially influenced by the cocoa and chocolate products used.

Cocoa products are used in the bakery industry as aromatic ingredients, coatings and for decorating purposes. In order to correctly process these high-quality ingredients, a baker must have fundamental information about the composition, suitability and technological properties of cocoa products.

Couverture and Chocolate Coatings

Joe says:
"I would use chocolate coatings only for coating purposes. They are easier to process than couverture. And, quality-wise, they are just as good. The customers will not notice any difference!"

What do you think?

Joe is right about the ease of processing and the high quality of chocolate coatings containing cocoa. But, he should also recognize the difference between couverture and chocolate coatings.

Couverture (60/40) is composed as follows:

Chocolate Liquor	*= 50%* }	→	*Fat = 27%*
Cocoa butter	*= 10%* }	→	*Fat = 10%*
Sugar	*= 40%*		
	100%		*37%*

Cocoa butter turns the dry components of the couverture into a homogeneous mass. Because of its properties, the cocoa butter also determines the state of the couverture.

Cocoa butter
— *is composed of about 60% of the solid fatty acids, stearin and palmitin. The third fatty acid component is primarily oleic acid,*
— *turns hard at room temperature,*
— *melts completely to form a tender substance at a temperature below that of the human body,*
— *melts clear in a narrow temperature range between 29 and 33°C.*

The fat of chocolate coatings containing cocoa has different melting characteristics than cocoa butter.

Palm oil and hardened palm oil
— *have a lower content of solid fatty acids than cocoa butter,*
— *melt slower over a wider temperature range than cocoa butter,*
— *have a considerable content of solid fat, even at a temperature above 35°C.*

When the proportion of solid fats at various temperatures is shown in per cent, a typical melting curve can be traced.

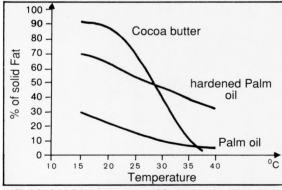

Table 146 Melting curve of fats contained in couverture and chocolate coatings

Food for Thought: *Which types of couverture are categorized as bitter and which ones as sweet?*

Chocolate coatings containing cocoa are considered as imitation chocolate. Chocolate coatings containing cocoa should not be used:
— for baked goods of special quality or when the label says "finest ingredients;" e.g., in the case of Sachertorte,
— for the production or coating of sweet goods; e.g., for products made with almond paste, almonds, chocolate,
— for durable baked goods in which high quality is stressed.

Otherwise, chocolate coatings containing cocoa can be used for baked goods and ice cream in products sold with a label indicating its use. This identification can take the following forms:
— in the case of baked goods offered for sale in unpackaged format, through a label beside the baked good or on the price tag saying "with chocolate coating,"
— in the case of food products sold in prepackaged format, through the words "chocolate coating" in the list of ingredients and the additional identification "with chocolate coating" in connection with the trade name of the baking product.

Composition

The couverture package reads "couverture 60/40." What does that mean?

Couverture is composed of chocolate liquor, cocoa butter and sugar. The identification 60/40 indicates the quantitative ratio of cocoa components and sugar. In our example, the couverture is composed of 60 parts cocoa components and 40 parts sugar. Other couverture varieties available on the market have a ratio of 70/30 and 50/50.

Through a third number (e.g., 70/30/38), the content of cocoa butter can be identified.

Other ingredients can be powdered milk (for milk couverture) or whipping cream (for whipping cream couverture).

For chocolate coatings containing cocoa, there is no identification of ingredients on the package. These coatings are made from a basic recipe comparable to that of couverture. However, the cocoa butter is either completely or partially replaced with substitute fats.

The type of substitute fats used determines the quality of the chocolate coatings.

➤ Fat mixtures that are very similar to cocoa butter give chocolate coatings the tenderness, shininess and firmness characteristic to couverture. These chocolate coatings must be processed in the same way as couverture.

➤ Palm kernel and coconut fats have a tenderness comparable to, and a firmness identical to, that of cocoa butter. They yield coatings resistant to the touch of a finger. They do not have to be processed in the same way as couverture.

➤ Fats that are similar to cocoa butter yield coatings that are easy to cut and very elastic. They are soft but not shiny. They are not very tender and have a limited chocolate flavor. They are easier to process than couverture.

Storage of Couverture and Chocolate Coatings

Couverture and chocolate coatings containing cocoa can be stored for a long time because they contain little water. Moreover, they have a high sugar content. However, the processing characteristics can be reduced through light, heat and moisture. Because they are sensitive to strong foreign odors, it is recommended to store products containing cocoa in a package in a cool, dark environment.

Processing of Couverture and of Chocolate Coatings Containing Cocoa

Chocolate coatings containing cocoa and couverture should be made into a liquid through heat application prior to further processing. The flowing capacity during the coating process depends on the fat content. Fat amounts to about 1/3 of the coating's mass.

Adding fat while dissolving the coating mass can increase the flowing capacity.

> * Respect the following rules:
> ➤ Couverture can be thinned only through the addition of cocoa butter.
> ➤ Chocolate coatings containing cocoa can be thinned with cocoa butter, but also through the addition of other fats.
> ➤ For couverture and chocolate coatings containing cocoa, no water should be added because the coating may coagulate.

Chocolate coatings containing cocoa are heated to about 40°C.

However, couverture must be tempered to crystallize the fat components of the cocoa butter.

How is tempering performed correctly?

→ Heat couverture to about 45°C; it turns liquid.

→ Cool couverture by adding firm, grated couverture pieces; it begins to solidify.

→ Heat couverture again to the desired temperature; it is now suited for coating purposes.

For tempering purposes, and instead of using grated couverture, put some of the dissolved couverture onto a marble slab and work it with a spatula until it solidifies. Then add it to the liquid couverture. A couverture tempering device is also very appropriate (see *Fig. 696*).

Fig. 696
A simple couverture tempering device with electric heating and water bath

Why does couverture have to be tempered?

➤ The cocoa butter can solidify in various crystallized shapes.

➤ The cocoa butter forms a solid coating without streaks only in a certain crystallized form.

➤ Through tempering, 3/4 of the cocoa butter is liquid and 1/4 of it is solid (in the form of crystals). Thus, segregation of the ingredients is prevented. Moreover, the crystalline cocoa butter parts provide stability to the still liquid components until they solidify.

The temperature at which couverture should be processed depends on the variety. Bitter couverture solidifies, for example, at about 31 – 33°C. Milk couverture solidifies at about 29 – 31°C.

The correct temperature for coating is established by means of test coatings. The expert uses the very sensitive tip of the little finger to determine the correct temperature for coating.

Figs. 697 to 699
Working steps in the coating process, dividing and decoration of a cake. Also take note of the tips on page 328!

Practical tips:

➤ *Do not overwork melted or tempered coatings or bubbles will form.*

➤ *Allow cold products to warm up to room temperature prior to applying the coating. Otherwise, the coating solidifies too quickly and cannot be smoothened out.*

➤ *When applying a coating to cakes, cover the sides first, then quickly smooth the coating using a palette knife. This way the walls are cleanly and completely coated.*

➤ *Pastries are dipped "head first" down to the bottom of the coating (perhaps by means of a fork). Thus, the sides are smooth and the excess coating can drip off on the grid.*

➤ *Score the surface into divisions with a heated knife after the coating has settled. This will prevent the coating from breaking when slices are cut.*

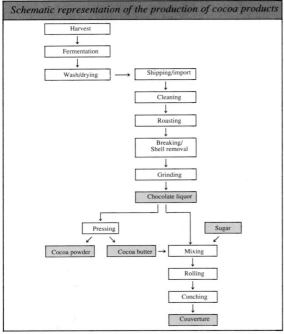

Fig. 700 **Cocoa fruit**

Table 147

Deficiencies of Couverture Coatings

Deficiency	Cause
➤ streaky-gray coating	➤ segregation of the cocoa butter due to insufficient temperature during tempering
➤ dull coating	➤ irregular fat crystals form due to excessively high temperature during tempering
➤ crumbly coating	➤ excessively high temperature during tempering or water in the couverture
➤ breaking of couverture	➤ coating applied to excessively cold parts

Cocoa Powder

The baker processes cocoa powder into pastes, fillings and glazings. A good aroma and smoothness without clot formation (lumping) is expected.

Cocoa powder is offered in two qualities:

➤ Cocoa powder containing at least 20% cocoa butter,
➤ Cocoa powder with at least 8% cocoa butter (low fat content, or oil removed to a large extent).

The quality type is indicated on the package. Other ingredients are listed as well, e.g., sugar (must be identified, if more than 5% is added), lecithin (= up to 1% is allowed) and aromatic substances.

Additional Information

The cocoa tree grows in Central America. The ancient tribes of the Toltecs and Aztecs used the cocoa beans as a currency. They also prepared a bitter, dark beverage from chocolate liquor. In the Aztec language, this beverage was called "xocoatl." Over the centuries, this word became "chocolate."

Between 1515 and 1520, cocoa was brought by the Spanish conquerors of Central America to the court of the King of Spain. For about 200 years, only the Spaniards traded cocoa. First, it was appreciated as a cure, due to its stimulating substances, caffeine and theobromine. Only after it became known that chocolate combined successfully with sugar did it become popular all over Europe. The Spaniards also developed chocolate as a solid bar-type product. In Switzerland, the process of milk chocolate preparation and conching was invented in the middle of the 19th century.

Production of Cocoa Products

The bittersweet cocoa products are obtained through a long refining process.

The cocoa tree grows in tropical countries, mainly in Ghana, Brazil, the Ivory Coast, Nigeria, Mexico and Venezuela.

The cocoa fruits grow directly on the trunk and thick branches of trees The growing and harvesting season lasts all year long.

The cocoa fruits have the shape of melons. They are about 25 cm long and 10 cm thick. About 25 to 50 cocoa beans are embedded in the pulp.

This is how cocoa products are produced:

— The cocoa kernels (cocoa beans) are removed, after the harvest, through a fermentation process of the fruit pulp. In the process, they receive their brown color and develop the first traces of aroma.

— After fermentation, the cocoa beans are washed and dried. Through the drying process, the beans become storable. At the same time, the aroma develops further.

— The cocoa beans are cleaned and roasted in the user countries. During the roasting process at 140 – 150°C, the color and the aroma develop further.

— The roasted cocoa beans are broken and removed from the woody shell. The broken cocoa is milled.

— The cocoa mass contains 50 – 54% cocoa butter, 20 – 23% albumen substances, 10 – 12% organic acids, 3.5% theobromine and caffeine, 2.5% water, 1% starch and 1% minerals.

— When heated to about 50°C, the cocoa mass turns into a mush and becomes "chocolate liquor." Through pressing, the cocoa butter is separated. The remainder is the pressed cocoa cake.

— *Cocoa butter* is packaged as a separate product (see *Fig. 703*). It is also processed further to produce couverture and chocolate.

— *Cocoa powder* is obtained through grinding the pressed cake. It contains about 10% cocoa butter when a large amount of the fat has been removed. It contains about 20 – 25% cocoa butter when only a small amount of the cocoa butter has been removed through pressing.

— *Couverture* or chocolate is made with chocolate liquor; an additional amount of cocoa butter and sugar are added. For special types of couverture, milk or whipped cream is added.

To make couverture, chocolate liquor, cocoa butter and sugar are mixed, rolled and conched. Conching is a stirring and grinding process performed in huge machines. Through grinding, ventilating and heating inside the conches, the chocolate particles are very finely and intimately mixed. The finished mass is shaped, cooled and packaged.

Countries where the cocoa tree grows

Mexico
Costa Rica
Columbia
Ecuador

Haiti
Jamaica
Grenada
Trinidad
Venezuela
Brazil

Ivory Coast
Nigeria
Cameroun
Ghana
St. Thomas
Congo

Ceylon

Java

Madagascar

New Guinea

Fig. 701   **Countries where the cocoa tree grows**

Fig. 702   **Fermented cocoa beans**

Fig. 703   **Cocoa butter and chocolate liquor**

Fig. 704   **Conching of chocolate**

Coatings and Decorations

Fig. 705 **Fondant Petite Fours**

Many cakes and desserts are given a cover, a coating or a glazing, and they are also decorated.

The coating
— gives the pastry firmness,
— gives the pastry a rounded flavor,
— protects the pastry from drying out,
— is used for decorating purposes.

Coatings and Glazings

Couverture, chocolate coatings, nut glazings, nougat coatings, fondant and sugar glazings are normally used for coating cakes and pastries. For further information about sugar used for decorating purposes, please refer to the chapter entitled **Sugar for Decorating Purposes**.

Special products:
— sugar coating paste containing cocoa (200 g powdered sugar, 100 g water, 50 g cocoa);
— Ganache = coating (250 g whipping cream boiled with 350 g couverture);
— Piping chocolate = a glazing suited for filaments (chocolate is mixed until smooth with warm simple syrup);
— Royal icing, white glazing = sugar glazing suited for filaments (mix 1,000 g powdered sugar with 250 g egg white until smooth).

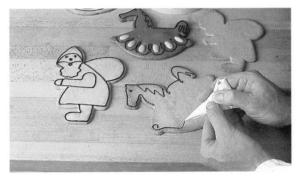

Fig. 706
Decorations with piping chocolate

Materials used for Decorating Purposes

After they have been assembled, cakes and pastries are often wrapped in, or covered with, marzipan. For this purpose, almond paste and powdered sugar are blended at a ratio of 1/1. When glucose or invert sugar are added, the blended marzipan remains fresh and moist. The marzipan cover can be coated, but it can also remain as the outer layer of the pastry.

Decorating Materials

Fruits, nuts, sugars, sprayed and piped ornaments and coating materials are used to decorate cakes and pastries.

Special products:

— Nougat (Nut crunch topping) = caramelized sugar, melted dry, with nuts or almonds. The hardened product is ground after it has cooled.
— Candied fruits = fruits or fruit parts cooked or thickened in sugar.

Use of Coloring Agents

For decorative purposes, fillings and coatings of baked products can be colored.

The coloring agents used for this purpose are food additives. Color substances such as carotene and caramel are generally used, but there are restrictions regarding specific food products. Refer to local authorities for regulations concerning the use of added coloring.

Publisher's Note:

So ends the first English edition of Baking, The Art and Science. We think Baker Smith sums up the book best:

"To be a good baker means much more than having the right equipment or knowing the right recipes. It takes a commitment to quality. Today's baker must respect the customer's need for the best quality ingredients, prepared with care in a sanitary environment. The baker should, whenever possible, prefer fresh ingredients over those that are frozen or preserved, and should offer finished products at the peak of their quality. Finally, bakers should be aware of changing consumer tastes, and offer their customers as much variety as possible. To follow these principles with pride is to be a successful baker."

The Multi-Phase Milling Process
(implified diagram)

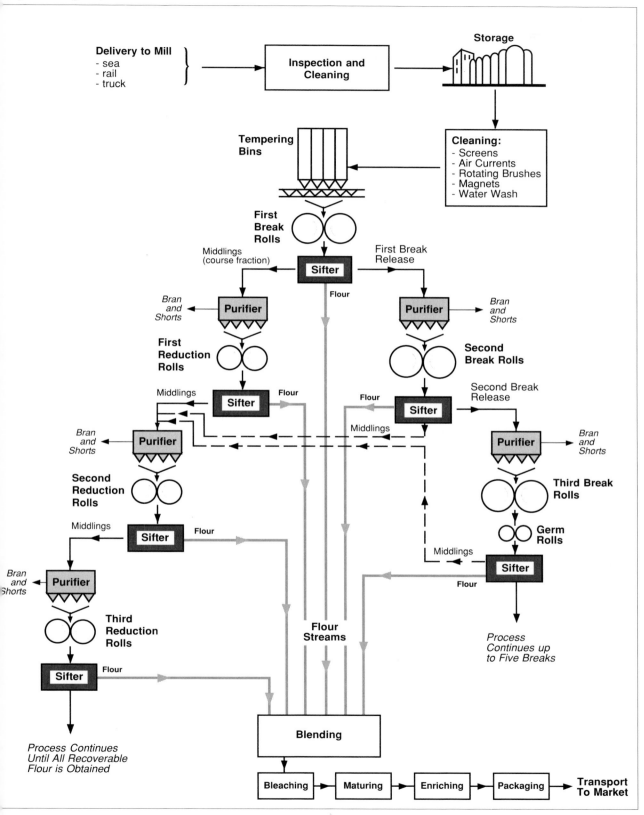

Acknowledgements

ABS Bakery Equipment Systems: Figs. 59, 111

Agefko - Carbon dioxide: Figs. 250, 251

Boehringer Co.: Figs. 2, 4, 6, 8 ,9, 66, 120, 128, 140, 141, 162, 163, 193, 211, 215, 216, 217, 219, 220, 221, 229, 230, 232, 233, 236, 237, 238, 246, 263, 271, 294, 295, 300, 307, 308, 309, 310, 311, 312, 351, 353, 368, 372, 378, 381, 382, 383, 385, 386, 387, 388, 396, 397, 398, 399, 400, 405, 409, 410, 411, 413, 418, 421, 422, 425, 647, 648, 649, 650, 651, Table 129

Brabender: Figs. 51, 52, 53, 54

Chocolate Information Centre of Germany: Figs. 700, 701, 702, 703, 704

Crespel & Deiters Co.: Figs. 609, 652, 689

F. Daub & Sons: Figs. 148, 327, 328, 329, 337

DEBAG Oven mfg.: Figs. 147, 204, 315, 319, 322, 323, 324, 332

Detia Safety Equipment: Figs. 60, 61, 62, 63

Dierks & Sons, Bakery Equipment: Figs. 126, 130, 133, 134, 135

Doehler Products: Figs. 575, 608, 636, 654, 664, 674, 684, 687, 708

Richard Doerr: Values for Fig. 673

G.L Eberhardt, Equipment mfg: Figs. 167, 171, 180

Eisvoight, Cooling systems: Figs. 199, 248

European Bread Museum (Ireks-Arkady collection): Fig. 314, bread stamper in Fig. 359

Food & Restaurant Association of Germany: Fig. 178

Fraunhofer Institute: Fig. 341

A. Fritsch, Equipment Mfg.: Figs. 501, 506, 526, 527

German Bakery Council: Fig. 338

German flour milling Co-operatives: Fig. 55

German Grains & Potato Institute: Figs. 313, 355, 356, 363, Table 42

German Agricultural Association: Figs. 370

Herlitzius Co.: Fig. 428

Hobart Equipment: Figs. 633, 634, 683

Fritz Homann Bakery Supplies: Figs. 3, 218, 468, 483, 484, 490, 492, 495, 513, 515, 516, 528, 533, 534, 560, 561, 581, 583, 603, 607, 637, 657, 662, 667, 680, 681, 709

IWEX Cooling systems: Fig. 242

Ireks-Arkady, Baking additives: Figs. 164, 165, 166, 258, 259, 260, 261, 262, 264, 265, 268, 395, 420, 427

G. Jansen: Fig. 613

E. Kemper, Equipment Mfg.: Figs. 138, 177

Koma (Netherlands) Melick: Fig. 200

Leutenegger & Frei (Switzerland): Figs. 186, 201

Margarine Institute of Germany: Figs. 470, 471, 472, 473, 566, 567, 568

Martin Braun Co.: Figs. 462, 614, 620, 625, 646, 660, 685, 686, 693, 695, 697, 698, 699, 706, Page 200

Meistermarken, Fats, Oils and Baking Institute: Figs. 195, 196, 197, 198, 434, 435, 436, 441, 496, 499, 509, 518, 519, 523, 530, 531, 532, 535 - 559, 563, 570, 571, 577, 578, 579, 580, 582, 584, 596, 597, 599, 611, 612, 616, 643, 655, 656, 661, 665, 668, 669, 670, 671, 675, 676, 677, 678, 679, 682, 691, 692

Kurt Neubauer: Figs. 573, 696

Dietrich Reimelt: Figs. 56, 57, 58, 574

Rico-Rego Equipment: Figs. 631, 632

E.O. Schmidt and Publipress: Figs. 615, 617, 618, 619

Seever, Bakery Equipment Mfg.: Fig. 524

Prof. Dr. Seibel: Figs. 349, 350

Dr. Spicher: Fig. 280

Stonemason-Patented milling: Fig. 416

Stephan & Sons: Figs. 131, 132

Ulmer Spatz, Bakery technology and supplies: Figs. 11, 12, 17, 23, 46, 113, 222, 223, 242, 256, 257, 291, 298, 303, 304, 321, 330, 365, 366, 367, 369, 379, 384, 389, 390, 394, 408, 423, 491, 493, 494, 497, 498, 500, 512, 529, 576, 602, 626, 627, 628, 629, 630, 663, 688

Uniferm Yeast: Figs. 82, 90, 91, 92

United Wheat, Market and Food Research: Figs. 1, 254, 255, 415

W. Vortmeyer: Figs. 562, 564, 565, 569

Kurt Warnke: Fig. 429

Michael Wenz, MIWE Oven Mfg: Figs. 317, 318, 326, 331, 334, 338, 339, 340

Fr. Winkler, Bakery Equipment: Figs. 148, 172, 173, 174, 183, 184, 194, 203, 206, 208, 299, 301, 306, 316, 320, 325, 333, 342, 360, 361

Dr. H.V. Zeddelmann: Figs. 587, 112-115

For the English version the following sources are also acknowledged:

Agriculture Canada

Approved Methods, Eighth Edition, American Association of Cereal Chemists

Canadian Standards Association

Canadian International Grains Institute, Winnipeg, Manitoba

Consumer and Corporate Affairs Canada

Metric Commission Canada

Index

334

Metric Conversion Tables

Basic Units
weight: grams = g
volume: litres = l
length: metres = m
temperature: degrees Celcius = °C

Weight
1 ounce	=	28.35 grams
1 gram	=	0.035 ounce
1 pound	=	454 grams
1 kg	=	2.2 pounds
1 kg	=	2.2 pounds

• One kilogram (1,000 grams) is slightly more than 2 pounds
• 30 grams is about 1 ounce

Volume
1 fluid ounce	=	29.57 millimetres
1 mm	=	0.034 fluid ounce
1 cup	=	237 millimetres
1 litre	=	33.8 fluid ounces

Length
1 inch	=	25.4 millimetres
1 centimetre	=	0.39 inch
1 metre	=	39.4 inches

• 1 centimetre (10 millimetres) is slightly less than half an inch
• 5 cm is about 2 inches

Temperature
To convert Fahrenheit to Celsius: Subtract 32, then multiply by 5/9.

To convert 400°F to Celsius:
$$400 - 32 = 368$$
$$368 \times 5/9 = 204°C$$

To convert Celsius to Fahrenheit: Multiply by 9/5, then add 32.

To convert 200°C to Fahrenheit:
$$200 \times 9/5 = 360$$
$$360 + 32 = 392°F$$

Common oven temperatures

°C	replaces	°F
100		200
150		300
160		325
180		350

°C	replaces	°F
190		375
200		400
220		425
230		450

Refrigerator temperature:	4°C	replaces	40°F
Freezer temperature:	−18°C	replaces	0°F